Excavations at Rhuddlan, Clwyd:
1969–73 Mesolithic to Medieval

Excavations at Rhuddlan, Clwyd: 1969–73 Mesolithic to Medieval

By Henrietta Quinnell (formerly Miles)
and Marion R Blockley

with
Peter Berridge

and
George C Boon, A Clark, Blanche Ellis, Ian Goodall,
T Holden, Bruce Levitan, Graham Morgan,
Wendy Owen, E J Pieksma, Alison Roberts,
D F Williams

1994

CBA Research Report 95   **Council for British Archaeology**

Published by the Council for British Archaeology
Bowes Morrell House, 111 Walmgate, York, YO1 2UA

ISBN 1 872414 40 0

British Library Cataloguing in Publication Data
A catalogue card for this book is available from the British Library

This book is published with the aid of a grant from Cadw: Welsh Historic Monuments.

Typeset by M C Bishop, Ryton, Tyne and Wear
Printed in Great Britain at Adpower, Halifax

Dedication

To J E Messham in tribute to his knowledge of the history of Flintshire and his generosity in sharing it

Contents

Preface ii
Addresses of contributors iii
Illustrations iv
Summaries viii

1   Introduction and background 1

2   Historical summary 7

3   Site A, Abbey Nurseries, Abbey Road. On the line of the Norman Borough Defences 11

4   Site T, Ysgol-Y-Castell, Lôn Hylas. On the line of the Norman Borough Defences 27

5   Site V, Area behind the Norman Borough Defences, Ysgol-Y-Castell, Lôn Hylas;
     Medieval pottery kiln 47

6   Site E, Ysgol-Y-Castell, Lôn Hylas. On the line of the Norman Borough Defences 57

7   Site M, Ysgol-Y-Castell playing fields. The Norman Church and prehistoric sequence beneath............72

8   Site D, Gwindy Street. The Edwardian Borough Defences...84

9   Minor Sites including Site S, Princes Road 92

10 The lithics 95
     Peter Berridge

11 The Mesolithic decorated and other pebble artefacts: synthesis
     Peter Berridge with Alison Roberts...115

12 Between the Mesolithic and the Iron Age with a study of a Bronze Age pottery
     group in Pit C46..132
     Peter Berridge

13 Iron Age and Romano-British artefacts and synthesis 140

14 The veterbrate remains...147
     Bruce Levitan

15 Botanical remains 160
     T G Holden, Graham Morgan with G Hillman and P Moore

16 Coins (George C Boon) and medieval small finds 164

17 Ironwork and metallurgy. Iron artefacts Ian Goodall with Blanche Ellis. Metallurgy and the
     use of coal..178

18 Medieval and post-medieval pottery 191
     Wendy Owen

19 Rhuddlan during the early Medieval period and the location of Cledemutha.............208

20 Rhuddlan between AD 1070 and 1277 214

21 Rhuddlan under Edward I and after..219

Bibliography...227
Index Peter Gunn...238

Preface

This report has been finally completed 23 years after the strategy for the initial excavation was planned. Inevitably, over such a lapse of time, methodology has advanced and much of the work done will appear deficient by the standards of today. Some reparation is made by the inclusion of specialist reports prepared comparatively recently, but there are bound to be areas of record or comment which will be viewed critically. With the advance of time goes increase in costs, and full coverage of every aspect of the excavation results has not been attempted. Instead the report has been planned to bring to the notice of those interested in the various periods, structures and artefacts, the full range of data available for study.

The report has suffered vicissitudes apart from the long time lapse. An initial stratigraphic draft with preliminary notes on finds was prepared by myself in 1976–8. In 1986 Marion Blockley was contracted by the Welsh Office to prepare for publication all but the earlier prehistoric material, for which Peter Berridge was engaged. She revised the stratigraphy and prepared notes on the small finds and history. Her greatest contributions to the final report were the identification of pre-Norman structures and artefacts which had not been recognized during the 1970s, and an alternative interpretation of the *Cledemutha* defensive circuit. Unfortunately Marion Blockley was unable to see the project through to publication due to illness. I was, in 1988, in a position to resume work on the report; I take full responsibility for the content of all sections apart from those written by specialist contributors, whilst acknowledging Marion Blockley's crucial contribution to the project as a whole.

I wish to thank a wide range of people and organizations who have helped in various ways with this complex and long-running project: the Flintshire Historical Society, who were most supportive throughout and whose officers administered the finances for 1971, 1972 and 1973; the numerous staff of the organisation which was, 20 years ago, the Ministry of Public Buildings and Works and which is now Cadw, in particular Jeremy Knight, Michael Apted and Richard Avent, and most especially Michael Yates who has constructively monitored work over the last five years; the staff of the Clwyd-Powys Archaeological Trust, past and present, especially Chris Musson, William Britnell and Chris Martin; the people of Rhuddlan for their support and hospitality, especially the late Mr J Beckett; all those who helped on the excavations in whatever capacity from supervising to tea-making; Trevor Miles for running the finds shed and for post-excavation work on the finds; the late Wendy Aldridge for general back-up over the years; M Lesley Simpson for preparing the first set of stratigraphic drawings and Brian V Williams for providing the final publication versions; all the specialists whose contributions are printed in this volume; J E Messham for all his help with the history and for his hospitality; Dr A J Taylor for help and encouragement; the Clwyd County Archaeological Service and especially John Manley who had to write up his own later excavations without full access to the data published here; Ken Brassil and Bob Higham, together with the anonymous CBA referee, for constructive comments on the text; Stephen Aldhouse-Green of the National Museum of Wales for facilitating the deposition of the finds and archive; finally my husband Norman Quinnell for help with the drawings and revision of the text, and for much-needed support during the completion of the final versions of the report. Additional acknowledgements for help in specialist areas are included at the ends of relevant chapters. I apologise to anyone whose contribution has been inadvertently overlooked with the passage of time.

Rhuddlan has proved to be a site of exceptional archaeological importance and is now well protected. It will one day yield enormous quantities of data. I wish all those who work there in the future every success in dealing with the wide range of material, the potential of which is only hinted at in this volume.

Henrietta Quinnell
1992

List of contributors

Henrietta Quinnell   9 Thornton Hill, Exeter EX4 4NN

Marion Blockley   Ironbridge Institute, Ironbridge Gorge Museum, Ironbridge, Telford TL8 7AW

Peter Berridge   Flat 3, Atlantic Road, Weston-s-Mare, Avon BS23 2DG

George Boon   43 Westbourne Road, Penarth, S Glamorgan CF6 2HA

Anthony Clark   19 The Crossways, Onslow Village, Guildford, Surrey GU5 5QG

Blanche Ellis   Candlespur, Acrise, Folkestone, Kent CT18 8LW

Ian Goodall   22 Elmlands Grove, York YO3 0EE

Tim Holden   Institute of Archaeology, 31–34 Gordon Square, London WC1H 0PY

Bruce Levitan   Mildmay Mission Hospital, Hackney Road, London E2 7NA

Graham Morgan   Department of Archaeology, University of Leicester, University Road, Leicester LE1 7RH

Wendy Owen   Clwyd-Powys Archaeological Trust, 7a Church Street, Welshpool, Powys SY21 7DL

Alison Roberts   Department of Prehistoric and Romano-British Antiquities, British Museum, London WC1

David Williams & E J Pieksma   Department of Archaeology, University of Southampton, Southampton SO9 5NH

List of Figures

1.1 Map of North Wales setting Rhuddlan in its topographical context and naming major medieval sites mentioned in the text.

1.2 Rhuddlan, Clwyd. Major medieval sites and structures and areas excavated up until 1988.

3.1 General plan of Site A.

3.2 Site A. Sections through *Grubenhaus* Structure 1 (C2) and X–Y through boundaries.

3.3 Site A. Sections through the Norman Borough Defence Ditch sequence.

3.4 Site A. Drying kiln C3 plan and sections.

3.5 Site A. House 1 plans and sections.

3.6 Site A. House 2 plan, including adjacent contemporary features, and sections.

3.7 Site A. Phase plans Mesolithic to Post-Medieval.

4.1 Site T. Plan of features likely to date before *c* AD 900.

4.2 Site T. Plan of features likely to date after *c* AD 900.

4.3 Site T. Sections AB and BC in north of the Site.

4.4 Site T. Sections EF, HG across the Norman Borough Defence Ditches and later features.

4.5 Site T. Plan of corn drying kilns 61 and 50.

4.6 Site T. Sections of corn drying kilns 61 and 50.

4.7 Site T. Phase plans Iron Age to post-Medieval.

5.1 Site V. Plan of probable prehistoric and Romano-British features.

5.2 Site V. Plan of medieval and later features.

5.3 Site V. Sections.

5.4 Site V. Plan and section of pottery kilns 51 and 4.

5.5 Site V. Phase plans.

6.1 Site E. Plan of features before *c* AD 1280.

6.2 Site E. Plan of features after *c* AD 1280.

6.3 Site E. Section AB through Ditches I to IV and overlying levels.

6.4 Site E. Section CD through Ditch V; also shows Mesolithic pit J92 and soil H39.

6.5 Site E. Phase plans Mesolithic to post-Medieval.

7.1 Site M. Proton magnetometer plot indicating Church and its location in the school playing field.

7.2 Site M. Plan of features pre-dating the Norman Church.

7.3 Site M. Section of the west side of the trench.

7.4 Site M. Plan of the Norman Church and burials.

7.5 Site M. Detailed plans of graves M115 and M117.

8.1 Site D. The Edwardian Borough Defences, Gwindy Street. Plan.

8.2 Site D. Features below, and on the inner edge of, the Edwardian Borough Inner Bank.

8.3 Site D. Features below and above the Edwardian Outer Bank in DP.

8.4 Site D. Sections through the Edwardian Borough Defences.

8.5 Site D. Phase plans.

9.1 Site S. Plan and section, Bryn Teg, Princes Road.

10.1 Mesolithic chert; preparatory pieces. Also standard conventions used in lithics illustrations.

10.2 Cores, tertiary flakes and plunging flakes.

10.3 (a) Chert waste flakes length. (b) Chert waste flakes width. (c) Chert waste flakes: length to breadth ratio.

10.4 No 29 core with crested ridge not removed; 30 flake with crested ridge not removed; 31–32 core rejuvenation tablets; 33–34 crested blades.

10.5 Microburins; 'miss-hit' microburins; flakes notched prior to microburin snap.

10.6 Microliths of various forms.

10.7 Scrapers; piercers/awls; utilised blades.

10.8 Scrapers; piercers/awls; edge ground pieces; fabricators; microdenticulates.

10.9 Axe-sharpening flakes; ? flakes derived from axes.

10.10 Leaf arrowheads; scrapers.

11.1 Mesolithic decorated pebbles SF1 and SF2.

11.2 Mesolithic decorated pebbles SF3–SF6.

11.3 Mesolithic utilised stones. SF7 quern. SF8 bevelled pebble.

12.1 Prehistoric pottery PP1–PP12 from pit C46, Site A.

12.2 Prehistoric pottery PP13–PP18 from pit C46, Site A; PP19 pit J102, Site E; PP20 soil H8, Site E; PP21 residual, Site D.

13.1 Iron Age and Romano-British copper alloy objects.

13.2 Rotary quern fragment SF10.

13.3 Iron ? adze SF 12.

13.4 Romano-British pottery.

14.1 Fragmentation of cattle bones.

14.2 Fragmentation of sheep/goat bones.

14.3 Fragmentation of pig bones.

14.4 Summary of butchery of cattle bones, late 13th century.

14.5 Proportions of major species varying through time.

14.6 Anatomical representation of major species, late 13th century.

16.1 MSF 1–13 Objects of copper alloy.

16.2 MSF 14–18 Objects of lead.

16.3 MSF 19 Glass linen smoother.

16.4 MSF 20 Part of clay loom weight.

16.5 Carving on bone trial piece MSF 21.

16.6 MSF 22–24 Bone objects.

16.7 MSF 25–26 Antler objects.

16.8 MSF 27 Stone weight.

16.9 MSF 28–30 Stone spindle whorls and gaming counter.

16.10 MSF 31–3 Bakestones.

16.11 MSF 34–9 Whetstones.

16.12 MSF 40 Whetstone used as a mason's 'trial piece'.

17.1 Medieval Iron objects. Tools nos 1–14.

17.2 Medieval Iron objects. Knives, shears nos 15–32.

17.3 Medieval Iron objects. Staples, hinges, bindings, nails, studs, bolts nos 34–72.

17.4 Medieval Iron objects. Candlesticks, handles, chains, ferrule nos 73–85.

17.5 Medieval Iron objects. Barrel padlock no 86.

17.6 Medieval Iron objects. Locks and keys nos 87–101.

17.7 Medieval Iron objects. Buckles, horseshoes, spurs nos 102–137.

17.8 Medieval Iron objects. Arrowheads nos 137–152.

18.1 P1–4 Saxo-Norman pottery.

18.2 P5–P10 V4 Kiln products.

18.3   P11–P22 V4 Kiln products.

18.4   P23–P24 V4 Kiln products.

18.5   P25–P35 Pottery from Site A contexts.

18.6   P36 Site A; P37–P57 Pottery from Site T contexts.

18.7   P58–P68 Pottery from Site E contexts.

18.8   P69–P93 Pottery from Site D contexts; P94–P95 Site S contexts.

List of Plates

1.1   Aerial view of Rhuddlan from the south showing the area of the Norman Borough with major excavation sites marked on.

3.1   Site A. Corn dryer C3.

3.2   Site A. House 1 before excavation.

3.3   Site A. House 1 excavated to show packing of Phase 2.

3.4   Site A. House 2, excavated to remove all soil from voids left by decayed timbers.

4.1   Site T. Ploughmarks T319, cut by base of palisade line T81.

4.2   Site T. East end, collage view from south.

4.3   Site T. Four-post structure T327-326-325-116 cut by palisade line T81.

4.4   Site T. Ditches II and III excavated (kiln T50 in foreground).

4.5   Site T. Kiln 61 completely excavated showing timber settings.

4.6   Site T. Kiln 50 during excavation (kiln 61 in background).

5.1   Site V. Hollow V24 during excavation; kiln V4 at level of cross baulks.

5.2   Site V. Kiln V4 during excavation.

6.1   Site E. Bronze Age posthole H42 with limestone packing.

6.2   Site E. Pit J21 with timber settings in corners.

6.3   Site E. Ditch IV with cleaning slot in base. G6 lane.

6.4   Site E. Ditch V. Mesolithic features J92 and J86 cause darkening on left ditch edge.

6.5   Site E. Lane G6 at east of Site.

6.6   Site E. Horseshoe no 117 on surface G6.

7.1   Site M. Mesolithic hollow M90 with subsidiary features in base.

7.2   Site M. Trench looking north showing slag-filled Church foundations and burials of Phase 3.

7.3   Site M. North Church foundation M4 with tap slag fill and small amount of mortared limestone rubble on top. Phase 3 burial M14 to right.

7.4   Site M. Burial M115 with sand-filled coffin stain, cutting burial M117 with coins of William II.

8.1   Site D. The Edwardian Borough Ditch fully excavated with the Outer Bank beyond.

11.1   SF1 Decorated pebble Site E. Side A.

11.2   SF1 Decorated pebble Site E. Side B.

11.3   SF1 Decorated pebble Site E. Side C.

11.4   SF1 Decorated pebble Site E. Side D.

11.5   SF2 Decorated pebble Mesolithic hollow M90. Side A.

11.6   SF2 Decorated pebble Mesolithic hollow M90. Side B.

11.7   SF6 Decorated pebble Site T soil T64.

11.8   Experimental engraved line made with bladelet, showing characteristic features. × 200.

11.9   Experimental engraving with bladelet showing characteristic features and accidents associated with overcutting lines. × 25.

11.10   Chert bladelet with edge ground due to experimental use as engraving tool. × 50.

11.11   Heavily ground edge of chert bladelet from Rhuddlan. × 50.

11.12   Detail of reverse side of SF2 showing area of overcutting and intersecting engraved lines. × 17.

11.13   Detail of reverse side of SF2 showing faint worn engraved lines cut by more clearly defined series. × 17.

11.14   Detail of the edge of SF3 showing engraved lines being cut by the break surface, the start of a line, and a faint worn line underlying several others. × 16.

11.15   Detail of SF5 showing the effects of erosion and abrasion on an engraved line. Apparent marks perpendicular to the engraved line are natural features. × 21.

11.16   Detail of the front of SF1 showing the termination of the engraving and natural bedding features. × 19.

11.17   Detail of the front of SF1 showing the termination of the engraving and natural bedding features. × 20.

11.18   Engraved lines made with a chert burin. × 25.

11.19   Engraved lines made with a flint burin. × 25.

16.1   MSF 21 Trial piece on calf radial bone.

16.2   MSF 34 Whetstone pit T349.

Summaries

Five seasons of excavation, mostly on the fluvio-glacial sand ridge above the Clwyd, revealed complex multi-period activity from the Mesolithic onward. The Mesolithic occupation dated to the earlier seventh millennium BC (radiocarbon years) and produced a rich chert industry, some possible structural features, and a series of decorated pebbles so far unique in Britain. The site, discussed at length, is considered to be a major centre of occupation. There was sporadic evidence for most subsequent prehistoric periods. An important feature was a large pit group of pottery dating to the later second millennium BC. The Iron Age was represented by traces of ploughing, four-posters and other structures, and artefacts including a decorated ring-headed pin and briquetage.

Activity during the Roman period was largely agricultural with pottery indicating an emphasis on the later centuries. There is a possible post-Roman timber building and system of plot boundaries.

Mercian influence is reflected in artefacts from the 8th century onward. The defences of the *burh* of *Cledemutha*, double-ditched with a timber-revetted bank, appear to have underlain those of the later Norman Borough and to have enclosed about 6ha; sunken-floored structures were found and a range of objects including ironwork. The probability of this siting for *Cledemutha*, as opposed to the 30ha site previously suggested, is discussed at length.

The ditch of the Norman Borough was located on sufficient sites for a 6 ha circuit to be suggested. The church, mentioned in Domesday Book, was trial dug. It was a large structure of simple two-celled plan, its limestone walls set over substantial foundation trenches filled with tap slag. The earliest inhumation found had been buried with two London-minted coins of William Rufus. The graveyard had been intensively used until c AD 1300. The areas dug were, by chance, mainly on the defensive circuit and little was learnt about its interior, or the vicissitudes forced on the community by the wars of the 12th and 13th centuries. The Borough Ditch was redug during Henry III's reoccupation of North Wales, and a pottery kiln dated to c AD 1250 found.

The defences of the Borough founded by Edward I in 1278 were sectioned and proved to consist of two similar broad banks either side of a wide flat-bottomed ditch. These defences were maintained, probably, up to the revolt of Owain Glyndŵr when they were slighted and never subsequently repaired. Outside Edward's masonry castle, started in 1277, levels of intense industrial activity, mainly smithing, were located. These were sealed by a lane and working area composed of chippings of the various stones used in the castle, which provides a horizon which can confidently be dated to around AD 1280. Elsewhere outside the Edwardian Castle and Borough two gable entrance houses built of staves and planks and three large corn drying kilns could be dated to the late 13th century. The late 13th century levels were rich in artefacts, particularly iron objects and their contexts allow fairly close dating. From the 14th century onward the reversion of the Norman Borough area to agricultural use was traced.

The preservation of features from so many periods had been made possible by a gradual build-up of soil, partly caused by sand blown from dunes when the coastline was close to Rhuddlan. This stratified occupation makes Rhuddlan arguably one of the most important archaeological sites in Wales.

Zusammenfassung

Im Laufe von fünf Grabungskampagnien, die zum größten Teil auf der fluvioglazialen Anhöhe über dem Clwyd durchgeführt wurden, ist eine Komplexe und über viele Zeiträume reichende, mit dem Mesolithikum beginnende Siedlungstätigkeit festgestellt worden. Die mesolithische Besiedlung datiert in das frühe siebte Jahrtausend v Chr (Radiokarbonjahre) und ergab eine reichhaltige Hornsteinverarbeitung sowie einige Anhaltspunkte für mögliche Bauten und eine Reihe von verzierten Geröllsteinen, die bisher in Großbritannien einmalig sind. Die Fundstelle die hier eingehend besprochen wird, wird als ein wichtiges Siedlungszentrum angesehen. Für fast alle nachfolgenden vorgeschichtlichen Zeitabschnitte kamen vereinzelte Funde zu Tage. Einen wichtigen Fund stellte eine zahlenmäßig reiche Keramikgruppe dar, die einer Grube des ausgehenden zweiten Jahrtausends entstammte. Die Eisenzeit ist durch Pflugspuren, vierpfostige und andere Bauten sowie Artifakten vertreten, unter denen sich eine verzierte Ringknopfnadel und Schamottbruchstücke befanden.

Die Nutzung in der Römerzeit war hauptsächlich landwirtschaftlicher Art, wobei der Keramikbefund auf ein Schwergewicht während der späteren Jahrhunderte hinweist. Ein möglicher nach-römischer Holzbau und ein System von Grundstücksbegrenzungen wurden festgestellt.

Vom achten Jahrhundert an spiegelt sich aus Mercia kommender Einfluß in den Artifakten wieder. Die Verteidigungsanlagen der befestigten Siedlung (*Burh*) *Cledemutha*, aus einem Doppelgraben und einem mit einer Holzwand verstärktem Wall bestehendm lagen als Vorläufer unter den Anlagen für den späteren normannischen Borough und scheinen ein Areal von ungefähr 6 ha eingefaßt zu haben. Es wurden Grabenhäuser und eine Reihe von Gegenständen, unter denen sich Eisenzeug befand, gefunden. Die Möglichkeit, daß es sich bei dieser Örtlichkeit um *Cledemutha* handelt, und nicht das wie bisher angenommen 30 ha umfassende Areal, wird eingehend besprochen.

Der Umfassungsgraben des normannischen Boroughs wurde an genügend Stellen geortet, um einen Umfang von 6 ha zu ergeben. Im Fall der Kirche, die im Domesday Buch erwähnt wird, wurden Sondierungsgrabungen durchgeführt. Sie war eine große Anlage mit einem einfachen zweiräumigen Grundriß. Ihr Kalksteinmauerwerk ruhte auf mächtigen Fundamentgruben, die mit Abstechschlacke gefüllt waren. Das früheste festgestellte Körpergrab enthielt zwei in London geschlagene Münzen aus der Regierungszeit von William Rufus. Der Friedhof ist bis ungefähr 1300 n Chr intensiv belegt worden. Durch Zufall lagen die Grabungsstätten zum größten Teil auf dem Verlauf der Verteidigungsanlagen. Aus diesem Grund hat man nur wenig über das Innenareal und die Schicksale, die die Bevölkerung während der Kriege des zwölften und dreizehnten Jahrhunderts befielen, erfahren. Der Umfassungsgraben des Borough war im Zuge der Neubesiedlung von Nordwales durch Heinrich VIII. erneut ausgehoben worden. Weiterhin wurde ein Töpferofen mit einem Datum von circa 1250 festgestellt.

Die Verteidigungsanlagen des von Eduard I. 1278 gegründeten Boroughs wurden durch Schnittgrabung untersucht und es zeigte sich, daß sie aus zwei gleich breiten Wällen bestanden, die zu beiden Seiten eines Grabens mit flacher Sohle angelegt waren. Diese Verteidigungsanlagen wurden wahrscheinlich bis zur Revolte des Owain Glyndŵr in Stand gehalten, in deren Verlauf sie zerstört und danach nie wieder erneuert wurden. Vor der Steinburg Eduards I., die 1277 begonnen worden war, wurden Horizonte intensiver gewerbliche Tätigkeit, hauptsächlich Schmiedearbeit festgestellt. Diese Schichten waren durch einen Weg sowie einen Arbeitsplatz überdeckt, der aus den Abschlägen der verschiedenen, bei dem Bau der Burg verwendeten Gesteine bestand. Dies lieferte einen Horizont, der mit Sicherheit in die Zeit um 1280 datiert werden kann. An anderer Stelle außerhalb der Burg Eduards und des Boroughs konnten zwei Häuser in Ständerbohlenbauweise mit Giebeltoren sowie drei große Trockenöfen für Getreide in das in das dreizehnte Jahrhunderts waren reich an Artifakten, besonders Eisenzeug, und ihr Fundzusammenhang erlaubte eine verhältnismäßig genaue Datierung. Vom vierzehnten Jahrhundert an konnte auf dem Gebiet des normannischen Boroughs eine Rückentwicklung zu landwirtschaftlicher Nutzung hin festgestellt werden.

Die Bewahrung von Befunden aus so vielen Epochen wurde durch einen allmählichen Bodenanstieg ermöglicht, der zum Teil durch Windverwehung von Dünen verursacht wurde, als die Küstenlinie noch in der Nähe von Rhuddlan verlief.

Diese stratifizierte Besiedlung läßt Rhuddlan zweifellos zu einer der wichtigsten archäologischen Fundstellen in Wales werden.

Résumé

Cinq saisons de fouilles, principalement sur l'arête de sable fluvio-glaciaire au-dessus de la rivière Clwyd, ont révélé une activité complexe pendant plusieurs époques à partir du mésolithique. L'occupation mésolithique remontait au début du septiéme millénaire av. J.-C. (datation au radiocarbone) et produisit une importante industrie de pierre de corne, quelques traits structurels possibles, et une série de cailloux décorés, uniques en Grande Bretagne jusqu'à présent. On considère que le site, dont on traite dans le détail, est un grand centre d'occupation. ll y avait des témoignages sporadiques d'occupation au cours de la plupart des époques préhistoriques suivantes. Une particularité importante était un grand groupe de céramiques découvert dans une fosse et datant de la fin du deuxième millénaire av. J.-C. L'âge du fer était représenté par des traces de labourage, par des structures à quatre montants et autres structures et par des objets façonnes comprenant une épingle à tête annulaire et du briquetage.

Au cours de l'époque romaine, l'activité était largement agricole avec de la céramique qui mettait l'accent sur les derniers siècles de cette époque. ll y a un bâtiment en bois post-romain possible et un système de bornage de parcelles de terrain.

Des objets façonnés datant du 8ème siècle et plus tard reflètent l'influence mercienne. Les ouvrages défensifs du *burh* [village fortifié] de *Cledemutha* qui ont un double fossé avec un remblai revêtu de bois semblent avoir été en dessous des ouvrages défensifs du Borough normand ultérieur et avoir entouré, une superficie de 6 ha; des structures à sol souterrain ont été découvertes ainsi qu'une gamme d'objets, y compris des objets en fer. On traite à fond de la probabilité de ce site étant celui de *Cledemutha*, à l'encontre du site de 30 ha qui avait été suggéré auparavant.

On a découvert le fossé du Borough normand dans assez de sites pour qu'on puisse suggérer un périmètre contenant 6 ha. On a fait des fouilles d'exploration de l'église, qui est mentionnée dans le Domesday Book. C'était une grande structure de plan tout simple à deux cellules, ses murs de calcaire construits au-dessus de grandes tranchées de fondation remplies de scories. L'inhumation la plus ancienne découverte avait été enterrée avec deux pièces de Guillaume le Rouge frappées à Londres. Le cimetière avait été utilisé de manière intensive jusqu'à environ 1300. Par hasard, les endroits où on a fait des fouilles se trouvaient surtout sur le pourtour défensif et on n'a appris que très peu de choses sur l'intérieur ou sur les vicissitudes éprouvées par la communauté à cause des guerres du 12ème et du 13ème siècle. Le fossé du Borough, fut creusé à nouveau quand Henry III réoccupa le nord de la Galles et on a trouvé un four à céramique daté à environ 1250.

On a fait des sections transversales des ouvrages défensifs du Borough fondé par Edouard I en 1278 et on a découvert qu'ils consistaient de deux larges remblais similaires de chaque côté d'un large fossé à fond plat. Ces ouvrages défensifs avaient probablement été maintenus jusqu'à la révolte de Owain Glyndŵr, lorsqu'ils furent, détruits et jamais réparés par la suite. En-dehors du Château de pierre d'Édouard, dont la construction commença en 1277, on a trouvé des niveaux d'activité industrielle intense, surtout des forges. Ces niveaux étaient recouverts d'un chemin et d'une aire de travail composés de fragments des diverses pierres utilisées dans le Château, ce qui donne une date limite d'environ 1280. Ailleurs, en dehors du Château d'Edouard et du Borough, on a pu donner une date de la fin du 13ème siècle à deux loges à pignon d'entrée construites de bâtons et de planches et trois grands fours à sécher le blé. Les niveaux de la fin du 13ème siècle étaient riches en objets façonnés, particulièrement en objets de fer et leurs contextes permettent de leur donner une date assez précise. A partir du 14ème siècle, on a pu tracer la réversion de la zone du Borough normand à l'agriculture.

L'accumulation graduelle de terre, causé en partie par du sable apporté des dunes par le vent lorsque la côte était près de Rhuddlan, avait favorisé la préservation des particularités de tant d'époques. On peut soutenir que cette occupation stratifiée fait de Rhuddlan un des sites archéologiques les plus importants du pays de Galles.

Crynodeb

Datguddiodd pum tymor o gloddio, yn bennaf ar hyd cefnen dywod y ffrwd rewlifol uwchben afon Clwyd, weithgaredd cymhleth amlgyfnodol o'r oes Fesolithig ymlaen. Dyddiai'r feddiannaeth Fesolithig yn ôl i'r seithfed milflwyddiant cynharaf C C (blynyddoedd radiocarbon) a chynhyrchodd ddiwydiant chert ffyniannus, ynghyd â rhai nodweddion strwythurol o bosib, a chyfres o beblau addurniedig sydd, mor belled, yn unigryw ym Mhrydain. Ystyrir fod y safle hon, yr ymdrinir â hi'n fanwl, yn un o brif ganolfannau'r feddiannaeth. Yr oedd yna dystiolaeth ysbeidiol ar gyfer y rhan fwyaf o'r cyfnodau cynhanes dilynol. Un nodwedd bwysig oedd grŵp pwll mawr o grochenwaith yn dyddio yn ôl i'r ail filflwyddiant diweddarach C C Cynrychiolid yr Oes Haearn gan olion aredig, strwythur pedwar postyn ymhlith strwythurau eraill, ac arteffactau'n cynnwys pin penmodrwy addurnedig a 'briquetage'.

Gweithgaredd amaethyddol yn bennaf a gafwyd yn ystod y cyfnod Rhufeinig gyda chrochenwaith yn dynodi pwyslais ar y canrifoedd mwy diweddar. Mae yna o bosib adeilad pren ôl-Rufeinig a system o ffiniau rhandir.

Adlewyrchir dylanwad Merciaidd yn yr arteffactau o'r 8fed ganrif ymlaen. Ymddengys fod gwrthgloddiau *Cledemutha*, gyda'u ffos ddwbl a thorlan gynnal o bren, islaw rhai'r Bwrdeistref Normanaidd mwy diweddar a'u bod yn amgylchu tua 6ha; darganfyddwyd strwythurau lloriau soddedig ac amrywiaeth o wrthrychau gan gynnwys gwaith haearn. Ymdrinir yn fanwl â'r tebygolrwydd mai dyma oedd safle *Cledemutha*, yn hytrach na'r safle 30ha a awgrymid cynt.

Lleolwyd ffos y Bwrdeistref Normanaidd ar nifer digonol o safleoedd i'w gwneud hi'n bosibl i awgrymu amdaith o 6ha. Cafwyd cloddfa brawf ar safle'r eglwys, y cyfeirir ati yn Llyfr Domesday. Yr oedd yn strwythur mawr ar gynllun syml dwy gell, gyda'i waliau carreg galch yn seiliedig ar ffosydd swmpus a lanwyd â sorod traw. Cafwyd fod y daeariad cyntaf a ddarganfyddwyd wedi'i gladdu gyda dau ddarn o arian a fathwyd yn Llundain yng nghyfnod Gwilym Goch. Gwnaed defnydd helaeth o'r fynwent tan oddeutu 1300 O C. Ar hap, yr oedd y safleoedd a gloddiwyd ar yr amdaith amddiffynnol yn bennaf ac ni ddarganfyddwyd llawer am y tu mewn, nac am y cyfnod helyntus a impiwyd ar y gymuned gan ryfeloedd y 12fed ganrif a'r 13eg. Ailgloddiwyd ffos y Bwrdeistref yn ystod ailfeddiannaeth Harri'r Trydydd ar Ogledd Cymru, a darganfyddwyd odyn crochendy yn dyddio'n ôl i 1250 O C.

Yr oedd amddiffynfeydd y Bwrdeistref a sefydlwyd gan Iorwerth y Cyntaf yn 1278 yn ranedig a chafwyd bod iddynt ddwy dorlan lydan debyg i'w gilydd y naill ochr a'r llall i ffos helaeth â gwaelod gwastad. Mae'n bur debyg i'r amddiffynfeydd hyn gael eu cynnal a'u cadw hyd at wrthryfel Owain Glyndŵr pan bylchwyd hwy, ac na chawsant eu trwsio wedi hynny. Y tu allan i Gastell feini Iorwerth, y dechreuwyd ei adeiladu yn 1277, cafwyd hyd i lefelau uchel o weithgaredd diwydiannol, gwaith gof yn bennaf. Yr oedd y rhain dan sêl lôn a lle gwaith a wnaed o sglodion y gwahanol feini a ddefnyddiwyd yn y Castell, sy'n darparu gorwel y gellir ei ddyddio'n bur hyderus i oddeutu 1280 O C. Mewn mannau eraill oddi allan i'r Castell a'r Bwrdeistref Iorwerthaidd gellid dyddio dau dŷ mynedfa piniwn a wnaed o estyll a dellt, a thri odyn mawr i sychu ŷd, i ddiwedd y 13eg ganrif. Yr oedd lefelau diwedd y 13eg ganrif yn gyfoethog mewn arteffactau, yn enwedig gwrthrychau haearn, ac mae eu cyd-destun yn caniatáu dyddio gweddol fanwl. O'r 14eg ganrif ymlaen gellid amlinellu dychweliad ardal y Bwrdeistref Normanaidd i drefn amaethyddol.

Gwnaed cadwraeth nodweddion cynifer o gyfnodau yn bosibl gan bentyrru graddol y tir, yn rhannol o achos y modd y chwythwyd tywod o'r twyni pan oedd yr arfordir yn agos at Rhuddlan. Gellid honni bod y feddiannaeth haenol yma yn gwneud Rhuddlan yn un o'r safleoedd archeolegol mwyaf pwysig yng Nghymru.

1   Introduction and background

1.1 General

The present town of Rhuddlan (Figs 1.1, 1.2) was founded by Edward I in 1278; now in Clwyd, it was in Flintshire until 1974. It was established north east of Edward's masonry castle. A motte and bailey castle lies 200m to the south and is surrounded by a fair amount of land, so far not built on. Domesday Book records a borough at Rhuddlan and a scatter of other documentary references suggest that the site was important to Welsh, Saxon and Norman activity in the area (Chapter 2 and Soulsby, 1983, 226–31). Until 1969 no formal excavations had taken place. In that year a building application for Site A (Fig 1.2) off Abbey Road prompted the then Inspectorate of Ancient Monuments, Ministry of Public Buildings and Works, to ask the author (HQ) to carry out excavations to assess the likely archaeological potential of this part of Rhuddlan. The results, multi-period prehistoric occupation (previously unsuspected) and complex medieval stratigraphy, caused the author to be asked to conduct further excavations on other threatened sites in 1970 to 1973 (Pl 1.1). The outcome of these later seasons confirmed the importance of this area as a multi-period site and resulted in the extension of statutory protection under the Ancient Monuments Acts. In 1971 the author was also asked to confirm the presumed earthwork remains of the Edwardian Borough Defences. Again positive results lead to the protection of this unbuilt area. Both an interim report and a popular account of the 1969–71 excavations were published in 1972 (Miles, 1971–2; 1972). Short reports on the subsequent seasons were presented in *Archaeology in Wales* (CBA II) and in *Medieval Archaeology*.

1.2 Topography and geology

Rhuddlan is situated on the right, east bank of the River Clwyd, four km south of its present estuary, at the lowest ford crossing and at the highest point reached by tides. It lies on a bluff at around 15m (45 to 50ft) OD looking north over the flatter lower ground of the Clwyd estuary at Rhyl. Its position was of importance for any communications in the area, situated on a route which skirted the hills to the south but which allowed crossing of a major river.

The Vale of Clwyd is a broad, down-faulted valley, floored by Coal Measures shales and Permo-Triassic sandstones which are overlain by a variable covering of drift. The valley is bounded on the

east by the Clwydian range with the foothills of Mynydd Hiraethog on the west. These areas of upland comprise Silurian sedimentary rocks with locally extensive drift deposits; along the valley edge are narrow outcrops of Carboniferous Limestone. At Rhuddlan rock exposures are absent; the geology, consisting of various Quaternary deposits, is dominated by boulder clays derived from Irish Sea or Northern Ice. As well as limestone and other local rock types, the boulder clays contain erratics originating in the Lake District, Northern Ireland and the west of Scotland; sand and gravel lenses occur within the boulder clay. Overlying the boulder clay are areas (Fig 1.2) of fluvial-glacial sands and gravels (Warren, Nutt & Smith, 1984). These sands have been locally reworked and deposited as wind blown sands as late as the Romano-British period. The freely draining sands give rise to soils described as sandy loams of the Newport series whilst the boulder clay is covered by permeable but seasonally waterlogged clayey loam of the Salop series (Ball, 1960).

Manley (1982b) has summarized the probable alterations to the local environment caused by sea-level change from the Mesolithic to the medieval periods. From the Mesolithic on there were a series of marine transgressions which flooded the low-lying Morfa Rhuddlan, the marsh west of the Clwyd estuary, and which, for long periods, brought the sea close to the bluff on which Rhuddlan is situated. Sea-level appears to have been locally at its highest, and Rhuddlan therefore closest to the sea, during the Roman and post-Roman periods. By the early medieval period the sea had retreated, possibly to the north of the present coastline, but the coastal lowlands were subject to periodic inundation. The situation only began to be stabilized by Edward I's work on the Clwyd (Chapter 2). The straightened course of the Clwyd below Rhuddlan is the work of the last two centuries.

The former bow below Twt Hill (Fig 1.2) appears as the main stream on a map of 1756. This map of 'Rhyddlan Estate....belonging to Mad'm Elinor Conway and the Heirs....of her son James Stapleton...' will be referred to as the '*Conway Map of 1756*'. The original is in the National Library of Wales; a copy is in the Clwyd Record Office referenced NT/M/94(ii).

Pl 1.1 Aerial view of Rhuddlan from the south showing the area of the Norman Borough with major excavation sites marked on. Published by permission of J K St Joseph.

1.3 Archaeology above ground

A useful general survey is given in Soulsby & Jones (1976), where some structures not detailed here are described, as are some by the Royal Commission (RCHM(W), 1912, 79–85). Comprehensive coverage is contained in the Clwyd County Council Archaeological Record housed at Shire Hall, Mold and at the Clwyd-Powys Archaeological Trust in Welshpool.

1.3.1 Twt Hill – motte and bailey castle

Twt (Toot or Bonc) Hill (SJ 026777) consists of a motte 6m high, about 30m across at the base and 9m at its slightly sunken top (profile with archive). It appears to have been largely built of sand, though traces of mortar have been noted (Soulsby & Jones, 1976, 27). On the west side the slope is continuous with the natural drop to the Clwyd. The bailey is in fact a platform 3m high with a very slight bank defining its crest on the north (RCHM(W), 1912, No 222).

1.3.2 The Town Ditch

The south and east sides of an enclosure of about 30ha survive intermittently, consisting of a broad (now shallow) ditch between two banks, each about 10m wide. It is known locally, and marked on Ordnance Survey maps, as the 'Town Ditch'. It was first recorded by Pennant (1784, 10) as 'a very deep foss which crosses from the margin of the bank, near the ascent of the present road to St Asaph, to another parallel road, near which it is continued, then turns and falls nearly into the southern part of the walled ditch of the castle: the whole forming a square area of very great extent'. The north side now is invisible, its position built over but confirmed by excavation (Site K Fig 1.2 and Chapter 9.3). The Town Ditch is not referred to by the Royal Commission (RCHM(W), 1912). Its south and east sides were investigated by J Manley in 1979–82 (Manley, 1987) and the earthwork interpreted as a Saxon *burh* (but see Chapter 19).

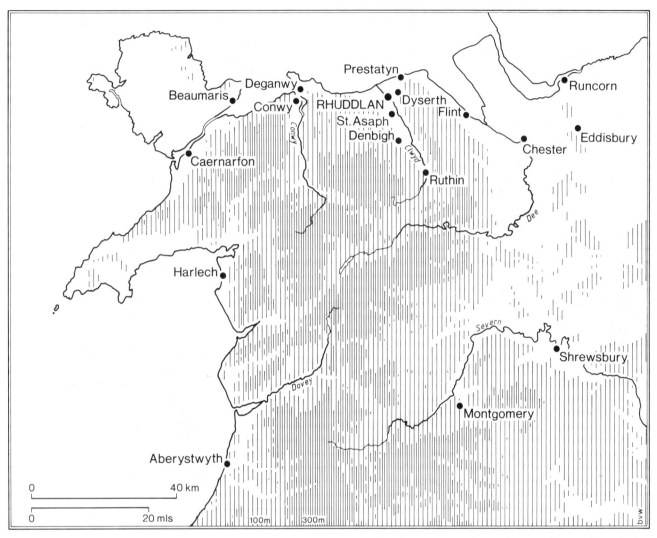

Fig 1.1 Map of North Wales setting Rhuddlan in its topographical context and naming major medieval sites mentioned in the text.

1.3.3 The Dominican Friary

Remnants of this survive in Abbey Farm, formerly known as Plas Newydd. Its date of foundation is given as AD 1258 by James (1968, 9) but is said to be uncertain by Soulsby & Jones (1976, 31). An engraving by Buck in 1742 shows most of the church standing, but this had disappeared by the time of Pennant's tour of 1784. Parts of the south cloister are incorporated in the present farm buildngs and some carvings are now in the parish church (James, 1968, 42). Fuller descriptions are given by the Royal Commission (RCHM(W), 1912, No 227) and by Soulsby & Jones (1976, 31–32). The Friary survived to the Dissolution in 1538. Sample pits dug by Manley in 1981, in advance of the erection of a new agricultural building, revealed nothing of significance (Manley, 1981). Results were also negative from 'keyhole' excavation in connection with electricity installation in 1987 (Brassil & Owen, 1987).

1.3.4 The Edwardian Castle

This concentric masonry castle was constructed by Edward I, on an apparently virgin site, largely between 1277 and 1280 as part his initial policy for the control of North Wales. Descriptions are given by Taylor (1956; 1963, 318–27). The castle remained a functioning entity throughout the remainder of the medieval period.

1.3.5 The Edwardian Borough and its defences

The present street plan of Rhuddlan reflects that of the Edwardian foundation of 1278, with the cross streets aligned with the River Clwyd. Part of the defensive circuit survives off Gwindy Street. Here there is a corner with a ditch 13m wide and an outer bank *c* 17m across. This corner was excavated in 1971 and the presence of an inner bank confirmed (Site D Chapter 8). It is now preserved as an open area. There are problems about the

4

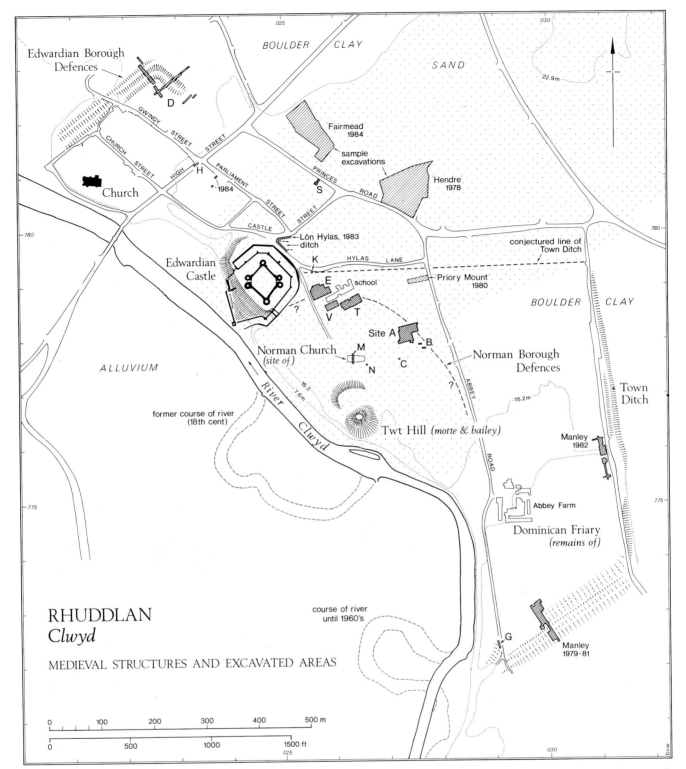

Fig 1.2 Rhuddlan, Clwyd. Major medieval sites and structures and areas excavated up until 1988. (Extent of glacio-fluvial sand after Manley 1984, Fig 1). Based on 1st Edition Ordnance Survey 25 inch plan with later additions.

exact line of part of the circuit, and about how far these defences were ever completed.

1.3.6 The Edwardian Parish Church of St Mary

The present church was founded in 1284 (Taylor, 1955) and contains much of the original 13th century architecture in the nave and chancel.

There were major alterations that doubled the width of both nave and chancel in the late 15th century (James, 1968).

1.3.7 Crosses with interlaced decoration

Two fragments, from different crosses with interlaced decoration, were found during the demolition of a wall near the Vicarage in 1936, and are now in the parish church. It is not known where they originated. They have been dated stylistically to the late 10th or early 11th centuries (Nash-Williams, 1950, 127) and are of importance for the pre-Norman ecclesiastical history of Rhuddlan.

1.4 Excavations between 1973 and 1988

1.4.1 Hendre 1978

Excavations (marked 'Hendre 1978' Fig 1.2) were carried out by J Manley in advance of building work to (a) establish whether this was the site of a documented hospital of St John of Jerusalem and (b) check how much of the multi-period occupation revealed in the 1969–73 excavations occurred this far east. Evidence for the hospital was negative (J E Messham in Messham, Manley & Morgan, 1980; this includes a comprehensive account of the documentary history of the hospital and suggests that it was sited at Spital SJ 035778 outside Rhuddlan). Positive results were a kiln of unknown function dating between AD 1680 and 1720 (*ibid*, 131), a samian sherd (*ibid*, 132) and an extensive Mesolithic assemblage (Manley & Healey, 1982). The excavations are fully published in these two reports.

1.4.2 The Town Ditch 1979–82

The south side was sectioned (Fig 1.2 'Manley 1979–81') and a possible entrance gap on the east (Fig 1.2 'Manley 1982') trial-dug by J Manley to provide a date for this earthwork. A series of radiocarbon dates and other details suggested that the Ditch was in fact the defence of the Saxon *burh* of *Cledemutha* (Manley, 1987; the full excavation report), but the evidence for an entrance was ambiguous. These excavations and the siting of *Cledemutha* will be discussed further in Chapter 19. There were a few Roman sherds, a brooch and two coins (*ibid*, 27, 36–7) from the trench across the south Ditch. Small quantities of lithic artefacts, suggested to be late Mesolithic, came from both the south and the east Ditches (*ibid*, 41). Arising from these excavations Manley published a general study of the *Cledemutha* problem (1984), a detailed study (1985a) based on an iron arrowhead found in his 1979–81 excavations (Fig 1.2), and an extended discussion of the radiocarbon dates and plant remains (1985b) as well as the final excavation report in *Medieval Archaeology* (Manley, 1987).

1.4.3 'Priory Mount', Abbey Road 1980

Trial excavations, four 2 by 2m squares within the area marked 'Priory Mount' 1980 on Fig 1.2, were carried out in advance of building work by K Brassil for the Clwyd-Powys Archaeological Trust because of its proximity to Site A. There was no *in situ* stratigraphy but a mixture of medieval, post-medieval and lithic artefacts were retrieved from mixed A–B soil horizons. (K Brassil in Manley & Healey, 1982, 46).

1.4.4 Lôn Hylas 1983

A salvage excavation at the junction of Castle Street and Lôn Hylas was organised by Clwyd County Council and the Clwyd-Powys Archaeological Trust after road widening had revealed stratigraphy ('Lôn Hylas 1983', Fig 1.2). A small Roman ditch contained late 1st to early 2nd century material; there was a single chert blade, probably Mesolithic. A large ditch, *c* 23m wide and 4m deep running east to west, was filled with slow silt and some deliberate dumping; there were possible traces of a bank on the inner, north side. This ditch was not dated but compared in the excavation report (Manley, 1985c) to that of the Edwardian Borough Defences on Site D (Chapters 8 and 21).

1.4.5 'Fairmead' 1984

Exploratory trenching in advance of building work, by K Brassil for the Clwyd-Powys Archaeological Trust, evaluated an extensive area just outside the presumed line of the Edwardian Borough Defences ('Fairmead 1984' Fig 1.2). Only a series of shallow ditches, possibly medieval field boundaries, were found (Brassil, 1984).

1.4.6 Parliament Street 1984

Trial excavations, by K Brassil for the Clwyd-Powys Archaeological Trust, on an open plot off Parliament Street within the Edwardian Borough produced little evidence for datable pre-Victorian activity ('Parliament Street 1984', Fig 1.2; Brassil, 1984).

1.5 Site and archive recording and the presentation of the report
1.5.1 Site records

All Sites were recorded in imperial measurements, plans normally at 1:24 and sections at 1:12. These were backed up by colour slides, but only for 1973 with a consistent black and white photographic record. Site A, 1969, was recorded with three major context sequences A, B, and C, and three minor ones, D, E, and F. Site E, 1970, had context sequences G, H and J. Site D, 1971 and 1972, was recorded in four sequences, O, P, Q and R. Sites M, 1971, S, 1972, T and V, 1973, had only single eponymous context sequences. The context sequences have been simplified slightly for publication, to avoid occurrences such as duplication of context numbers for the same feature, and the archive has been clearly annotated to show which context numbers are used for publication.

All finds were marked RHU 69 etc and given a number sequence, independent of context, enclosed within a rectangle. This finds number sequence runs continuously through the excavation series. The finds numbers in rectangles were used both for small finds and for groups of finds excavated in any one day from one context. Few items were treated as individual small finds. A finds list filed with the archive gives contexts for all finds numbers.

1.5.2 Changes during report preparation

During work on the excavation report some alternative labelling for Sites was adopted and then abandoned. Some of this labelling was used in the interim report (Miles, 1971–2) and re-used by other workers. In this interim report 'B' on present Fig 1.2 was separated into B and C, present 'C' was D, 'K' was F, and the various trenches of Site D named J, K, L and N.

During early preparation of the report, an attempt was made to simplify the presentation of the data by complete renumbering of contexts in stratigraphic order. Mesolithic contexts from all Sites were prefixed 'Me' in a single sequence, later prehistoric 'Br' as most were thought at the time to be Bronze Age, and Roman period contexts 'Rb'. For all Sites the contexts dating after the Roman period were renumbered in chronological order starting with the earliest; for Sites where there had been several context sequences, a single letter was selected, A, E, and D. When work resumed on the report in 1986 this re-enumeration was found to be basically flawed, and restrictive in regard to chronology. It was therefore abandoned. It was extensively used in interim records and all finds packaging marked with it. A reference book with full correlations is filed with the archive.

1.5.3 Presentation in this report

The stratigraphic data is presented in Chapters 3 to 9, and with it is included discussion relevant to distinctive contexts and structures. General discussion, particularly that concerning possible relationships between features and stratigraphy found on more than one site, is reserved for separate Chapters in chronological sequence. This sequence links finds and general discussion by period from the Mesolithic onward. Only Chapters 14 on animal bones and 15 on botanical remains cover material ranging from prehistoric to medieval; these reports are positioned after the Chapters on prehistoric and Romano-British finds and discussion, and before those on aspects of the medieval period.

1.5.4 Radiocarbon dates

All dates represent radiocarbon years and none have been calibrated, unless expressly stated. The general discussion in Chapters 11–12 refers to uncalibrated centuries; elsewhere, such discussion refers to calibrated, chronometric, centuries.

1.6 Deposition of records and finds

It is understood, at the time of going to press, that Clwyd County Council is considering donation to the National Museum of Wales.

2   Historical Summary

This chapter is intended to provide a general background to the chapters on stratigraphy and finds. Important aspects are expanded in Chapters 19–21. Any information not referenced comes from Lloyd (1939). Soulsby (1983, 226–231) presents a convenient summary.

2.1 Before AD 1073

The earliest documentary reference to Rhuddlan records 'bellum Rudglann' in AD 796; the actual reference in the *Annales Cambriae* (Morris, 1980, 88) refers to AD 797 but is accepted as being a year out. In the late 8th century there was a protracted struggle between the Welsh and the Mercians for control of this area of North East Wales; Offa's Dyke was built in the 780s as a barrier between the two. The north end of this frontier is now suggested to have been at Basingwerk, the north end of Wat's Dyke (Hill, 1974) rather than on the line between Newmarket and Prestatyn (Fox, 1955, Fig 6). Offa of Mercia mounted attacks on Wales in AD 778, 784, and 795. In 796 he gained control of the cantref of Tegeingl (Englefield) west of the Dyke, which included the site of Rhuddlan (Davies, 1987, Map 2). AD 796 was the year of the important battle 'bellum Rudglann', said to have been fought on the marsh of Morfa Rhuddlan, probably for control of the north end of the Vale of Clwyd and the river crossing. The full *Annales Cambriae* entry for 796 (797) reads 'an. Offa rex Merciorum et Morgetiud rex Demetorum morte moriuntur, et bellum Rudglann' (Morris, 1980, 88). Some of the English placenames to the west of Offa's frontier as defined above may relate to this phase of Mercian advance (Tait, 1925,1).

The Mercians appear to have controlled Tegeingl and increased their control over North Wales until the mid 9th century, with the frontier advanced perhaps to the Conwy. In 798 Caradog, King of Gwynedd, was killed by them, and in 816 they invaded and annexed Rhufoniog between the Clwyd and the Elwy (Morris, 1980, 89). In 822 the Mercians destroyed the Welsh fortress at Degannwy, and also broke the control of the Kingdom of Powys. By the mid 9th century Mercian dominance was contained by the rise of Rhodri Mawr (king of Gwynedd 844 to 878), and affected by the ascendency of Wessex and the intensification of Norse raids; it was Rhodri, who in 856, defended the North Welsh coast against the Vikings at Great Orme. In 880 the Mercians were defeated at the battle of Conway (Morris, 1980, 90) and in 893 the

Welsh allied with the English to repulse the Vikings after the battle of Buttington. In the following year Anarawad repulsed the Norse raiders who were plundering North Wales for provisions, though the Scandinavians made further attacks on Anglesey and Chester in 902. By this time Wessex had become the strongest English power and the focus of resistance to Viking raiding and settlement.

The alliance of the Viking kingdoms of York and Dublin in 919 must have increased the pressure on the north west frontiers of Wessex and Mercia. Edward the Elder built a *burh* at Thelwall, Merseyside and repaired that built at Manchester by Aethelflaeda, probably in response to Norse attacks from the Irish Sea. These two *burhs* completed a line of defence south from the Mersey to the Dee, linking Chester (restored 907) with Eddisburg (914) and Runcorn (915). Clearly the Vale of Clwyd provided a potential foothold for the Vikings, who had already occupied the Wirral, and whose influence is still reflected in placenames beyond Edward's frontier. The foundation of a fortified *burh* at Rhuddlan, to guard the Vale of Clwyd, would have been a logical progression. The Welsh had formed an alliance with Edward in 918 because of the Viking threat and presumably supported the system of a fortified frontier.

The foundation of a *burh* at *Cledemutha* by Edward is recorded for 921 in the Mercian Register of the Anglo-Saxon Chronicle (Whitelock, 1955, 199). Its location was not specified, but the argument, on etymological grounds, by Wainwright (1950) that it was situated at the mouth of the Clwyd seems to have gained general acceptance. The question has been recently reviewed by Taylor (1984), with new documentary evidence. Taylor proposed that *Cledemutha* was not at Rhuddlan itself, but on the coast at the north end of the estuary (see 19.3). The situation, historically and archaeologically, may be more complex than previously supposed. *Cledemutha* probably did not prosper long, whatever its precise site, since no products from its Saxon mint are known despite the legal obligation of *burhs* to possess one (Stenton, 1971, 527–8). The unstable frontier zone location of Rhuddlan, still subject to Norse raids, could not have been conducive to the success of a new town.

During the late 10th or early 11th century Tegeingl was regained by the Welsh. Any co-operation between Welsh princes and Wessex had broken down. The revolt of Idwal in 942, the death of the anglophile Hywel Dda in 949/50 and the resulting civil war, and finally the death of Edgar in 975, contributed to a weakening of English influence in the Rhuddlan area. In 1015 Llywelyn ap Seisyll of Gwynedd built a stronghold (palatium) at Rhuddlan, perhaps sited on Twt Hill which commanded the Clwyd ford. Gruffudd ap Llywelyn of Gwynedd (reigned 1039 to 1063) was the dominant figure in mid 11th century Wales. He co-ordinated response to Norse raids, personally launched attacks into England and was for the last eight years of his life regarded as the paramount ruler of Wales. By the 1050s the principal base for his *llys* was Rhuddlan. In 1063 Harold Godwinson mounted a successful campaign to contain Gruffudd's growing power; this included a raid on Rhuddlan, which was burnt with most of Gruffudd's ships. Gruffudd escaped in a single ship and was killed soon after and Harold forced the Welsh rulers to acknowledge English overlordship. Although the position in Tegeingl after Harold's victory is unclear in detail, Earl Eadwine of Mercia appears to have had some control, but much of its territory was held by Edwin ap Gronw (of Tegeingl) from the Welsh ruler Bleddyn ap Cynan.

2.2 Between AD 1077 and 1277

William the Conqueror quickly established a policy for regaining control of the Welsh Marches. In the North this was energetically pursued by Hugh of Avranches, made Earl of Chester, who swiftly consolidated rule over the lowlands west of the Dee as far as Basingwerk (Davies, 1987, 31) and then advanced around the coast to reach Rhuddlan by about 1073. A motte and bailey castle was built at Twt Hill, presumably on the site of the former Welsh *llys*; this castle was strong enough to repel a Welsh attack in 1075, when Hugh of Chester had been supported in his advance by his cousin Robert, who subsequently built a forward base at Deganwy, staking a claim to the whole of Gwynedd. Domesday Book records a small borough at Rhuddlan within the hundred of Atiscross, which was a holding divided between Hugh and Robert, now known as 'of Rhuddlan'. The borough had 18 burgesses, a church and a mint (see 20.1).

Rhuddlan appears to have remained under continued Norman control until Welsh recovery under Owain of Gwynedd (reigned 1137–1169) after the death of Henry I. Owain appears to have siezed Rhuddlan and Tegeingl about 1140 and held it until Henry II regained them in 1157. The foundation of the See of St Asaph directly by Canterbury in 1143 (Davies, 1987, 189) may be viewed as part of the complex interaction between the Anglo-Normans and the Welsh. Henry, realising Rhuddlan's strategic importance, made it a royal castle. In 1167 after a three-month siege, Owain Gwynedd and Rhys ap Gruffudd destroyed the castle and seized control and after Owain's death his son Dafydd controlled the area. Married to Henry II's half-sister Emma, he made Rhuddlan his principal residence. Dafydd entertained Baldwin, Archbishop of Canterbury, on tour raising support for a crusade, in Easter week 1188. Baldwin's companion, Giraldus Cambrensis, described Rhuddan as 'a noble castle on the river Cloyd... where we were handsomely entertained that night'. Baldwin proceeded next day to celebrate mass at St Asaph Cathedral, thus emphasing that Welsh cathedrals came under his jurisdiction. Rhuddlan remained in Welsh hands until 1241, with the exception of the years 1211–1213, when King John briefly regained it, to be retaken by Llywelyn ap Iorwerth, who maintained a strong grip on North Wales until his death in 1240. Subsequent to the Domesday Book entry there is no reference to the borough at Rhuddlan. James (1968, 9) asserts that non-Welsh inhabitants of Tegeingl evacuated the district after Owain's advance around 1240. In view of the encouragement of markets and small towns by Welsh rulers that is evident by the 13th century (Soulsby, 1983, 17), the possibility of settlement around Rhuddlan castle during periods of Welsh control must be allowed for.

In 1241 Henry III secured Rhuddlan and much of Gwynedd, taking advantage of the difficulties that arose after the death of Llywelyn ap Iorwerth. There are records (Taylor, 1956, 4) of payments for timber to repair wooden works at Rhuddlan castle in 1241–2. The church was presumably still functioning as Henry is recorded as appointing a priest to 'one portion' of the rectory about 1252, previous to which the names of four incumbents are known (James, 1968, 20). The portionary holding of the church continued the situation described in Domesday Book and suggests that the church was maintained as a structure; records certainly indicate that the church subsequently existed until its relocation by Edward I between 1284 and 1301. In 1281 Richard Bernard was appointed rector, with no mention of portions (James, 1968, 21).

The centres for Henry III's control after 1241 were the new royal stone castles at Degannwy and at Diserth. Diserth commanded the Diserth Gap on the Rhuddlan to Chester road, and in 1248 a small borough was founded there (Soulsby, 1983, 130). There appears to be no surviving reference to a borough at Rhuddlan under Henry III, but the sparcity of detailed records for the area until the arrival of Edward I makes the value of negative evidence difficult to assess.

Llywelyn ap Gruffudd of Gwynedd emerged as the major Welsh leader in 1255, and by late in 1256 had retaken all of North East Wales (including Rhuddlan) except the castles at Deganwy and Diserth. The latter reverted to Welsh control in 1263 and Llywelyn's predominance was complete in the area.

The Dominican Friary at Rhuddlan was in existence by 1258, possibly founded in that year by Llywelyn (Gumbley, 1915, 34–49). The Friary grew and flourished through the period of Welsh control in the later 13th century, a period for which there is again no record of a borough at Rhuddlan, but during which encouragement of this form of settlement by Welsh rulers is possible. Rhuddlan and North Wales remained under Llywelyn's control until the campaigns of Edward I in 1277.

2.3 Edward I

Edward I's initial campaign against Llywelyn and Gwynedd led to the latter's submission to English terms in November 1277. Edward re-established total control as far as the Conwy, Llywelyn holding western Gwynedd under him. New stone castles, both with boroughs attached, were constructed by Edward at Flint and Rhuddlan. Work on Rhuddlan Castle started in August 1277. The key element, the canalisation of the Clwyd, straightening it and bringing it directly below the new castle, began in November 1277. Rhuddlan would now act as an effective port. The old ford lost its importance and a bridge was built on the site of the present Rhuddlan Bridge.

The borough of Rhuddlan on its present site was founded in 1278. Burgages were granted in February of that year (Taylor, 1963, 322), and a charter of liberties issued in the following November. Edward's plan at this time was to make Rhuddlan the major administrative centre for North East Wales and in 1281 he applied to the papacy for the transfer of the see of St Asaph (Taylor, 1955). Edward also appears to have intended that Rhuddlan, rather than Flint, should have shire town status (Waters, 1929). By March 1279 burgages were being erected near the castle (Taylor, 1963, 322). In August 1279 the men of Rhuddlan were granted the fee farm of the town for seven years, which because of expenses the burgesses incurred was deferred until 1286 (Taylor, 1963, 322).

The total outlay between December 1277 and March 1279 came to over £3160 for work on the castle, town defences and the diversion of the river. Expenses specifically for the fortification works around the town occur in the Royal accounts for the period from March 1279 until March 1282. There is no reference to masons working on the town defences, but the records mention a ditch and a palisade.

In 1282 a major Welsh revolt was spearheaded by Llywelyn of Gwynedd and in March of that year the rebels attacked Rhuddlan, besieging and probably temporarily capturing the castle, and causing sufficient damage for the church of St Mary (presumably still on its Norman site) and the Dominican Friary to receive 50 marks and £17 10s respectively in compensation (Taylor, 1963, 322 with refs). The town was under English control again by the end of April. Edward then proceeded to subdue the whole of Gwynedd. Llywelyn was killed in December 1282 and the final Welsh submission came in June 1283. Edward now decided to

hold Gwynedd with a network of new castles, and Rhuddlan, while retaining importance as a port and point of control, was no longer the main centre and arrangements were dropped for moving the see from St Asaph.

It is unclear how far the town defences were completed. At the end of June 1282 arrangements were being made to accelerate the haulage of timber from Delamere Forest for the town defences. In July a clerk was sent to Lancashire to supervise the cartage of timber earmarked for the Rhuddlan palisade. This arrived in Rhuddlan on 6th and 7th of August 1282 and was transported up from the river in 20 carts and from September 6th until December 24th a watchman was paid for guarding it. In December another clerk was sent to see to the carting and shipment of further wood for the palisade and on December 26th boats were sent to bring it to Rhuddlan. On 20th June 1283 the King ordered that all the material prepared for the town's enclosure should be sent forward to where it was more urgently needed and on July 5th payment was made for shipping nine shiploads of timber from Rhuddlan to Caernarfon.

The parish church of St Mary's seems still to have been on on its original site in October 1282 when, because of the 'insufficiency of the cemetery of Rhuddlan church for burying the dead' (Haddan and Stubbs, 1869, 540) the King ordered a cemetery site for the new borough to be found on the outskirts of the town. This would have surely been unnecessary had a church in the new borough been available. By 1284 plans for the cathedral had been abandoned, and arrangements in 1296 reduced the church to a chapelry of St Asaph Cathedral. The present St Mary's church in the Edwardian borough was probably under construction by 1301 (James, 1968, 22).

By 1292 the new borough housed 75 taxpayers (refs in Soulsby, 1983, 231). By its charter of 1278 it enjoyed the usual commercial privileges, with weekly markets, annual fairs, and the monopoly of all trade in western Englefeld; the monopolies included the baking of bread and the brewing of ale.

2.4 The fourteenth and fifteenth centuries

During the first half of the 14th century the borough grew in prosperity, renting mills at Pentre and Diserth for £24 in 1301 and for £40 in 1348 (*Flints Ministers Accounts*). The Black Death affected its success, so that by 1385 rents for mills had been reduced to one third. There was friction between the burgesses and the Welsh population of the surrounding area, leading to riots in 1344 and 1370. In 1380 a market was granted to St Asaph. Burgesses from Rhuddlan and Conwy petitioned against this grant; in evidence they said they would lose trade from brewing and selling ale as the Welsh would prefer to use St Asaph; the tenants of surrounding areas would no longer bring their peas and beans, oats, wheat and other produce for sale to Rhuddlan; the burden of paying rents for mills was becoming too great and many were giving up their dwellings and departing from the district (information from J E Messham from *Flints Plea Rolls and Welsh Church Records*). In 1388 (information J E Messham) the borough petitioned the King for a reduction in the rent of mills; the subsequent inquisition stated that 'the greater part of the people who had used to bring their corn to be ground had died of pestilence' and 'that whereas 20 or more brewers once lived there now there were only five or six'.

In September 1400 came the rebellion of Owain Glyndŵr. In that year the rebels' activities are described as 'a demonstration in arms before the castle and town' (Messham, 1968, 2). In 1403 the rebels burnt Rhuddlan and slew some burgesses, followed by at least a second attack (Messham, 1968, 14), although the castle held out against them. English control was regained during 1406–7 but the rebellion had a long-term effect on Rhuddlan. Only 37 burgesses are listed in a survey of 1428 (Jones, 1915). This survey shows that all the street names have changed since that date with the exception of High Street and Castle Street. It also refers to tenements 'upon le Ditch' and in 'le Oldtown'.

Rhuddlan continued as a small trading centre through the succeeding centuries. Lead mining contributed to the economy in the 16th century (Soulsby, 1983, 231) and its quay served as a small port until the arrival of the railway in the 19th century.

Acknowledgments
We are most grateful to J E Messham for providing us with references to unpublished information, and for general guidance over Rhuddlan's history.

3 Site A, Abbey Nurseries, Abbey Road. On the line of the Norman Borough Defences

3.1 Introduction (Fig 3.1)

About 900 sq m were excavated in advance of the construction of new greenhouses on pile-driven foundations; the shape of the excavation was determined by the plan of the new buildings, with small extensions to allow the complete excavation of significant features. The work took place over four weeks at Easter 1969 and was the first of the excavations published in this report to take place.

A ridge of hard, concreted fluvio-glacial sand ran nearly due north across the Site. Eroded by horticultural activities, this was covered by topsoil only 0.25–0.35m thick. To the west the sand became softer, and dipped below a subsoil c 0.20m thick and topsoil up to 0.40m. The fluvio-glacial deposits contained bands of red clay on the east and south west edges of the Site. A major complex of ditches lay to the east of the hard sand ridge. These were unexpected, with no surface indication of their presence on the Site or anywhere else in Rhuddlan. This, the third defensive circuit at Rhuddlan, is interpreted below as the Norman Borough Defences which previously had been assumed to be the earthwork known as the Town Ditch (Fig 1.2).

3.2 Mesolithic (Fig 3.7 no 1)
3.2.1 Stratigraphy

Three features, all filled with leached buff sand fading to white at their bases, were almost certainly of Mesolithic date as their fills were similar, and two produced large quantities of Mesolithic material. Pit C25, 1.05m deep, contained 101 pieces of worked chert and flint, pit C38, 0.52m deep, 86 pieces, but pit C77, 0.10m deep, only six; there were no artefacts later than Mesolithic. 309 chert/flint pieces were residual in later contexts.

3.2.2 & 3 Dating and interpretation

See Chapters 10 and 11.

3.3 Bronze Age (Fig 3.7 no 2)
3.3.1 Stratigraphy

Pit C46, 0.55m deep, was filled with medium brown sand mixed with burnt pebbles, and contained sherds from a minumum of 15 vessels attributable to the Earlier Bronze Age (Chapter 12). Posthole C58, 0.45m deep, had medium brown sand packing around a postpipe 0.15m across filled with lighter sand. Cut by C46, it produced no finds; its similarity of fill to C46, particularly when compared to the leached sands in the Mesolithic pits, suggests a Bronze Age date. Pit A51, 0.07m deep, was cut by Ditch I in the Norman Borough Defence sequence, and on similarity of fill may tentatively be assigned to the Bronze Age.

3.3.2. & 3 Dating and discussion

See Chapter 12.

3.4 Iron Age and Romano-British (Fig 3.7 no 3)
3.4.1 Stratigraphy

A series of gullies had similar grey-brown silty sand fills with depths varying between 0.60 and 0.07m, and were presumably for drainage. The more complete gullies present a sequence of C43, C9 and C124. C9 defined an oval area 8m across, C124 a circle 6m in diameter. Pits C45, C9A, C134, C131 and C132 had fills similar to those of the gullies, and three (C45, C131, C132) were cut by the gullies. The area was rapidly dug at the end of the excavation and some data may have been missed.

Pit C44, 0.50m deep, filled with mixed dark brown and light yellow sand with pink clay lumps, contained eight large sherds of a grey-ware jar RP 1 (Fig 13.3). The relationship of pit C44 to the series of intercutting curvilinear gullies could not be determined during excavation, but it seems probable, that, had gully C9 cut pit C44, some Romano-British sherds would have eroded into its fill.

3.4.2 Dating

The only datable material, RP 1 from C44, has a broad range within the Roman period. Only gully C43 produced scrappy sherds which might be Iron

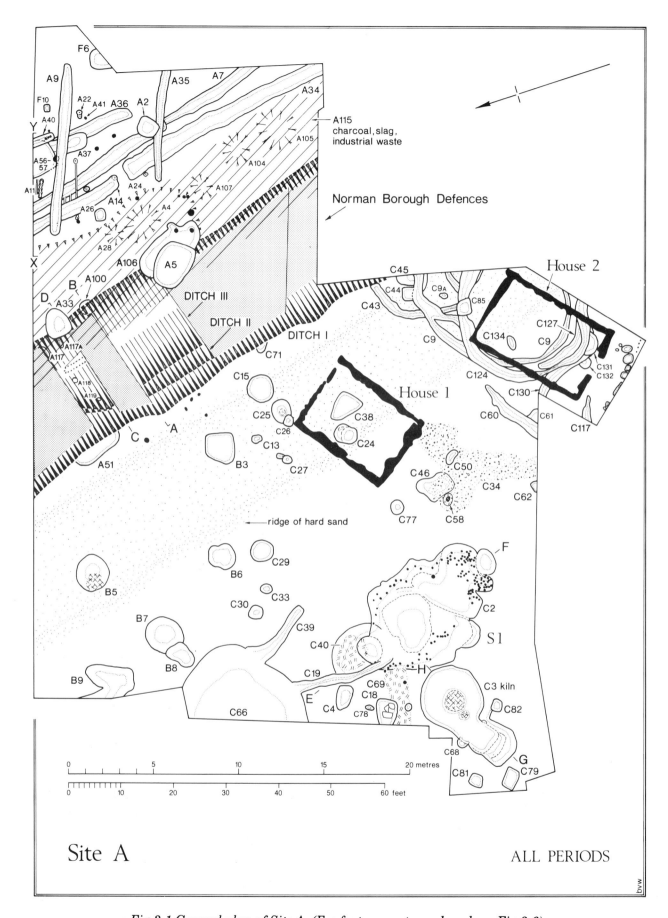

Fig 3.1 General plan of Site A. (For features not numbered see Fig 3.6).

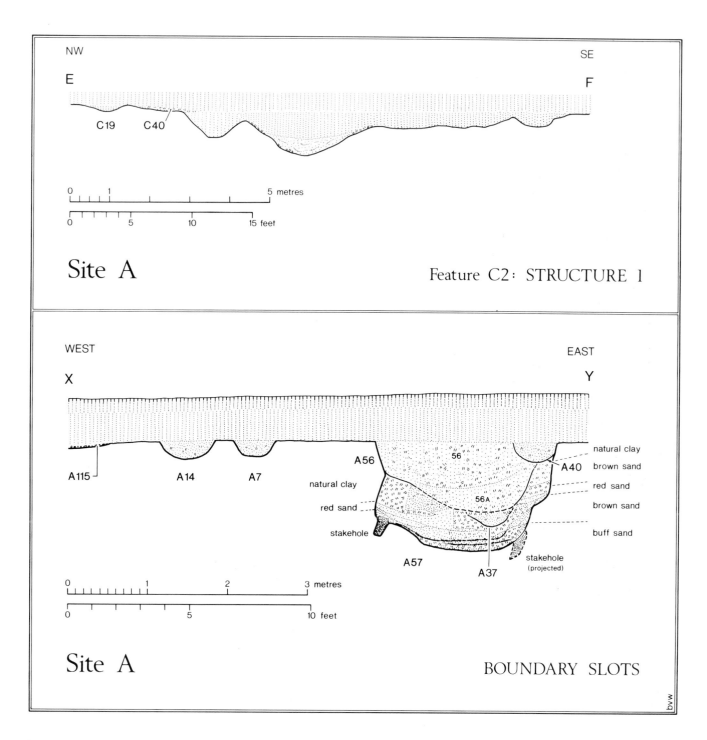

Fig 3.2 Site A. Sections through Grubenhaus *Structure 1 (C2) and X–Y through boundaries in the north corner of the Site.*

Age. On balance the gullies are regarded as Iron Age and pit C44 the only feature of certain Roman date (Chapter 13).

3.4.3 Discussion

See Chapter 13.

3.5 Between the Romano-British period and the Norman Conquest

(Fig 3.7 no 4)

3.5.1 Structure 1 (C2 and related features) Stratigraphy (Fig 3.2)

Structure 1 (S1) survived as an irregular hollow C2, 10m long and 5.5m wide, with its maximum depth of 1.20m in a central depression around which were traces of red clay. At the south end was a more distinct oval depression 0.20m deep, at the north another 0.40m deep; these may have once been postholes. There were a large number of stakeholes up to 0.10m deep around the inside of the edge. The central depression contained grey sandy silt, but the remainder of the hollow was filled with homogenous brown sandy soil. Gully C19, 0.30m deep filled with similar brown soil, ran north, and slightly downhill, into C66, a hollow 4 m across and 0.50m deep containing grey-brown silty sand. A length of gully C39, 0.25m deep with a brown sand fill, also ran into C66. The fills of features C2, C19, C66 and C39 appeared to have been contemporary. It is possible that C2 was used for some time as a building, and then its hollow left open for a while to form part of a complex holding water. Alternatively the gully C19, linking C2 to C66 may have been intended to provide a drain from the Structure. It is possible that the fill of C2 may postdate the initial Structure by some length of time. The complex underlay red clay features C40 and C69 which may relate to kiln C48.

3.5.2 Dating

The only distinctive artefact from any of these interrelated features is iron spur 136 of, most probably, 10th century type. The spur came from infilling of C2 and its deposition may have post-dated the initial use of Structure 1. The C2 infill contained other iron artefacts and several pieces of cut antler. A Saxo-Norman sherd P4 (Fig 18.1) came from C69. Other evidence for the 10th and 11th centuries from Site A consists of residual Saxo-Norman sherds in A5 and A11 (Table 18.2) and a penny of Edward the Confessor (Chapter 16.1) from topsoil removed by machine.

3.5.3 Discussion

Structure 1 has the classic appearance of a *Grubenhaus*, with rounded depressions suggestive of settings for gable-end posts at either end of the long axis. The 10m length is at the upper recorded limit of size for *Grubenhäuser*. Generally the larger *Grubenhäuser*, dating late in the Saxon period, represent the cellars of timber buildings. Examples have been excavated at Canterbury (Blockley, forthcoming), Chester (Mason, 1985), and at Upton, Northants, (Jackson, Harding & Myres, 1969). The association with worked antler is discussed in 16.7.

3.6 The Norman Borough Defences
(Figs 3.3, 3.7 no 5)
3.6.1 Stratigraphy

A substantial ditch with two obvious recuts ran almost north–south across the site. On topographi-

cal grounds the bank should have existed on its western, inner, side but the ditch silts gave no indication of the direction from which they had been derived. On the line of the presumed bank was a ridge of concreted sand, either influencing its siting or caused by percolation of water through the bank. The line of the ditches south of Site A was confirmed by two small machine cuts, B on Fig 1.2, both within the grounds of Abbey Nurseries.

The lower levels of the ditches were not given context numbers during excavation, their fills being described on section drawings; only those contexts numbered on site are numbered on Fig 3.3.

Ditch I

This, the earliest ditch detected, was between 2.20 and 2.50m deep with an irregular profile; it had probably been about 5m wide originally. The primary silt, very pale fine brown sand, passed gradually upwards into a darker sand, beneath A84/A84A, grey-brown sand with some lumps of pink clay. A78 was light brown sand with occasional concreted lumps. The upper fill A80 was of mid-brown silty sand. An oval post socket A119 was set 0.20m deep at an angle of 45° into the west side of the ditch.

Ditch II

Ditch II, cut through Ditch I, was originally about 7m wide and 2.50m deep. To the north it narrowed, possibly nearing an entrance. In the north section (Fig 3.3, C–D) the bottom deepened 0.50m to the butt end of a slot, possibly intended to take a horizontal sleeper beam as no vertical post settings were noted; its fill was sharply distinguished vertically between a very clean sand on the east, and greyish sand with lumps of pink clay and charcoal on the west. A posthole A118, 0.25m deep, was adjacent to the end of the slot in the ditch bottom.

The ditch bottom was infilled with mixed deposits, which appeared to have been deliberately and rapidly dumped, over which were silting layers of fine brown sand and soil with occasional clay lumps. These were covered by brown silty soil with frequent pink clay lenses A91/97, and then by a darker brown sandy silt A89. The top of the ditch was backfilled by grey-brown sandy loam with occasional mussel shells, charcoal and clay lumps A79/101.

Ditch III

This was 2.10m deep and 6m across, with a fairly regular V-shaped profile, which, in the south section, broadened into a flat-bottomed channel filled with mixed clay and sand A102. Two probable post sockets A117 and A117A, each 0.10m deep, were cut in its east side. In the north section primary sand silt was covered by brown-grey silty

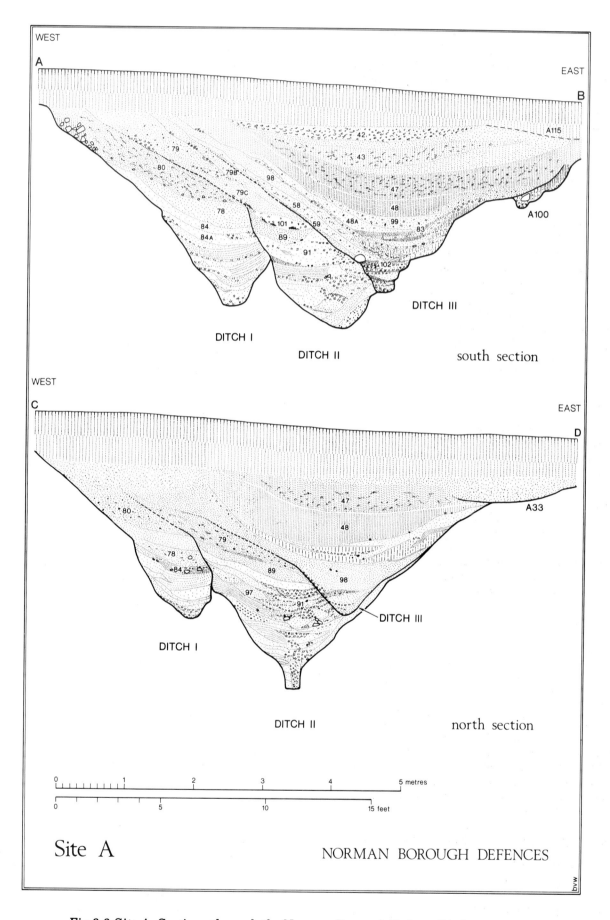

Fig 3.3 Site A. Sections through the Norman Borough Defence Ditch sequence.

Pl 3.1 Site A. Corn dryer C3 fully excavated with raised burnt patch on base. View from west. Scale in ft.

sand A98; in the south A98 was greyer and contained charcoal and mussel shells, with light clean sands A58/A59 beneath. A98 was covered by hard, brown slightly gritty silts with some pink clay lenses, enumerated as A83/A48A/A99 in the south section. The upper silts were composed of brown sand with charcoal, red clay and mussel shells, A48 passing up into a darker layer A47, which in the north section continued up to the top of the ditch. In the south section the upper layers were mixed fine gravel and red clay A43 and a dump of mussel shells A42. A43 looked like a deliberate infill or spread. The upper levels of the ditch were fully excavated across Site A. South of section A–B the top of A42 slumped down to a depth of 0.50m, and above it the ditch hollow was filled with dumps of soil with charcoal and ash A82 which mounded up over the ditch top in places to merge with the brown sand soil at the base of topsoil. (The sections Fig 3.3 AB, CD were reconstructed back to ground surface to show the depth of overlying levels).

3.6.2 Dating

The earliest datable object from the ditches was the unfinished decorated bone trial piece MSF 21

from A78 Ditch I, probably 10th century or earlier (16.5). Ditch I produced no pottery, nor, probably, did Ditch II, P25 being almost certainly intrusive. They could be pre- or post-Norman, and are fully discussed in Chapters 19 and 20 with relevant evidence from other Sites. Ditch III produced 13th century sherds from levels A98 upward. The upper levels and dumps contained material of kiln V type as well as other 13th century sherds, and the ditch by some date in this century was no more than a rubbish tip.

3.6.3 Discussion

The possible historical contexts for the ditches and correlations with those found on other Sites is discussed in Chapters 19 and 20. It is concluded that the later phases at least formed part of the defensive circuit of the Norman Borough; consequently the ditches are referred as the Norman Borough Defences both in the subsequent text and on relevant illustrations.

3.7 Kiln C3 (Figs 3.4, 3.7 no 6; Pl 3.1)
3.7.1 Stratigraphy

Kiln C3 was sited just west of Structure 1, which may still have formed a slight depression. A roughly circular steep sided pit 5m across was dug to a depth of 1.30m. An area left raised in the centre of the base was heavily burnt. The main circular pit or firing chamber was approached by two rough steps in an extension to the west. At the junction of the approach and the chamber, where there could have been a stoke pit arch, were two small sockets on the north side and one on the south. C68 and C82, 0.30m deep, may have held posts connected with the arch or another part of the superstructure. Irregularities around the steps suggest that these had been redug or reduced in size. In places (not shown on section) the vertical kiln wall was lined with up to 0.20m of mixed clays, which had shrunk slightly to leave gaps against the original pit edge which had become filled with fine black soil.

The main pit was backfilled with a mixed deposit of pink clay and sand (3a), interspersed with runs of charcoal containing some grain (3b) and bright red clay (3c); a thin spread of dark sandy soil with some lumps of natural yellow sandstone (3d) was next thrown in from the western end. A thick dump of mixed pink clay and sand (3e) was thrown into the hollow, and then a layer of medium brown sandy soil with lumps of natural sandstone (3f). A dark brown humic sandy soil (3g) accumulated in the top of the backfilled hollow.

Various features around and to the north of kiln C3 may have been related to it, forming the damaged remains of structures. C81 and C79, 0.30m deep, were filled with black soil and could have been structural. North of the kiln was an area of pink clay, C69, 0.05m thick, laid directly on the

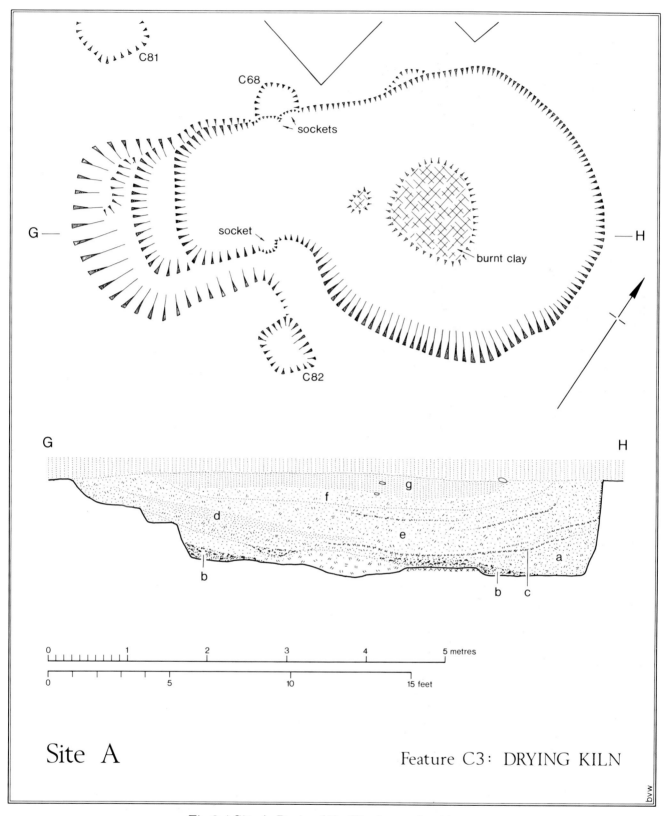

C81

C68

sockets

G

socket

burnt clay

H

C82

G

H

d

b

f

g

e

a

b

c

0 1 2 3 4 5 metres

0 5 10 15 feet

Site A

Feature C3: DRYING KILN

bvw

Fig 3.4 Site A. Drying kiln C3 plan and sections.

sandy subsoil; its south edge was well defined in a
straight edge through which two stakeholds were
cut. Part of clay C69 overlay the edge of the fill of
Structure 1. An area of similar clay C40 filled a
small pit cutting the north end of the Structure. A

substantial posthole, C18, 0.75m deep with
limestone packing stones, cut through clay C69.
The packing stones were set in a matrix of greenish clay and the socket, from which the post had
been withdrawn, was filled with black soil flecked

with pink clay. Further to the north were two postholes filled with dark brown sand, C78 and C4, 0.20 and 0.15m deep respectively.

3.7.2 Dating

Both C3e and C3f produced glazed jug sherds of 13th century date. Posthole C18 contained P29, and floor C69 P36 as well as residual Saxo-Norman P4; these could also be 13th century.

3.7.3 Discussion

C3 is interpreted as a corn drying kiln similar to 13th century kilns T50 and T61. The sockets, at the base of the steps, probably held uprights for the stoke pit arch; the largely destroyed clay lining, perhaps with light internal timbering, could have supported the main weight of the dome. There is no surviving evidence for how the drying floor was supported. The raised central floor area had been hardened by burning and would be appropriate for frequent lightings of a small fire. Only a small amount of grain was identified from the fill (Chapter 15.3). Fuller discussion of drying kilns follows descriptions of the Site T kilns 51 and 60 (Chapter 4.9.3).

3.8. House 1 (Figs 3.5, 3.7 no 6; Pls 3.2, 3.3)

3.8.1 Stratigraphy

The House, situated on the ridge of hardened sand forming the highest part of the Site, had been substantially eroded and no interior levels remained. It was of at least two phases with internal dimensions of 5.50m (18ft) by 3.70m (12ft). Its wall timbers had been ground set, in an irregular slot varying between 0.15m and 0.60m in depth. The north corner had been cut away by a modern disturbance. The irregularity of the slot related to the method by which it was initially dug; it had been cut down almost vertically on the outer edge,

Pl 3.2 Site A. House 1 before excavation. View from east. Scale in ft.

presumably with a sharp edged spade, and blocks of the cemented sand subsoil levered out, causing the subsoil to break unevenly along the inner edge. The slot fill was dark brown sandy soil containing frequent lumps of cemented sand and pink clay. There were a number of packing stones of white Carboniferous Limestone with some of purple Carboniferous Sandstone.

Phase 1 Corner Posts

The corners of the House had originally been supported by posts set into distinct circular postholes. The south east posthole, 0.25m deep, had contained a circular post 0.20m across set on a flat stone and wedged in place by vertical packing stones. The south west posthole, 0.30m deep, had held a circular post 0.20m in diameter, with a base stone but no vertical stones. The north east posthole, 0.27m deep, appeared to have been damaged by the removal of the post and only two packing stones remained. The north west posthole had been completely destroyed by modern disturbance. The south east and south west postholes were filled with fine dark soil without any clay or cemented sand lumps; the filling of that on the north east corner was of dark sand mixed with cemented sand and clay lumps, indistinguishable from that of the slot on either side.

Phase 2 Corner Posts

A single flat limestone block had been wedged in the tops of all three surviving corner postholes. Those on the north east and south east projected, above the level at which the slot was detectable, into the base of topsoil. It is likely that these slabs supported the bases of posts during a second phase of the building. It is not clear which structural elements of the wall slots were contemporary with the two phases of corner posts.

Wall slots

The wall slot varied in depth from 0.15m to 0.45m. The basal packing stones lay mainly flat on its base, in fairly straight lengths on the west, more irregular on the east. Most of the packing stones on the south were concentrated around a posthole (a) in the slot bottom and 0.45m deeper than it. The slot on the north was irregular and discontinuous, the only packing stones in a short stretch in the centre in positions indicating the presence of two separate posts. In a gap was a distinctive posthole, (b), 0.25m deep, sloping west at an angle of 45°. The mixed homogeneous fill and the irregularity of the packing stones suggest that the posts of the Phase 1 building had been dug out. A number of distinct circular depressions, 0.05m to 0.15m across and with the same range of depths, occurred along the base of the slot, and were filled with soft dark brown soil. They were all straight-sided but came

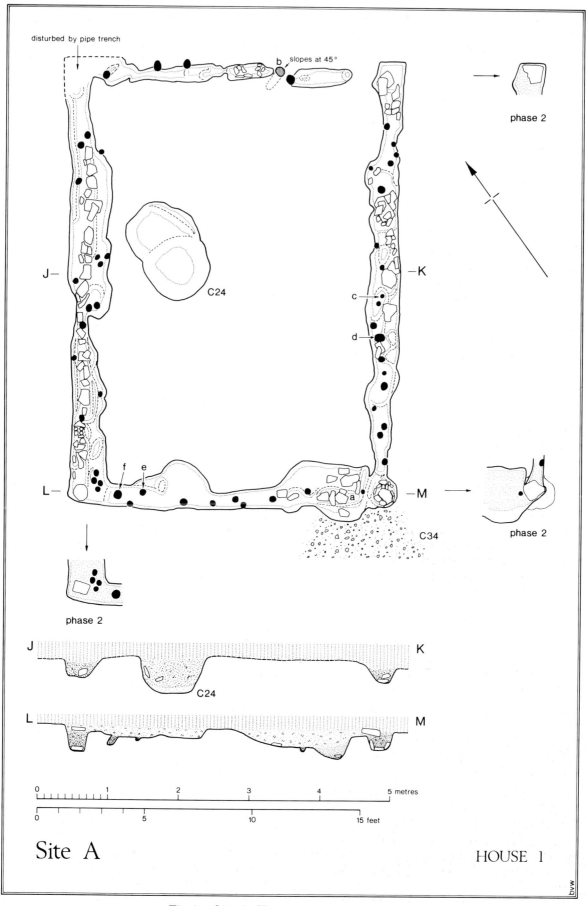

disturbed by pipe trench

slopes at 45°

b

phase 2

J—

C24

—K

c

d

f e

L—

a

—M

phase 2

C34

phase 2

J   K

C24

L   M

0   1   2   3   4   5 metres

0   5   10   15 feet

Site A

HOUSE 1

Fig 3.5 Site A. House 1 plans and sections.

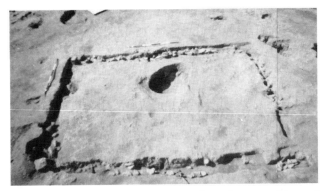

Pl 3.3 Site A. House 1 excavated to show packing of Phase 2. View from east. Scale in ft.

to a point at the base. None were sealed by packing stones. Four appeared to have held diagonal, not vertical posts; (c) and (d) were 30° from vertical, leaning north; (e) was 25° from vertical to the west and (f) 45° from vertical to the east. These holes appeared to have been produced by ramming in pointed stakes, which did not relate in any way to the surviving arrangements of packing stones. They may relate to Phase 2 of the House.

The entrance

The position of the entrance in either phase cannot be established with certainty. The pebble spread C34 outside the south east corner may have been a path leading to an entrance. The pebbles did not continue within the House and presumably were contemporary with it. They were deposited in the base of a depression, in a matrix of brown soil, and pressed into the sand subsoil. They probably indicated a worn pathway subsequently filled with pebbles. An entrance in the south east would presumably have belonged to the second phase, because of the presence here of the substantial post setting (a) with undisturbed packing stones suggested as typical of the first phase. It is also possible that there had been an entrance central to the south side, as the slot widened either side of the centre, and to the west deepened by 0.07m; this may have been to hold posts for a doorway. The slot ran across the presumed entrance, and the lack of packing stones or post sockets suggests that any door posts had been removed. Another possible site for an entrance was the discontinuous slot at the north east corner. This separate section of slot, only 0.13m deep, could have been cut in the second phase to provide seating for rammed stakes.

Possible hearth C24

Pit C24 within the House may have been related to it as it produced fragments of both the limestone and the sandstone used in the packing slots. Its fill was of black sandy soil with charcoal flecks, over a thin layer of light brown sand. The maximum depth was 0.50m but on the north there was a flat shelf only 0.35m deep. The fill was homogeneous

and the small pieces of stone in its fill did not appear to be packing stones for posts. There were no traces of burning. Pit C24 produced four joining fragments of a heavily burnt sandstone bakestone (Chapter 16.8, MSF 31; Fig 16.9) and may have been sited next to a hearth now removed by erosion.

3.8.2 Dating

From pit C24 came a glazed jug sherd and from the wall slot a waster of kiln V type. These suggest a 13th century date.

3.8.3 Discussion

The plan and the method of construction are similar to the better preserved House 2 (Chapter 3.9.3).

3.9 House 2 and adjacent features

(Figs 3.6, 3.7 no 6; Pl 3.4)

3.9.1 Stratigraphy

House 2 lay parallel to House 1 but was situated in a slight depression and so had not suffered from erosion; its floor level was sealed by decay and destruction material C7 beneath brown sandy soil C12. It was single phase, its internal dimensions 6.60m (21ft 2in) by 3.80m (12ft 6in). The northern end had been levelled back 0.15m into a slight rise. The timber uprights had been set in a square cut slot (C52, 53, 54, 73) between 0.25m and 0.40m deep and packed with small, waterworn lumps of white limestone in pink clay. The four corner posts appear to have been rectangular and more deeply set than the side walls. The walls were composed of planks and staves, apparently set edge to edge, irregularly interspersed with larger posts. The positions of the planks were marked by a band of fine dark soil C31, in places no more than 0.03m wide, running vertically down through the clay slot packing to their base. The character of soil C31 is indicative of woodwork decaying in position, although ragged hollows around some larger posts suggest that they may either have been dug out or have collapsed, damaging their settings. In places compression of the clay packing, subsequent to the rotting of the planks, had twisted from vertical C31, the soil representing their position.

Doorway

The entrance was central to the south wall. The west doorpost had consisted of a squared timber set 0.35m deep; the setting for that on the east was badly damaged, probably during the removal of the post. The surface in the entrance had been worn slightly hollow and a dirty trampled surface extended south to the edge of the excavated area (not on plan).

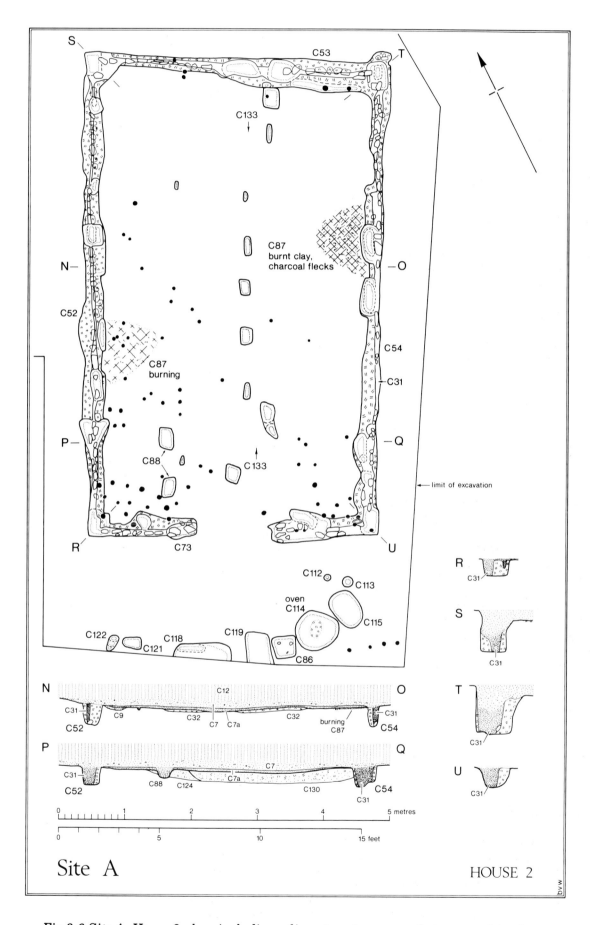

Fig 3.6 Site A. House 2 plan, including adjacent contemporary features, and sections.

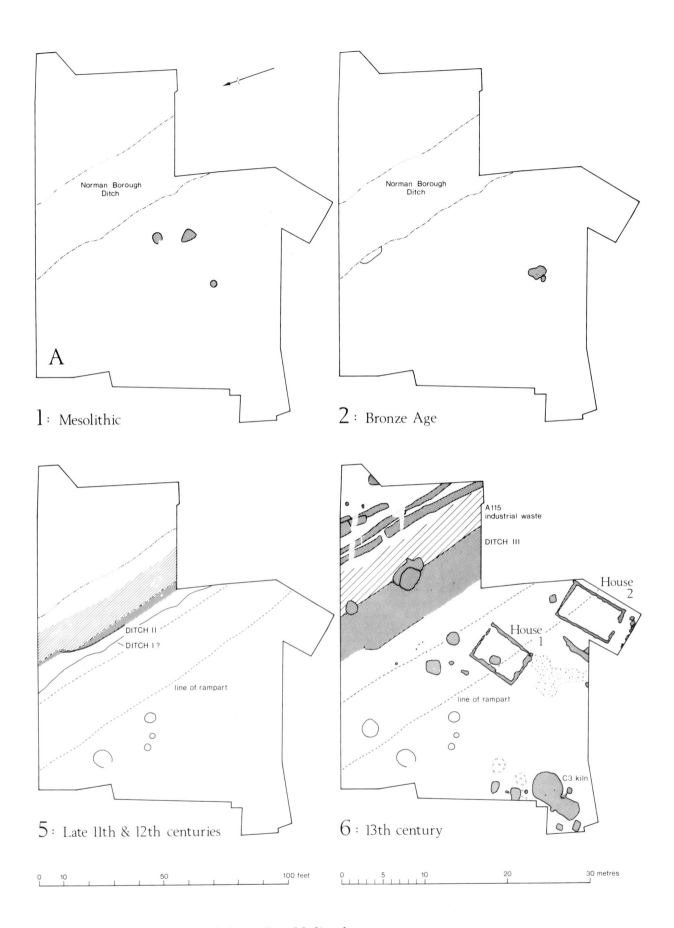

Fig 3.7 Site A. Phase plans Mesolithic to Post-Medieval.

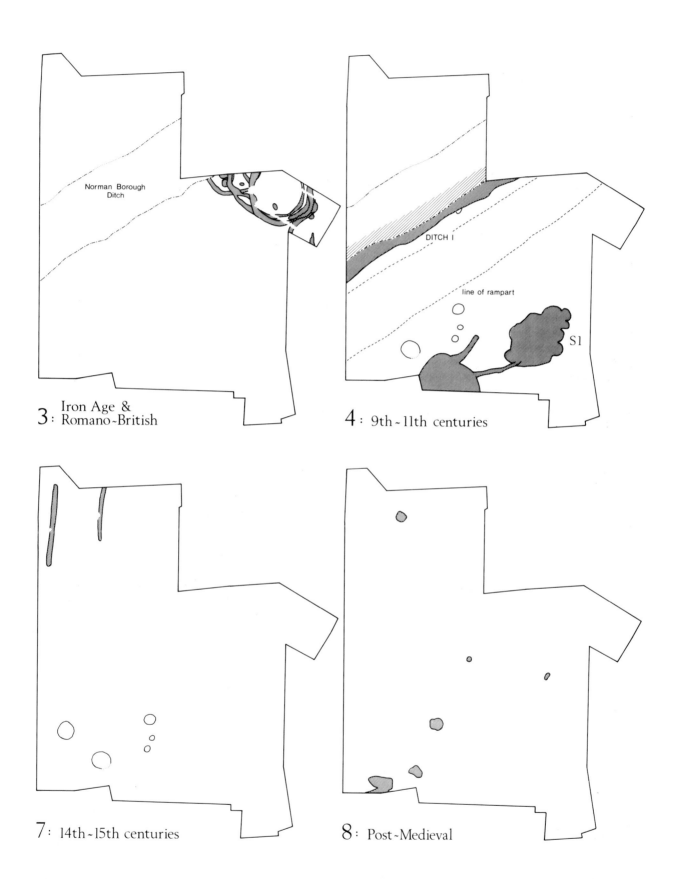

3: Iron Age &
   Romano~British

4: 9th~11th centuries

Norman Borough
Ditch

DITCH I

line of rampart

S1

7: 14th~15th centuries

8: Post~Medieval

Pl 3.4 Site A. House 2, excavated to remove all soil from voids left by decayed timbers. View from south. Scale in ft.

Floor, possible hearths, interior post-holes and stake holes

The interior surface was laid with patches of pink clay where sand formed the subsoil, or over the Romano-British gullies C9 etc. The surface of these patches together with that of the clay subsoil formed a floor C32, worn, compacted and dirty, with much charcoal trampled into it in places. Areas (C87) against the east and the west walls had been so heavily burnt that the material beneath was red to a depth of 0.05m (Section N–O).

The interior had been subdivided by a line of posts (C133), set in sockets about 0.10m deep, running down the long axis of the building. A slight depression 0.03m deep running along much of the inner side of slot C53, with two stakeholes in it, may have held an interior fitting. There were also two postholes C88, 0.15m deep, and a large number of stake holes, mainly on the west side, varying between 0.05m and 0.07m in depth. They presumably represented the positions of interior fittings.

South Annex and other contemporary features

Outside, and 1.50m south, of the entrance was an arc of postholes and stakeholes cut into the trampled surface running out from the entrance; they apparently formed an enclosure or annex. The features, C122 to C115, were all probable post settings up to 0.45m deep. C114 was a possible oven. This was a pit 0.20m deep, lined with clay 0.07m thick, with, on the bottom, a dome of clay heavily burnt on its top. C85, to the north of the House (Fig 3.1), was a possible posthole 0.85m deep.

Occupation and destruction deposits

A thin soil C7A, almost black, up to 0.05m thick occurred all over the interior floor C32, presumably dirt trampled onto the floor. A layer of dark brown sandy soil C7, mixed with extensive spreads of dirty yellow clay, covered the interior of the House, spread over the lines of its walls and, on the south, continued to the limits of the excavated area. To the north and west it faded gradually against the rising slope, to fill the hollow caused by the levelled house platform. This deposit presumably built up as House 2 decayed after it became disused.

,25

3.9.2 Dating

A few glazed jug sherds, were found in the floor trample C7A and a single sherd in C31, the fine soil marking the line of the decayed east wall. Destruction deposits C7 produced a small group of similar glazed sherds and P34, a rim sherd from an alkaline-glazed bowl provisionally dated by J G Hurst to the 14th century. The House may have been built during the 13th century; its site was accumulating debris during the 14th. The parallel layout of Houses 1 and 2 suggests they were standing at the same time.

3.9.3 Discussion

The plans of both Houses, with entrances in the gable ends, appear unusual for their date, although these types occur for example in 10th century Dublin (Murray, 1981). The central line of post-holes in House 2 is uncommon, but the irregularity of the holes suggests an internal division rather than support for the roof ridge.

The soil-filled voids within the wall trenches probably represented vertical planks between load bearing staves along the length of the walls, with posts at the corners (clearly with House 2, most probably with House 1); the planks may well have been fitted into grooves in the staves.This type of building construction is well known in Western Europe from the 6th century onward, although by the 12th–13th centuries its use had become restricted (Chapelot & Fossier, 1985, 273), and it was mainly used in churches, especially in Scandinavia (Bugge, 1935). The 11th century church of Greensted in Essex (Christie, Olsen & Taylor, 1979), in its earliest phase, is similar to House 2 as it had thick vertical staves set in a wall trench, rather than a cill beam; it differed in not having more substantial posts along its walls. This technique survived in rural ancillary buildings (which tend to continue traditional techniques) in the Alpine region; in the late 12th–13th century German settlement of Ostfriesland (Chapelot & Fossier, 1985, 262) the upright plank panels between posts were set into wall trenches in the same way as in House 2. The use of a foundation trench for the walls was replaced by a cill beam into which vertical timbers were slotted, and by the late medieval period the cill beam was frequently placed on a stone wall base to protect it from contact with damp (le Patourel, 1973, 96, Fig 30).

Part of an earthfast plank and stave structure was recently excavated at Ironmonger Lane, London (pers comm Valerie Horsman). A more complete example of late Saxon stave-built building set on timber baseplates 0.24m wide was excavated at Pudding Lane, City of London during 1981 (Horsman, 1985); this had the entrance in the gable end. Well preserved 10th–11th century stave-built structures are also known from Dublin, some with alternate staves and planks tongue and groove

jointed (Murray, 1983) and Coppergate, York (Hall, 1984a). Earlier examples, from the 6th and 7th centuries come from Chalton, Hants, (Addyman & Leigh, 1973) and Thirlings, Northumberland (Miket, 1974).

House 2, and probably House 1, appear to show a survival of an archaic, mainly urban, British building technique generally assumed to be current from the 7th–11th centuries, with a concentration in the 9th–11th centuries. The Houses are most likely to relate to Edward I's occupancy; their siting shows the Norman Borough Defences well out of use and House 2 at least survived to have rubbish dumped in the 14th century. There may well have been personnel with a wide range of European backgrounds at Rhuddlan by the late 13th century and a consequent wide range of architectural traditions to draw on.

This discussion assumes that the Houses do not relate to Welsh traditions. It is possible that they were constructed during the period of Welsh ascendency before AD 1278. Knowledge of 13th century Welsh building traditions is only gradually accumulating. Excavation of a farmstead at Cefn Graenog, Clynnog, Gwynedd (Kelly, 1982, Fig 5) revealed an end-entrance house of timber construction beneath a later one of stone. This was of 12th or 13th century date but its construction appears to have involved cruck timbers. Kelly's discussion of the Cefn Graenog buildings (ibid, 882–5 with references) presents a comprehensive summary of the available evidence from Wales, and while structures with end-entrances may occur, stake-built structures have not so far been located.

3.10 13th Century activity post-dating the Norman Borough Defences (Fig 3.7 no 6)

3.10.1 Stratigraphy

After Ditch III had almost entirely silted up, a trampled surface A115 formed over its top and extended 4 to 5m north east; in places it formed depressions in the subsoil with a few stake holes and postholes A26 and A24. Associated with A115 were a run of shallow pits, the bottoms of which had well-trampled patches of gravel, spreads of charcoal, but no traces of burning, and of mussel shells. The scoops were A33 0.25m deep, A28 and A4 0.07m deep, A106 0.30m deep with two post sockets on its east side, A107, A104 and A105 all 0.15m deep. A28 and A4 had iron slag in their fills. Pit A5, 0.35m deep, cut into the top of A106, was lined with 0.05m of pink clay and had a number of stakeholes in its base. The fill of A5 was dark brown sandy soil mixed with charcoal and lumps of slag and burnt clay but there was no burning on its clay lining. Clay lumps in this pit had been mixed with straw or other vegetable filler, and were curved as though they had come from some form of superstructure.

Surface A115 extended east to A14/34, one of a series of slots. These, parallel to the line of the Norman Ditch, were filled with brown sandy soil and lumps of pink clay and around 0.30m deep. While no positions of upright posts were detected, the fills gave the impression of having been deposited quickly after the slots were cut, and may have been packing for timbers. Slot A36, the furthest east, started a complex relationship between the slots and pit A56/57 (Fig 3.2). A36 was cut through by, or ran up to, pit A57; this had stakeholes in its base and was infilled with mixed layers, probably dumped, of sand and clay. Slot A37 was dug through these layers, but was subsequently truncated by the recut A56/A56A of pit A57 (section X–Y, Fig 3.2; the recut A57 co-incides so closely with the original pit A56 on plan Fig 3.1 that it is not shown as a separate line). Slot A40 finally cut the infilled pit A57/A56. The slots seem best interpreted as a series of successive boundary lines, associated with pit A57/56 which initially had contained some form of structure. Minor features such as A11 and A37 hint at some complexity.

3.10.2 Dating

Pits A33, A28 and A106 contained sherds kiln V type, and a few other sherds including P30. A10 produced jug P31 and a green-glazed Saintonge sherd, A5 numerous sherds and wasters of kiln V type, and jug P32. The comparatively large amount of pottery in these features suggests a date late in the 13th century.

Slots A34 and A14 contained sherds of kiln V type, and A7 P33 similar to kiln V material; there were a few other 13th century sherds. The dating of the slots is consistent with the material from the scoops associated with surface A115, although they contained less ceramic material.

3.10.3 Discussion

Surface A115 and associated features are similar in position and dating to levels over the infilled Norman Borough Defences on Sites T and E, although these produced more iron slag. This possible industrial phase is discussed in Chapter 20. The slots may have represented successive boundaries between an area of industrial activity over the infilled ditch, and a plot used for other purposes to their east.

3.11 East–west slots A9 and A35

(Fig 3.7 no 7)

These had similar fills, sandy with clay lumps, to the north–south slots they truncated. A9 had a maximum depth of 0.30m, and A35 of 0.20m. The slots could have formed part of a timber building. However traces of gullies filled with dark soil on a similar alignment were noted during machine clearance, and this alignment is that of plot boundaries as recorded on the *Conway Map of 1756*. A9 and A35 may therefore be the deeply dug and surviving remnants of the division of the former Norman Borough into small fields. A single medieval glazed sherd was the only artefact recovered. Given the complexity of the sequence that A9/A35 postdated, a sequence which started in the late 13th century, a 14th or 15th century date might be possible.

3.12 Miscellaneous pits and features of probable medieval date

(Fig 3.7 no 7)

A scatter of pits across the site could not be related to any structure. B5, 0.20m deep, had a patch of heavy burning on its base and was filled with dark brown sandy soil and charcoal; it may have been used as an oven. C15, 0.25m deep, was filled with dark brown sandy soil mixed with lumps of concreted sand and pink clay and contained a sherd from of kiln V type. B7, 0.30m deep, contained a thick layer of charred grain on its base beneath a fill of almost black sandy soil (Chapter 15.5).

Other pits etc are described in the archive as they could not be dated or related to any phase of activity.

3.13 Post-medieval features

(Fig 3.7 no 8)

A few pits had post-medieval material in their fills: B9, B8, B6, C26, A2 and C50.

3.14 Site C (Fig 1.2)

A trench 2m by 2m by 2m deep was dug during 1969 for rubbish disposal. This revealed a pit of unknown date over 2 m deep.

Acknowledgements
We are grateful to Mr Hurst of Abbey Nurseries for permission to excavate; Charles Young and Ian Young were supervisors. Valerie Horsman was most helpful with comparanda for Houses 1 and 2.

4 Site T, Ysgol-Y-Castell, Lôn Hylas. On the line of the Norman Borough Defences

4.1 Introduction (Figs 4.1–3; Pl 4.2)

Site T, together with Site V, was excavated from March to May 1973, covering sufficient area to allow for immediate and medium term expansion of school buildings and an extension of the playground. Topsoil clearance was started by hand, but it became apparent that up to 0.60m of spoil, from school foundation trenches and playing field levelling, had been recently dumped over the lower, east end of the site. Beneath the dumped material was a post-medieval soil 0.60m thick which covered the whole area. These levels were removed mechanically, after which a substantial ditch was observed running diagonally across the eastern part of the site (Norman Borough Defences). Section lines were laid out across the ditch, but, to the west, where no features were immediately apparent, a grid was established parallel to the trench edge and used initially as a control for excavation.

Prior to the recent dumping, the site had sloped gently downhill from west to east, dropping by about 1m over 40m. The recent dumping levels have been omitted from the published section drawings. The subsoil was fine yellow compact sand, very soft on the west, with pink clayey patches to the east.

4.2 Mesolithic (Fig 4.1)

No features were located, but 1351 pieces of chert and flint (Chapter 10) and decorated stone SF 6 (Chapter 11) were found in residual contexts. It is just possible that T208, a patch of yellow sandy soil at the base of the stratigraphy in the extreme south corner of the site was the remnant of a Mesolithic soil such as M26.

4.3 Iron Age (Figs 4.1, 4.7 no 1)

4.3.1 Stratigraphy

A number of features were sealed by, or appeared to pre-date, soil T64, preserved by the bank associated with the Norman Borough Defences, and were cut into either a sandy soil T322 (Fig 4.3) or into peri-glacial sand. Relationships suggest a sequence of some duration. The earliest post-Mesolithic artefacts are of Iron Age type and relate to features early in the sequence.

The lowest surviving soil level T322, immediately west of the ditches, was preserved beneath soil T64, itself protected by the associated rampart T69. Soil T322 was orange-brown and sandy, 0.10m thick; to the west of the rampart line the soil had remained unsealed and could not be distinguished as a separate layer in the lowest soil identified T178 (see 4.5).

Curved gully T127 and associated features (Pl 4.1)

Gully T127, 0.20m deep, with sloping sides and a curved base, was filled with compact mixed brown sands and pebbles with no trace of post settings. It terminated in a butt end to the north east but curved round to the north west where it had been removed by ploughing T319; it surrounded an area

Pl 4.1 Site T. Ploughmarks T319 parallel with marker, cut by base of palisade line T81.View from south.

28

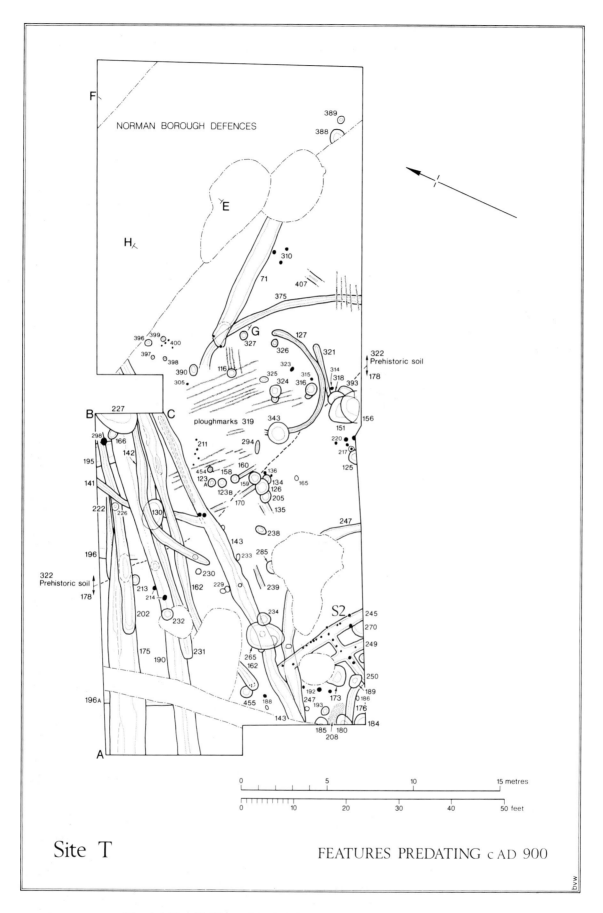

Fig 4.1 Site T. Plan of features likely to date before c AD 900.

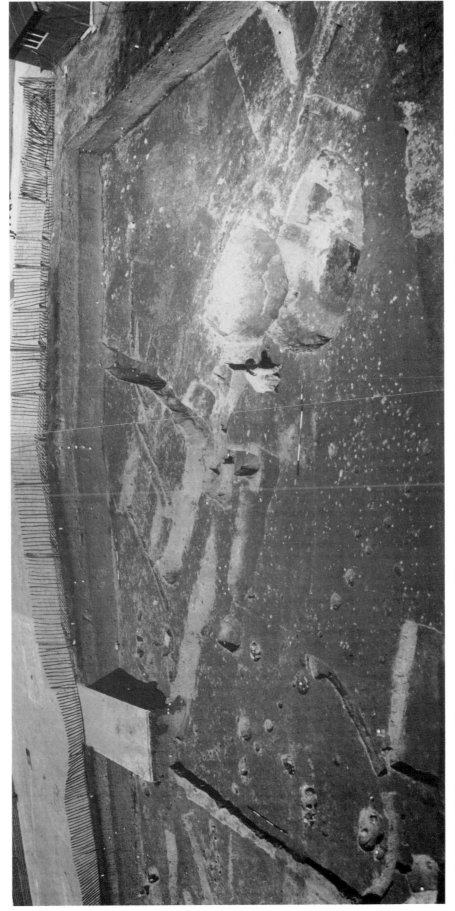

Pl 4.2 Site T. East end, collage view from south. Kilns 50, 61 in process of excavation, compound slots T34 etc excavated. Infilled Ditches lie beneath, top right. Palisade line T81 and prehistoric features gully T127 etc. Scale in ft.

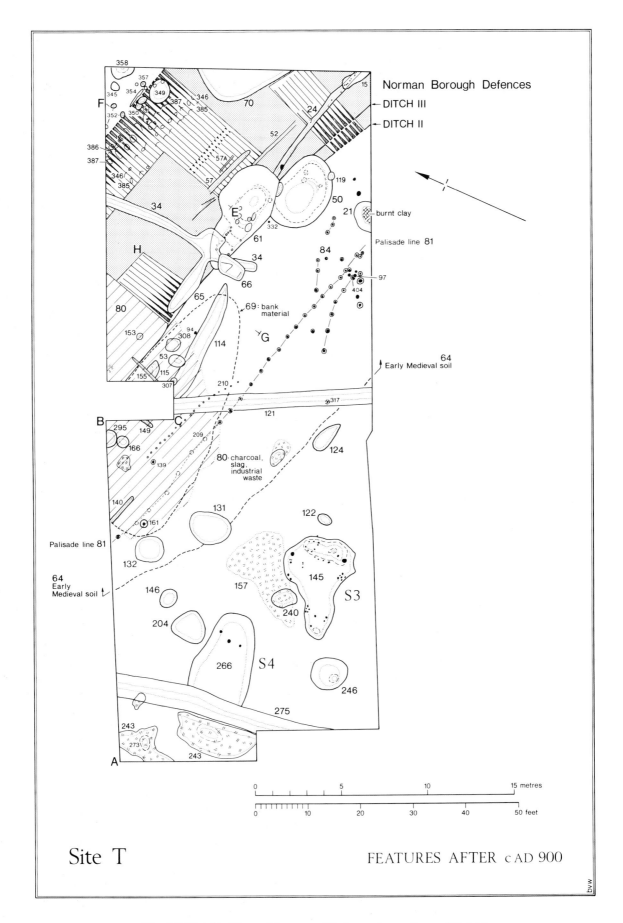

Site T

FEATURES AFTER c AD 900

Fig 4.2 Site T. Plan of features likely to date after c AD 900.

6 or 7m in diameter. To the north east was a stretch of similar but straighter gully T375 down-slope beyond T127, and a fragment of gully T407. T127 cut gully T321, 0.10m deep and filled with brown sandy soil, with occasional pink clay lumps and small pebbles, with again no trace of post settings.

All four features cut soil T322 and were covered by soil T64.

Ploughmarks and agricultural activity

(Pl 4.2)

Cutting through soil T322 and gully T127, and observed over the fill of T375, were a number of dark parallel striations T319, only preserved where overlying soil T64 was protected by the later rampart. These consisted of a series of slight depressions in T322 about 0.07m across and deep and between 0.08m and 0.20m apart. The main group ran approximately north west–south east, a second at right angles with only a slight overlap. These striations are interpreted as ploughmarks. None of the marks appeared double, suggesting that no furrow had been ploughed twice. Two slight gullies T170 and T160 ran parallel to and slightly west of the main group of marks; these were approximately 0.05m deep and filled with a brown sandy soil. They may either have been exceptionally wide furrows or the remnants of demarcation gullies or field boundaries.

The suggested ploughmarks were indicated by dark marks on the apparent top of soil T322. This suggests that they were formed at the bottom of a soil profile with humus from the top becoming displaced. The soil above must have been continually disturbed to prevent the marks showing at a higher level. The soil above is T64, and it is probable that part of this at least represents the disturbed upper part of the prehistoric soil.

Remnants of features to the north suggest an extension of the agricultural system (Fig 4.3). T195, 0.25m deep, may have been a broader demarcation gully; its top was levelled with a layer of clay and pebbles. T196 and T196A were slight scarps running roughly north–south with drops of 0.15m; each was filled with sandy soil slightly darker than T322/178 into which they were cut; these may have been negative lynchets. These three features appeared the earliest in this complex part of the site. A short length of round-bottomed gully T135 ran east–west to the west of the ploughmarks and may also have been connected with agricultural activity.

Possible four-post stuctures (Pl 4.3)

Four-postholes, T327-T326-TT325-T116, formed a 2.10m square within the curve of gully T127. All four contained limestone packing. The southern pair T325 and T326 were 0.40m deep, T327 and T116 only 0.15m. The similarity of the four sug-

Pl 4.3 Site T. Four-post structure T327-326-325-116 cut by palisade line T81. View from east. Scale in ft.

gests that they had formed a structural unit. T116 definitely cut through the ploughmarks T319 which had eroded gully T127. Four small pits or postholes T396–99, north of ploughmarks T319, were filled with charcoal flecked brown sandy soil and c 0.15m deep. They may also have formed a four-post structure, though much smaller than the T325 unit. Both quartets were sealed by soil T64 and cut into T322.

Miscellaneous features

Other features cut soil T322 and were overlain by T64. Within the area of T127 but cutting through the ploughmarks were two similar postholes T324 and T316 with fills of limestone packing, 2.10m apart centre to centre and 0.30m and 0.22m deep respectively. They both replaced to the east smaller, shallower postholes. Four stakeholes T400 were adjacent to the suggested four-poster containing T399; each had traces of charcoal at its base suggesting driven stakes with fire-hardened charred tips. Two small pits T389 and 388 were truncated by medieval Ditch II.

A series of features in the south west corner of the site was covered by soil T178, cut by the wall trenches of Structure 2 and by early medieval pits T180 and T189; the features cut into the sand subsoil, T322 not being clearly distinguishable in this area. Their compact brown sand fills were consistent with those of the suggested Iron Age features securely sealed beneath soil T64. T176, a curved flat-bottomed gully 0.32m deep, had a pale brown sand fill with frequent small pebbles which, although there was no trace of post settings, seemed more like deliberate packing than rain-

32

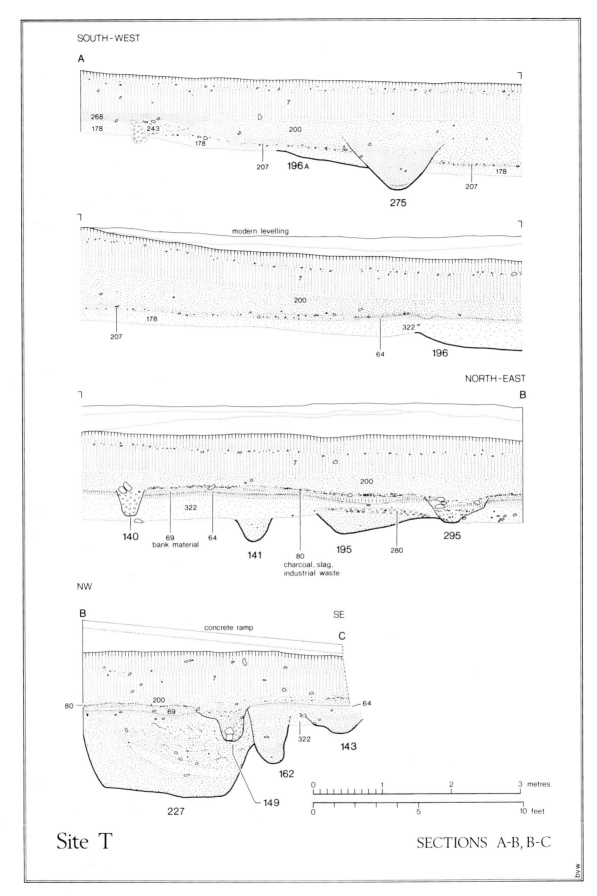

SOUTH-WEST

A

268
178
243
178
7
200
207
196 A
275
178
207

modern levelling
7
200
178
207
64
322
196

NORTH-EAST

B

7
200
140
69
bank material
64
322
141
80
charcoal, slag,
industrial waste
195
280
295

NW

B
concrete ramp
SE
C

7
80
200
69
64
322
143
162
149
227

0   1   2   3 metres
0   5   10 feet

Site T

SECTIONS A-B, B-C

bvw

Fig 4.3 Site T. Sections AB and BC in north of the Site relating the soil levels and rampart
material to gullies T162 etc.

washed silt. T184 and T185 were shallow depressions 0.15m deep filled with brown sand containing fire-cracked pebbles. T193, T186, T192 and T188 were small post or stakeholes filled with charcoal-flecked sand with depths from 0.05 to 0.15m. Curving gully T247, round-bottomed and up to 0.30 deep, was of uncertain relationship with Structure 2.

4.3.2 Dating

The most distinctive Iron Age object is the ring-headed pin SF9 residual in T64 (13.1.1).

The 23 fragments of salt container ceramic from Site T, including two possible rims, constitute 50% of the total assemblage from the 1969–73 excavations (13.1.4). Contexts containing this were: soil T322, posthole T126, gully T142, stakehole T220, four-poster posthole T326, gully T222, curved gully T127, posthole T328 (details 13.1.4). This material could be of any date from the 5th century BC to the 1st century AD, but is most probably from the 3rd to the 1st BC. The long date range allows for some centuries of Iron Age activity. It is possible that some features without close stratigraphic relationships could be of pre-Iron Age date.

4.3.3 Discussion

See Chapter 13.3.

4.4 Romano-British (Figs 4.1, 4.7 no 2)

4.4.1 Stratigraphy

Gully T71, the most securely dated Romano-British context, was flat-bottomed, 0.35m deep, and filled with brown sandy soil. It shallowed to the north west to form a clear butt-end with two small postholes in the base, each a further 0.10m deep. T71 cut soil T322 and gully T375 and was sealed by soil T64, and most residual Romano-British pottery occured in its area. Pit T151 with part of a (?) steelyard, SF 11 (13.3.1), and stakehole T305 with a samian sherd may be Romano-British, as may some of those features cutting ploughmarks T319 beneath soil T64 or those without relationships in soil T178.

4.4.2 Dating

Samian sherds suggest activity during the 2nd century but most other datable pieces, both from T71 and residual, were of late 3rd or early 4th century date. (13.2.3).

4.4.3 Discussion

See 13.3.

4.5 Between the Roman period and *c* AD 900 (Figs 4.1, 4.7 no 3)

4.5.1 Stratigraphy

Gullies, pits and postholes

A series of gullies in the west corner of the site ran roughly north east to south west; most appeared to have been intermittently recut. Fills were of pale brown rain-washed sandy silts, and depths varied between 0.85m and 0.20m. They formed several groups but details were difficult to disentangle. T222, cut away by T175 later cut by T202, formed the earliest group, on the north of the complex. This group was cut across by T141 on a different alignment. T141 was in turn cut by the group of T190, T231, T162 and T142 in sequence; T162 cut pit T227 (which contained a sherd of Saxo-Norman ware), flat-bottomed, around 1.0m deep, and filled with a series of grey and brown sand bands which appear to have been tipped in from the northern edge. The relationship of T143, on the south east of the group, to the others can not be ascertained; its junction with T141 was cut away by later pit T131. The gully system as a whole underlay soil T64.

Soil T64/178

Soil T64 (Fig 4.3), preserved beneath the line of the rampart south of the Norman Borough Defence ditches, formed a band 11m wide between 0.10m and 0.25m thick parallel to the ditches. It was of medium brown sand, passing downwards without any marked break to the lighter soil T322. T64 appears, in its surviving form, to represent a period of inactivity, separating the features it sealed and the features cut into it. Some of it must have been in position in the Iron Age to allow plough marks T319 to have been preserved. Beneath T69, a surviving patch of rampart, T64 was heavily compacted with discontinuous iron pan on its surface; the soil profile was incomplete, suggesting that turf had been stripped prior to rampart construction. South of the rampart line, soil T64 was continued by T178, up to 0.30m thick, sealed intermittently by a horizon of pebbles and pieces of broken stone T207.

Structure 2

Structure 2 (S2) was situated in the south corner of the site, cutting through T178 but below pebble layer T207. Its relationship with gully T247 was unclear, but it was cut through by gully T143. It contained no datable artefacts, so its date can only be suggested from the chronology of the gully system and the nature of its plan.

S2 consisted of three contemporary elements, T245, T249 and T250. These were round-bottomed trenches with a maximum depth of 0.30m, filled with medium brown sandy soil with darker lenses. In the base of the trenches were impressions of pointed stakes up to 0.10m deep; the fill of these stakeholes was dark brown charcoal-flecked sand which in some cases could be traced running up through the trench fills. The stakes were placed centrally within T250 and ? T249, but along the outer edge of T245. S2 was therefore constructed by driving stakes into prepared trenches which were then back-filled around them. The building plan was complex with T245 and T249 parallel but only 1m apart and T250 at right angles to them. The building was at least 5.75m long, and may be presumed to be the corner of a much larger structure. It was cut through by a later pit T246.

Miscellaneous features

A number of postholes, small pits and stakeholes were scattered, cutting through T322, and sealed by T64:- T126, T159, T123A, T123B, T158, T134, T205, T318, T136, T454, T211, T294, T323, T315, T314, T305, T163, T393, T310; these may be any date before the earliest construction of the Defences. Beyond T64 were others:- T151, T238, T285, T125, T165, T233, T217, T220, T214, for which the potential date range may extend even longer. Detailed descriptions can be found in the archive.

4.5.2 Dating

T222 and T142 contained salt container ceramic but no Roman sherds. Gully T222 and pit T227 each produced a small sherd of Saxo-Norman ware. The gullies T162 etc truncated the Iron Age/ Romano-British surface with ploughmarks and lynchets yet lay beneath soil T64 and rampart material T69. They appeared to pre-date the construction of the defensive system by the time necessary for soil T64 to form. Assuming that the Saxo-Norman ware is not intrusive, their date seems to be bracketed between the earliest date for this pottery and that of the earliest defensive phase. The pottery is unlikely to pre-date the 9th century and is more probably 10th. The earliest defences could be 10th or 11th century (Chapters 19 and 20). There is also the problem of gully T143 cutting through Structure 2, and of the gully group being cut by *Grubenhaus* S4 which is dated below to around the 10th century.

4.5.3 Discussion

The problem of the similarity of the gullies as a group to those on Site M and Site V assigned to the Iron Age is discussed in 13.3. They may all be interpreted as field or plot boundaries many times recut. All other comment depends on the dating.

Post-in-trench Structure 2 could, from its technique, be Roman (see eg Building R7 at Prestatyn; Blockley, 1989, Fig 22) but the absence of Roman pottery seems to rule out this period. The technique is also appropriate for Saxon structures from

perhaps the 6th century onward (Miket, 1974; Rahtz, 1976), while nothing is known in detail of Welsh building traditions in lowland areas at this period.

On balance it is suggested that the most appropriate interpretation for the features discussed in 4.5 is for the gullies to represent a long-maintained boundary in the post-Roman period. Structure 2 should be contemporary with part of this as it was cut through by T143, the latest of the sequence. The whole gully system should have been out of use by the time of Structure 4, probably 10th century. (The Saxo-Norman sherd in gully T222, very early in the sequence, and that in pit T227 would then be interpeted as intrusive.) This would provide possible evidence for occupation and activity at Rhuddlan, which could be linked with the fact that the site was already known by the time of the *Annales Cambriae* reference of AD 796. This interpretation would allow for the period of inactivity indicated by soil T64 before the construction of the defences.

4.6 Sunken-floored structures or *Grubenhäuser* S3 and S4
(Figs 4.2, 4.7 no 4)
4.6.1 Stratigraphy
Structure 3

This Structure related to a sunken area T145, an irregular triangular hollow 7m by 4.5m with an average depth 0.30m, dropping gradually from the east, more steeply from the west. It was partly within soil T178, partly apparently overlain by it and covered by T207. At either end of the long axis were two postholes, that on the east 0.30m deep, that on the west 0.10m. Scattered around the margins of the hollow and specifically within the deeper hollow in the eastern half were a number of small stakeholes. A linear depression around the posthole at the east end was filled with sticky brown soil and lenses of sand. The main hollow was filled with brown sandy soil which became lighter towards the base, with a number of scattered pebbles. Structure 3 exhibits the classic plan of a Saxon sunken-floored hut or *Grubenhaus*. The only find was an offcut strip of waste lead (16.2, MSF 15).

Structure 4

Structure 4 (T266) was a subrectangular hollow with surviving dimensions of 6m by 4m; its west end was truncated by a post-medieval boundary T275. Its stratigraphic position was the same as Structure 3. The hollow T266, 0.35m deep, had on its base a triangular area of pebbles 1m across, with, to the west, charcoal in brown loamy soil with occasional fired clay flecks and small pebbles T276. These basal layers were sealed by dark brown sandy soil which infilled the hollow. There were

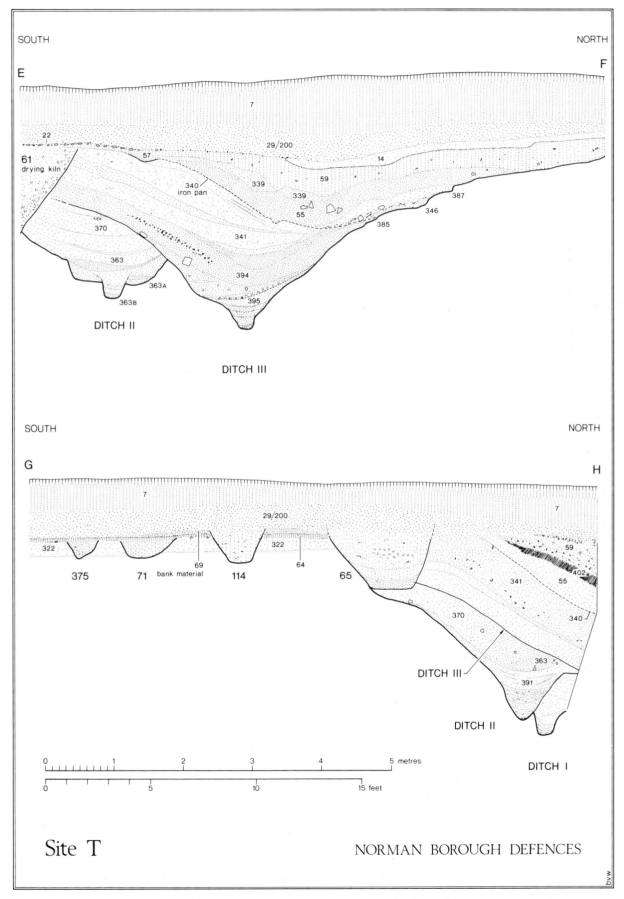

Fig 4.4 Site T. Sections EF, HG across the Norman Borough Defence Ditches and later features.

three stakeholes in its base, but the postholes and scatter of stakeholes associated with standard *Grubenhäuser* were absent. Iron artefacts were found in the basal layers, nos 52, 67, 68 and no 15, a knife of Saxo-Norman type.

4.6.2 Dating

The stratigraphic position of Structures 3 and 4, and the iron artefacts in the latter, are consistent with the date suggested by their structural form, that is centring on the 10th century (see Chapter 19).

The only other artefacts from Site T of this general date are loomweight MSF 20 (16.5) from posthole T97 and twelve Saxo-Norman sherds (from seven vessels); of these, three vessels were in contexts predating the defences, the remainder either insecurely stratified or residual (Table 16.2). At present a date within the range early 10th to mid 11th century would be acceptable for these sherds (18.2.1).

4.6.3 Discussion

The Structures are most conveniently discussed together with the initial date for the Defences in Chapter 19.

4.7 The Norman Borough Defences

(Figs 4.4, 4.7 no 5)
A substantial ditch cut north west to south east across the west side of the site, parallel to the band of soil T64 preserved beneath surviving rampart material T69. Three main ditch phases, I, II and III, were distinguished, with probable recutting within the phases.

4.7.1 Stratigraphy
The rampart

The line of the rampart was preserved by the soil T64 (Fig 4.3). The only clearly defined rampart material T69, of yellow-brown sand, was preserved where sealed by overlying post-Edwardian industrial waste T80. T69 represents only a fragmentary patch from a sequence of ramparts which the ditch stratigraphy suggests would have been complex. T51, a more poorly preserved extension to the south east, is not shown on Fig 4.2. Soil T64 gave the impression of having been stripped of its upper, more humic, layers, before the rampart was built.

Possible palisade(s) (Pl 4.2)

A row of 23 postholes T81 about 0.80m apart ran north west to south east parallel to and 5.5m inside the edge of Ditch II, and cut soil T64. Each had a round postpipe 0.15m across filled with brown sandy soil set in a circular pit packed with lighter brown sand and clay. Depths from the surviving top of soil T64 varied between 0.10m and 0.25m. Six of the line were covered by rampart material T69 and their posts did not appear to have projected through this. Two postholes contained a small sherd of medieval pottery, probably intrusive. The position and alignment of the postholes suggests either a palisade or a timber strengthening to a rampart.

A line of nineteen stakeholes T210 0.15m deep ran roughly parallel to the suggested palisade line T81, again mainly beneath rampart material T69. These may be the remnant of a slighter palisade or again of strengthening to a rampart.

Other postholes similar to the T81 with defined pipes and comparable depths formed patterns not easy to relate to the defensive system. T404 formed a curved line of six holes. T84 represents eighteen holes without obvious plan; Fig 4.2 shows which were stakeholes and which postholes with pipes; T139 and T161 are similar postholes beneath rampart material T69. These postholes are presented on Fig 4.2 because of their similarity to those in the T81 line, and more importantly, because they cut soil T64.

All those postholes shown on Fig 4.2, and rampart material T69 which sealed some of them, were covered by soil T29 of probable 14th century date; it will be demonstrated that the area was subject to considerable erosion and disturbance during the medieval period.

Ditch I (Fig 4.4 G–H)

Ditch I was only located in the northern of three cuttings across the defences (Fig 4.2). It was about 3m deep. The Ditch had a flat-bottomed slot 0.30m deep in its base, presumably from cleaning. Ditch fill was light brown sand with slight silting lines of humic material and clay. There were no artefacts.

Ditch II (Fig 4.4 E–F,G–H; Pl 4.4.)

Ditch II occurred in all three cuttings, although not with a complete profile because of removal by Ditch III and later features. In section EF it originally had a broad flat bottom and was 2m deep. The primary silt of sand with some humic material T363A was cut through by a narrow flat-bottomed cleaning slot filled by sand T363B with less humic material than T363A. In section GH, and in the south cutting, Ditch II had a smooth V-shaped profile with no slot or obvious recut; its fill, T391, was more clayey than 363A/B. These differences hint at some complexity of recuts or cleaning. The upper fills of Ditch II were similar in all three cuttings, 363 grey humic material mixed with sand below 370 lighter grey-brown sandy silts with occasional darker humic lines.

Ditch III (Fig 4.4 E–F, G–H; Pl 4.4)

Ditch III preserved an almost complete wide V-

Pl 4.4 Site T. Ditches II and III excavated (kiln T50 in foreground). Pit 349 and slot-lines 387 etc on far side of Ditches. Note rubbish levels in top of Ditch III. View from west. Scale in ft.

shaped profile, surviving to a maximum depth of 2.70m. Primary silt 366, homogeneous dark and sandy, was absent in EF, removed by a shovel-width cleaning slot filled with banded grey sandy silts 395. Sealing the slot were banded grey silts 394 with much clay. Above, in all sections, were yellow sand silts 341 with some humic bands, charcoal flecked with mussel shells. The top of 341 was marked by a hard compact surface with iron pan 340, indicating a break in the deposition of silts. The compaction and iron pan continued out over the outer ditch lip and natural sand up to the edge of the trench.

Above surface 340 Ditch III was infilled by a grey silt layer T55. In EF T55 was overlain by dumps of clean pale brown sand 339, elsewhere by a soil 402 thick with charcoal. The top of the ditch was backfilled with dumps of mixed deposits T59, mottled brown sands with mussel shells and possible industrial waste of slag and charcoal. The

surface of T59 was compacted and mixed with humic material; it may have been a surface for some time. The centre of the infilled ditch in EF was levelled up with clean yellow sand T14.

Lines of sockets on the north edge of Ditch III (Pl 4.4)

The iron pan of surface 340 was interrupted by three lines of sockets or scoops cutting natural sand on the edge of Ditch III. Most seemed designed to hold posts for a series of timbers. The sockets were irregular and tended to increase in depth towards the upper edge of the slope. They were all filled with dark brown sandy soil. The inner line 385 consisted of nine partial and two complete sockets each about 0.05m deep. The next line T346 had six partial and six complete sockets, about 0.05m deep. Line 387 was more irregular with single complete and partial sockets, double sockets and double partial socket, again 0.05m deep. Line 386 was very fragmented.

The most likely interpretation of these sockets is that they were for lines of timber forming an outer defence to the Ditches. Because they seem shallow for their size, it is possible that they belong with an early Ditch phase and were truncated by Ditch III.

4.7.2 Dating

The earliest context with pottery is T370, high and probably intrusive in Ditch II (Table 18.2). The next context, middle silts T341 in III, produced a few sherds of the kiln V type, suggesting a 13th century date for these levels and for the formation of the surface T340. This 13th century dating for III leaves a wide range of earlier possibilities for I and II.

Dump deposits T55 contained material of kiln V type and P37, P38 and P39 (Fig 18.6). Layer T59 contained an Edward I penny issued about AD 1280 (16.1, No 6) and about 60 sherds, including P40 to P44 and some of kiln V type. A Mediterranean import of probable 14th century date, P46, came from sand layer T14 over T59. Layer T14 also produced fragments of purple roofing slate most probably from the Cambrian deposits of the Bethseda-Nantlle belt (identification M Owen).

4.7.3 Discussion

Comparanda for the palisade line and for outer timbering, chronology of the Ditches and their correlations with the phases indentified on Sites A and E are discussed in Chapters 19 and 20.

4.8 The site during and immediately after the Norman Borough Defences (Fig 4.7 no 6)

The scant amount of rampart material *in situ* and the fact that structures such as kiln 50 both cut from the top of the ditch silts and from a surface from which the rampart had been removed suggested a phase of erosion after the use of the Defences, perhaps some deliberate levelling. Features inside the Defences and contemporary with them were difficult to identify. Soil T178 may have continued to accumulate; pebble layer T207 above it could relate to a period of levelling.

4.8.1 Stratigraphy
Pit T349 and related features

This pit, 0.70m deep, cut the east side of Ditch III. The sand at its base was heavily scorched, although no charcoal was present. Several runs of lead weighing 5kg appeared to have been poured into the pit in a hot, molten state and had preserved the negative impression of a piece of stone or wood. The lead was sealed with burnt sand and

ash. On this a whetstone (MSF 34, 16 no 9), barrel padlock (17: no 86), and a charred wooden object were deposited. The pit was subsequently backfilled with layers of clean and dirty sand and a 0.10m thick layer of mussel shells mixed with a few bone fragments. Scattered throughout the fill of the pit were a number of lumps of white limestone, some quite large.

Posthole T350, 0.30m deep, with limestone and burnt pebble packing, was cut by T351 with a similar fill but only 0.15m deep; both were cut in the top silts of Ditch III. Outside the Ditch was a series of slots, pits and postholes T354, 357, 352, 345, 358.

Narrow slots T24 etc (Fig 4.4 EF)

Cutting into the top of the backfilled ditch was a series of narrow slots T24, T52, T57 and T57A. These were shallow, less than 0.10m deep, and filled with dark sandy soil. They were difficult to follow and appeared discontinuous. It is likely that only some of the features originally present were detected. These slots may represent fence lines, insubstantial boundaries perpetuating the line of the ditch.

4.8.2 Dating

All these features post-date the late 13th century final filling of Ditch III. The slots precede the drying kilns (4.9) which may be either late 13th or very early 14th century.

4.8.3 Discussion

Pit T349 with its strange association of objects suggests more than the burial of unwanted objects, possibly an act with 'magic' overtones, but comparanda are not easy to find.

4.9 Drying kilns T6l and T50
(Figs 4.5, 4.6; Pls 4.1, 4.5, 4.6)
4.9.1 Stratigraphy

Kilns T61 and T50 which cut Ditch III and slots T24 and T52 had a complex interrelationship.

Kiln T61 was set in a sub-rectangular pit 3.50m by 3m by 2m deep which was dug with a 3m long sloping ramp to the west. Two lines of sockets 376 and 377, all 0.15m deep, appear to have held timbers down either side of the westerly extension or flue. The south line terminated at a block of limestone with burning on its north face. The socket lines continued into the pit with three post settings on each side. To the south 380 appeared to have held both a post and a driven stake, the former set 0.20m deep; 380 and 379 were 0.15m and 0.20m deep respectively. To the north 381–383 were all simple postholes 0.20m deep. The timbers held in these sockets would have been necessary to

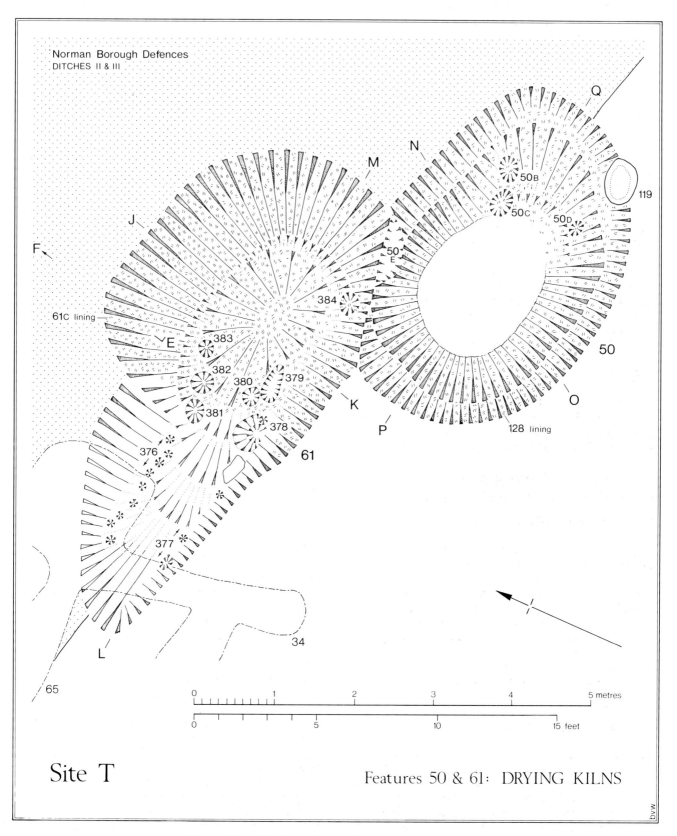

Norman Borough Defences
DITCHES II & III

Fig 4.5 Site T. Plan of corn drying kilns 61 and 50.

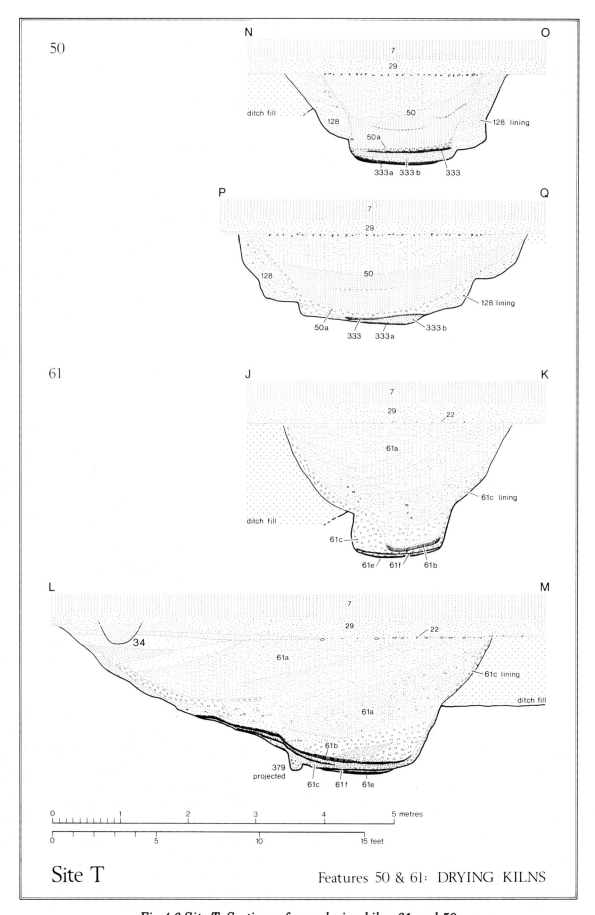

Site T

Features 50 & 61: DRYING KILNS

Fig 4.6 Site T. Sections of corn drying kilns 61 and 50.

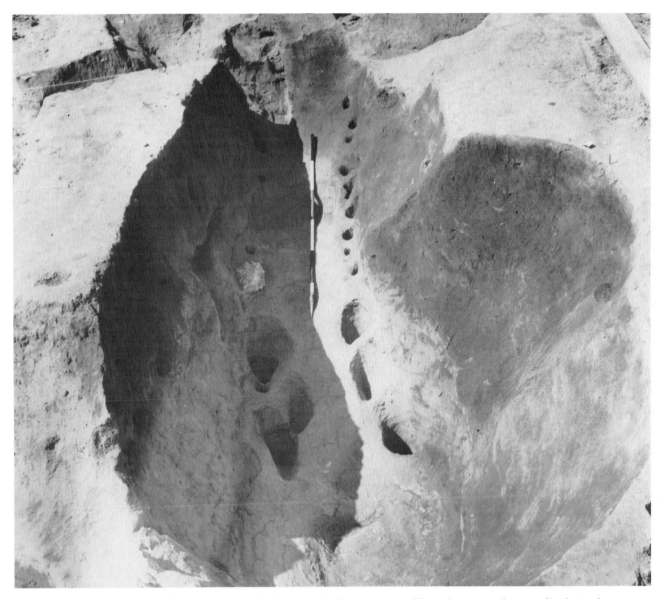

Pl 4.5 Site T. Kiln 61 completely excavated showing timber settings. View from south east. Scale in ft.

support the soft sand sides of the kiln pit during any initial phase of operation. They presumably relate to a system inside the main kiln pit of which T384 is the only remnant; posthole 384, 0.15m deep, was sealed by lining 61C and so belonged to an early phase.

The sand at the base of the pit was scorched bright red (61E), indicating heavy burning *in situ*, covered with 61F, 0.10m of fine charred material interleaved with thin lenses of sandy silt and grey clay. Two samples of charred grain were studied from this deposit (K1 and K2). The species present suggested a crop predominantly of oats, grown in partially waterlogged fields (Chapter 15.2).

A thick lining 61C of mixed soil and clay was added to the sides and base of the pit (over the basal deposits 61E/F) but did not extend into the flue, and respected the positions of all postsockets except 384. Lining 61C, of mixed silty soil and yellow sand mixed with green clay, was thickest

over the area where the kiln cut through Ditches II and III. The top of this lining on the kiln base was heavily burnt with an accumulation of charcoal over it.

As the kiln was going out of use, 61B, layers of charcoal and sand and bands of clay, accumulated on its base, covering all postsockets. The kiln was backfilled with clods of green clay and dark, redeposited sandy silt 61A packed solid, with above looser brown and grey sandy soils interspersed with rainwashed bands of dark grey silt.

Kiln T50 was subsequent in construction to T61 as its pit cut through lining 6lC of the former. In its first stage T51 was 3m by 4.5m by 1.40m deep. It had a stepped profile all round, cutting into soft, natural sand and the edge of Ditch III. At the east end were three 'steps' for access. There was one small posthole 50D, 0.10m deep, south of these 'steps' and two to the north, 50B and 50C both 0.20m deep, all filled with dark grey silty soil.

Pl 4.6 Site T. Kiln 50 during excavation (kiln 61 in background). Lining 128 partly sectioned to right. Charred material 333 on base. View from south east. Scale in ft.

These are likely to be traces of a timber revetting system for the 'steps'. The kiln had a lining T128 of fine brown sandy soil with patches of green clay, banded with yellow sand and grey silt T128. This lining was banded horizontally and, in places, showed slight horizontal grooves on its surface as though it had been tamped in behind a structure with horizontal timbers. Parallels for a timber lining are discussed below; repeated use and cleaning out of the bottom could have removed any evidence for slight vertical supports. In its surviving form lining T128 bulged to project over basal deposits. This may be because it sagged when a timber structure rotted or was removed. It is also possible that lining T128, like that in kiln 6l, was secondary and represented rebuilding after a period of use. Lining T128 peeled cleanly off lining 61C. At the junction of kilns 50 and 6l was depression 50E 0.10m deep; the side adjacent to 6l dropped steeply, that towards 50 was almost flat and formed a continuous level with the top of lining 128. Presumably 50E held a timber around which the lining was packed.

On the base of kiln 50 was a 0.12m thick deposit of charred material with sand lenses T333A. The sand beneath was heavily burnt. Charred material T333A was sealed by grey silty soil 333B, 0.10m thick, heavily burnt and fire-reddened. Subsequently a second layer of charred material T333, 0.10m thick, was deposited. Charred layer 333 was sealed by compact green clay 50B.

Kiln 50 was partly backfilled with a dump of dark brown sandy soil with occasional lenses of light green clay, partly with a dump of looser brown sandy soil and a few small stones and some sand patches and silt lenses; finally rubbish including mussel shells and animal bone fragments in dark soil was dumped to fill up the depression; T50 is applied to all these fill layers. The fill was continuous with that of T61 across depression 50E.

The kilns seem to represent three phases of use. First T61 was used with some kind of interior timber lining. In a second phase this lining was reinforced by one of soil/cob. Thirdly kiln T50 was constructed, but the linking feature of 50E and the continuity of the backfills suggests that both kilns were in use together in the third stage. There may be significance in the fact that the entrance to the later kiln, 50, was in the opposite direction to that to 61.

4.9.2 Dating

Both kilns were cut into Ditch III after it was completely infilled, providing a late 13th century *post quem*. Kiln 61 was in turn cut through by structure T34/65 which contained a coin of Edward I (16.1, no 7). Both kilns were covered by T29, soil of late 13th and 14th century date, and both contained pottery. Both probably date to the late 13th century, although the early 14th century would be possible.

4.9.3 Discussion

Kiln 61 comprised the classic features of a keyhole shaped oven or kiln, while 50 had a modified plan without the elongated approach; both, from the analysis of the charred material they contained, are presumed to have been used for grain drying. Both had timber revetted entrances, timbering for stokehole arches, and firing chambers lined eventually with clay mixed to a kind of cob. There was heavy burning on the bases, a distinctive feature of firing chambers where the walls may not show evidence of intense heat. The flue arches would have had to be sturdily constructed since they would have supported much of the weight of the clay domes which covered the drying chamber. It seems likely that there would have been suspended floors above the kiln pits. The large air space beneath such floors would have acted as a heat-mixing chamber, so that the heat reaching the drying chamber would have ensured fairly even parching or drying of all its contents. Suspended floors would have been made of combustible material, such as planks covered with straw or horsehair, so there would have been a constant risk of fire. Low temperature controllable fires would therefore have been necessary for the successful working of the kilns. Excavation near Fishergate, Nottingham in 1973 revealed a very well preserved corn drying kiln of this type, of 13th century date, (pers comm C S B Young). The Nottingham example had collapsed, preserving the remains of the suspended floor in the firing chamber; the floor had been made of re-used joists covered with branches and straw or horsehair. Quantities of grain were recovered from above the remnants of the flooring material. The firing chamber was lined with a wicker framework covered with raw clay. This framework was built inside the firing chamber leaving a gap between it and the pit edge which was subsequently backfilled with rubbish. Ten other Saxon and medieval corn drying kilns found in Nottingham were of similar type but the evidence for the wicker framework was less clear. It is possible that the Rhuddlan kiln linings were constructed on a wicker framework of which no trace survived except as horizontal impressions on lining T128.

There must have been some form of dome covering the drying chamber. The clods of green clay in the kiln infills may have come from the collapsed domes, which probably would have consisted of raw clay over a wicker framework as at Fishergate, Nottingham.

Analysis of grain samples (15.2.3) shows that none contained weed heads, or larger chaff fragments; the grain had been winnowed and coarse sieved. A number of oat grains were still within their leemas and had not been dehusked, a state in which it is unlikely that grain would have been stored. The grain was likely to have been charred accidentally during parching in a drying kiln, and was intended for human consumption as it was being parched within its lemmas to aid the removal of the latter during husking.

The secondary deposits from kiln 50 were the exception to this. Analysis of T333 showed that it consisted mainly of oats which had not been dehusked and a number of weeds indicative of partially waterlogged fields (15.2.3); a sample from 333A had a large number of straw nodes present which suggests a less rigorous cleaning regime than for other charred deposits. This might indicate that the crop had been prepared for livestock rather than human consumption.

The similarity of the kilns to those from Nottingham and the indications that they may have had roofs link them to English influence and activity outside the Edwardian Borough. They appear similar to kiln C3 on Site A which can be given a general 13th century date. Britnell (1984) has recently contrasted such kilns with the unroofed structures recorded in more recent rural Wales with particular reference to a stone-built example excavated at Collfryn, Powys.

4.10 Later medieval activity

(Fig 4.7.7)

4.10.1 Stratigraphy
Soils T29 and T200

A thin layer of pebbles T24 (Fig 4.4 E–F) was laid down, perhaps as a surface, after kilns 61 and 50 had been backfilled, and over the Ditch line, now a slight hollow in the contemporary ground surface. (Sand T14 over the Ditches may also have been an attempt to counteract a muddy surface.) Above the pebble horizon a dark brown sandy soil, T29, started to accumulate. The soil was most clearly defined in the hollow above the Ditches and kilns and where sealed by subsequent layers such as the deposit of late medieval industrial waste T80. Soil build-up continued, after the deposition of T80, over the whole site as T200.

Timber Structure T34/65 (Pl 4.2)

After soil T29 had accumulated, a substantial timber structure was erected cutting through the

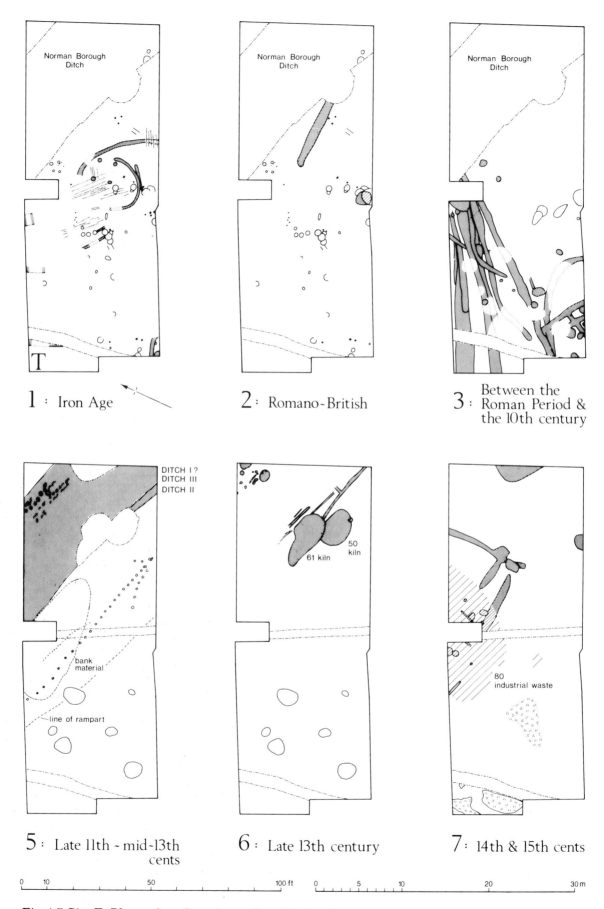

1 : Iron Age

2 : Romano~British

3 : Between the Roman Period & the 10th century

5 : Late 11th ~ mid~13th cents

6 : Late 13th century

7 : 14th & 15th cents

Fig 4.7 Site T. Phase plans Iron Age to Post-Medieval.

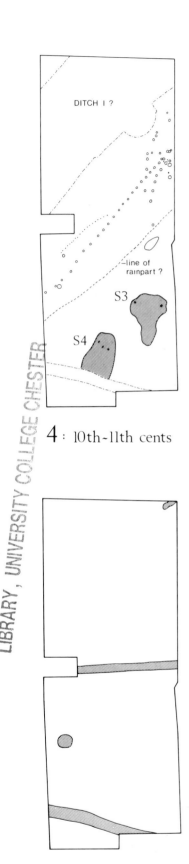

4 : 10th~11th cents

8 : Post~Medieval

west end of kiln 61. This structure consisted of a series of broad trenches with homogeneous fills of mixed brown sands with charcoal flecks and occasional clay lumps. The east side was formed by slot T34, its base fairly flat although the depth varied between 0.20m and 0.50m. At the junction with T65, the south side, T34 projected eastwards, 0.40m deep. T65 formed a contemporary junction with T34 but its base sloped steeply from 0.30m at the junction to 0.70m towards its projecting east butt end. The separate length of slot to the south T114 had a fairly even base 0.50m deep. The area enclosed by these slots was at least 9m by 10m. A single posthole T153, 0.15m deep, further to the west, had a similar fill to the trenches and was cut from the same level; it may have been part of this structure. There was no evidence for vertical post emplacements within the trenches so they may have held cill beams which were subsequently removed. Given its size, the structure may well have been an unroofed compound rather than a building. A quantity of domestic rubbish had been thrown back into the trenches after robbing.

Industrial Activity

Against the north side of the site, over the Ditches and soil T29, was a spread of dark soil T80 (Fig 4.3) mixed with unburnt clay, charcoal, iron slag lumps, and scraps of possible paving of limestone and pink Carboniferous Sandstone; some of the stone has been identified (M Owen) as medium-grained grey sandstone possibly from the Upper Coal Measures but not used in the Edwardian Castle. Part of T80 rested directly on top of the eroded rampart T69. The soil in T80 was around 0.10m thick, with clay and ash occurring in separate spreads. The clay, mainly pink, but some white and all unburnt, sometimes infilled shallow pits.

T155, T140 and T149 were narrow steep-sided slots cut from the surface of T80, 0.20m, 0.40m and 0.40m deep respectively. They were filled with stones and pink clay. Although no actual post settings survived, they may have held uprights, and have been the foundation for a compound, shelter or baffles associated with the industrial activity suggested by the iron slag.

Pits or postholes were cut from the surface of T80 and may have been associated with industrial activity: T115 0.30m deep; T53 0.25m deep; T307 0.30m deep; T166 0.30m deep; T295 0.40m deep; T308 0.20m deep; T124 0.40m deep and T122 0.15m cut from the base of soil T200. Oven T21, on the south of the site, underlying soil T200, may have been contemporary and connected with industrial deposits T80; 0.30m deep, it was flat-bottomed and lined with clay burnt bright red, covered with a charcoal spread and then by unburnt white clay and dark, charcoal-flecked sandy soil. Posthole T119 cut the edge of kiln T50, 0.13m deep, and was filled with lumps of burnt clay and charcoal-flecked dark soil. T70 was a large sub-rectangular depression 0.25m deep; its flat bottom was covered with sandy soil slightly darker than T29 into which it was cut; it underlay soil T200. Pit T70, 0.25m deep, cut into compound slot T34 and was filled with charcoal-flecked brown soil and lumps of pink clay.

Elsewhere was a series of features which may be roughly of the same period, as they predated the accumulation of soil T200; they postdated soil T178 and pebble layer T207. Pit T246, 0.60m deep, cut down through Structure 2. On the west of the site was a series of unburnt clay spreads T157 and 243. T157 filled a depression 6m by 4m and 0.10m deep and covered shallow pit T240. T243 was a series of thicker (0.15 m) patches of unburnt pink clay in depressions in T200, which may have been eroded remnants of a larger clay area. The clay covered small depressions; T273, 0.15m deep, was possibly a clay-filled posthole with Carboniferous Sandstone fragments; further stones were scattered on the surface around it beneath clay T243. T243 was overlain by dark sandy charcoal-flecked soil T268 up to 0.10m thick, co-extensive with T243 but merging with T200 further east.

4.10.2 Dating
Soil T29

The soil produced Ewloe material (18.2.2) of 14th to 15th century date as well as many sherds of kiln V type; it may have started to develop in the late 13th century and continued through the 14th.

Timber structure T324/65

Artefacts included a coin of Edward I (16.1 no 7) and some pottery (Table 18.2). An early 14th century date may be appropriate as the structure cut soil T29; the coin may either have been residual or had a long period of use locally.

Industrial deposits T80 etc

T80 contained P53, 14th or 15th century Ewloe, as well as about 70 medieval sherds. A few 18th century Buckley sherds may be intrusive. A 14th or 15th century date would seem reasonable, and material from T243 and T268 would be consistent (Table 18.2).

Soil T200

Soil T200 contained Ewloe sherds of 14th or 15th century as well as other medieval material. Sherds of 17th century Buckley wares in the upper levels suggest that upper soil levels may still have been forming in the 17th century.

4.10.3 Discussion

These features relate to activity outside the Edwardian Borough and are discussed in Chapter 21.

4.11 Late medieval/post-medieval
(Fig 4.7 no 7–8)
4.11.1. Stratigraphy

Cutting into the late medieval soil T200 were two ditches running north west to south east across the width of the site. Ditch T275, 0.80m deep, was filled with dark silty soil. It cut from below the top of T200 through earlier medieval and prehistoric levels into natural sand. Ditch T121 to the east was much more tenuous. For most of its length it was barely detectable in soil T200 but showed clearly for a short stretch cutting into T80, the industrial waste layer, and underlying rampart material T69; its maximum depth was 0.20m. It is likely that other late features with dark soil fills were removed by machine or could not be detected in the dark soil of T200.

Two other features contained post-medieval finds and were cut from a high level in soil T200. T15, a pit in the east corner of the site 0.50m deep, contained a fill of dark soil with frequent limestone lumps. T132, 0.50m deep, cut down into the west edge of rampart material T69. Pits T204 and T131 were cut from levels within soil T200.

Soil build-up continued as layer T7 which was scattered with post-medieval material with a depth of between 0.70m and 1.10m over the whole site.

4.11.2 Dating

Ditch T275 contained no post-medieval material and might be assigned to a late medieval or possibly 16th century date. T121 contained a single sherd of a 17th century Buckley slipware dish. Soil T7 contained a wide range of ceramics from medieval to 20th century.

4.11.3 Discussion

The two boundaries T110 and T121 fit in well with the alignment of fields east of the Edwardian Castle marked on the *Conway Map of 1756*. The build-up of soil with a high humic content suggests agricultural use.

Acknowledgments
We are grateful to Clwyd County Council (formerly Flintshire) for permission to excavate and to Mr Morgan, Headmaster, and all staff at Ysgol-Y-Castell. Site supervisors were Jenny (Thompson) Britnell, and Pat (Downham) Loscoe-Bradley. M Owen (British Geological Survey) provided identifications of building stone. All other specialist contributions have been acknowledged in the appropriate chapter.

5 Site V, Area behind the Norman Borough Defences, Ysgol-Y-Castell, Lôn Hylas; Medieval pottery kiln

5.1 Introduction

Site V, situated immediately west of T (Pl 5.1) lay entirely within the Norman Borough Defences. It was excavated together with Site T during spring 1973 in advance of extensions to Ysgol-Y-Castell. The ground sloped up hill to the west by 0.75m, but had been truncated to the north by the scarp for the school playground. Because of this slope and the soft fluvio-glacial sand on the site, allowance must be made for the erosion of deposits in interpreting the stratigraphic record. There were considerable but discontinuous build-ups of soil, mostly post-dating the medieval occupation. The top 0.70m of this build-up was removed by a Hymac excavator.

5.2 Mesolithic (Fig 5.1, 5.5 no 1)

In the north east corner a patch of orange sand V94 survived up to 0.15m thick. It merged gradually downwards into the paler sand subsoil and was sealed by the early medieval soil horizon V30. V94 contained a scatter of pebbles, some fragmentary and burnt, and eleven pieces of struck chert and flint. V94 is presumed to represent the only surviving area of Mesolithic soil in V, equivalent to soils H39 and M26. No definite Mesolithic

Pl 5.1 Site V. Hollow V24 during excavation; kiln V4 at level of cross baulks. Site T in foreground with removal of soils T200 and T178. View to west to Edwardian Castle. Scale in ft.

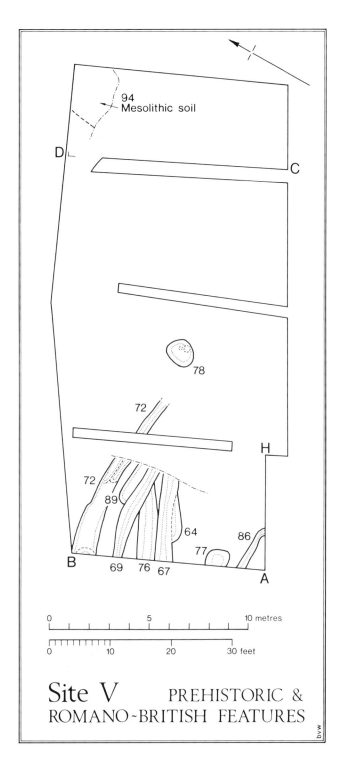

Fig 5.1 Site V. Plan of probable prehistoric and Romano-British features.

features were identified but residual worked chert and flint occurred frequently (257 pieces) in later contexts.

5.3 Iron Age/Romano-British

(Fig 5.1, 5.5 no 2)

5.3.1. Stratigraphy

There was no identifiable trace of a later prehistoric or Romano-British soil horizon, such as M53. The lowest general soil horizon V30 sealed a group of features cut into the sand subsoil. These features had fills of much cleaner sand than those of later stratigraphic contexts. V86 was a slot with V-shaped profile 0.30m deep. Its fill was homogeneous light grey-brown sand with some large pebbles; its profile, and possible packing stones, suggests that it may have been structural. A spread of clean sand V86a, possibly wind blown, survived in a hollow over the top of the slot. The sand V86a was cut through by V77, a pit or the butt end of a gully filled with light brown sand with some silting lines. To the north of V77 was a series of gullies V64, V67, V76, V69, V89, V72 with silty fills of pale sand. Relationships between the gullies were difficult to establish. The gullies had been cut away by the medieval ditch V13 and removed to its east both by general erosion and by wear around the hollow V24. V76, cut by V67 and V69, appeared to be the earliest of the series. Both V67 and V69 were apparently recuts of earlier features, V64 and V89 respectively. The northernmost gully V72 had two grooves in its base for most of its length, indicative of a possible recut. V77 survived to a maximum depth of 0.60m, V76 0.30m, V67 0.65m, V69 0.30m and V72 0.25m. V78, a pit truncated by hollow V24, had two small sockets each 0.07m deep in its base; its fill contained many burnt pebble fragments.

5.3.2 Dating

The dating evidence for these features is somewhat equivocal. Gully V64 produced three sherds of salt container ceramic and pit V78 four. Six sherds were residual in V68, V73, V24, and V20. This material is likely to date between the 5th century BC and the 1st AD (13.1.4). The gullies may be Iron Age, or the ceramic may be residual.

Three Romano-British sherds, from 2nd to 4th century date, came from V4, V37 and V39, the latter dating to after AD 370 (13.2.3).

5.3.3 Discussion

The gullies are presumed to represent frequently renewed plot boundaries, comparable to those beneath the church on Site M. If an Iron Age date is accepted for them, there should be a reason for their similar alignment with the gullies in Site T. If the pottery is accepted as residual and the gullies regarded as continuations of those in Site T, it may seem strange that post-Roman features are the earliest on Site V (except Mesolithic V94). The reason is probably to be found in the position of the site with erosion downhill removing earlier levels. These problems regarding the gullies in Sites T and V are discussed in 13.3.

5.4 Between the Roman period and the 12th/13th Centuries
(Fig 5.2, 5.5 no 3)
5.4.1. Stratigraphy
Soil V30

A light brown sandy soil V30 lay directly over the natural sand subsoil, covering Iron Age features for the western 7m of the site. V30 was sealed by V68, the probable floor of Structure 5. Soil V30 had largely been eroded from the east of the site, where its remnants survived at the base of V20. The soil contained no medieval artefacts, and presumably accumulated possibly during, but more probably after, the Romano-British period.

Structure 5

Structure 5 V68–V29 was post-built and rectangular, 6m by at least 4m. Its floor consisted of V68, a rectangular area of compact dark brown sand with charcoal. There was a dense charcoal patch V27 within it but no obvious hearth. Postholes V52–V40 cut through the edges of floor V68 and were not detected at a higher level. V52, 0.18m deep, and V48, 0.25m deep, had grey-brown sandy fills with a few pebbles. V45, 0.40m deep, had a circular post-pipe of grey-brown sand 0.22m across and packing of darker sand and pebbles. V34, 0.28m deep, and V39, 0.20m deep, had fills as V52. V40 replaced V39; its fill was identical to that of V45 with a postpipe. Within the Structure, cutting through the floor, were two stakeholes V29 0.08m and 0.15m deep. Structure 5 was sealed by soil V20.

Probable postholes

V43, V88, V71, V75, V74 were cut into soil V30 or the sand subsoil south and west of hollow V24. V43 was 0.25m deep, V88 0.20m, V71 0.25m, V75 0.15m, and V74 0.30m. All the postholes were sealed by the soil V20, but clearly postdated erosion which removed soil V30 in their area. They could relate to the phase of occupation represented by Structure 5, or might be considerably later.

Structure 6

This Structure was post-built and set on a levelled area at least 5.5m across, cut back up to 0.25m into the slope. Its north edge was cut away by V47, a late medieval trench, and its south by medieval hollow V24. Three postholes in line, V82, V80 and V81, appeared associated with the cut and may have formed part of the north wall of a building set endways into the slope; the south side had been removed by erosion connected with V24. V82,

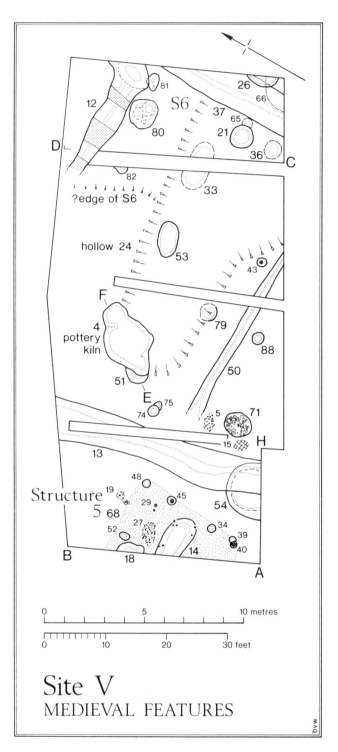

Fig 5.2 Site V. Plan of medieval and later features.

0.25m deep, had a dark brown silty sand fill and appeared to have been recut. V80 had a similar fill, was 0.30m deep, and had the settings for, or the impressions of, four-posts in its base. V81, 0.30m deep and filled with light brown sand and pebbles, had two post sockets a further 0.10m deep in its base. There was no sign of any compaction or flooring. The levelled area was back-filled with a brown sandy soil V73 which postdated the use of the Structure.

Hollow V24 (Pl 5.1) truncated a series of features which produced no dating material but which may, stratigraphically, relate to Structure 6 or another early structure. V79, 0.08m deep, was filled with light brown sand; V33, 0.15m deep, contained dark brown sand and pink clay; V36, 0.40m deep, had layers of alternating dark and light sands; V65, 0.20m deep, had a fill of light brown sand and burnt pebbles; V66, 0.30m deep, contained large pebbles and pink clay.

5.4.2 Dating

The sherd postdating AD 370 (13.2.3) from posthole V39 is obviously insufficient for dating Structure 5. It can only be loosely placed somewhere between the Roman period and the 13th century (when pottery becomes common). No datable objects came from Structure 6 or from V73 which infilled its levelled area. A Type A nail (17.1.3) was found in V81. The absence of pottery would again suggest a pre-13th century date, although how much earlier remains unknown. Of the features possibly related, only V36 produced a small sheet of lead which had been wrapped around a stick to form a hollow spiral cone.

5.4.3 Discussion

Since Structure 5 overlay the V64 gully sequence it is possible that it represented a late or sub-Roman structure. However soil V30, 0.22m thick, had developed over the gullies before the wear resulting in floor V68 and this suggests some interval between the gullies and Structure 5. The form of the Structure is so simple that no chronological deductions can be made from it.

Little can be said of Structure 6 because of disturbance by later features. However structures terraced into slopes are a common vernacular type from the early medieval period onward in the Principality (Lewis, 1976, 26). The function and relationship of features such as V33 to the suggested Structure is quite unclear.

5.5 Hollow V24 and other features sealed by soil V20 (Fig 5.2, 5.5 no 4)
5.5.1. Stratigraphy

V24 (Pl 5.1) was a worn hollow widening and deepening from west to east to a maximum depth in the subsoil of 0.69m. Its area as a definable depression with separate infill is shown on Fig 5.2, but it is probable that further wear around its edges was responsible for the removal of much of soil V30 and the Iron Age gullies to the west. The hollow was filled with light grey-brown sand with occasional darker charcoal-flecked bands concentrated towards its top.

Features V26 0.20m deep, V21 0.60m, and V52 0.35m deep, were cut into the fill of hollow V24 and were sealed by V20, but could not be otherwise dated in the absence of finds.

5.5.2 Dating

From the fill of the hollow came two wasters and about seventeen other sherds from the pottery kiln V4. It is likely that these sherds were intrusive as the fill was fairly soft, and separated stratigraphically from the kiln by the suggested agricultural soil V20. (It should be noted here that there may be other pottery kilns, not yet located, of different dates but producing visually similar products). It would seem probable that hollow V24 predated the V4 kiln by some considerable period. The latest possible date, allowing for the accumulation of soil V20 before the presumed mid 13th century kiln V4, would be early 13th century; the earliest date depends on the date of Structure 6 and associated features, which might be well back in the pre-Norman period. A date bracket of perhaps the 9th to early 13th centuries is therefore possible.

5.5.3 Discussion

The hollow would appear to have been too regular for a sand quarry scoop, and appears most like a track or hollow way; its west end may have been eroded by the agricultural episode of soil V20. Its alignment would be appropriate for a track around the interior of the Norman Borough Defences.

5.6 Medieval soil V20 (Fig 5.3)
5.6.1 Stratigraphy

A brown sandy soil covered the whole site to a maximum depth of 0.35m. It was brown and sandy with a substantial humic content, but also had lenses of clean sand and lumps of pink clay indicating a disturbed soil profile.

5.6.2. Dating

The soil contained 68 sherds from pottery kiln V4 which was cut into it; waste products from the kiln may have been discarded onto its surface; there was also some intrusive post-medieval material. The soil may have built up during the 12th and early 13th centuries.

5.6.3 Discussion

The disturbed soil is presumed to represent reversion of the site to agricultural use. This would explain the truncation of the underlying deposits and features.

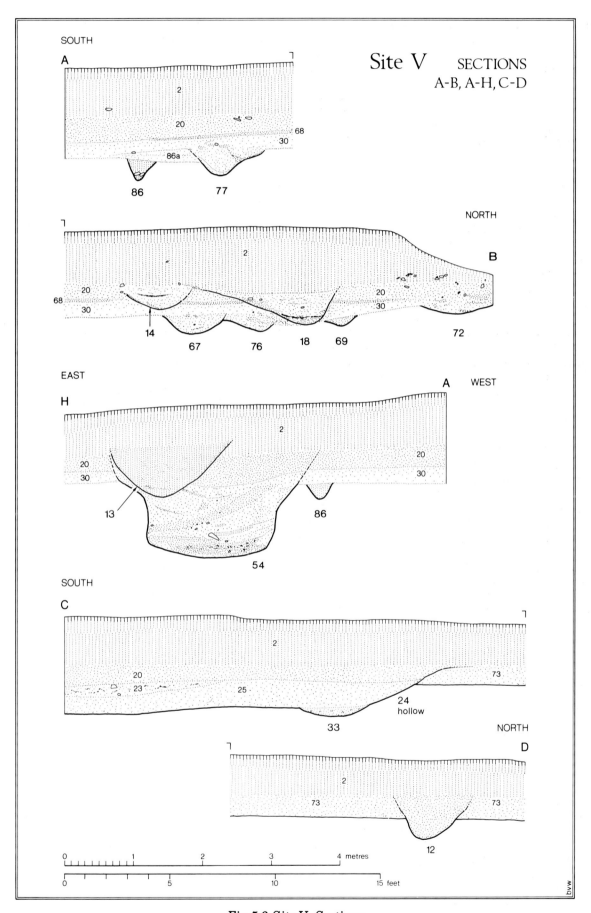

Fig 5.3 Site V. Sections.

Pl 5.2 Site V. Kiln V4 during excavation. Stones in pile come from kiln infill. View to west. Scale in ft.

5.7 Pottery kilns V51 and V4
(Fig 5.4, 5.5 no 5; Pl 5.2)
5.7.1 Constructional details

The construction pit for the kilns had been cut from the surviving surface of soil V20, but no contemporary surface could be identified. The backfill of the kilns consisted of sherds which projected upwards above the edges of the pit into the overlying soil V2. It is likely, therefore, that the ground surface contemporary with the kilns had been removed by subsequent, presumably agricultural, activity.

Phase 1: Kiln V51

The first phase was represented by V51, a pit 1.29m in diameter and 0.35m deep. It was cut from the surviving top of V20, and was backfilled with wasters, lumps of fired clay, small limestone chunks and black charcoal-rich soil. The pottery in its backfill was indistinguishable from that in the main kiln V4. This primary phase of the kiln was partly sealed by a dump of pink unburnt clay V41.

Phase 2: Kiln V4 used with two stoke-holes

The main kiln pit V4 was 4m overall in length with a central firing chamber and stoke-holes or flues at either end to the north east and to the south west. The firing chamber was 2.40m in diameter at its surviving top, 1.55m at its base. A few limestone pieces had been set, apparently at random, into its floor, and single blocks of heavily burnt limestone placed in the fired clay either side of the junction between the firing chamber and the stoke-hole.

The sand base of the firing chamber had been burnt bright orange-red (V4a) to a depth of 0.10m. Its surface was in places consolidated with splashes of glaze, although the sand itself was not vitrified. The burnt sand became shallower towards the flues; the bases of the stoke-holes showed little trace of burning. The north east stoke-hole appears to have been filled in at this stage. Its base was spread with 4d, black soil, ash and wasters below an infill 4e of brown sand with burnt sand streaks, burnt clay lumps, limestone and a few waster fragments; 4e was covered by a spread of burnt sand 4f which ran down over the primary surface of the firing chamber 4a beneath a second surface 4b, relating to the subsequent use of the kiln.

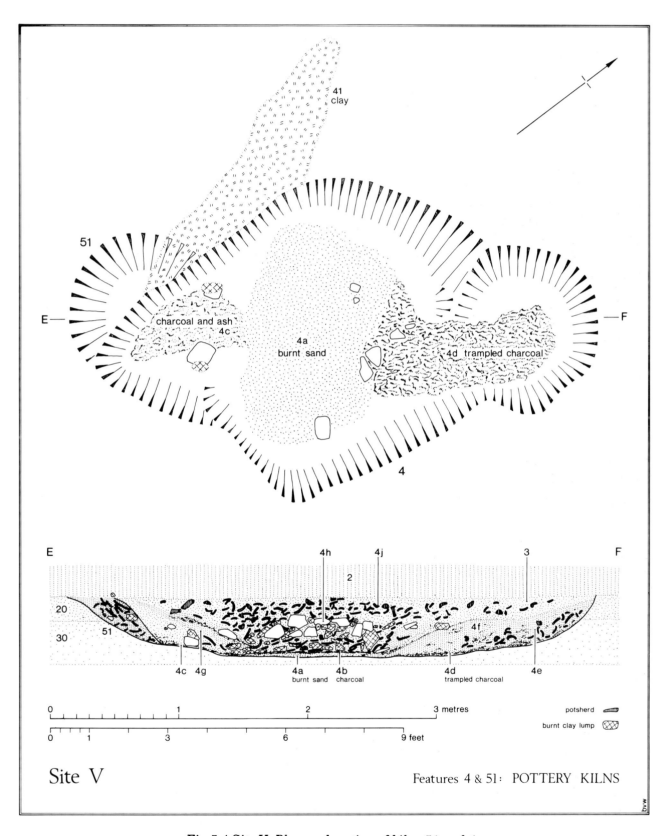

41
clay

51

E —

charcoal and ash
4c

4a
burnt sand

4d trampled charcoal

— F

4

E   4h   4j   3   F

2

20

30   51

4f

4c 4g   4a   4b   4d   4e
        burnt sand charcoal   trampled charcoal

0   1   2   3 metres   potsherd

0   1   3   6   9 feet   burnt clay lump

Site V   Features 4 & 51: POTTERY KILNS

Fig 5.4 Site V. Plan and section of kilns 51 and 4.

Phase 3: Kiln V4 used with one stoke-hole

The surface V4b, irregular over loose sand, heavily burnt bright orange with much charcoal, ran over the end of 4f infilling the north east stoke-hole.

The south west stoke-hole had subsequently been filled with 4c, a layer of black soil, ash and charcoal mixed with wasters which covered its base over 4b on the firing chamber floor. Over this was 4g, brown sand and wasters and a layer of black charcoal-rich soil, ash and much pottery. The chamber itself was partly backfilled with a dump 4h of waste sherds mixed with burnt limestone and formless lumps of burnt clay, some shaped as crude tile, under a level of dark brown sand, charcoal and sherds 4j. Most of the pottery and kiln furniture studied from the kiln derived from 4h.

Features posibly connected with the Kilns

Three areas of burnt clay V5, V15 and V19 (Fig 5.2) were situated, as were the kilns, on top of soil V20. The clay appears to have been placed in scoops in the soil which had subsequently been much eroded. A number of small stakeholes cut the clay of V5. In V19 there was a single stakehole together with a group of stones on one edge, possibly the remains of a posthole.

Also cut into soil V20 and cutting through Structure 5 was pit V14 (Fig 5.3 AB), 0.35m deep with seven detectable stakeholes in its base. Its lower fill was of light brown sand with occasional burnt patches, covered by a dump of red, burnt sand, whose top was infilled with runs of charcoal-black and white sand. Pit V18, 0.45m deep, had lumps of iron slag and charcoal in its dark brown sand fill. Pit V54, 1.50m deep, had been largely infilled soon after its excavation with runs of charcoal-flecked brown sand; the hollow left in its top had accumulated a dark brown sandy silt.

5.7.2 Dating

The Rhuddlan kiln products (here designated MA2) belong to a broad group of sandy red wares produced widely in North and West Britain (18.2.2). Sandy red wares had a long life, possibly from the 12th to the 14th centuries, with the main peak during the 13th. The Rhuddlan types are also consistent with broadly accepted datings for pottery in the rest of Britain (Vince, 1985, 43–50) and the North West of England in particular (Davey, 1977).

It can be difficult to separate visually the products of different kilns producing these wares, and therefore the identifications of probable Rhuddlan kiln products cannot be regarded as certain. It is also likely that other kilns exist at Rhuddlan apart from the complex excavated and that their products, indistinguishable from those from V4/5l, may be of slightly different dates. Hurst (1969, 95) has pleaded for caution in relating archaeological contexts and the pottery contained in them to historical events, and caution needs to be exercised in establishing the probable date of the Site V kilns.

On Sites T, A and E probable kiln sherds were found both in the silts of Ditch III and in the rubbish dumps filling its top. On Site E these levels were sealed by a surface dated to c AD 1280 and the construction of Edward I's stone castle. On Site D kiln products were incorporated in the bank of the Edwardian Borough Defences. It will be argued (Chapter 20) that Ditch III represents Henry III's activities at Rhuddlan from 1241 to 1256. If this is accepted, pottery was being made at Rhuddlan by the time this Ditch was silting up. The potter(s) who set up the Rhuddlan kilns may have been imported from Cheshire to supply the needs of Henry III's campaign. Some corroboration for a Henrician date comes from Diserth. Diserth Castle, started by Henry III in 1241 and destroyed by Llywelyn ap Gruffudd in 1263, (Cox, 1895; Edwards, 1912; Hewitt & Morgan, 1977) has produced pottery visually identical to that from the Rhuddlan Kiln. The Diserth pottery was unfortunately not reliably stratified although it is assumed (Hewitt & Morgan, 1977) to belong to the 22-year English occupation of the castle.

It may be that Welsh lack of interest in pottery has been overstressed, particularly in this region of the Principality subject to Anglo-Norman influence, a view supported by the gradual monetisation of North Wales during the 13th century (Davies, 1987, 162). Establishment of pottery kilns at Rhuddlan under Welsh rule cannot be ruled out.

The amount of kiln V4/5l pottery from the dump levels in the top of Ditch III, ascribed to Edward I's occupation from 1277, is probably sufficient to indicate a kiln operating in the late 1270s. The Site V kilns seem close to the activity surrounding the building of Edward's castle. For the present it is suggested that the Site V kilns relate to AD 1241–53, but that other kilns were in production under Edward I. Pottery may have continued to be made and used, once local manufacture was established, whether Welsh or English were in control.

5.7.3. Discussion

The Rhuddlan kiln in Phase 2, fits into Musty's type 2a (Musty, 1974, Fig 1, 44) consisting of a firing chamber joined by arched flues to two opposed stoke-pits or stoke-holes. Originally this type was classified as a through- or horizontal-draught kiln, implying that there was a fireplace in one stoke-hole and a chimney or exhaust vent at the other (eg Webster, 1960, 109–111). However it is now clear that both stoke-holes would have served as fireplaces. Although a common type for pottery production on a professional-scale, there were two disadvantages with the design. Firstly the fire would be in direct contact with the oven floor, and therefore the lowest level of pots would

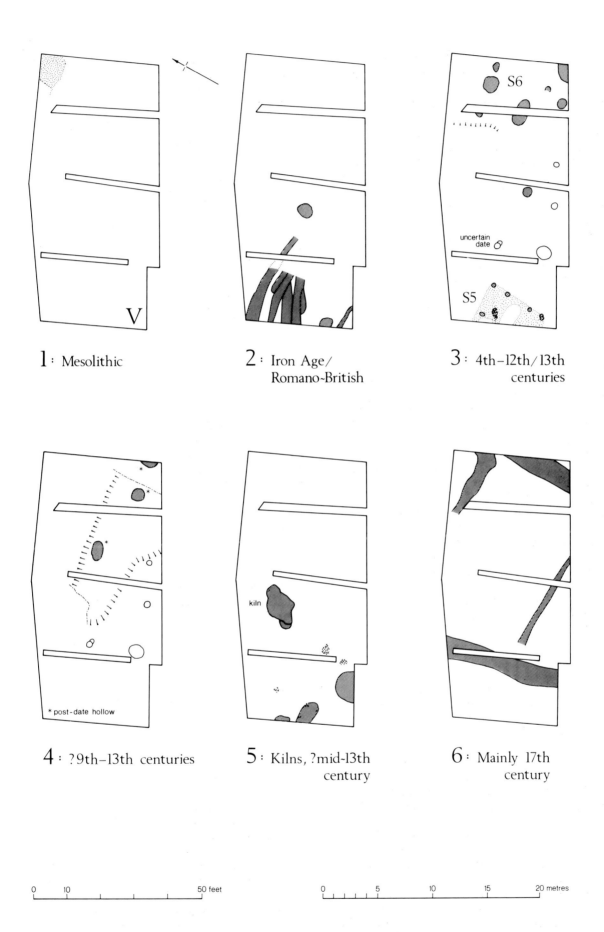

1: Mesolithic

2: Iron Age/
Romano-British

3: 4th–12th/13th
centuries

4: ?9th–13th centuries

5: Kilns, ?mid-13th
century

6: Mainly 17th
century

Fig 5.5 Site V. Phase plans.

suffer considerable temperature fluctuation and inevitably be covered with ash (Musty, Algar & Ewence, 1969, 86, Pl XIII); hence the large number of wasters within the kiln. Secondly raking out the ashes would be difficult, as the stoke-pit arches had to be cleared out without damaging the pots placed behind them. To counteract these two problems, specially made pre-fabricated kiln furniture (Fig 18.3 nos 21–2) was used to facilitate loading and draught circulation among the stacked pots. The specially thrown Rhuddlan kiln props or saggars bore either runs of glaze or the glazed impression of jug rims that had fused to the props, indicating that props were placed among the (inverted) vessels to allow warm air from the furnace to pass freely between them. Tile-like rectangular fired clay slabs may have been used to bridge the gap between stacked pots and to block the flue during cooling (*ibid*, 90) so as to prevent 'cold spots' and failure of the vessels closest to the flue during the crucial 48 hour cooling period (Mayes, 1967, 94–7; Bryant, 1973, 113–116). Remnants of such slabs may not have been recognised among the large quantity of burnt clay fragments in the kiln pit infill. The pottery kilns at Audlem and Ashton in Cheshire both made use of cylindrical kiln props (Webster, 1966, 113, 118, Fig 42 Nos 30–31; Newstead, 1933).

The superstructure of the Rhuddlan kiln would probably have been a low clay dome resting on the flue arch between stoke-hole and firing chamber. It is likely that the two burnt limestone blocks *in situ* either side of the south west flue formed footings for the flue arch and that an extra reinforcement of withies would have been necessary to enable the flue arch to withstand the full weight of the dome. Failure of the flue arch to carry the load was the most frequent cause of collapse of Romano-British kiln superstructures (Swan, 1984, 32). Once the correct temperature had been reached the flue arch would have to be temporarily blocked, perhaps with raw clay mixed with fragments of burnt clay and wasters. The flue would have needed frequent cleaning during firing as the accumulated ash would reduce the draw. The area from which the kiln was serviced, with its soft sandy soil, would quickly have become dirty and trampled; at Rhuddlan such an area had eroded together with the surface at which the kiln activities occurred.

There was no sign of a clay lining to the firing chamber, presumably since the structure was well insulated below ground in the natural sand. The greater capacity and efficiency of the double-flue pot kilns suggests the concentration of pottery manufacture in the hands of a few producers. What significance, if any, there is in the Rhuddlan kiln operating in its final phase as a single stoke-hole kiln is unclear.

All the essential requirements for pottery manufacture were available at Rhuddlan, suitable secondary clay deposits, tempering material (if needed) from the local sand subsoil, water (for use in production and for transport), fuel either from forests nearby or using reeds, chaff or coal.

The products of the Rhuddlan kilns have much in common with those of the contemporary kiln at Audlem (Webster, 1960, 109–125), and the double-flue contruction was similar. A new 13th century pottery kiln site has recently been found east of Chester (pers comm J A Rutter) which produced pots very similar to those at Audlem. The master potter controlling the production of pottery at Rhuddlan may well have come from Cheshire at the request of Henry III.

5.8 Boundary ditches and activity post-dating the kilns
(Figs 5.2–3, 5.5 no 6)
5.8.1 Stratigraphy

Kiln V4 and related features were covered by a sandy soil V2. This soil was darker than V20 and had an increasing humic content towards the top of its 0.80m thickness. The accumulation of this soil must have followed a period of erosion, possibly agricultural activity, as soil V20 beneath it and the kiln complex had been truncated.

A series of probable boundaries ditches V12, V37, V50 and V13 were cut as this soil began to form. All were filled with dark brown sandy soil. The four gullies together, if contemporary, may have delineated a plot.

5.8.2.Dating

The lower part of soil V2 contained sherds of kiln V4 type, and the upper part of some 17th century material. V50 had 17th century sherds in the central part of its fill only, suggesting some recutting. V13 had 17th century material scattered along its length, although its profile in places indicated recutting. The date of layout of the gullies is hypothetical, but they certainly seem to have been in use during the 17th century.

5.8.3 Discussion

The gullies may have been connected with agriculture outside the Edwardian Borough, as is suggested for those on Site E (Chapter 21).

Acknowledgements
We are grateful to Clwyd County Council (formerly Flintshire) for permission to excavate, and to the Headmaster, Mr Morgan, and the staff of Ygol-Y-Castell for their co-operation. The supervisor was Richard White. Full acknowledgment of all who have helped with the pottery is given in Chapter 18.

6 Site E, Ysgol-Y-Castell, Lôn Hylas. On the line of the Norman Borough Defences

6.1 Introduction

Site E was situated north west of Sites T and V in the grounds of Ysgol-Y-Castell in Lôn Hylas, and reached within 25m of the outer wall of the Edwardian Castle. The ground sloped down gently from the west, outside the Castle. Excavation of approximately 600 sq m took place during spring 1970 in advance of extensions to the school. Up to 1.5m of sandy soil had accumulated over the site since the medieval period; this was thickest at the west and thinned to around 1m to the east; this was cleared mechanically to a depth of approximately 1m. Extremely soft yellow or buff fluvioglacial sand underlay the whole site.

6.2 Mesolithic (Figs 6.1, 6.3, 6.5 no 1)

6.2.1 Stratigraphy

A thick but uneven soil H39 survived across the site, except at the east end where it had been removed by medieval activity. H39 was of orange sand which passed gradually downward into the undisturbed buff-yellow sand beneath. It was generally around 0.30m thick to the west but in places increased to at least double that depth. Around the west end of Ditch IV (Fig 6.3) it appeared to infill a depression at least 1m in depth. At its top H39 merged into a rather browner sand soil H8. H39 contained quantities of struck chert and flint, and some carbonised hazelnut shells, and is presumed to be of Mesolithic date. There may have been periods of erosion between its formation and that of H8.

J104, a hollow 2.40m by 1.40m and 0.50m deep, appeared to cut the top of sand soil H39. Its sides were fairly steep but indefinite, its bottom flat and irregular. The lower 0.25m of the fill was of mixed yellow and grey sand with a lens of almost black sand; the top consisted of very coarse orange sand.

J92 (Fig 6.4, Pl 6.4) was a pit at least 1.30m across and 0.60m deep cut away by medieval Ditch V. Cut from the top of H39, it was flat bottomed, had a primary fill of very dark grey sand, overlain by patchy yellow and grey sand. J86 was a round bottomed pit adjacent to J92; cut by Ditch V, it survived to a depth of 0.25m and was 0.60m in diameter. The pit was entirely full of black sandy

soil. These Mesolithic features had extremely indistinct edges. There had clearly been a great deal of leaching and mineral movement within the soil since their infill; lines of fine silt were observed running across them and through the sand layers on either side. This effect was noted to a lesser extent in most other Mesolithic features on Sites A and M.

6.2.2 Dating

A large quantity of struck chert and flint material came from this area. Soil H39 produced 3626 pieces, pits J104 1604, J92 49, and J86 19; all were of early Mesolithic date. 3110 pieces were residual in later contexts.

The lens of black sand within hollow J104 contained charred hazelnuts which produced a radiocarbon determination of 8739 ± 86 BP (BM–691), although most of the lithics appear to be about a millennium earlier (Chapter 10). Two late Mesolithic microliths were residual in the later soil H8. The incised pebble SF1 almost certainly came from H39 (11.1). There was no material later than Mesolithic from either H39 or the three pits.

6.2.3 Discussion

See Chapter 11.

6.3 Bronze Age (Figs 6.1, 6.3, 6.3 no 2)

6.3.1 Stratigraphy

Sand soil H8 represented the remnant of a phase in soil development within the Bronze Age. H8 consisted of soft orange sand, as did the underlying H39, but with some admixture of grey humic matter. Around postholes such as H38 and H34 soil H8 was 0.20m deep, and contained a large quantity of burnt and broken pebbles. These occurred occasionally in the soil elsewhere, where it was thinner or indistinguishable from overlying soil G143 containing medieval artefacts. In all areas of the site H8 merged upwards and downwards without clearly defined interfaces.

Pit J102, c 0.25m in diameter and surviving 0.15m deep, contained the lower part of a small collared urn (Fig 12.2 no 19) set upright, contain-

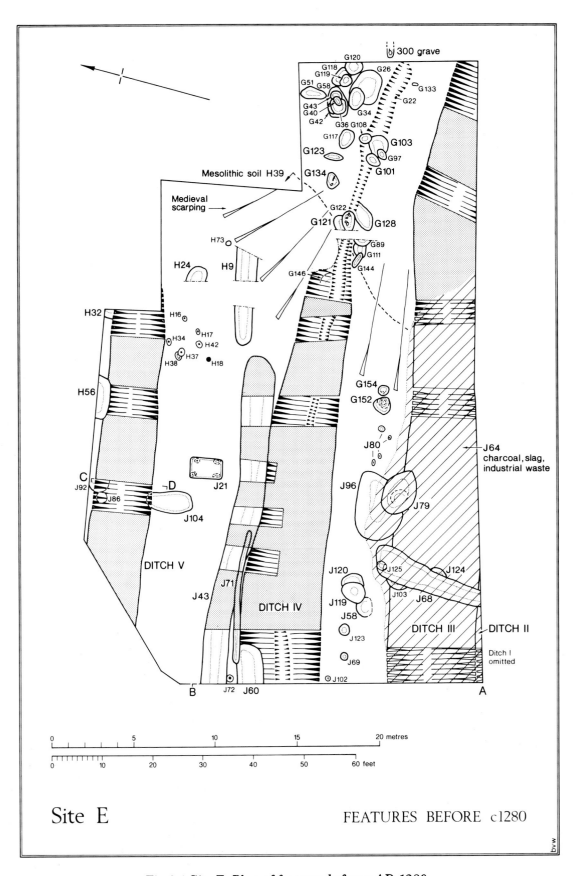

Fig 6.1 Site E. Plan of features before c AD 1280.

Pl 6.1 Site E. Bronze Age posthole H42 with limestone packing; postpipe excavated. View from west. Scale in ft.

ing some cremated bones mixed with brown sand. The pit lay beneath a slight hollow where the soil H8 was missing, and therefore only survived cut into the underlying H39. A few sherds from the upper part of the vessel were found in the base of medieval soil G143 above it. There had clearly been medieval activity in the area which had both removed the Bronze Age soil H8 and damaged the upper part of the vessel.

Postholes H38–H17 occurred in the area where soil H8 was most distinct. H38, 0.25m deep, contained a few burnt stones in its brown sand fill. H37, 0.45m deep, which cut or replaced H38, was tightly packed with small burnt pebble fragments which defined a post socket 0.18m in diameter filled with grey brown sand. H34, 0.28m deep, contained a few burnt pebbles in its grey brown sand fill. H42 (Pl 6.1), 0.38m deep, had a ring of packing stones at its top, around a possible post socket 0.20m in diameter, filled with grey brown sand. H16–H18 were similar; H16 was 0.27m deep, H17 0.30m deep, H18 0.15m deep. Each had a small black sand patch a few cms thick above a grey brown sand fill, but no other trace of a post socket. H16 and 17 had some scattered burnt pebbles, possibly disturbed packing stones, but there were none in H18. (H73 was probably of later date.) Pit H24 was 0.25m deep and filled with dark brown sand.

Other probable Bronze Age postholes are J72, J69 and J123, 0.30m, 0.18m and 0.20m deep respectively, because their fills of grey brown sand and a few burnt pebbles were similar to those of the preceding group, and they appeared to be cut within soil H8.

6.3.2 Dating

J102 contained collared urn no 19 (12.1) of the Earlier Bronze Age. H38, H37, H34 and H24 contained sherds probably dating to the later 2nd millennium BC. The remaining features are assumed to be of Bronze Age date because they were cut from the same level as these and had the same type of fill.

6.3.3 Discussion

See Chapter 12.

6.4 Romano-British

Six sherds of Romano-British pottery were residual in medieval contexts (13.2.3), but no features could be definitely assigned to this period. It must be stressed that surviving deposits are unlikely to represent the full range of activity on this site; the slope of the ground would have been conducive to erosion whenever surface vegetation was disturbed.

6.5 Between the Roman period and the 11th century (Figs 6.1, 6.5 no 3)
6.5.1 Stratigraphy

A grey-brown sandy soil, G143, was found over most of the site except where cut away by later features; this gradually merged downwards into the prehistoric soils beneath but the junction was nowhere distinct. It was extremely soft and irregular and undoubtedly some disturbances within it were not detected. On the west G143 was up to 0.60m thick but thinned eastwards to 0.30m. At the east end it had been entirely cut away by scarping or levelling (Fig 6.1). The surface of G143 was sealed over most of the site by G6 and associated levels, almost certainly dated c AD 1280. The nature of the soil means that no finds from it can be used to provide a definite date, and the small amount of pottery appears to postdate many of the features cut through it.

Pit J21 (Pl 6.2) was rectangular, 2 by 1.3m, with almost vertical sides and a flat bottom. It had a detectable depth of c 0.5m and was only noticed after the removal of G143. There were postholes in each of the corners; north east 0.15m deep, south east 0.20m deep with a recut, south west 0.15m deep and north west 0.10m deep with a recut. The postholes were filled with dark brown coarse sandy soil, the pit fill itself was finer and greyer. The fill of the postholes was not detected above the level of the pit bottom. The vertical edges and clean nature of both sides and bottom of the pit suggest that these may have been lined with timber. Other possible early features include posthole H73, 0.13m deep with unclear stratigraphic relationships, and

Pl 6.2 Site E. Pit J21 with timber settings in corners. ? 8th/9th centuries. View from south.

pits such as G128 and G146 cut by Ditch IV (see below).

6.5.2 Dating

Because J21 was covered by the full surviving thickness of G143, and produced no medieval finds, it may date early in the post-Roman medieval sequence and perhaps be pre-Norman. Iron knife no 23 (17.1.2) could be pre-Norman in date.

6.5.3 Discussion

Pits similar in size to J21, with postholes at the corners, are frequently found on Saxon sites. A good example is pit F54 from Hamwih; Holdsworth, (1976, 40–1) in his discussion of this pit and parallels on other sites, lists suggested uses as, cellars, storage, retting, scudding or fulling trough or weaver's pit, while pointing out that there is no evidence to support any of these functions.

6.6 The Norman Borough Defences
(Figs 6.1, 6.3, 6.4, 6.5 no 4)

6.6.1 Stratigraphy

Parts of five distinct ditches were located; I, II and III appeared to represent an original line twice recut. Ditches IV and V lay to the north, on the outer side of the defensive circuit.

The relationship between soil G143 and Ditches I and II had been cut away by Ditch III (Fig 6.3); Ditch III was cut from its top. Ditch IV predated III since its line was only clear when c 0.10m of G143 had been removed. Further Ditch IV was cut away at its east end by the scarping of soils G143 etc, which III post-dated. Ditch V cut through the top of G143 but its relationship with IV was not ascertainable.

Ditch I (Fig 6.3)

Ditch I, at least 2.40m deep, was only found in the section at the west of the site, south of II and III. Only a primary deposit of light brown sand with some grey patches survived, without fine silt horizons or layering. In the base of the Ditch was a double groove. (Ditch I is not shown on plan).

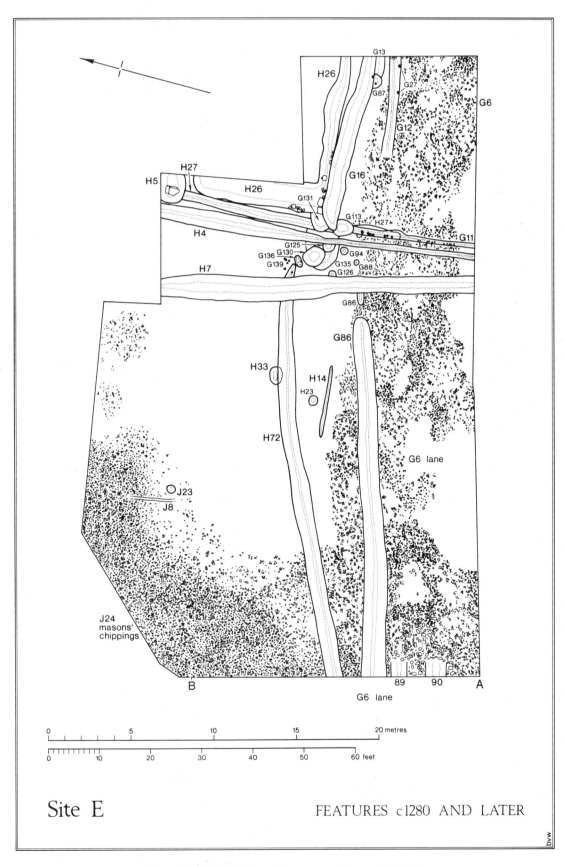

Fig 6.2 Site E. Plan of features after c AD 1280.

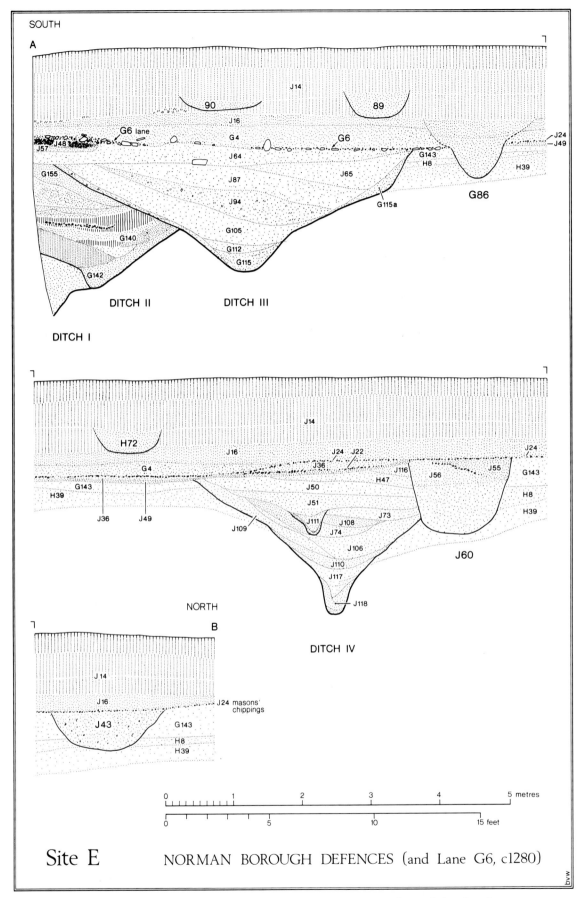

SOUTH

A

90

J14

89

J16

G6 lane

G4

G6

J24
J49

J48
J57

J64

G143
H8

H39

G155

J87

J65

G86

J94

G115a

G140

G105

G112

G115

DITCH II

DITCH III

G142

DITCH I

H72

J14

J16

J24 J22

J24

G4

J36

J116

J56

J55

G143

G143

H47

H8

H39

J36

J49

J50

J51

J111

J73

H39

J109

J108

J74

J60

J106

J110

J117

J118

NORTH

DITCH IV

B

J14

J16

J24 masons'
chippings

J43

G143

H8
H39

0   1   2   3   4   5 metres

0   5   10   15 feet

Site E   NORMAN BOROUGH DEFENCES (and Lane G6, c1280)

bvw

Fig 6.3 Site E. Section AB through Ditches I to IV and overlying levels.

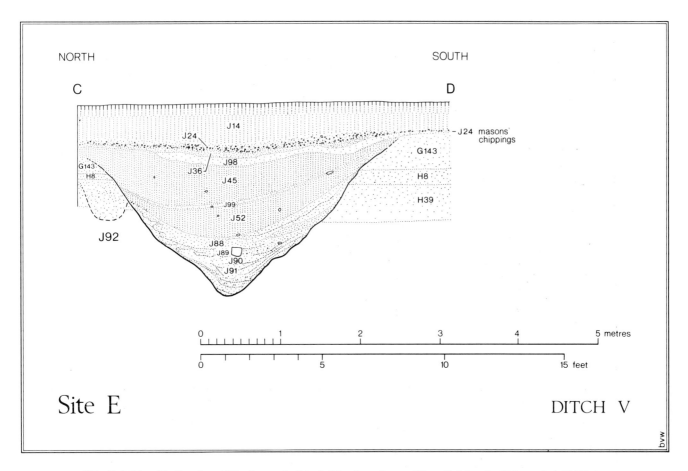

Fig 6.4 Site E. Section CD through Ditch V; also shows Mesolithic pit J92 and soil H39.

Ditch II (Fig 6.3)

Ditch II was located in all the sections across Ditches I–III, except that at the east end (it is only shown on Fig 6.1 where it cut into the subsoil). Its north edge was III, its south edge lay under the baulk, so no complete profile was obtained. It appeared to have had a regular wide V-shaped profile, about 2m deep. Primary sand silts G142 appeared to have been partly removed by a recut in which silts G141 were deposited. G141, in the base of the recut, was of clean fine orange sand, overlain by a lens of sticky black soil beneath light brown sand silt. G140 above was hard, almost black sand with a lens of mussel shells. G155, filling the top of II, of hard greenish-grey brown sand beneath lighter, softer grey-brown sand.

Ditch III (Fig 6.3)

Ditch III ran roughly east–west along the south of Site E, appearing to turn south at the east end. Its profile was wide and V-shaped, consistently *c* 1.90m deep even in the area of scarping. There was evidence for a recut. The original brown sand primary silts G115/G115a were discontinuous with the deposits above. The primary sand silt of the recut G112 lay under sand silt layers increasingly

dark and humic, G105, J94, J87 and J65. Levels J94 upward had the appearance of deliberate backfill. G105 contained a quantity of Carboniferous Limestone in small lumps.

Ditch IV (Fig 6.3, Pl 6.3)

Ditch IV, 4.5m north of III, had a steep V-shaped profile with a narrow slot at the base. On the west IV was 2m deep, but in the trench to the east its depth dropped to 1.50m and then decreased rapidly. The decrease in depth started before the scarping which cut through it. The slot at the base of the ditch survived the scarping and was 0.80m to 1m deep. The basal slot was filled with two separate deposits sharply divided; J118, light brown sandy silt, under J117, a cleaner sand. This looked like the setting for timbers, which had been removed, but as it continued right across the site is more likely to have been a cleaning slot. Sealing the slot were light brown sandy silts J109, J110, beneath clean sandy silt with darker lenses J106 and darker sandy silts J74, J108, J73. A narrow trench J111 0.50m deep was cut into J73, only detected against the west baulk. Above were sandy silts increasing in humic content towards the top, J51, J50, H47 and J116, the upper two of which may have existed as a ground surface for some time.

Pl 6.3 Site E. Ditch IV with cleaning slot in base. G6 lane and basal layers about 1 ft below top of marker. View from east. Scale in ft.

Ditch V (Fig 6.4, Pl 6.4)

Ditch V, along the north edge of the Site, was 2m deep with a regular V-shaped profile. Primary sand silts J9l to J88 became gradually darker upwards. The upper part of the Ditch appeared to have rapidly silted up with grey-brown sand with a few lighter sand streaks (J52–J45), beneath clean yellow sand J98 and yellow clay J36. There was no indication of any recuts. J45 contained lumps of coarse-grained sandstone, probably from the Millstone Grit.

6.6.2 Dating

All the Ditches had become completely infilled before surface G6/J24 was laid; it will be argued below that this dated to c 1280, and therefore provides a *terminus ante quem* for them.

Ditches I and II contained no pottery or other datable artefacts. Insufficient of I was removed for this to be meaningful, but II appears aceramic and therefore 12th century or earlier. Both predated the scarping. IV also predated the scarping; from its upper fill J50 came a single sherd, and from H47 above several sherds including one of Site V kiln type, and two of Ewloe type of probable 14th century date. These are the only Ewloe type sherds to underlay surface G6 and are probably intrusive. If they are so regarded, IV can be placed 12th century or earlier in the ditch sequence with I and II, although there is no way of deciding its comparative date.

Ditch III produced several small sherds from G112, in the primary fill, and several more including some kiln V type material from J94 and above (Table 18.5). It seems probable that the Ditch was dug at a date when more pottery was around, probably during the 13th century. This would be consistent with its postdating the scarping which truncated II and IV.

Ditch V has datable material comparable to that from III. A single sherd from J88 in the primary silts underlay more material including kiln V type sherds from J45 (Table 18.5). Again a 13th century date is probable, but there is no way of directly comparing its date with III.

6.6.3 Discussion

The historical contexts for the Ditches, and the

Pl 6.4 Site E. Ditch V. Mesolithic features J92 and J86 cause darkening on left ditch edge. View from west. Scale in ft.

possible links with sections cut on other sites, are covered in Chapters 19 and 20.

6.7 Medieval features predating the c AD 1280 surface (Figs 6.1. 6.5 no 5)

6.7.1 Stratigraphy

Fills were of various grey-brown sands, often with mussel shells, unless otherwise stated; surviving depths are given in brackets after each feature number. Features not mentioned are described in the archive.

Pits pre-dating the Ditches

G146 (0.15m), filled with brown sand, and G128 (0.15m), with light brown sand, were cut by Ditch IV, pit H32 (0.45m) by Ditch V.

Pits in the area of scarping

These either post-dated Ditch IV or the scarping of the area; some may have been the bases of features predating the scarping. They ranged in surviving depth from 0.13m to 0.60m, with most between 0.25 and 0.30m. G134 (0.30m) contained large stones including a rough limestone block and a water-worn boulder. The number of recuts suggest either a long or very intensive period of use. These features were sealed by the make up layers J15, J22 for the c 1280 lane.

Pits between Ditches III and IV

All appeared to have been cut through soil G143. G154, G152 and J80 may have been structural, 0.10m–0.30m deep, with slight depressions, probably postsockets, in their bases. J120, J58 and J119 (c 0.30m) were filled with dark grey sandy soil with a quantity of mussel shells.

Features north of and cutting Ditch IV

J60 (Fig 6.3) was either a pit or butt end of a gully; gully J43 (0.60m) contained a large quantity of cockle shells, perhaps related to H9 which was virtually filled with similar shells. Both J60 and J43 and Ditch IV were cut by narrow gully J71 (0.30m).

Pl 6.5 Site E. Lane G6 at east of Site. View to west. Scale in ft.

Metalworking area over Ditch III

Layers and features linked by large quantities of iron slag and charcoal overlay Ditch III and were sealed by G6, the *c* AD 1280 lane. Gully J68 (0.45m), and earlier features J124 and J123, cut Ditch III; this had a primary deposit of grey-brown sandy soil 0.25m thick, very clayey at the butt end, with a few burnt limestone lumps. The upper fill was sandy soil almost black with charcoal, slag and burnt limestone. Posthole J125 (0.15m) cut into J68. Pit J96 (0.30m), cut by J79 (0.50m), contained charcoal and slag.

The fill of J68 was continuous with a charcoal-rich soil J64 containing iron slag. Above J64 in the south west corner of the site were grey-brown clay soil J57 and J48, a layer of almost pure charcoal.

6.7.2 *Dating*

H32, G26, G103, G101, G89, J79, J60, J43, J71, and H9 all produced small amounts of pottery (Table 18.5) and are likely to be of 13th century date. Those features post-dating Ditch III should also belong to the 13th century; J68 and J64 both contained single sherds.

6.7.3 *Discussion*

The various pits defy constructive interpretation. The slag-bearing deposits such as J64 suggest an industrial episode after the infill of Ditch III. All the slag appeared to be from iron working and included smithing hearth bottoms and hammer scale. The presence of charcoal (15.2) and coal (17.3) are consistent with the working of iron. All processes, apart from smelting, could have been carried out, from processing blooms to the manufacture of artefacts. Analyses of slag from J68 and J79 are given in Table 17.3. Similar industrial episodes are evidenced on Sites A and T over the infilled Ditch III.

6.8 The *c* AD 1280 lane G6 and associated deposits

(Figs 6.2, 6.5 no 6; Pls 6.5, 6.6)

6.8.1 *Stratigraphy*

Initially a 'lane' J22 *c* 6m wide was laid east–west across the site, and after some usage, was remade with a more solid surface G6 and an extension J24. The material used in both phases was stone chippings of the various kinds of stone used in the Edwardian Castle (6.8.2).

Some turf and topsoil were probably stripped before the surfaces were laid. At the east end the basal sand of the lane, J49, rested on clean natural sand topped by thin iron pan. Stripping would account for the apparent cutting of almost all medieval features under J22/G6 from the same level, from the top of soil G143.

'Lane' J22 of stone chippings overlay a hard greenish grey sand J49 (Fig 6.3); hard orange sand J98 in the top of Ditch IV may have been contemporary. The surface of J49 was dirty and compacted with a number of slight ruts; it lay adjacent to the north edge of Ditch III, in the area where charcoal

Pl 6.6 Site E. Horseshoe No 117 on surface G6.

soil with iron slag J64 may still have being accumulating. To the east J49 directly overlay the silts of Ditch III. Subsequently pink sandstone chippings J22 were deposited over the length of J49, not sealing Ditch III except at the east end. The surface of J22 was also dirty, compacted and rutted. Over its east end, down slope, G5 silt with mussel shells accumumlated on J22 where it overlay the line of Ditch III.

Next, sand J36, white to bright yellow in colour with some pink sandstone chippings, was deposited under the upper lane G6 and extension J24; it did not occur under the stone spreads on either side of the west end of lane G6. The surface of J36 was clean and the main layer of stone fragments G6 was dumped directly on it. Lane G6 consisted of one thickness of white limestone fragments, with some sand at the east end. The G6 lane was 7–8m wide running east–west, widening out on the west to form a yard surface J24. The surface of G6 was compacted and heavily worn. In the south west the limestone was in large blocks and the surface included some iron slag.

Much dark soil was found between the stones, probably mud accumulated during use, and produced artefacts. A dark brown sandy soil G4 built up in the hollow formed in the surface of G6, which contained much debris, and the soil passed upward into J16.

6.8.2 Dating and 6.8.3 Discussion

J49 produced sherds of kiln V type, as did silt G5 between the two lane surfaces and sand J36, make-up for lane G6 and G6 itself. Silt G4, above, produced kiln V type sherds, among much other material including Saintonge sherds and some presumed intrusive post-medieval pieces.

The limestone and sandstone chippings forming the lane and yard surface were of the same stone types as those used in the Edwardian Castle. The fragments appeared to be masons' chippings, waste from the construction of the Castle, used to surface both a working area and a track coming from the Castle. This would indicate a date of around AD 1280 for the track and metalled surface.

Samples of the stone in G6/J42 were examined by M Owen, who also re-examined the building stones in the Edwardian Castle. He confirms that the majority in both were of the local Carboniferous Limestone. Most of the 'pink' rock is identified by M Owen as fine to medium-grained, purple micaceous sandstone, similar to that used in the Castle, and probably from the Upper Coal Measures outcropping along the Dee estuary and along the Elwy. The other coloured stone is a slightly micaceous sandstone which matches exactly Carboniferous Gwespyr Sandstone from near the Dee estuary. Neaverson (1947) identifies four major building stones in the Castle, but M Owen (pers comm) does not agree that Triassic Sandstone was used. He sees three main building stones in the Castle, all of which have fragments in G6/24. He also identifies a few fragments of bluish-grey roofing slate probably from Ordovician and Silurian deposits in the areas of Blaenau Ffestiniog and Corwen.

It is of course possible that the chippings were spread at a later date, but the artefacts appear to support late 13th century deposition. In this report, the c AD 1280 date is put forward as a moderately secure horizon, and is regarded as the most firmly based of those examined during the excavations.

6.9 Soils J16 and J14 over the AD 1280 surfaces (Fig 6.3)

6.9.1 Stratigraphy

Soil J16 continued above G4, which infilled the lane hollow, as a grey, increasingly humic sand; it passed upwards gradually into the overlying soil J14, and disturbances may have been missed.

6.9.2 Dating

J16 contained a quantity of sherds, some of kiln V type, some likely to be of 14th or 15th century date (pers comm M Blockley), with some possibly intrusive post-medieval material. It is likely, therefore, that the soil started to form around AD 1300, after major work on the Edwardian Castle ceased. It may have continued to build up until the late 15th century, the latter sherds being intrusive. J14 contained a wide range of sherds, from green-glazed Saintonge to local 18th century wares, and would thus date from the 13th to the 18th centuries.

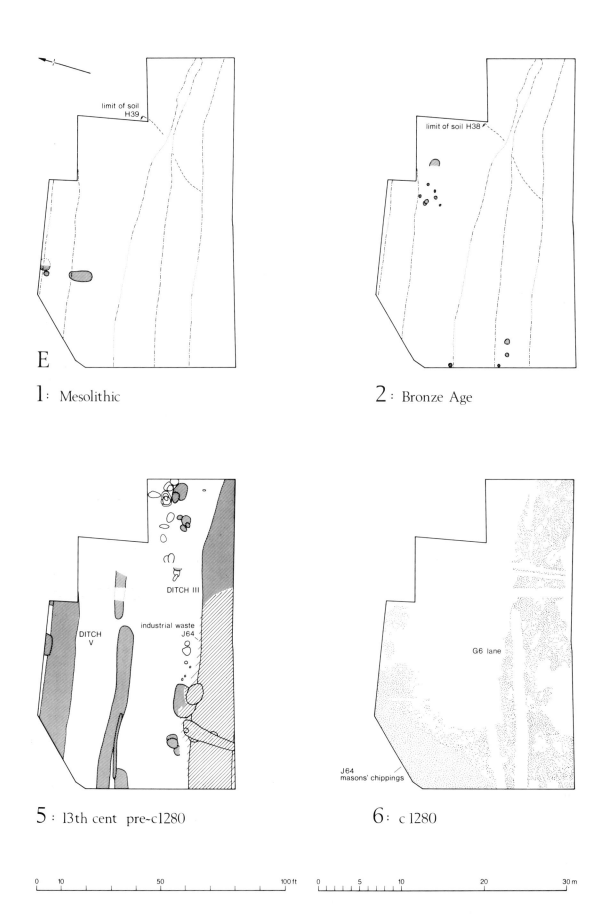

E

1 : Mesolithic

2 : Bronze Age

DITCH III

DITCH V

industrial waste J64

G6 lane

J64 masons' chippings

5 : 13th cent pre-c1280

6 : c 1280

limit of soil H39

limit of soil H38

| 0 | 10 | | 50 | | 100 ft |

| 0 | 5 | 10 | 20 | 30 m |

Fig 6.5 Site E. Phase plans Mesolithic to post-medieval.

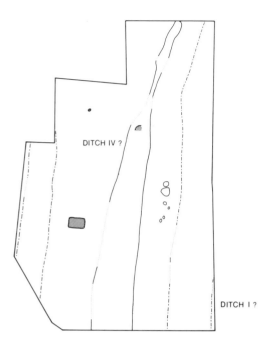

3 : ?10th/11th cents to c1070

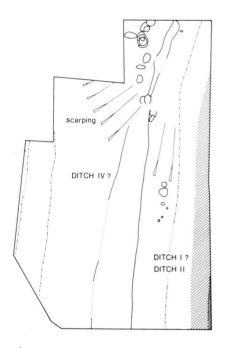

4 : Late 11th/12 centuries

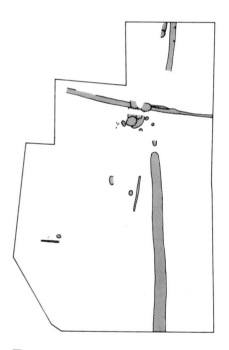

7 : c1300 ~ 1500

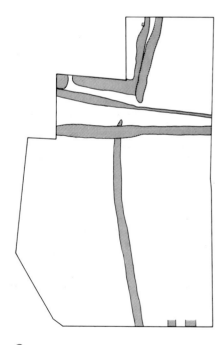

8 : Post-Medieval

6.10 Late medieval boundaries

(Figs 6.2, 6.5 no 7)

6.10.1 Stratigraphy

After soil G4 had mostly formed, a series of boundary trenches were cut as the soils above continued to build up. The tops of many were not clearly defined since their fills were similar to overlying soil J16.

Pit G135 may have been one of the earliest features in the sequence cut through soil G4. At least 0.50m deep, it was filled with mixed layers of brown and yellow sand, little of which survived since it was largely destroyed by later features. This large pit seems to have been the focus of most of the presumed boundary slots.

Slot H27, north to south, was the first to be cut after pit G135 had been partially backfilled; H27 cut soil G4 and was covered by soil J16; 0.30m deep, it was filled with brown sand. H27 continued south of pit G135 as G11 with scattered stones and a series of stakeholes in its base.

The earliest slot to the east of G135 was G12; its dark sandy fill contained three limestone chunks, possibly packing for a posthole, and stakeholes G27. The slot west of G135 was G86, 0.85m deep. G86 appeared to have been cut from soil J16, although it could have been recut.

A series of small pits or postholes G126, G88, G94, G125, G130, G131, G113, G136 were cut in the top of, and around, pit G135. These were an average of around 0.50m deep, and filled with mixed grey-brown sandy soils.

Also cutting soil G4 were miscellaneous features H14, H23, H33, J8, J23, G13, G87; stakeholes, pits and a trench.

6.10.2 Dating

These features contained a little kiln V type material, together with some sherds which may be 14th or 15th century and a few of post-medieval fabrics (Table 18.5; pers comm M Blockley). If soil G4 was forming by the 14th century, some of the material may be residual, and some intrusive.

6.10.3 Discussion

It is suggested that pit G135 was a marker, at the junction of four separate plots of land, and was part of the division of the area into arable parcels after the establishment of the Edwardian Borough. The boundaries were maintained until, probably, the early 20th century. Agricultural activity within the plots would account for the gradual build-up of soil with a mixed range of artefacts.

6.11 Post-medieval boundaries and structure (Figs 6.2, 6.5 no 8)

6.11.1 Stratigraphy

The north–south boundary H27 was replaced by gully H4 (0.50m) which cut through soil J16 and was filled with dark brown sandy soil. East of H4 was trench H26, which appeared to be the south and west foundation of a rectangular structure cut into J16. The building would have been 7m wide by at least 10m long, but had been extensively robbed. H26 was infilled with dirty brown sand, with sufficient masonry *in situ* to indicate that the walls had consisted of rough limestone blocks bonded with grey-white mortar. Postpit H5 (0.60m), adjacent to the north west corner of the suggested building, had on its base two unmortared limestone blocks on top of each other, which may have been a post pad. These features appeared beneath soil J14.

The remaining gullies were cut after soil J14 had formed, and varying amounts of overlying soil J16 had accumulated. J14 was very dark grey-brown, its junction with underlying soil J16 not clearly defined except by a thin spread of red clay in the south west of the site.

Gully H72, (0.40m), ran roughly east–west and was filled with dark grey brown sandy soil; there was a single stakehole in its east end. Gully G16, (0.50m), to the east contained very dark brown sandy soil, and cut the foundation trench H26. Gully H7, (1.0m), redefined the north–south boundary line; it postdated all other gullies as it was cut from topsoil over soil J14. Gullies (or possibly pits) H89 and H90 could only be traced running a short distance east of section AB; they cut from a level high in soil J14. The soil build-up continued on the site until recent times with up to 0.50m of sandy soil over J14.

6.11.2 Dating

H4 contained pottery of varied dates up to the 18th century; it may have been cut (into soil J16) at any date from the late 15th century and had silted up by the 18th. Pit H5 produced Ewloe P68 (Fig 18.7), perhaps 15th century. A late 15th or 16th century date for the structure H26 is postulated from the level at which it cut into soil J16.

Soil J14 contained material ranging from the medieval period to the 19th century. Gully G16 contained mainly residual medieval pottery with a few probable 17th century sherds.

6.11.3 Discussion

The building in H26 was constructed at the extreme south west corner of a plot of land. Its function may have been agricultural rather than domestic although the two could easily have been accommodated under one roof. There was no apparent trace of flooring material; either this had been removed during the comprehensive robbing of the walls or through erosion, or perhaps, a rush strewn, beaten earth floor had sufficed. The building does not appear on the *Conway Map of 1756*.

Boundary gully H7, late in the sequence, almost certainly continued in Site V as V13. This boundary is clearly marked on the *Conway Map of 1756* and also on the Tithe Apportionment Map of 1839. The 1.50m accumulation of soil since the medieval period was caused presumably by the continuance, from the later medieval period, of agricultural activity.

Acknowledgments
We are grateful to Clwyd County Council (formerly Flintshire) for permission to excavate and for the co-operation of Mr T Charles, Headmaster of Ysgol-Y-Castell, and his staff for this, the first excavation in school grounds, which, timed to take place during the Easter vacation, extended into the summer term. Ian Young, David Freke and the late Eleanor (Muers) Saunders acted as site supervisors. M Owen of the Geological Museum (National Environmental Research Council) provided valuable help with the identification of building stones.

7 Site M, Ysgol-Y-Castell playing fields. The Norman Church and prehistoric sequence beneath

7.1 Introduction

The site lies in the playing field of Ysgol-Y-Castell, which Flintshire (now Clwyd) County Council was considering levelling in 1969. At that time the surface of the field was irregular, rising by about 3.30m from Site T north west to Site E and by about 1.50m to the south, towards Twt Hill. The southern part of the field had previously been lowered, probably by at least 0.30m to 0.60m, and the soil dumped in the lower, north east area. In 1959, probably just after this levelling, goal posts were set up at the southern end of the field, in the process of which human bones were found. A small trial excavation (Fig 1.2 N) was organised by P Hayes, then at the Flintshire County Record Office (7.7.1). A geophysical survey was subsequently carried out by A J Clark of the Department of the Environment Ancient Monuments Laboratory (now Historic Buildings and Monuments Commission for England) (7.2). This survey indicated a very strong anomaly at the southern end of the field close to the find of human bones; its plan indicated a two-cell building about 27m long aligned very nearly east to west, reasonably interpreted as a Church. At Easter 1971 a single trench 15m by 1.50m was cut towards the west end of the presumed nave of the suggested Church, west of a possible south doorway.

The purpose of this excavation was to confirm the presence of a Church, to investigate the reason for the strong geophysical anomaly and to obtain information on the nature, depth and significance of archaeological deposits under the playing fields. The trench in fact confirmed the presence of a Church over up to 1.50m of stratified levels and in view of the importance of these it was agreed that the field should not be levelled. The presumed area of the church and cemetery surrounding it was subsequently scheduled as part of Ancient Monument No 129.

7.2 The geophysical survey (Fig 7.1)

by A J Clark (1978)

The geophysical survey of the school playing field was carried out by A J Clark and D Haddon-Reece of the Geophysics Section, Ancient Monuments Laboratory, with the assistance of P Humphries of the Inspectorate of Ancient Monuments for Wales. Measurements were made with an Elsec proton magnetometer at 5 ft (c 1.5m) intervals. An initial small-scale dot-density plot showed fairly weak indications of possible ditches and other features, but the outline of the Church stood out with a clarity that was baffling until excavation revealed that the foundations were composed of iron slag. A portion of the dot-density plot was published (Miles, 1972, 247). The contour plot used to illustrate this report was prepared as follows.

After correction for diurnal drift, the magnetometer results were smoothed by replacing each reading by the mean of itself and the four adjacent readings, and then computer plotting, using contours at 30 gamma intervals (approximately half the standard deviation). The best delineation of the Church seems to be provided by the 150 gamma contour, which has therefore been thickened.

The other, weak, indications, where excavated in Sites T and E, overlay areas of complex stratigraphy and did not correspond to specific features.

7.3 Mesolithic (Figs 7.2, 7.3)

7.3.1 Stratigraphy

M26, a soft orange-brown sandy soil with little humic matter, lay everywhere directly over the glacial yellow sand subsoil, except where cut away by later features. It merged upwards into the late prehistoric/Iron Age soil M55, except at the southern end of the trench where pebble horizon M64c intervened. M26 contained 786 fragments of worked chert and flint (10.1) and occasional burnt or utilised pebbles.

A series of features M52, M46, M50, M60, M122, M123 and M90 cut into the sandy soil in the southern part of the trench and were only detected after M26 was removed. M52, a posthole 0.12m deep, was filled with orange-brown sand; its relationship to posthole M46, 0.10m deep, with a fill of yellow-brown sand and pebbles, could not be determined. M50 was a hollow or pit at least 1.70m across and 0.30m deep filled with reddish (burnt?) sand. M60, up to 0.18m deep, had three slight depressions, possible post sockets, in its base

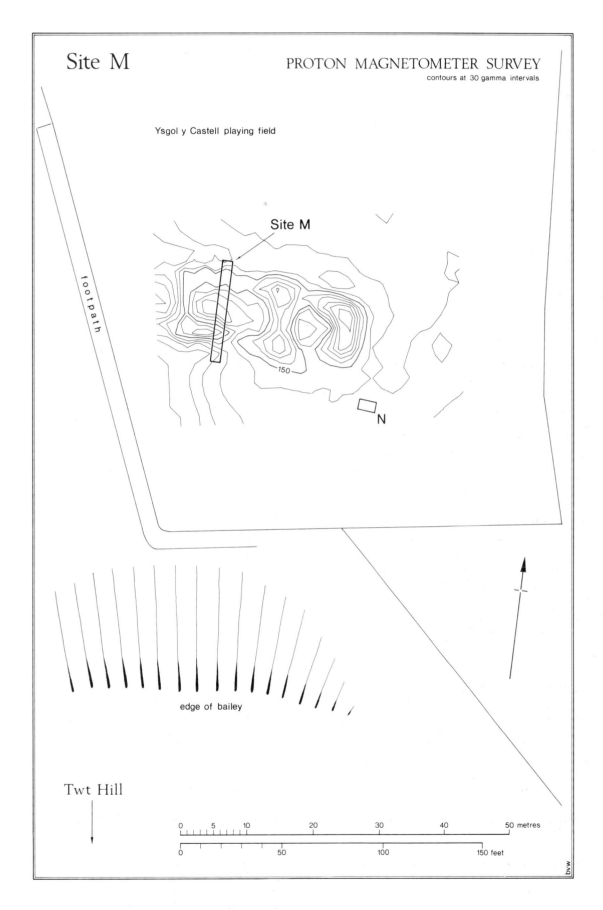

Fig 7.1 Site M. Proton magnetometer plot indicating the Church and its location in the school playing field. (From data supplied by A Clark).

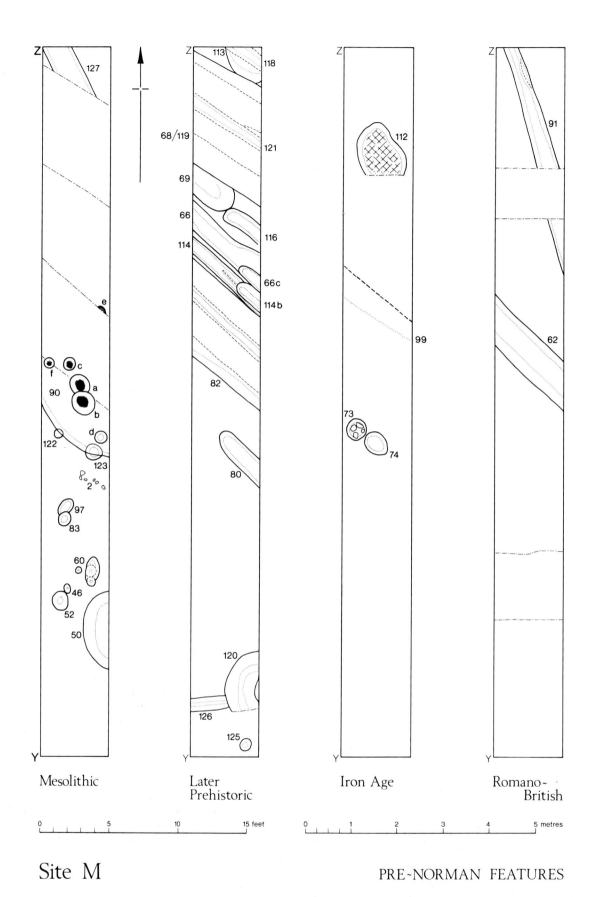

Site M

PRE-NORMAN FEATURES

Fig 7.2 Site M. Plan of features pre-dating the Norman Church.

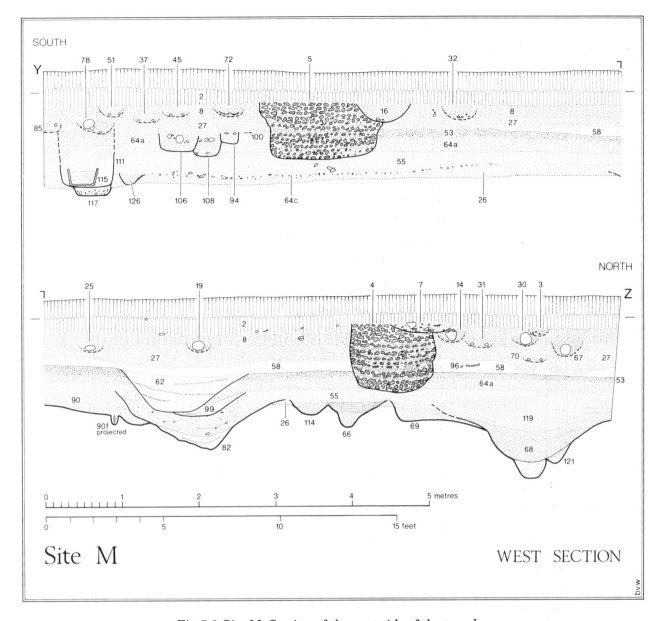

Fig 7.3 Site M. Section of the west side of the trench.

containing reddish sand. M122, a small pit or post base 0.10m deep filled with dark orange sand, and M132 with a brown sand fill 0.18m deep, were both largely cut away by the M90 complex.

M90, cut from a higher level through part of the soil horizon M26, was a flat-bottomed hollow at least 0.30m deep and 3m wide (Pl 7.1). There were six small pits or hollows in its base. Pits 90a, 90b, 90c, 90f, 0.17m, 0.25m, 0.20m and 0.15m deep respectively, were filled with sand, coloured almost black at their centres but fading to light brown at the edges and base. Pit 90e, 0.18m deep, had an almost black sand fill, but 90d, 0.18m deep, had an even fill of hard brown sand. The dark centres of all but 90d appeared to contain minute flecks of charcoal. The main light brown sand fill of M90 contained a large quantity of worked chert and flint, incised pebble SF2 (11.1) and some carbonised hazelnut shells. The upper part of M90 was cut

away by a later, prehistoric, gully M82. M83 and M97, intercutting postholes 0.10m and 0.05m deep filled with orange brown sand, and gully M127, 0.10m deep filled with orange sand and pebbles, were all cut from much the same level as M90.

7.3.2 Dating

A radiocarbon determination of 8528 ± 73 BP (BM–822) was obtained from hazelnut shells in M90. No finds were later than Mesolithic, and the nature of the lithics suggested a date somewhat earlier than the single radiocarbon date.

7.3.3 Discussion

The nature of the Mesolithic occupation, better preserved than on any other site, is discussed in Chapter 10.

Pl 7.1 Site M. Mesolithic hollow M90 with subsidiary features in base; gully M82 cuts through with sandblow M58 and gully M62 above. East side of trench. View from south west. Scale in ft.

7.4 Later prehistoric (Figs 7.2, 7.3)

7.4.1 Stratigraphy

It is probable that there were considerable episodes of erosion as there are no features subsequent to the Mesolithic which can definitely be dated before the Iron Age. There was a slight discontinuity between Mesolithic soil M26 and the slightly darker soil M55 above it which contained no datable material. At the south end of the trench this separation was emphasised by M64c, an undated brown sandy soil and pebble horizon which overlay a slight depression and sealed a short slot M126, 0.13m deep, and a possible post setting M125, 0.05m deep; M125 and 126 were filled with orange-brown sand and light brown sand respectively, but contained no datable material. Pit M120, 0.15m deep with dark brown sand fill, cut M126 but underlay soil M64c. These features may be of any pre-Roman but post-Mesolithic date.

A sequence of small ditches or gullies M80–M113 ran north west to south east across the northern half of the trench cutting into the Mesolithic deposits beneath. Their fills were all of mixed sand with some silting lines; M82, 0.60m, was the deepest (Pl 7.1). As a group they gave the impression of a boundary line many times recut. Because of the similarity of their fills, distinction of details was difficult.

The overlying hard light brown sand M55 was thickest (up to 0.25m) towards the south where it filled the hollow over M120, but thinned and faded towards the north. It was heavily iron panned in places, particularly in the vicinity of the north wall of the later Church, the foundation trenches of which were filled with iron slag.

Two postholes and a pit M73, M74 and M112 were cut into M55. M73 was a posthole 0.30m deep with large pebble packing stones, M74 a hollow or shallow pit 0.08m deep with brown sand fill. M112 was an irregular pit 0.25m deep with a fill of brown

sand flecked with charcoal and occasional pebbles; its base was heavily burnt and it may have been a hearth. These three features were sealed by a more humic sand soil horizon M64a which merged into an old ground surface M53.

7.4.2 Dating

A quantity of salt container ceramic came from M99, the latest of the gully series. There were no other datable finds. The long-lived gully sequence may have started well before the Iron Age, to which this ceramic should be dated (13.1.4). Soil M55 represents broadly a horizon at the end of detectable Iron Age activity. Posthole M73, cut into it, contained a broken Iron Age quern SF11 (13.1.2) among its packing. The overlying layer M64a produced Romano-British material.

7.5 Romano-British (Figs 7.2, 7.3)

7.5.1 Stratigraphy

Features such as M73 and soil M55 were covered by a more humic sand soil horizon M64a which merged into an old ground surface M53. M53 had a well defined horizon of iron panning at its top, which looked like a fully developed old land surface; the iron panning again probably related to the slag in the Church foundation. Soil M53 survived over the northern two thirds of the trench, the surface of which sloped down towards the north. Surface M53 was sealed by a covering of clean, wind-blown, sand M58.

Two features cut wind blown sand M58. M62 was a flat-bottomed gully 0.45m wide. To the north was a second flat-bottomed gully M91 running approximately north–south. Both were filled with very clean sand interspersed with slight grey brown silt lines, suggesting rapid silting; their fills merged at the top with sand M58 (Pl 7.1). M58, with M53 beneath it, had been removed at the south end of the trench by later levelling or erosion. Sand M58 merged gradually upwards into darker sand soil M27.

7.5.2 Dating

The lowest context to produce definite Romano-British material was M64a, with sherds from several vessels which suggest a late 2nd to mid-3rd century date for activity predating the development of humic soil M53 (13.2.3).

This later soil M53, a probable old ground surface, which immediately predated wind-blown sand M58, contained pottery of probable late 3rd or early 4th century date (13.2.3). M62, the late gully cutting through M58, contained a single body sherd of samian, presumably residual. The gully M91, in a similar stratigraphic position, contained two small body sherds of black-burnished ware. A 4th century date for the features cutting sand M58 would seem reasonable.

7.5.3 Discussion

See 13.3.

7.6 Between the Roman and the Norman periods (Fig 7.3)

Soil build-up continued subsequent to the Romano-British sandblow M58 with M27 and M8. The stratigraphy was confused by the later insertion of a complex series of burials outside the Norman Church. Levels were clearer in the centre of the trench, within the Church walls, where there had been fewer burials. The lowest soil level, M27, was of yellow-brown sand (0.20m thick) into which M58 merged gradually; in the centre of the trench it was lighter and sandier than at the ends. M27 passed upwards into a browner sandy soil M8, 0.30m thick, which was heavily disturbed by burials. Soil M8 had accumulated to at least the height of the tops of the Church foundation trenches M4 and M5 by the later 11th century. It may have been even higher. There had been some subsequent removal of soil in the Church area as its interior, as surviving, appeared to be below the level of any floor. The accumulation of soils M27 and M8 seem to have occurred gradually over some centuries, with no suggestion of any specific activity. They contained about a dozen sherds of Romano-British pottery of various dates, but nothing else which need be pre-Norman.

7.7 The Norman Church (Figs 7.3, 7.4)

The historical background to the foundation of a Norman Church at Rhuddlan, first referred to in Domesday Book, is given in 2.2.

7.7.1 Stratigraphy

The Church foundations M4 and M5 (Pl 7.2)

The foundation trenches M4 and M5 had been cut from at least the top of soil M8; M4, the north foundation, was 1.05m wide and 0.85m deep, M5, that on the south, 1.35m wide and 0.75m deep. Both had been filled with tap slag from iron working, mixed with small amounts of charcoal. The slag had been rammed flat in layers, in the process of which thin spreads of sand had accumulated from the foundation trench sides. Traces of white mortar with a few small lumps of the local limestone adhered to the top of the slag in the fill, indicating that the walls of the superstructure had cores of rough limestone lumps set in mortar. Mortared limestone lumps were also contained within the fill of graves M117, M108, and M106, some of the earliest graves; Ml17 and Ml08 also contained a few small fragments of tap slag. This suggests that a stone structure, either that represented by foundation trenches M4 and M5, or an earlier one on the same line, was extant before the first burials found were inserted. This relationship

Pl 7.2 Site M. Trench looking north showing slag-filled Church foundations and burials of Phase 3.

is also supported by the alignment of some of the earliest burials on foundation M5.

A single posthole M13, 0.15m deep, filled with slag and limestone packing, was cut within the Church into the surviving top of layer M8.

The burials

A total of 45 graves was found but further individuals were represented by disarticulated bones redeposited in grave fills. The graves have been divided into four phases on the basis of their stratigraphic relationships, depths, and to some extent their fills. This division assumes that the graves became successively shallower and their

78

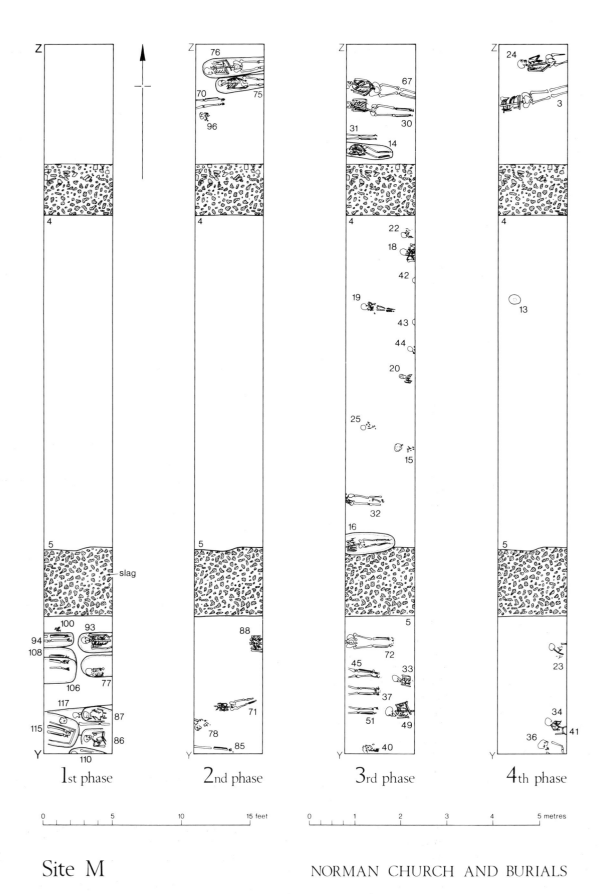

Site M NORMAN CHURCH AND BURIALS

Fig 7.4 Site M. Plan of the Norman Church and burials.

fills darker and less sandy with time. However this phasing can only be tentative for those graves without stratigraphic relationships, as in many cases the level from which the grave had been cut could not be determined, and depths of grave pits may not have been consistent at any period. As a minimum the phasing may be regarded as a suitable way of presenting a series of burials which were in fact a continuous sequence. In each suggested phase, except perhaps the first, the layout was essentially regular without overlaps. There was no suggestion of any prolonged gap in the use of the cemetery, although different areas of the grave yard may have been used cyclically. The area north of the Church contained only three burial phases, lacking the suggested first phase. South of the Church the Phase 1 burials such as M117 were deeper than any to the north and had cleaner sandy fills. The earliest phase to the north, (Phase 2, burials 70, 75, 76, 96) cut into layer M27 and M58 and may be contemporary with burials 71, 78, 85, 88, on the south side of the Church. The sparse burials within the Church (burials M16–M22) are included with Phase 3 burials cutting only down into M8. Phase 4 consisted of burials M23, M34, M36 and M41 to the south, and M3 and M24 to the north. These burials were cut from the top of M8, at a level at which there was a lot of scattered debris. The distinctive alignment of M3 and M24 off the line of the Church should be noted.

The term 'grave pit' is used where the cut for the burial was detected. This only occurred for some of the early burials cutting into the lower lighter sandy soils.

Burials of Phase 1

Burial M117 (Fig 7.5; Pl 7.4) was the deepest, and may be the earliest, burial found, although the presence of juvenile bones in its grave fill indicated that others elsewhere predated it. Only 0.11m of its grave pit survived since it had been largely cut away by burial M115. The grave pit had been lined with lumps of mortar, lime, unburnt limestone and a charred wooden object. A layer of pink sand was spread over this material, on top of which an adult male was buried. The sand immediately beneath the bones, and also over the top part of the right leg bone, was stained green to a depth of 0.03m. Two coins of William Rufus (issued c 1092–1095) (16.1, Nos 2–3), a rock crystal and a fragment of decayed leather, perhaps the remains of a purse or pouch, were found in the area of the left inner thigh. The grave fill contained some tap slag fragments. M117 had been partly cut away by burial M115, the grave pit of which, M111, contained the skull and other bones of M117 and had tap slag in its fill.

Burial M115 (Fig 7.5; Pl 7.4), in grave pit M111 0.95m deep, was an adult in the only coffin detected, which survived as a brown stain. This was trapezoidal and wider at the top than at the bottom, and as there were no nails, probably had

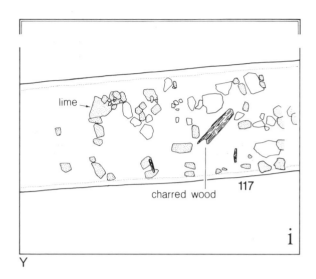

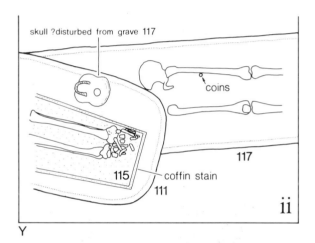

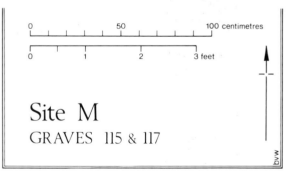

Fig 7.5 Site M. Detailed plans of graves M115 and M117.

been pegged or jointed together. The coffin had an infill of clean whitish-yellow sand, overlain by a compact band of brown staining, possibly the collapsed coffin lid, which sloped down over the bones to touch the base of the coffin at one side. Further clean sand covered the decayed coffin lid and filled grave pit M111, which contained some parts of skeleton M117. Close to the bones of M115 were slight traces of green staining similar to that

Pl 7.3 Site M. North Church foundation M4 with tap slag fill and small amount of mortared limestone rubble on top. Phase 3 burial M14 to right. View from east. Scale in ft.

in burial M117. There was tap slag in the fill.

Burial M108 was of an adult, of unknown sex, since only the legs survived, due to later disturbance by burials M106 and M94. The fill of the grave contained mortar and some tap slag.

Burial M106 was in a detectable grave pit M105. Only the feet of the burial survived indicating the occupant was an adult. Juvenile bones were also found in the grave fill. Skeleton M106 was covered with limestone and mortar lumps adhering to tap slag.

Burial M94 lay in grave pit M95. Legs only survived and were those of an adult of unknown age. There was tap slag in the grave fill.

Burial M100 was a mass of small bones, without a detectable grave pit. The bones included those of an infant around two years old, another of twelve months and some foetal bones.

Burial M93 was the upper torso of an adult male in a grave pit.

Burial M77 lay in grave pit M102, its base covered with pebbles, limestone fragments and a few pieces of mortar to a depth of 0.5m; approximately 0.10m of brown sand sealed the pebbles. On top of the sand the bones of a three-year old infant

were laid against the southern side of the grave. Bones of other skeletons came from the grave fill, which had probably been disturbed. The fill contained tap slag.

Burial M110; skeleton in a grave pit, not lifted since it was mainly under the south baulk.

Burial M86; the upper part of an adult female.

Burial M87; very disturbed, bones of an infant around three to five years old, legs cut away.

Burials of Phase 2 south of the Church

Burial M88; grave with limestone in base. Adult with bones (?skull) of infant about four years old. The head of the adult was cut away by burial M72.

Burial M71; skeleton of an infant around six years old, skull removed by burial M51, adjacent to the foot of which skeleton the skull was found. Tap slag in fill.

Burial M78; grave containing part of adult female, with adult skull, possibly from same skeleton out of position. Tap slag in fill.

Burial M85; left leg only, adult; traces of mortar in grave fill.

Burials of Phase 2 north of the Church

Burial M75; grave pit containing child, about nine years old; limestone pieces in fill.

Burial M76; grave pit with bones, adult male. Tap slag in fill.

Burial M70; adult.

Burial M96; skull and upper rib cage only.

Burials of Phase 3 south of the Church

(Pl 7.2)

Burial M72; grave containing adult male, with bones of another adult and an infant less than twelve months old in the fill, also tap slag.

Burial M45; legs of an adult.

Burial M37; grave with tap slag, limestone and mortar in primary fill; adult legs, with an infant about six years old in fill with tap slag.

Burial M51; grave with tap slag and limestone in fill; child about fourteen years old, with an infant about four years old in the fill.

Burial M40; grave with tap slag in fill; infant three or four years old with the bones of a child of about thirteen years old in the fill.

Burial M49; grave of an adolescent sixteen years old, with child about ten years old in the fill with tap slag.

Burial M33; child about six years old.

Burials of Phase 3 north of the Church

Burial M14; grave cutting footings of north wall of Church; adult. Tap slag in fill. (Pl 7.3).

Burial M31; adult female. Tap slag in fill.

Burial M30; adult female. Tap slag in fill.

Burial M67; grave of an adult male, with remains of a second adult male in fill. Tap slag in fill.

Burials of Phase 3, interior of the Church

These burials are assigned to Phase 3 because of their appropriate depth.

Burial M16; grave pit cutting foundation of south wall of Church; child about nine years old. Tap slag in fill.

Burial M32; child about eleven years old. Tap slag in fill.

Burial M15; infant less than twelve months.

Burial M25; infant, probably new born. Tap slag in fill.

Burial M20; grave with slag and mortar in fill; infant about two years old.

Burial M44; grave with fill containing slag; infant about one year old. Tap slag in fill.

Burial M43; skeleton not lifted, only top of skull visible; mainly under baulk.

Burial M19; grave with slag in the fill, infant about three years old. Tap slag in fill.

Burial M42; skeleton not lifted; only top of skull visible, mainly under baulk.

Burial M18; grave with tap slag in fill; child

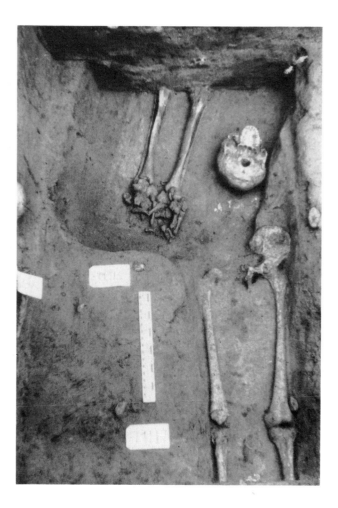

Pl 7.4 Site M. Burial M115 with sand-filled coffin stain, cutting burial M117 with coins of William II. View from east.

about five years old, with the bones of an adult male in grave fill.

Burial M22; grave with fragments of tap slag in fill; child about four years old.

Burials of Phase 4 south of the Church

Burial M36; grave with tap slag and mortar in fill; adult male, with the bones of one child aged about nine years and of two infants aged three years and twelve months respectively in fill.

Burial M34; grave with mortar fragments; child about four years old, with the bones of another child of about six years and of one other individual in the fill. Cut by M41.

Burial M23; grave with tap slag in fill; adult male.

Burial M41; grave with tap slag in fill; adult with infant about two years in fill.

Burials of Phase 4 north of the Church

Burial M3; adult male.

Burial M24; adolescent female. Tap slag in fill.

The demolition of the Church

It is presumed that the Church was demolished when the present church of St Mary's was built in the Edwardian Borough. Building materials were almost certainly removed from the site, as little limestone or mortar was found in soil M2 which overlay the foundations, nor in the topsoil. A spread of limestone chippings was noted outside the Church. A shallow trench M7 cut into the footings of the Church north wall, and may have been dug to remove re-usable building materials as its bottom was mortar from which limestone blocks had been removed. Its fill contained quantities of tap slag, limestone and mortar among brown sand.

Site N 1959 Excavations

The following account is based on notes (in the Clwyd County Record Office, Hawarden) made by P Hayes about his trial excavation after human bones were noticed when pits were dug for the erection of goal posts in the School playing field.

The excavation was about 2.50m square and natural sand was recorded at a depth of 1.05m. No prehistoric levels were distinguished. The bottom 0.80m was of 'dark sand' with occasional pieces of limestone and slag, with only topsoil recorded above it. Five skeletons without defined grave pits were found, one at the bottom of the excavation cut into natural sand, three at the same level in the middle of the 'dark sand' and one cutting into its top. The bones have not been submitted for anatomical comment as insufficient were lifted. The finds, preserved at the County Record Office, Hawarden, consist of some probable 13th century sherds, an iron knife and arrowhead and a small fragment of samian.

7.7.2 Dating

Interpretation and dating are uncertain because the later graves obscured the tops of the earlier ones, because it was difficult to see anything cutting through soil M27, and because soils M27 and M8 contained material which was almost certainly intrusive.

Soils M27 and M8 contained medieval and post-medieval sherds as did some burials of Phases 3 and 4. It seems improbable that most material can be anything but intrusive in the soft sand soils; 17th century material was found with several Phase 3 burials and there are no documentary references to a burial ground of this date anywhere at Rhuddlan than the Church of St Mary's in the Edwardian Borough.

The two coins of William Rufus (1092–1095) with the skeleton in M117 (16.1) provide a reasonably firm date for the earliest grave located. Grave M117 was lined with lime, limestone, mortar and a few fragments of tap slag, which seems to link it closely with the slag foundations for a mortared limestone building. Another early grave M108 also

contained lumps of mortared limestone in its fill. The evidence is consistent with the documentary references to the Church in the Norman Borough in use from the late 11th to the late 13th centuries, but evidence from a narrow trench is bound to be inconclusive. The possibility that there were burials here preceeding the Norman Borough can not be discounted, nor that the foundations found replaced an earlier structure.

7.7.3 Discussion

The structure excavated may reasonably be linked to the Church at Rhuddlan mentioned in Domesday Book. The geophysical plot indicates a building about 27.5m long with a nave about 9m wide. It had a small rectangular chancel inset on the eastern end. (The geophysical plot could be interpreted as showing an apsidal-ended chancel.) The Church was built of mortared local limestone, with no evidence of ashlar work. Some fragments of black roofing slate, possibly from Silurian strata of the Corwen-Llangollen area, were found, notably in grave M33. The simple bipartite rectilinear plan is common for early Norman churches, and its size should be considered in relation to churches of Norman urban centres. Welsh churches tend to be much smaller and no standing masonry structure can be definitely dated to the 11th century (Radford, 1963). Recent excavations such as those of the church at Capel Maelog, Llandrindod Wells, Powys (Britnell, 1990) and at Llanychlwydog, Dyfed (Murphy, 1987) are likely to be more relevant to any church eventually established as preceding the Rhuddlan Norman foundation. The shafts of two crosses (1.2.7), now in the present St Mary's Church, of the late 10th or early 11th century may relate to such an earlier religious establishment.

The Rhuddlan Church was located adjacent to the east side of the footpath running from Hylas lane to Twt Hill and eventually Abbey farm. This footpath may represent the course of one of the streets of the Norman Borough.

During the use of the grave yard the burials seem to have become increasingly shallow. It is probable that the surface of the cemetery became gradually heightened during its period of use, and that the area is now lower than it was when the cemetery ceased to be used. Burial grounds generally have heightened surfaces if they are in use for any period of time. A certain amount of material was removed from the site during the levelling of 1959. Soil M2 had the appearance of truncating all features beneath it, perhaps through late- and post-medieval agricultural use. It is likely that the soft sand of the area would have provided an irregular surface during the medieval period, and that this would have been much affected by prolonged use for farming. There is no evidence for any use but farming in the period after the foundation of the Edwardian Borough.

Acknowledgments
We are grateful to Clwyd County Council (formerly Flintshire) for permission to excavate and the Headmaster, Mr T Charles and the staff of Ysgoll-Y-Castell for their suppport. The project was initiated by the geophysical survey carried out by A J Clark and his team. Ian Goodall and the late Eleanor (Muers) Saunders were site supervisors. M Owen provided geological identifications. Comments on the slag are covered in 17.2. Initial identifications of the skeletons were provided by Dr R S Connolly, Department of Anatomy, University of Liverpool.

8 Site D, Gwindy Street. The Edwardian Borough Defences

8.1 Introduction (Fig 8.1)

The north corner of the Edwardian Borough Defences, to the north east of Gwindy Street, forms the only surviving section of the earth and timber town defences built by Edward I in North Wales. The earthworks described here as the Edwardian Borough Defences had been identified as such because of their position on the edge of the Edwardian Borough and their alignment with its street plan. The historical evidence for the existence of such Defences is summarised in 2.3. The Department of the Environment (now Cadw) was considering their preservation as an Ancient Monument when, in 1971, two separate building schemes were proposed; Plot O adjacent to Gwindy Street, privately owned, was to be sold as building land, and Plot R on the inner corner of the Defences was to be used for an extension to the Telephone Exchange; the future of Plot P/Q, to the south east, was undecided by its owners, the then Flintshire County Council. The Department decided to excavate to obtain confirmation of the nature and date of the earthworks. Excavation took place for four weeks in spring 1971 and was continued on the site of the Telephone Exchange extension for three weeks in spring 1972. The extension has now been built, but the other building scheme was not proceeded with. The Defences were subsequently scheduled as part of Ancient Monument No 68.

The surviving earthworks in Plot O consisted of a ditch about 15m wide and 1m deep, rising without a berm to an outer flat-topped bank of similar width to the ditch and surviving 1m high; there were only slight traces of an inner bank. Both ditch and outer bank stopped a little east of Gwindy Street, possibly the site of an entrance. To the north east the ditch deepened slightly and turned, with the bank, through an angle of about 75° before passing into Plot P/Q, where both faded out. Plot O had a neglected rough grass cover, Plot R mown grass with recently planted trees, while Plot P/Q was close-grazed.

The hedge line dividing Plot R from O and P/Q is shown on the *Conway Map of 1756*; Plot R was in the Conway's possession, Plot O belonged to J Egerton Esq and Plot P/Q was Glebe. On the Tithe Apportionment Map of 1839 the boundaries and ownership appear to have been maintained, Plot R being labelled 'Gadles nr the town'. At the time of

the excavation, the boundary between R and P/Q was a modern fence contemporary with the construction of the Telephone Exchange in 1969.

Trenches DO and DP, each 3.66m (12ft) wide, were sited across the best preserved sections of earthwork in Plots O and P/Q. The turf was removed by a mechanical excavator ditching blade. The presence of an inner bank was confirmed after cleaning, and both banks were excavated entirely by hand. A 1m wide trench was hand-dug across the top of the ditch down to the primary silt levels in both trenches, and the remainder of the upper silts then removed mechanically; the primary silts were all hand-dug. 1m wide extensions were dug north from trench DP to check for any outer ditch; their location was determined by modern obstacles. Trench DQ was dug, in two parts to avoid modern boggy ground, in the south of Plot P/Q to check on the continuation of the ditch. The initial cruciform trenches in Plot R were designed to obtain the best continuations for the sections in DO (C1 to D) and DP (Fl to G) whilst avoiding flowering trees. In 1972 permission was given by the Post Office for the removal of some of the trees so that a small area could be cleared to check for the presence of a corner tower, and also for linking trenches north to DO as the hedge had been now replaced by a concrete post fence.

The natural in all trenches was a pinkish compact silty boulder clay 2m thick, forming part of the local glacial deposits. Beneath the clay was a layer of fine sand about 0.5m thick above more clay which drained badly and retained water in the ditch bottoms.

8.2 Prehistoric occupation

No features appeared to be of prehistoric date, but a residual scatter of lithic material (10.1), a Bronze Age sherd PP21 (Fig 12.2) and a scrap of samian show some pre-medieval activity in the area. The lithics are almost all of Neolithic date (12.2.1).

8.3 Features predating the Edwardian Defences
(Figs 8.2, 8.3, 8.5 nos 1–2)
8.3.1 Stratigraphy
Old land surface

A buried soil O41, O36, P37, P48, R14, (Fig 8.4) of

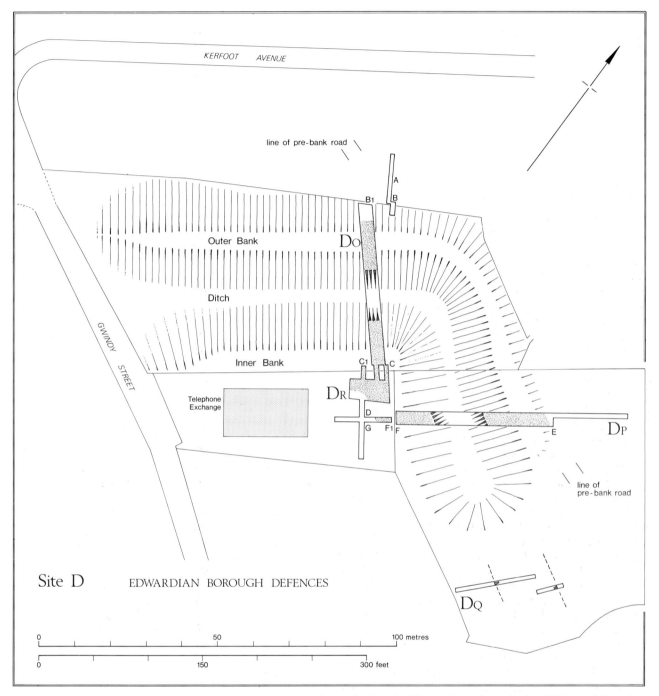

Fig 8.1 Site D. The Edwardian Borough Defences, Gwindy Street. Plan of earthworks in 1971 and location of trenches and section lines.

light brown sand with clay patches survived beneath the banks. It had probably been truncated as there was no noticable increase in humic material towards its top and most features beneath the banks, whatever their stratigraphic relationships, appeared cut from its surface. Features R97, and R84 (Fig 8.2), also R30 and R31 adjacent to section point Fl but not shown on published plans, were sealed by varying thickness of buried soil.

Features beneath the inner bank in DO/DR (Fig 8.2)

Some difficulty was encountered in clearly distinguishing features sealed by the tail of the inner bank. In the area covered by the clay layer O18/P16 (Fig 8.4) the stratigraphy was clear. The basal bank layer of redeposited soil O46/P12 extended irregularly up to 4m beyond the higher bank levels, and was not thick as it had been badly effected by later erosion. It was difficult to judge whether features seen clearly cutting into the old ground surface and the pink clay subsoil were in fact cut

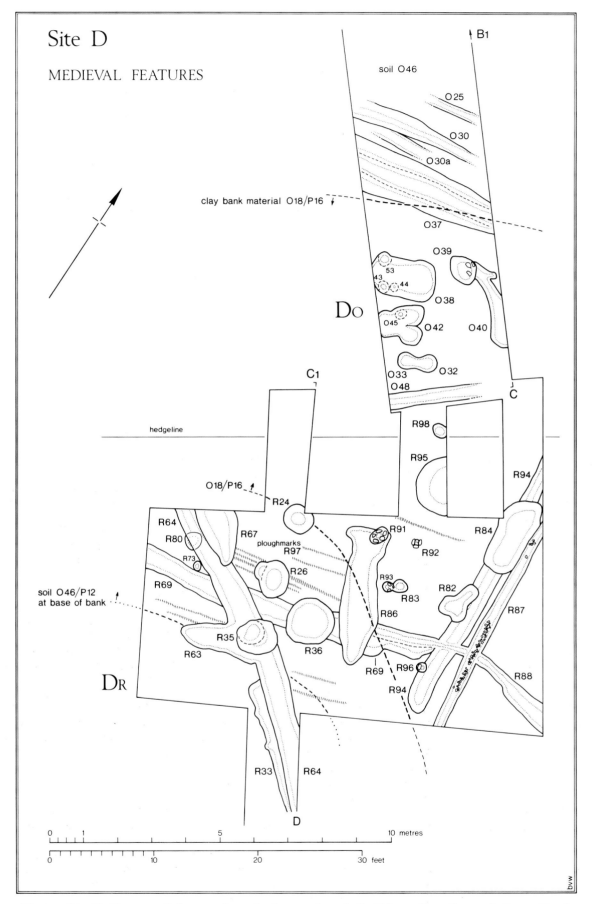

Site D

MEDIEVAL FEATURES

Fig 8.2 Site D. Features below, and on the inner edge of, the Edwardian Borough Inner Bank.

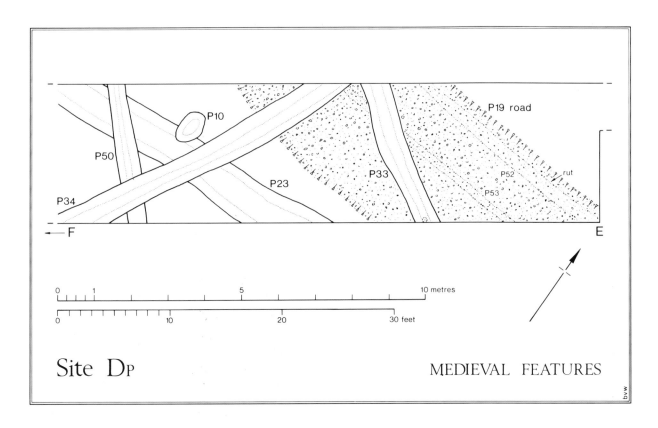

Fig 8.3 Site D. Features below and above the Edwardian Outer Bank in DP.

through layer O46/P12. It should be noted that no feature definitely sealed by the upper layer O18/P16 contained medieval pottery and that gully R64 appeared to follow the curve of the back of the bank. Where there is doubt, features are presented as subsequent to the Defences.

The earliest and most definite feature below the inner bank was a system of rectilinear plots. One plot was defined on its north side by a series of gullies such as O37, several times replaced and well sealed beneath the bank. The east side was marked at different times by R94 and R87, the relationship of which to the south boundary R69/88 was unclear; R88, R87 and R94 were well sealed by the bank. These gullies were filled with brown to grey sandy silt. Ploughmarks R97 aligned on these plot boundaries and may be of a similar period. This R97 series of striations in the subsoil, each approximately 0.05m deep, were filled with soil similar to the old land surface R14. They differed from those located on Site T (4.2) as there was no indication of cross-ploughing. No features predated any of those connected with the plot boundary system, which may be presumed to represent the earliest, undated, use of this area. The amount of recutting suggests a reasonable duration.

A second pre-bank phase included shallow pits such as R86 and R84, which cut gullies of the plot system; features such as O38 may relate to this phase. Another activity involved the erection of posts. Posthole R91 cut pit R86 but others such as O45 pre-dated a pit. A long period of use, the

details of which cannot be disentangled, may again be indicated.

All remaining features on Fig 8.2 are presumed to postdate the inner bank and are discussed below.

P26–P31 (not on plan) in trench DP was a line of stakeholes, 0.10m deep, running north east to south west beneath the inner bank.

Early Road (Fig 8.3)

In trench DP a gravel-filled hollow P19 was found beneath the outer bank. It ran north west to south east and consisted of a depression in the subsoil 4.5m wide and 0.20m deep, covered with 0.03m of gravel metalling. Two ruts P52 and P53, 1.35m apart centre to centre, were filled with similar metalling. About 0.10m of clayey silt P18 had accumulated in the hollow over the road. A similar feature on the same alignment in the continuation of trench DO was less deep.

8.3.2 Dating

As no datable artefacts were found in any of the features discussed above, including road P19, no chronology can be suggested. Earlier phases could be of prehistoric date. Later phases, and road P19, are perhaps more likely to be medieval and relate to activity outside the pre-Edwardian Borough to the south.

8.3.3 Discussion

The features beneath the bank represent a long period of use. The ploughmarks in one direction only are similar to those found in a post-Roman context outside Chester (Mason, 1985, 4) in strips 12m wide, a width similar to that defined by the O37 and R88 group of boundaries. Single direction ploughmarks have been identified elsewhere in pre-Norman Wales and West Britain, at Hen Domen (Barker & Lawson, 1971) and Gwithian, Cornwall (Fowler & Thomas, 1962). It may tentatively be suggested that the Site D ploughmarks are more appropriate to this chronological period than one of prehistoric date. The subsequent features, non-structural, emphasise the intensity of use of this area of Rhuddlan, well north of the main early established centres of activity, in the pre-Edwardian period.

8.4 The construction of the Edwardian Defences
(Figs 8.4, 8.5 no 3; Pl 8.1)
8.4.1 Stratigraphy

The Defences consisted of two similar banks with a ditch between them.

The outer bank was 12.20m across and 1.25m high in trench DO, 13.70m wide and 0.60m high in trench DP. Its basal layer O14/P9 was a spread of dark grey-brown soil, presumably redeposited topsoil from the ditch. In trench DO this was covered by a series of tips; O8 which sealed O14 consisted of tips of dark grey clayey soil, the middle band darker than those above and below. O17 consisted of mixed dumps of red and yellow stiff clay and were sealed by O19, a layer of stiff red clay which formed the surviving capping to the outer slope of the bank. O28, (Fig 8.4), a gully 0.5m deep with a dark brown sandy silt fill, ran north east to south west across trench DO, apparently defining the limit of *in situ* bank layers. It is just possible that O28 had some structural signficance, but the absence of a comparable feature in DP makes it more likely to have been a boundary feature adjacent to but later than the bank. Layers within both banks produced medieval pot sherds.

In trench DP the outer bank was more eroded and P8, a layer of red-brown clay, formed the only surviving layer over re-deposited topsoil P9 .

The inner bank was 18m wide and 1m high in trench DO and 13.40m wide and 0.50m high in trench DP. The additional width in DO was due to the corner as the Defences turned south east. The construction of the inner bank was similar to that of the outer, with an equivalent level of dark redeposited topsoil at its base. In DO this primary deposit O46 was covered by O27, a layer of dark brown soil, and then by O18, mixed red and yellow clays. In trench DP greater erosion had left only a trace of P16, the mixed clay layer, over the rede-

Pl 8.1 Site D. The Edwardian Borough Ditch fully excavated with the Outer Bank beyond. Trench O looking North. Scale in ft.

posited topsoil P12. No trace of timber lacing or evidence of a palisade was found in either bank, if O28 is accepted as a later boundary ditch.

The tail of the inner bank was found in Plot DR but had been greatly eroded.

The Ditch (Pl 8.l) was of similar width, 14m, and depth, 2.75m, in both trenches DO and DP but was more asymmetrical and irregular in profile in the latter. In both the bottom had been cut down through a fine, wet unstable sand. Both trenches indicated fairly rapid silting with no obvious recutting. In trench DO the sequence was a streaky dark grey-brown primary silt O29, overlain by O35 (see below). In trench DP the sequence was similar, layers P70 and P45 formed the primary silt whilst layer P73 towards the inner edge was equivalent to O35 though less clayey.

In trenches DQ silt deposits were removed to a depth of 1.5m and contained post-medieval material. Both edges of the ditch were located but severe water-logging prevented complete excavation.

the features postdating the outer bank itself produced post-medieval material. Pit P10 (Fig 8.3) contained an iron stud No 61 (17.1.3) of probable late 13th or 14th century date.

8.5.3 Discussion

The main silt deposit in DO, O31, was sandwiched between layers of clayey material that might be either bank slip or deliberate slighting; the same sequence was apparent, though less obvious in DP. This allows for the possibility of neglect/damage to the Defences both fairly soon after their destruction and late within the medieval period. The possibility that a destruction episode may relate to the activities of Owain Glyndŵr in the early 15th century is considered in Chapter 21. The upper silts O11 and P43 accumulated slowly during the post medieval period.

There appears to have been considerable activity inside the inner bank from soon after its constructon. Several features contained medieval pottery (Table 18.7). Plot boundary O28 in DO may be of similar date. Subsequently both inner and outer banks appear to have eroded, or possibly been levelled, within the medieval period; this would be consistent with the evidence of neglect and possible destruction in the ditches.

8.6 Post-medieval activity

(Fig 8.3 no 6)

A few features such as P2 produced post-medieval material. O2, on the line of the hedge boundary shown on the *Conway Map of 1756*, contained 19th century material. Activity within the post-medieval period included ploughing (at a period when the banks were much at their present level) and boundary gullies; this suggests that the area reverted to agricultural use.

Most of the post-medieval material from Site D came from the upper ditch silts.

Full discussion of the Edwardian Defences and features relating to the later history of the Borough is given in Chapter 21.

Acknowledgments
We are grateful to Mr J Owens for permission to excavate on Plot O, Clwyd County Council (formerly Flintshire) for Plot P/Q, and the Post Office for Plot R. Site supervisors were Ian Young, Richard White and Brian Williams.

9 Minor Sites including Site S, Princes Road

9.1 Site S, Bryn Teg, Princes Road

(Fig 9.1)

9.1.1 Introduction

Princes Road continues the projected line of the north east side of the Edwardian Defences. The road for much of its length is slightly sunken, the ground rising by about 1m on the south west, inner side, rather less on the north east. In 1972 Bryn Teg, a house immediately south west of Princes Road, was pulled down prior to rebuilding. A trial excavation on its site was organised to check whether the sunken roadway was due to the ditch of the Edwardian Defences and the rise to its south west to an eroded inner bank.

The garden of Bryn Teg ran fairly level towards Princes Road, where the drop was revetted by a recent wall. Foundation trenches for the new house were eventually cut just south west of the excavation; observation of these showed no rampart material nor any archaeological feature. The subsoil was extremely soft yellow sand.

9.1.2 Mesolithic

An incised pebble (Fig 11.2 SF4), lithic material, burnt and utilised pebbles were scattered through soil horizons S31 and S25 across the extension of the trench at the top of the slope. Similar material was residual in later features, making a total of 105 lithic pieces.

9.1.3 Medieval

Dating of soils and features was difficult due to the soft soil which was much disturbed by roots and animals.

Two merging soil levels survived in the level south west part of the trench. The lower, S31, of light brown sand was 0.15m thick; it contained only lithic material and pebbles and may be the remains of a prehistoric or early medieval soil. The upper horizon S25 was darker in colour, contained fewer pebbles and a medieval sherd P94. The slope beneath the recent garden soil S9 was covered by a thin layer of light brown sand S21; this produced 17th century pottery, perhaps intrusive.

Four possible post sockets, S8, S4l, S45, S45A, in a rough line along the upper edge of the slope, were largely cut away by gully S6; it was clear that S45 cut soil S25 and was sealed by soil S3. These sockets were originally around 0.45m deep. Two further features, S43, a posthole with a limestone packing block, and S24A with a dark sandy fill, also contained no finds. Because post medieval pottery was fairly common later in the stratigraphic sequence, all those described here, without it, may be of medieval date.

9.1.4 Post-medieval

Soil S3, the uppermost in the south west end of the trench, contained mixed medieval and later material. A series of pits and postholes such as S40, S4 cut post medieval soils S3 or S21, and were all post medieval in date; all features not individually mentioned are in this stratigraphic position. Pit S29 contained the skull from a horse burial. These pits were postdated by four gullies S6, S27, S24 and S37 filled with dark soil containing 17th and 18th century pottery. S24 was probably the earliest of the sequence and was the edge of a levelled area rather than a gully proper. These features were probably connected to horticultural activities connected with the house Bryn Teg which was constructed immediately south west of S6 sometime before 1756 when it appears on the Conway Map. Sometime then or slightly later a narrow limestone wall was built at the bottom of the slope along Princes Road and a deposit of garden soil S9 accumulated against it.

9.1.5 Conclusions

Soils S31 and S21 might have been preserved by the covering by rampart material. The slope to the north east appears too gentle to have been the top of a ditch in its surviving form. Excavations by the Clwyd-Powys Archaeological Trust in 1984 at 'Fairmead' north east of Princes Road also produced no definite evidence for the line of the Edwardian Defences.

9.2 Site H High Street (Fig 1.2)

A telephone cable trench 12m long was dug to a depth of 0.75m across the projected line of the north east side of the Edwardian Defences, through the pavement on the north side of the High Street. A watching brief was held during excavtions on

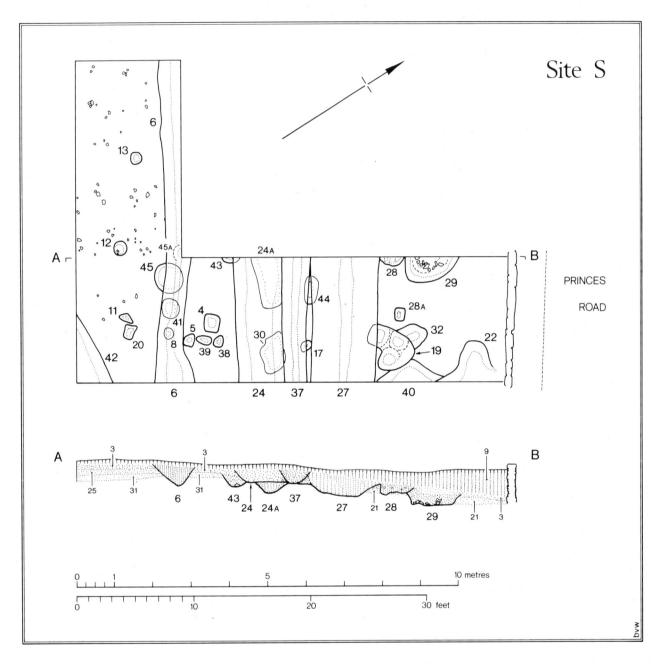

Fig 9.1 Site S. Plan and section, Bryn Teg, Princes Road.

Site D in 1971 but no archaeological features were revealed; the trench cut through boulder clay.

9.3 Site K, Castle Hill, Lôn Hylas

(Fig 1.2)

The line of Lôn Hylas is sunken and appears to run east–west in approximately the position of the earthwork seen by Pennant (1784, 117) in the 18th century. An earthwork at this point would complete a 60 acre quadrilateral enclosure against the River Clwyd; the two extant sides are marked as 'Town Ditch' on Fig 1.2. Trench K was dug in 1970 in the grounds of 'Castle Hill' immediately adjacent to

and south of Lôn Hylas which at this point lay 1.30m lower than the surface of the garden. Trench K was 1m by 2.60m in area and was taken to a depth of 2.95m without reaching undisturbed soil.

The lowest layer K10 was of soft brown silty sand sloping towards the north; this was covered by a 0.25m thick layer of clean orange sand K8. At the north end, filling the hollow left by the surface of the underlying deposits, was a dump of mixed yellow sand, gravel and small stones K7 0.30m thick. This was overlain by a layer of orange-brown sandy silt K6 0.20m thick which merged upwards into a brown silt K5 0.35m thick. This was overlain by K4, 1m of dark sandy soil containing charcoal fragments and occasional lumps of brick, which merged upwards into a very dark brown soil K2 0.70m thick below topsoil.

Layers K6 and K5 produced only small sherds of medieval pottery, while K4 and K2 produced post-medieval material ranging from the 17th to 19th centuries.

The stratigraphy suggests the presence of a large feature, probably a ditch, of medieval date, which could not be bottomed for safety reasons, cut into glacial sands.

9.4 Site G, Abbey Road (Fig 1.2)

The continuation of Abbey Road to the south, forming a medieval route to St Asaph, passes through the suggested line of the 'Town Ditch' close to its west, river, end. The road here becomes deeply cut or worn and south of the line descends rapidly to the Clwyd and the ford of Rhyd-y-Boncas. The earthworks at their junction with the road are not clearly defined. The main bank appears to die out immediately south of the road and above a steep drop to the Clwyd. North of the road there is a short length of bank, curving to the north east, apparently providing protection on this side of the road. From present surface indications it is unclear whether this bank is natural. In 1970 roadworks widened the road all the way south of Abbey Farm (the site of the Dominican Friary) by about 1m. Nothing was found until the bank north of the road was cut into at G for a length of 13m, allowing inspection of a sloping section some 1m in height. This was cleaned, revealing a 0.20m thick layer of red clay with a few pebbles overlying one of grey-green sandy clay, with pebbles and charcoal again 0.20m thick. The land surface beneath these appeared to have been truncated, as only the base of a soil profile was noted over boulder clay. A single sherd of kiln V type in topsoil was the only find.

Acknowledgments
We are grateful to the owner of the Bryn Teg site, Mr G Parry, and to the owner of Castle Hill for permission to excavate. The late Eleanor (Muers) Saunders supervised the Bryn Teg excavation and Ian Young that at Castle Hill.

10 The Lithics
Peter Berridge

10.1 Introduction

The lithic and other prehistoric material came from excavations primarily concerned with the investigation of medieval activity. This later activity was so extensive and destructive that prehistoric levels survive only as truncated fragments and over 47% of the lithic material was residual. The excavations took place at a time when the practice of individually recording lithic pieces was not general. At Rhuddlan pieces were recorded only by general context and sieving was not employed. Less information was therefore retrieved than would be expected from sites investigated during the 1990s.

The excavations produced 13,330 pieces of chert and flint including 8408 (63%) from Site E, and 2637 (20%) from Site M. Table 10.1 presents a generalised analysis of the lithic material. The vast bulk of this material dates to the Early Mesolithic, as will be discussed below.

10.2 Raw materials

Nearly 84% of the lithic assemblage (11,175 pieces) is of Carboniferous chert, sometimes referred to as Gronant chert (Sargent, 1923). Flint makes up nearly 15% of the assemblage (1,964), while the remainder includes rhyolite (17), and uncertain rock types (174). The percentages of flint and chert differ little from those from the adjacent Mesolithic site of Hendre, Rhuddlan (Manley & Healey, 1982), with chert 87% and flint 13%. Carboniferous chert was also predominant at the nearby Later Mesolithic site at Prestatyn (Clark, 1938).

The chert originally derives from the Carboniferous Limestone which bounds both sides of the Vale of Clwyd. It is perhaps unlikely to have been quarried but was probably collected from the scree slopes below the limestone cliffs. Most of the chert would appear to have been obtained in thin slabs. The length and width range of these slabs is difficult to assess but measurements of waste flakes give some indications (see Table 10.5). The longest piece in the collection is a thin slab (Fig 10.1, no 3) 115mm long, it is also one of the widest at 58mm. As evidence for larger blocks is absent, this piece may represent the upper size range in length and width. The thickness range can be estimated as the knapping technique involved removing highly characteristic flakes which retain the cortex from both the upper and the lower surfaces of the parent block. The sample of all such flakes from layer H39 Site E shows that original slabs rarely exceeded 40mm thickness; 95% are thinner than 40mm, 70%

thinner than 30mm while none are less than 10mm (Table 10.5a, Column 3). Thickness variation is well illustrated by Fig 10.1, Nos 2–7.

The colour and quality of the chert varies considerably. Chert from the adjacent Later Mesolithic site, Hendre (Manley & Healey, 1982, 21–4) was divided into two types (1) 'black or dark brown fine-grained' and (2) 'gritty or granular...of grey and greyish white', with some spatial variation noted between the use of the two. (1) represented nearly 69% of the chert (60% of the total assemblage), and (2) 31% (27% of the total assemblage). This simple division does not adequately cover the variation from the 1969–73 Rhuddlan sites. In this far larger sample at least four main groups can be identified. The first has alternating grey and black bands, an occasional browner zone along which slabs often split, and has a dull appearance. This comprised the bulk of the material (61% from the sample context H39). The second is dense and black with occasional grey banding near its edges. It is lustrous, of high quality, and forms 12% of the H39 sample. These two groups roughly equate with Healey's group (1). The third is of variable quality, grey and often granular with frequent bedding or fracture planes; its appearance is lustrous (22% of the H39 sample). The fourth is white to creamy yellow and markedly granular (5% of the sample). The second two groups roughly equate with Healey's group (2).

Though the chert can be divided into these four broad groups, the material probably represents a single range as there are a few pieces which display features of two groups. The value of dividing the chert into groups can therefore be questioned, but at Hendre there were some spatial variations in the frequency of use of the two types recognised (Manley & Healey, 1982, 21–4). Though time did not permit a detailed spatial analysis of the chert types, this may be a useful future research topic. For example, type (2) chert occurred in high proportions on Site A, notably from pit C25, 62% of the chert assemblage including three microliths (Fig 10.6, nos 91, 93–94).

A pebble origin for most of the flint is suggested by areas of surviving cortex. The flint was either obtained from beaches to the north or from local drift deposits; flint is attested from the Anglesey drift (Smith & George, 1961, 84). One or two non-pebble cortices may indicate a non-local source. The quality of the flint varies but is generally good. The largest flint artefact, 70mm long (Fig 10.8, no 143), shows that some sizeable pieces of raw

Table 10.1 Analysis of lithic material from all Sites, by context, major typological divisions and raw materials

	Parent Waste	Product Waste	Utilised Retouched	Total	Raw material Chert	Flint	Other
SITE E							
H39	165	3294	167	3626	3289	329	8
J104	80	1454	70	1604	1437	161	6
J92	1	46	2	49	34	15	0
J86	0	18	1	19	16	3	0
Post-Meso	176	2777	157	3110	2780	320	10
Totals	422	7589	397	8408	7556	828	24
SITE M							
M26	24	731	31	786	535	214	37
M52	0	4	0	4	4	0	0
M46	1	2	0	3	2	1	0
M50	0	1	0	1	1	0	0
M122	0	1	0	1	1	0	0
M123	0	19	0	19	18	1	0
M90	12	651	24	687	491	138	58
M83	2	4	0	6	6	0	0
M127	0	1	0	1	1	0	0
Post-Meso	66	1005	58	1129	764	305	60
Totals	105	2419	113	2637	1823	659	155
SITE T							
Post-Meso	80	1197	74	1351	1045	305	1
SITE A							
C25	9	84	8	101	92	9	0
C38	1	78	7	86	65	20	1
C77	0	5	1	6	4	2	0
Post-Meso	15	272	22	309	246	53	10
Totals	25	439	38	502	407	84	11
SITE V							
V94	0	11	0	11	9	2	0
Post-Meso	23	213	21	257	215	42	0
Totals	23	224	21	268	224	44	0
SITE D							
Post-Meso	7	21	10	38	5	33	0
SITE K							
Post-Meso	0	19	2	21	20	1	0
SITE S							
Post-Meso	9	88	8	105	95	10	0
TOTALS	671	11996	663	13330	11175	1964	191
	5.0%	90%	5%		83.8%	14.7%	1.4%

'Other' includes 17 rhyolite pieces; locations given in text.

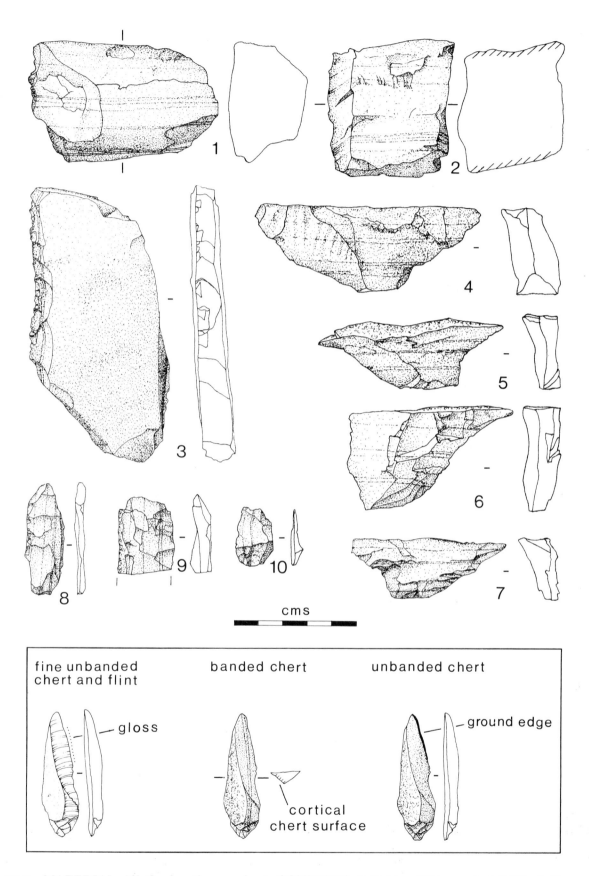

Fig 10.1 MATERIAL All Carboniferous chert. CONTEXTS 1–2 Mesolithic context M26, 3 Bronze Age context H24 E, 4–6 Mesolithic soil H39 E, 7, 10 Mesolithic pit J104 E, 8 residual E, 9 Mesolithic context M26. TYPES 1–3 parent slabs; 4–7 winged flakes; 8–10 preparatory flakes struck lengthways down slab. All 2:3. Also standard conventions used in lithics illustrations.

Table 10.2 Contexts divided according to raw material and major typological divisions

Site	Parent Waste		Product Waste		Utilised/Retouched		Total	
	Chert %	Flint %	Chert %	Flint%	Chert %	Flint %	Chert %	Flint %
E Mesolithic	86.6	13.4	91.8	8.2	68.5	31.5	90.4	9.6
E Post-Meso	84.7	15.3	90.8	9.2	76.4	23.6	89.7	10.3
M Mesolithic	82.5	17.5	77.5	24.5	59.3	40.7	75	25
M Post-Meso	81	19	72.2	27.8	57.6	42.4	71.3	28.7
T All contexts	71.3	28.7	78.4	21.6	69.6	30.4	77.4	22.6
A Mesolithic	80	20	84.4	15.6	81.2	18.8	83.9	16.1
A Post-Meso	86.7	13.3	84.4	15.6	54.5	55.5	82.3	17.7
V All contexts	82.6	17.2	85.7	14.3	61.9	38.1	83.6	16.4
D All contexts	–	–	9.5	90.5	20	80	13.2	86.8
K All contexts	–	–	94.7	5.3	–	–	95.2	4.8
S All contexts	–	–	90.9	9.1	–	–	90.5	9.5

(NB all % calculated exclude unattributable pieces and % only calculated if 10 or more pieces contained in category.)

material were available.

Flint comprises nearly 15% of the assemblage. This figure may be slightly inflated because of difficulty in distinguishing between flint and chert of the fourth category, especially among burnt pieces.

The proportions of flint and chert are fairly consistent from most contexts, with the exception of Site D (Table 10.5). Here a small group contained 33 flint pieces (87%) as opposed to 5 of chert. This group differs from those of the other sites in further ways (see below) and the disparity is almost certainly chronological.

While the percentages of raw materials are fairly consistent from most contexts on most sites, Table 10.2 shows that the percentage of flint to chert rises amongst utilised and retouched pieces as opposed to waste (except Site D). This could be partly due to the comparative ease with which utilisation and minor retouch can be detected on flint, but the percentage of flint to chert is also higher for artefacts such as scrapers and microliths (Table 10.3). It is probable that flint was preferred for certain artefacts.

Preferential use of flint is also apparent at other Mesolithic sites. In the Hendre assemblage 87% of the assemblage is chert but 42% (11 out of 26) of the microliths are of flint. The same trend occurs in some Yorkshire Mesolithic assemblages dominated by Carboniferous chert. Flint comprised only 2.1% of the 1369 piece lithic assemblage from Blubberhouse Moor, yet two of the five microliths were of this material (Davies, 1963); at Broomhead Moor Site 5 (Radley, Switsur & Tallis, 1974) flint comprised only 6.1% (100 items) of the total assemblage of 1652 pieces but 14 of the 37

Table 10.3 Scrapers and microliths: proportions of raw materials in Mesolithic and post-Mesolithic contexts

	Total Numbers	Chert	Flint	Unattributable
Scrapers				
Mesolithic Contexts	70	59.7 (62.3)	36.1 (37.7)	4.2
Post-Meso Contexts	96	53.2 (53.8)	45.7 (46.2)	1.1
Microliths				
Mesolithic Contexts	101	66.7 (69.4)	29.4 (30.6)	4
Post-Meso Contexts	67	60.6 (63.5)	34.8 (36.5)	4.5

Figures in brackets indicate % calculated excluding unattributable pieces.

microliths (37.8%) were of flint. A preference for flint artefacts is also found on sites where other types of chert are the predominant material as at some sites in east Devon (Berridge, 1985). It is apparent that in areas where the major lithic resource is relatively poor, better quality materials such as flint were often chosen for some tool types, particularly microliths, during the Mesolithic.

Seventeen pieces have been identified as rhyolite. The most striking is a yellow-grey crested blade from Site T (Fig 10.8, no 148). At 123mm it is the longest piece in the assemblage. The other pieces range from blue-grey to greenish-grey in colour. Site E produced five from H39 and eight from J104, Site M one each from M26 and M90B, Site A one from C38.

Dr M F Howells (British Geological Survey, Wales) has examined the rhyolite pieces and reports that macroscopically they all appear similar to No 152 which was thin-sectioned. He reports on this thin section: 'Rhyolite No 152 thin section. The rock is a fine-grained acidic tuff. The cut surface of the small section would suggest this composition without looking at the thin section. The rock is medium grey in colour with a narrow bleached weathered rim. The surface colour, slightly ochreous-pale brown, is the result of the soil. The rock comprises fine-grained sherds which were originally volcanic glass fragments (ash) produced by the explosive eruption of an acidic-magma; quiescent effusion of this magma would have produced a rhyolite lava, the explosive eruption produced a pyroclastic rock (tuff). The original volcanic glass has been devitrified and recrystallised and mineralogically the rock is dominated by quartz, chlorite with some feldspar. The sherds are the remains of the walls of bubbles (vesicles) due to exsolution of volatiles as the magma was rising in its conduit, prior to its explosive eruption. The sherds are characterised by cuspate shapes which are still discernible. They are extremely fine-grained and could represent distal fall out ash from the volcano but there are mechanisms which could have this result. Such tuffs are common in the Ordovician sequence of Snowdonia'.

10.3 Waste material

The 12,639 pieces categorised as waste can be divided into parent and product waste following Saville (1979). Parent waste comprises cores, core fragments and rough-flaked lumps or nodules. Product waste covers material struck from the parent blocks and the by-products of tool manufacture.

Terms such as waste or debitage do not have any implications for the functions of the pieces concerned. Microwear studies, not feasible for the Rhuddlan collection, make it increasingly apparent that significant numbers of items with no trace of use visible to the naked eye have been used as tools.

10.3.1 Parent waste (Figs 10.1–2)

There are 299 cores and 372 core fragments and flaked lumps. In Mesolithic contexts with more than 25, parent waste averages 3.8% with only one context having more than 5%. The exception is C25, Site A with 9%. In contrast the average figure for post-Mesolithic contexts is 8%, with only Site A having a lower proportion at 3%. Among these

Table 10.4 Cores

	Single Platform		Double Opposed Platform		Double Unopposed Platform		Triple		Keeled		Total
Mesolithic Contexts											
Site E Pit J104	21		11		2		1		0		35
Site E Soil H39	41		23		7		2		1		74
Site M Pit M90	4		0		1		0		0		5
Site M Soil M26	8		4		3		0		0		15
Others	4		1		2		0		0		7
Totals	78	(57.4%)	39	(28.7%)	15	(11.0%)	3	(2.2%)	1	(0.7%)	136
Post-Mesolithic Contexts											
Site E	52		39		2		1		5		99
Site M	5		8		0		1		0		14
Site T	21		5		3		0		1		30
Other	12		6		1		0		1		20
Total	90	(55.6%)	58	(35.2%)	6	(3.7%)	2	(1.2%)	7	(4.3%)	163
Grand total	168	(56.2%)	97	(32.4%)	21	(7.0%)	5	(1.7%)	8	(2.7%)	299

post-Mesolithic contexts Site D has an unusually high proportion of parent waste, 18.4% (7 out of 38 pieces).

Of the cores the single platform type is by far the most numerous (eg Fig 10.2, nos 11–12, 15, 17). Cores with two platforms at opposed ends are the next in frequency (eg Fig 10.2, nos 13–14, 16, 18). The predominance of these types is a reflection of the fact that the industry was principally aimed at producing blades.

10.3.2 Product waste (Figs 10.1–3)

The 11,996 pieces can be broadly divided into four types: 2798 complete flakes and blades; 8761 broken flakes and blades; 415 core preparation and rejuvenation flakes; and 22 microburins and related forms.

Study of the chert product waste, particularly of the banded type, is informative about the nature of the raw material and the knapping method employed. The majority of banded chert pieces have the banding running parallel to the bulbar axis (eg Fig 10.2, nos 19–24). It seems probable that it is easier to strike along the banding than across it, though this has not been established by experiment. On a number of pieces the banding is at right angles to the bulbar axis (eg Fig 10.1, nos 4–7). As these have been struck across the thickness of a slab they are short compared to pieces struck along a slab. The distal ends of these flakes widens markedly, giving them a distinctive winged appearance. This appears to be because the force of blow is initially sufficient to cut across the bands, but then is increasingly affected by the banding and spreads out to the sides. In some cases this effect can be extremely pronounced.

The majority of the cross-banded flakes were clearly produced at an early stage in the knapping process. They are presumably initial preparation flakes removed along the side of a slab to produce an even flaking face and possibly to create crested ridges, which would aid the removal of blades (Fig 10.1, no 3 depicts a slab at an early stage of preparation, with the removal of winged flakes along the edge showing clearly). None of these winged flakes have scars on their dorsal surfaces running parallel with the banding. This supports the idea that they represent an early stage of the knapping process. In contrast a small number of flakes/ blades with banding running parallel to the bulbar axis show contrary scars on the dorsal surface (eg Fig 10.1, nos 8–10). These represent the first flakes struck lengthways after the initial removal of flakes from across the thickness of a slab.

To examine this variation in the chert waste flakes, all complete, clearly banded, flakes from H39 Site E (424 pieces) were divided on the basis of the orientation of their banding: 254 pieces (59.5%) had banding parallel to the bulbar axis; 83 (19.4%) at right angles to the axis; and 90 (21.1%) in other directions. The length and breadth of the first two groups were compared (see Table 10.5 and Fig 10.3). There are clear major differences between the two groups as emphasised by the length to breadth ratio. The differences in length are clearly a factor in the varying dimensions of the raw materials, in particular the thickness of the slabs which places an obvious constraint on the length of the cross-banded pieces. The differences in breadth however seems likely to relate to the physical properties of the chert, as described above, by which the layered or banded nature influences the shape of struck pieces.

The presence of at least two distinct populations of waste flakes among the chert affects the overall figures. Table 10.5, column 1, analyses all complete chert waste flakes (1013) from contexts H39 and J104 Site E, and demonstrates, together with the Fig 10.3 graphs, that the figures for this complete sample lie roughly between those of the two banded groups. Although the primary aim of the industry was to produce blades, this is slightly obscured in the overall waste dimensions due to the physical properties of much of the chert and the initial method of knapping which combined to produce broad preparatory flakes.

The biasing effect of the broad preparatory waste flakes affects comparison of the waste flake dimensions from Rhuddlan with those from other sites with other raw materials. The shape of waste flakes has been demonstrated to be a useful chronological indicator (Smith, 1965; Pitts, 1978a; 1978b; Pitts & Jacobi, 1979). The shape of waste flakes changed gradually from the long narrow forms typical of the Late Glacial blade industries to shorter, broader forms in Postglacial assemblages. The waste flake figures from Hendre, mainly of Carboniferous chert, appear to be in broad agreement with those from Later Mesolithic assemblages, mainly of flint, from Southern Britain (Manley & Healey 1982, 28). If this agreement were valid, the Site E waste flakes, clearly of the Earlier Mesolithic (see below), should include a larger proportion of long narrow blades. Table 10.6 compares the waste flakes from Site E and from Hendre. The figures for blades (length more than twice breadth) for Site E show only a 0.4% increase over those from Hendre, while at the other end of the shape range there are far more flakes whose breadth exceeds their length from Site E than from Hendre. Overall the two sets of figures for chert are broadly similar and reflect the constraints imposed by the raw material type. For flint, in contrast, there are marked differences which are consistent with a later date for Hendre than for Site E.

10.3.3 Core Preparation and Rejuvenation Pieces (Figs 10.2, 10.4)

There are 253 crested blades/flakes (eg Fig 10.2, no 27; Fig 10.4, nos 33–34: and Fig 10.7, no 127). The formation of crested pieces occurs, normally, in the process of preparing a core for blade removal, often

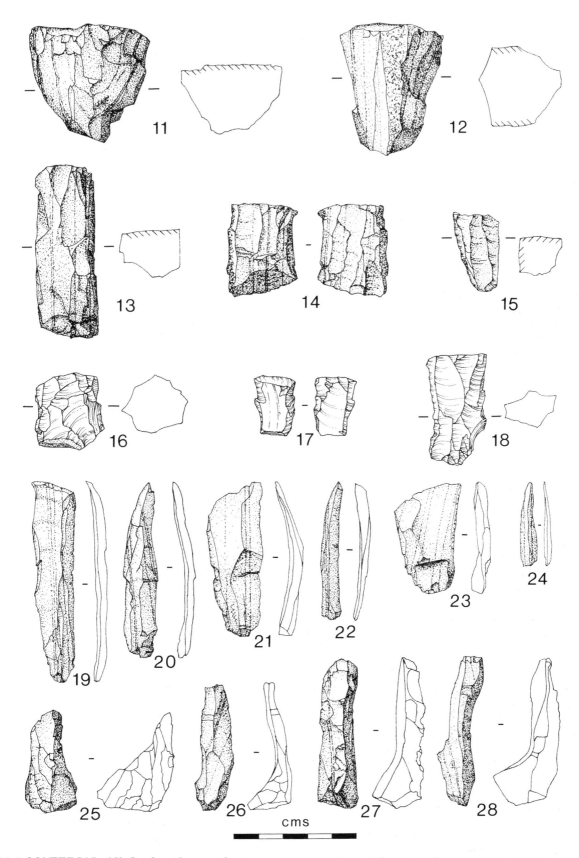

Fig 10.2 MATERIAL All Carboniferous chert except 16–18 flint. CONTEXTS 11–16, 18–24 Mesolithic pit J104 E, 25, 27, 28 Mesolithic soil H39 E, 26 E residual. TYPES 11, 12, 15, 17 single platform cores; 13, 14, 16 cores with platforms at opposed ends; 19–24 typical tertiary flakes struck from cores; 25–28 plunging flakes (27 is also crested). All 2:3.

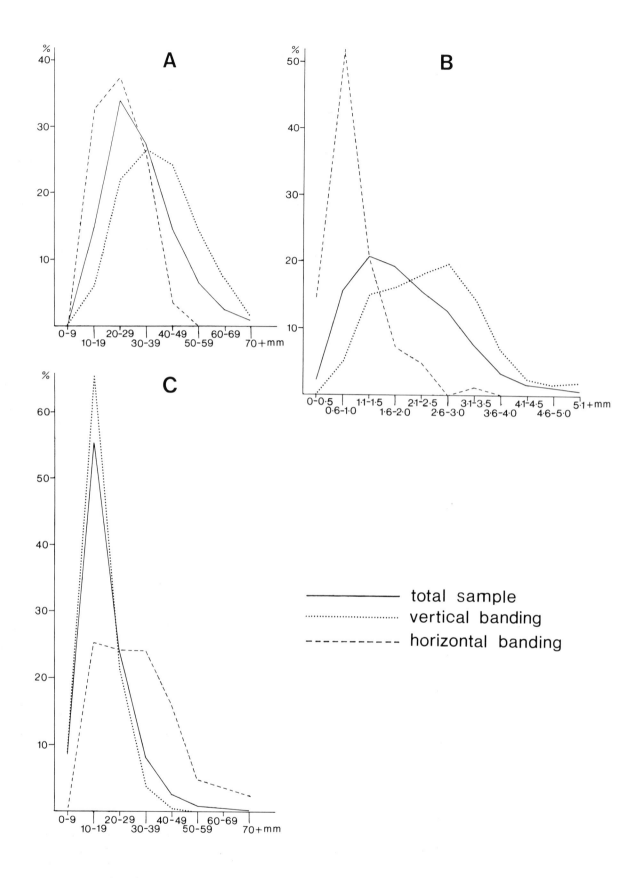

Fig 10.3 (a) Chert waste flakes length. (b) Chert waste flakes width. (c) Chert waste flakes: length to breadth ratio. Sample consists of all material included in Table 10.5.

Table 10.5 Waste flake measurements

	Chert H39 & J104 All Types		Chert H39 Banded parallel to bulbar axis		Chert H39 Banded across bulbar axis		Flint H39 & J104	
Length (mm)								
0–9	–	–	–	–	–	–	–	–
10–19	148	14.6%	16	6.3%	27	32.5%	25	18.8%
20–29	343	33.9%	56	22.0%	31	37.3%	59	44.4%
30–39	275	27.1%	67	26.4%	21	25.3%	37	27.8%
40–49	146	14.4%	56	22.0%	3	3.6%	8	6.0%
50–59	67	6.6%	37	14.6%	1	1.2%	4	3.0%
60–69	25	2.5%	18	7.1%	–	–	–	–
70–79	7	0.7%	4	1.6%	–	–	–	–
80–89	2	0.2%	–	–	–	–	–	–
Totals	1013		254		83		133	
Breadth (mm)								
0–9	86	8.5%	22	8.7%	–	–	13	9.8%
10–19	563	55.6%	166	65.4%	21	25.3%	85	63.9%
20–29	243	24.0%	55	21.7%	20	24.1%	32	24.0%
30–39	81	8.0%	10	3.9%	20	24.1%	2	1.5%
40–49	25	2.5%	1	0.4%	13	15.7%	1	0.8%
50–59	8	0.8%	–	–	4	4.8%	–	–
60–69	5	0.5%	–	–	3	3.6%	–	–
70–79	–	–	–	–	–	–	–	–
80–89	1	0.1%	–	–	1	1.2%	–	–
90–99	1	0.1%	–	–	1	1.2%	–	–
Totals	1013		254		83		133	
Length to Breadth								
0–0.5	21	2.1%	–	–	12	14.5%	1	0.8%
0.6–1.0	158	15.6%	12	4.7%	43	51.8%	21	15.8%
1.1–1.5	210	20.7%	38	15.0%	17	20.5%	24	18.0%
1.6–2.0	195	19.2%	40	16.0%	6	7.2%	33	24.8%
2.1–2.5	158	15.6%	45	18.0%	4	4.8%	32	24.1%
2.6–3.0	129	12.7%	50	19.7%	–	–	9	6.8%
3.1–3.5	76	7.5%	37	14.6%	1	1.2%	8	6.0%
3.6–4.0	33	3.3%	17	6.7%	–	–	3	2.3%
4.1–4.5	15	1.5%	6	2.4%	–	–	1	0.8%
4.6–5.0	11	1.1%	4	1.6%	–	–	1	0.8%
5.1–5.5	3	0.3%	1	0.4%	–	–	–	–
5.5–6.0	2	0.2%	2	0.8%	–	–	–	–
6.1–6.6	2	0.2%	2	0.8%	–	–	–	–
Totals	1013		254		83		133	

at an early stage in the knapping sequence. This does not seem to be true for the Rhuddlan chert, where it has been suggested above that removal of the distinctive winged flakes in the initial knapping stages was related to the production of crested ridges. In the Rhuddlan chert it seems probable that classic crested blades were made late in the knapping sequence as a method of core rejuvenation (Fig 10.4, no 29 shows a core with a crested ridge), or of converting flakes to cores (Fig 10.4, no 30 is a flake on which a crest has been formed).

The 50 core tablets recorded (eg Fig 10.4, nos 31–2) are flakes detached from core platforms to improve the flaking angle. A core can have a series of such flakes removed, strikingly shown at Thatcham where four such flakes, successively removed during rejuvenation episodes of a single core, were refitted (Wymer, 1962, 340–1).

The remaining core rejuvenation category are plunging flakes, with 134 clear examples identified

Table 10.6 Comparative flake size ratios from Site E and Hendre

Length to Breadth Ratio	Chert		Flint	
	Site E	Hendre	Site E	Hendre
Broad 0–1.0	17.7%	6.0%	16.6%	17.0%
Medium 1.1–2.0	39.9%	52.0%	42.8%	55.7%
Narrow 2.1 +	42.3%	41.9%	40.8%	27.1%

Table 10.7 Core Preparation and Rejuvenation Flakes

	Crested 1 Direction	Crested 2 Directions	Crested/ Plunging †	Crested Total	Core tablet	Plunging
Mesolithic Contexts						
E: Pit J104	27	1	(2)	28	2	7
E: Soil H39	78	2	(11)	80	18	29
M: Pit M90	11	2	(–)	13	4	–
M: Soil M26	11	–	(2)	11	1	10
Others	5	–	(–)	5	1	2
Totals	132	5	(15)	137	26	48
Post-Mesolithic Contexts						
E	51	2	(3)	53	15	31
M	25	–	(4)	25	4	9
T	24	–	(–)	24	3	17
A	3	–	(–)	3	1	6
V,D,K,S	11	–	(–)	11	1	1
Totals	114	2	(7)	116	24	64
Grand Total	246	7	(22)	253	50	112

† these are included in figures for crested 1 direction and crested 2 directions

(eg Fig 10.2, nos 25–8). Traditionally these are interpreted as deliberately struck to produce a new platform (eg Clark, 1954, 100). Although their removal can produce an efficient platform, the effect is probably unintentional. As Tixier (1974, 19) has pointed out, a plunging flake 'is nothing more than an accident....as anyone who tries flaking experiments will discover sooner or later to his cost'. The removal of a plunging flake from a small blade core can be counter-productive as it will substantially shorten the core. At the Mesolithic site on Hengistbury Head the refitting of flakes to two cores indicated that plunging flakes led to abandonment, not rejuvenation (Barton, 1992, 210 Fig 5.7). At Rhuddlan a significant proportion of cores were abandoned after the removal of a plunging flake. A total of 22 plunging flakes were also crested (eg Fig 10.2, No 27) and thus relate to the core rejuvenation process although the plunging effect was presumably accidental. Fig 10.2 no 28 probably resulted from an attempt to convert a flake into a blade core.

10.3.4 Microburins and related forms

(Fig 10.5)

Microburins are waste products created during the manufacture of microliths (Tixier, 1974, 17). There are 9 classic microburins, with a half notch and a sharply angled snap, 7 proximal, and 2 distal or mesial (eg nos 36–8, 43). A further 9 pieces are 'miss-hits' where the break runs across and is not angled (eg nos 35, 42). 4 blades have complete notches and may relate to the production of microliths (eg nos 39–41).

The number of microburins and related types is small compared with the 168 microliths. One reason for scarcity may be the absence of sieving, but relatively small microlith fragments were retrieved. Another may relate to the nature of the main raw material. The coarseness of some of the chert can make the removal of standard microburins difficult; relatively few microburins were recognised in the Hendre assemblage despite extensive sieving (Manley & Healey, 1982), four in relation to 26 microliths (a ratio of 1:6.5, the overall ratio for the Rhuddlan 1969–73 assemblage is 1:7.6). The lack of flint microburins is even more marked; Rhuddlan 1969–73 produced only three

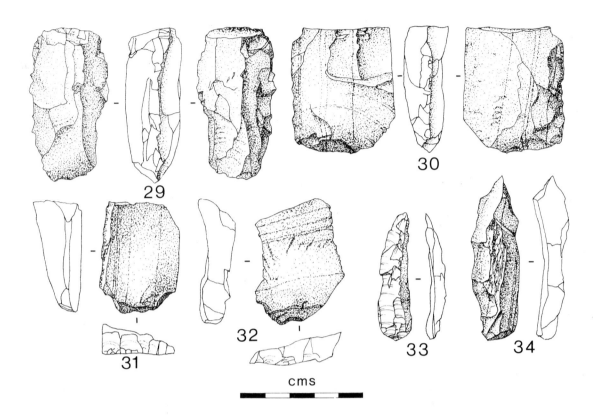

Fig 10.4 MATERIAL All Carboniferous chert. CONTEXTS 29–30 residual E, 31–34 Mesolithic soil H39 E. TYPES 29 core with crested ridge not removed; 30 flake with crested ridge not removed; 31–32 core rejuvenation tablets; 33–34 crested blades. All 2:3.

flint microburins to 53 microliths (1:17.7), and Hendre one microburin to eleven microliths. Microburin scarcity is clearly a reality, suggesting that either microliths were principally manufactured without the removal of a microburin (unlikely in the light of current evidence), or, more probably, that microliths were rarely made in the immediate area.

A review of the literature reveals a significant number of other sites with relatively few microburins. Such sites include nearby Prestatyn with a microburin/microlith ratio of 1:6.6 (Clark, 1938), Iwerne Minster (Dorset) 1:11 (Higgs, 1959),

Star Carr 1:9.2 (Clark, 1972), Morton (Fife) 1:4.6 (Coles, 1971), Abinger Common (Surrey) 1:5.7 (Leakey, 1951), and Mount Sandel (Co Derry) 1:110 (Woodman, 1985). All the sites mentioned are low lying and are relatively large scale.

10.4 Utilised and retouched pieces

A total of 663 pieces show signs of apparent utilisation or retouch, just under 5% of the assemblage. This is similar to 4.7% at Hendre (Manley & Healey, 1982). Following Saville (1979) utilised pieces have not been distinguished from those with

Table 10.8 Microburins and Related Forms

	Microburins	Miss Hits	Notched Blades	Totals
Mesolithic Contexts				
E: Pit J104	1	1	–	2
E: Soil H39	3	4	1	8
M: Pit M90	1	1	–	2
M: Soil M26	1	1	–	2
Post-Mesolithic Contexts				
E	1	–	1	2
M	1	–	1	2
T	1	2	1	4
Totals	9	9	4	22

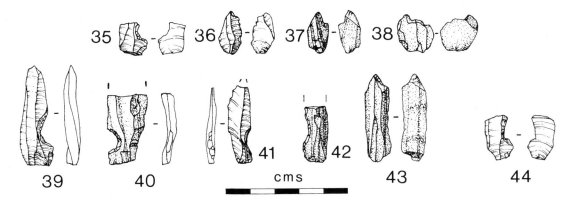

Fig 10.5 MATERIAL All Carboniferous chert. CONTEXTS 35, 36, 38, 43 Mesolithic soil H39 E, 41 residual E, 37, 39, 42, residual T, 40 residual M. TYPES 36–38, 43 classic microburins; 35, 42, 44 'miss-hit' microburins; 39–41 flakes notched prior to microburin snap. All 2:3.

apparent retouch as it is becoming increasingly clear that the grounds for such distinction are subjective and imprecise. Apparent utilisation and retouch traces can be caused by post-depositional occurrences (Tringham *et al*, 1974) or spontaneously during knapping (Newcomer, 1975). Chopping can also cause utilisation marks which could be mistaken for regular retouch (Barton, 1986).

10.4.1 Utilised/Retouched

A total of 264 pieces do not fall into any classifiable tool category (eg Fig 10.7, Nos 116–117, 126–127). It is not possible at present to provide realistic figures for the percentage of the assemblage which has been used, but the microwear study of the Mount Sandel assemblage may provide some indicators (Dumont, 1985). There, of 31 edge-damaged or casually retouched pieces examined for microwear, only 20 produced convincing traces. Perhaps up to 35% of the pieces identified macros-

Table 10.9 Analysis of tool types by contexts

	Ut/Ret	Microlith	Scraper	Awl	Notched	Fabricator	Ground	Md†	AxeR†	Arrow†	Totals
Mesolithic Contexts											
E: Pit J104	25	31	11	2	–	–	–	–	1	–	70
E: Soil H39	70	40	40	4	3	–	7	–	3	–	167
M: Pit M90	4	12	6	2	–	–	–	–	–	–	24
M: Soil M26	12	10	9	–	–	–	–	–	–	–	31
A: Pit C25	1	5	1	–	–	–	–	–	1	–	8
A: Pit C38	1	3	2	–	–	1	–	–	–	–	7
Others	3	–	1	–	–	–	–	–	–	–	4
Totals	116	101	70	8	3	1	7	0	5	0	311
Post-Mesolithic Contexts											
E	76	26	41	2	5	–	4	3	–	–	157
M	20	15	17	3	1	–	1	1	–	–	58
T	31	15	18	4	3	1	–	2	–	–	74
A	7	7	4	–	1	–	–	1	–	2	22
D	4	–	5	–	–	1	–	–	–	–	10
V	6	3	8	–	4	–	–	–	–	–	21
K	2	–	–	–	–	–	–	–	–	–	2
S	2	1	3	1	–	–	–	1	–	–	8
Totals	148	67	96	10	14	2	5	8	–	2	352
Grand Totals	264	168	166	18	17	3	12	8	5	2	663

Md† = Microdenticulates   AxeR† = Axe sharpening flakes   Arrow† =Arrowheads

copically as 'utilised' may not in fact have been used, though some as yet unknown factors obscuring microwear traces may be involved.

A flint flake, from H39 Site E, has distinct traces of gloss or polish down the left hand edge of its ventral surface together with some edge damage (Fig 10.8, no 143). Such gloss has been shown by experiment to be associated with plant-gathering and this may apply in the Rhuddlan example (eg Unger-Hamilton, 1984).

10.4.2 Microliths (Fig 10.6)

Microliths are usually the largest group amongst the classifiable retouched pieces, but in a few contexts they are less numerous than scrapers (Table 10.10).

The two largest groups from Mesolithic contexts came from H39 (nos 45–57) and J104 (nos 58–79), Site E. Both are dominated by obliquely blunted forms; 73.5% in H39 (nos 45–51) and 82.6% in J104 (nos 58–9, 61–76). J104 contained no triangles, but

H39 produced five, one scalene (no 52) and four isoceles (eg nos 53–55). Types with abrupt retouch forming a convex edge, some with additional retouch on the opposite edge (lanceolate forms), come from both contexts; four from H39 (eg nos 56–7) and three from J104 (nos 60, 77–8). J104 also produced a straight-backed form (no 79).

Pit M90, produced the third largest group of twelve microliths, six (54.5%) obliquely blunted points (nos 80, 82–3, 85–7), four (36.4%) curved backed and lanceolate forms (nos 81, 84, 88–9), one isosceles triangle (no 90), and one too fragmentary for classification. Layer M26, produced ten microliths, six obliquely blunted points, one curved back form, and three fragments.

The only other Mesolithic contexts with microliths were pits C25 and C38 on Site A. C25 contained four obliquely blunted points (nos 91–3) and a lanceolate form (no 94). C38 produced two obliquely blunted points (nos 95–6) and one fragment.

The main microlith groups from Rhuddlan fit

Table 10.10 Microliths

	Oblique	Isosceles	Scalene	Curved	Straight	Rhomboid	Classifiable	Unclassifiable	Total	Chert	Flint	?
Mesolithic Contexts												
E: Pit J104	19 (82.6)	–	–	3 (13)	1 (4.3)	–	23	8	31	23	8	–
E: Soil H39	25 (73.5)	4 (11.8)	1 (2.9)	4 (11.8)	–	–	34	6	40	25	14	1
M: Pit M90	6 (54.5)	1 (9.1)	–	4 (36.4)	–	–	11	1	12	7	4	1
M: Soil M26	6	–	–	1	–	–	7	3	10	6	3	1
A: Pit C25	4	–	–	1	–	–	5	–	5	5	–	–
A: Pit C38	2	–	–	–	–	–	2	1	3	1	1	1
Totals	62 (75.9)	5 (6.0)	1 (1.2)	13 (15.7)	1 (1.2)	–	82	19	101	67	30	4
Post-Mesolithic Contexts												
E	13 (61.9)	2 (9.5)	1 (4.8)	4 (19)	1 (4.8)	–	21	5	26	20	6	–
M	7	–	–	2	1	–	10	5	15	8	5	2
T	8 (66.7)	–	2 (16.7)	1 (8.3)	–	1 (8.3)	12	3	15	9	6	–
A	5	–	–	1	–	–	6	1	7	3	3	1
V	–	–	–	1	–	–	2	1	3	1	2	–
S	1	–	–	–	–	–	1	–	1	–	1	–
Totals	34 (64.7)	2 (3.9)	3 (5.9)	9 (17.6)	3 (5.9)	1 (2)	52	15	67	41	23	3
Grand totals	96	7	4	22	4	1	134	34	168	108	53	7

Figures in brackets represent percentages of major groups

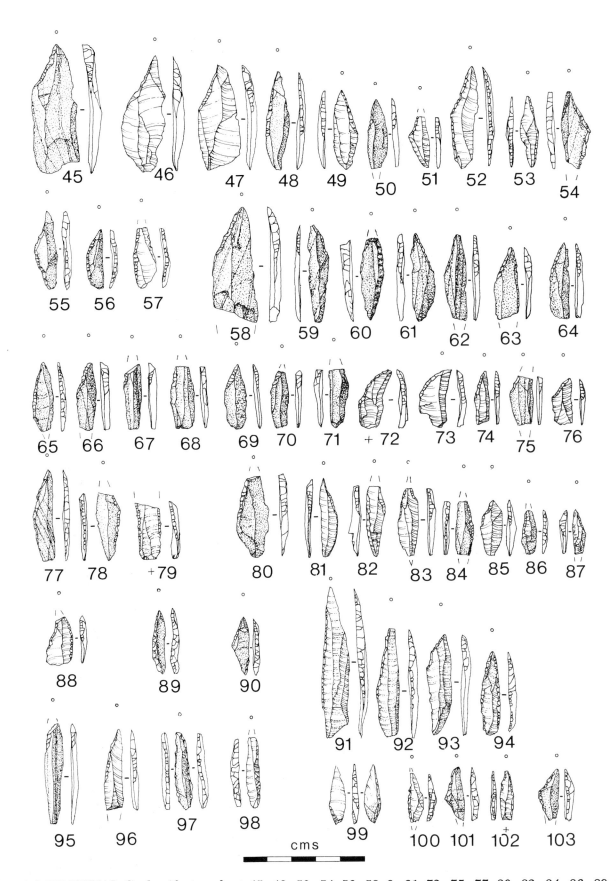

Fig 10.6 MATERIAL Carboniferous chert 45, 48, 50, 54–56, 58–9, 61–72, 75, 77–80, 82, 84, 86, 89–95, 97–99, 101, 103; remainder flint. CONTEXTS 45–57 Mesolithic soil H39 E, 58-79 Mesolithic pit J104 E, 80–90 Mesolithic pit M90, 91–94 Mesolithic pit C25 A, 95–96 Mesolithic pit C38 A, 97–98 residual M, 99 residual T, 100–102 Bronze Age soil H8 E, 103 residual A. TYPES All microliths of various forms. All 2:3.

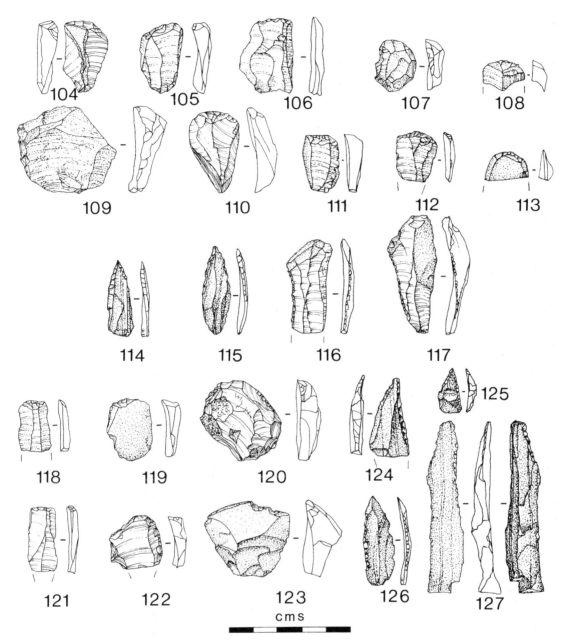

Fig 10.7 MATERIAL Carboniferous chert except 104, 107, 110, 116–7, 119–122 flint. CONTEXTS 104–117 Mesolithic pit J104 E, 118–127 Mesolithic pit M90. TYPES 104–113, 118–123 scrapers; 114, 115, 124, 125 piercers/awls; 116, 117, 126, 127 utilised blades. All 2:3.

firmly into the tradition of broad blade microlith assemblages, dominated by obliquely blunted points, recognised as typifying the Early Mesolithic of Britain and Northern Europe (Jacobi, 1973; 1976). (Further discussion Chapter 11).

67 microliths were recovered from post-Mesolithic contexts. While most are similar in type and form to those from the Mesolithic contexts, a few are distinctive. From Site E comes a small straight backed form (no 100), a small lanceolate type (no 102), a small isosceles triangle (no 101) and a small scalene triangle (no 103); from T an obliquely blunted point with inverse retouch at its base (no 99); and from M a straight-backed form (no 98).

The small size and form of these microliths indicates that they may be Later Mesolithic. A Later Mesolithic site, Hendre, does of course lie adjacent to the sites under discussion here (Manley & Healey, 1982). The microlith No 99 is of interest as the first recorded example in North Wales of a form recognised as a feature of some Later Mesolithic Cotswolds assemblages (Saville, 1984).

It has generally been accepted that most microliths formed parts of projectile points, acting as barbed insets. Despite Clarke's (1976) suggestion that they could form parts of other tools, particularly those for food processing, surviving hafted examples, experimental work and other

Table 10.11 Scrapers

	End	Double End	End And Side	Disc	Side	Broken	Total	Chert	Flint	?
Mesolithic Contexts										
E: Pit J104	6	1	–	–	–	4	11	6	4	1
E: H39	25	4	2	–	1	8	40	26	14	–
M: Pit M90	2	–	–	–	1	3	6	1	3	2
M: Soil M26	4	3	–	–	2	–	9	5	4	–
Other	4	–	–	–	–	–	4	4	–	–
Totals	41	8	2	0	4	15	70	42	25	3
Post-Mesolithic Contexts										
E	20	1	3	1	2	14	41	28	12	1
M	8	2	–	–	1	6	17	6	11	–
T	9	–	1	–	1	7	18	8	10	–
A	2	–	1	–	–	1	4	2	2	–
D	3	–	1	–	–	1	5	–	5	–
V	2	–	1	1	1	3	8	4	4	–
S	–	–	–	–	–	3	3	3	–	–
Totals	44	3	7	2	5	35	96	51	44	1
Grand totals	85	11	9	2	9	50	166	93	69	4

lines of evidence continues to support the traditional interpretation of microliths as armature for arrows (Barton, 1992, 219–26).

10.4.3 Scrapers (Figs 10.7–8)

A total of 166 formal scrapers were recognised (Table 10.11). Simple end-scrapers of typical Mesolithic form, with minimal retouch restricted to the working edge and rarely extending onto the edges, predominate in all contexts (eg Fig 10.7, nos 104–113, 118–123; Fig 10.8, nos 128–133). One scraper, from a post-Mesolithic context in Site V, shows invasive retouch and scalar flaking suggestive of a Later Neolithic or Earlier Bronze Age date (Fig 10.10, no 160).

The traditional interpretation of scrapers for working hides has been partly verified by recent microwear studies, though these also indicate other uses. Dumont (1989) in a microwear study of the Star Carr lithics reported hide polish to be the most frequently identified, but that significant numbers of scrapers had been used on wood, antler and especially bone. Scrapers used for working hides differ from those used on bone and antler; those used on antler have least curvature on the retouched edge, those on bone more, and those on hide the most. Thus likely functions for some Rhuddlan scrapers based on edge curvature would

be for nos 108, 110, 113 and 120 (Fig 10.7) use on hides, and nos 106, 111 and 123 on antler.

10.4.4 Notched pieces

Seventeen pieces have notches which are dissimilar to those formed in the microburin process. The only Mesolithic context to produce any was H39, Site E. When considering an interpretation of such pieces it is important to remember that regular notches showing several removals can form in incidental ways (Newcomer, 1975).

10.4.5 Awls (Figs 10.7–8)

Eighteen pieces can be classified as awls (eg Fig 10.7, nos 114–5, nos 124–5; Fig 10.8, nos 134–6). A small, narrow, and abruptly retouched piece may be a 'meche de foret' (Fig 10.6, no 97); wear and rounding of the tip is clearly visible. Such forms were common among the Early Mesolithic assemblage at Nab Head, possibly used in the manufacture of shale beads, of which large numbers were found (Gordon-Williams, 1926; Jacobi, 1980, 154; David, 1989).

Microwear studies, on some Mesolithic assemblages, have confirmed that pieces classified on typological grounds as awls were principally used for boring and piercing, particularly for bone, and,

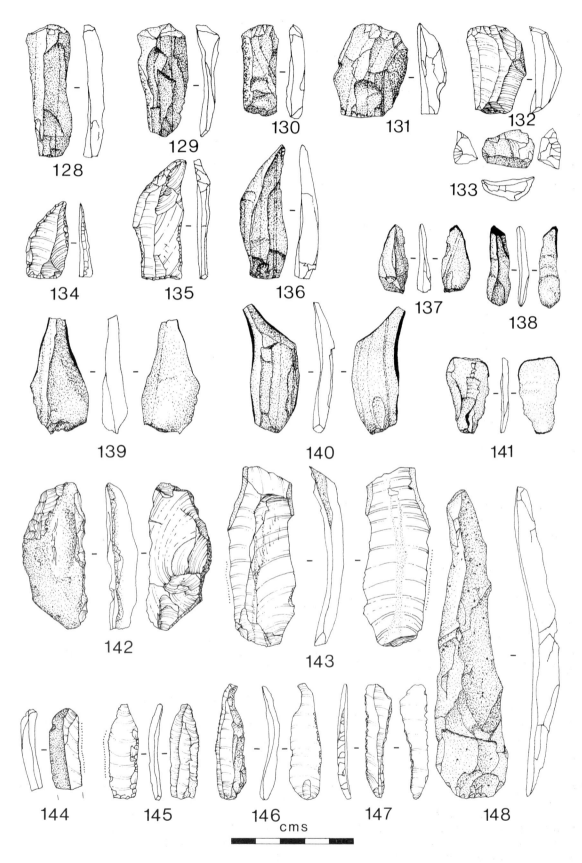

Fig 10.8 MATERIAL Carboniferous chert 129–131, 133, 136–141, 146, rhyolite 148, remainder flint.
CONTEXTS 128–141, 143, 148 Mesolithic soil H39 E, 142 Mesolithic pit C38 A, 122, 144, 146 residual E,
145, 148 residual T, 147 residual M. TYPES 128–133 scrapers; 134–6 piercers / awls; 137–141 edge ground
pieces; 142–143 fabricators; 144–147 microdenticulates; 148 ? All 2:3.

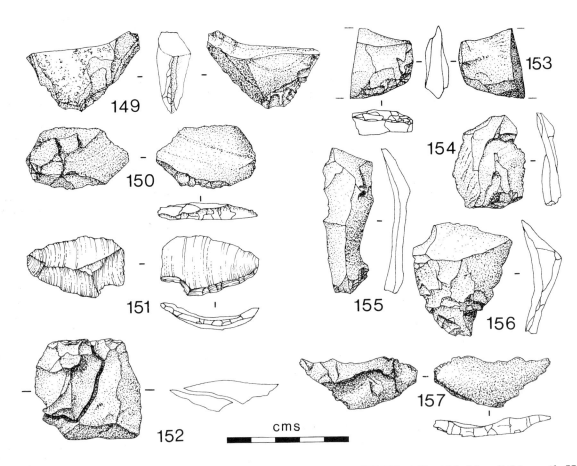

Fig 10.9 MATERIAL 149–157 rhyolite, remainder flint. CONTEXTS 149–151 Mesolithic soil H39 E, 152–156 Mesolithic pit J104 E, 157 Mesolithic pit C25 A. TYPES 149–151, 153, 157 axe-sharpening flakes; 152, 154–156 ? flakes derived from axes. All 2:3.

to a lesser extent, wood and hide (Dumont, 1987).

10.4.6 Worn/Ground Edge Pieces (Fig 10.8)

Twelve pieces have rounded or ground edges which seem likely to be the result of excessive wear (Fig 10.8, nos 137–141). These are sometimes called 'pieces emousées' and are fairly frequent on Mesolithic sites (eg Saville, 1977; Wymer, 1962, 342). Eleven come from Site E (seven from soil H39 and four from post-Mesolithic contexts) and one from Site M (post-Mesolithic context). Ten are of chert and two of flint.

On two complete and three fragmentary examples the wear is restricted to one end (eg Fig 10.8, no 141). Two others have wear at their distal ends, accompanied in one case by wear part way down one edge and in the other by wear down both edges and on the dorsal ridges (Fig 10.8, nos 137 and 138 respectively). The other five pieces have wear all along one or both edges; four of these have one or both ends missing so only on one is the wear definitely confined to the edges. On two wear is very pronounced, and striations clearly extend from the edges onto the dorsal surface indicating some use with a sideways motion (Fig 10.8, nos 139 and 140).

For such wear traces to form it seems logical to conclude that the pieces have been used to work some relatively hard material. The presence, at Rhuddlan, of pebbles decorated by scoured lines clearly points to one possible use. Experimental work has certainly shown that ground edges will form on flint or chert pieces used in this way though it has not yet been demonstrated that such traces precisely equate with those seen on the archaeological specimens (A Roberts Chapter 11; pers comm).

10.4.7 Microdenticulates (Fig 10.8)

Eight pieces, all from post-Mesolithic contexts, can be classified as microdenticulates (Fig 10.8 nos 144–7). Such pieces, with minute regular serrations, occur often, though not exclusively, in Mesolithic assemblages (eg Clark, 1954, 105–6; Rankine, 1952). Only one has serration on both long edges (Fig 10.8, no 145). One is steeply retouched along the edge opposite the serrations implying it may have been hafted.

Microwear analysis has so far proved inconclusive (Dumont, 1983; Barton, 1992). Experimental work, however, has clearly shown that such pieces can only have been used to cut relatively soft materials, though perhaps not as soft as meat but rather fresh plant material such as bracken or green wood (*ibid* 241–7).

10.4.8 Fabricators (Fig 10.8)

Three pieces may be termed fabricators. The best example, from pit C38 Site A, is made of flint and is battered and worn at both ends (Fig 10.8, no 142). One from Site D, again of flint, is bifacially worked and of a type typical of Later Neolithic and Earlier Bronze Age assemblages (Fig 10.10, no 163). Ideas about the precise function of fabricators vary though their use clearly involved some form of heavy percussive use.

10.4.9 Axe/adze sharpening and thinning flakes (Fig 10.9)

Five pieces may represent sharpening flakes from axes or adzes. All come from Mesolithic contexts: one from J104 Site E; three from H39 Site E; and one from C25 Site A (Fig 10.9, nos 149–51, 153 and 157). Of these three are of Carboniferous chert (Fig 10.9, nos 149–50, and 157) and two are of rhyolite (Fig 10.9, nos 151 and 153). Five further pieces from Mesolithic contexts in Site E have also been identified as rhyolite. These appear to be axe/adze thinning flakes. Though no axes or adzes were actually found, their presence is attested by the above pieces.

The use of volcanic, metamorphic and even sedimentary rocks for Mesolithic axes, as opposed to flint or chert, is attested elsewhere in Wales. A rhyolite axe of apparent Mesolithic type is reported from Benton Castle, Pembs (Grimes, 1951, 14, Fig 10.7, no 2; Wainwright, 1963, 112) and an axe of tuff (as well as one of black Carboniferous chert) was among the Mesolithic assemblage excavated at Trwyn Du, Aberffraw, Anglesey (White, 1978; Jacobi, 1980, Fig 4.20; Bevin pers comm). A flake of tuff is also reported from a surface Mesolithic collection from the same site (Ireland & Lynch, 1973). A tuff axe was also among the Mesolithic assemblage from Nab Head Site 1, while both Nab Head and Daylight Rock, Pembs, have examples said to be of a, 'partly mineralised siltstone' (Jacobi 1980, 166). Nab Head Site 2 has produced two pecked and ground axes or adzes made of 'igneous material' (David, 1989).

10.4.10 Arrowheads (Fig 10.10)

From post-Mesolithic contexts on Site A came a complete leaf-shaped arrowhead and an almost certain fragment of a second (Fig 10.10, nos 158–9). Leaf-shaped arrowheads are typical of the Earlier Neolithic, though it has been suggested that they may have persisted in use into the Later Neolithic and even into the Earlier Bronze Age, though the evidence for the latter is very tenuous (Green, 1980).

NOTE Pieces of possible rhyolite etc submitted for examination not illustrated have been given numbers 166 to 174.

Acknowledgments
A Goode (British Geological Survey, Exeter) and

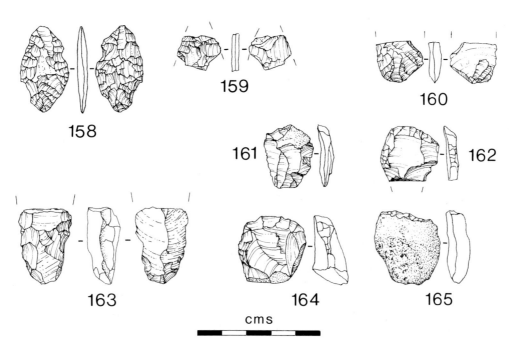

Fig 10.10 MATERIAL All flint. CONTEXTS 158, 159 residual A, 160 residual T, 161–165 residual D. TYPES 158–9 leaf arrowheads; 160–165 scrapers. All 2:3.

114

Dr R E Bevans (National Museum of Wales) provided preliminary comments on the petrology. Dr M F Howells (British Geological Survey, Aberystwyth) arranged for thin-sectioning and detailed petrological comment. The drawings are by Andy Brown.

11 The Mesolithic decorated and other pebble artefacts: synthesis

Peter Berridge with Alison Roberts

11.1 Decorated pebbles (Figs 11.1, 11.2)

Peter Berridge

11.1.1 Description

The recognition of a series of decorated pebbles during the excavations provided the most exciting evidence from prehistoric Rhuddlan. The first pebble was found only during the backfilling of Site E, in the second season 1970. In subsequent seasons pebbles of all sizes were routinely retrieved and examined, on Sites D, M, T and V, and another four with decorations were identified. A quantity were kept for study during post-excavation work which resulted in the recognition of a sixth piece. It is possible that pebbles were missed during the excavation of Site E and Site A in 1969, both of which took place before the existence of pebbles with fine decorative markings was recognized.

In the following descriptions of the decorated pebbles the terms top, bottom, left and right (unless otherwise stated) relate to their arrangement as seen in the illustrations.

SF1 (Fig 11.1, no 1; Plates 11.1–4)

SF1 from Site E was retrieved during backfilling of soil which came mainly from prehistoric horizons H8 and H39. It is a pebble of slightly micaceous silty sandstone with a mostly subrectangular cross-section and breaks at both ends which have clearly occurred after decoration. It is 80mm long.

All four main surfaces are decorated with a 'tree' motif made up of a central line parallel to the main axis of the pebble from which shorter lines branch on either side. Two opposing faces, B and D, have two motifs running in opposite directions as do the single motifs on the other pair of opposing faces, A and C. None of the six survive complete. If the motifs are viewed as though their bases are in the central area of the pebble, then in five of the six (the exception is that on A) the lowest branch lies to the left of the centre line. The fragmentary nature of the motif on A makes its detailed design uncertain; the lowest branch is probably on the right but, given the complexities of pattern on the other examples, it is possible that the right hand of the two lines parallel to the pebble axis is in fact

the central stem in which case it would conform to the others. On face B the second branch of both motifs is on the right, and the third and fourth branches leave the main stem at the same point. On D the second branch is on the left in both motifs. These similarities, at least in the initial stages of the paired motifs, suggest that the branches in the patterns were not laid out entirely at random.

SF2 (Fig 11.1, no 2; Plates 11.5–6)

SF2 from the Mesolithic hollow, M90, is a pebble of slightly micaceous, silty sandstone. It is of flattish oval section, narrowing to a 'neck' ending in a break, which again occurred after decoration. It is 82mm in length. Both broad faces, A and B, are decorated with the design extending to one of the narrower sides.

Face A has two decorated areas. The lower has two roughly parallel lines, 10–12mm apart, which run across the pebble. Then 30 lines were drawn between them, roughly at right angles; of these, 26 run all or most of the way between the two cross lines, while four extend only for short stretches. The upper decoration on A lies on the narrow neck, broken across, and is made up of three elements. The left hand element consists of two lines converging 16mm below the break. The 'V' so formed is crossed and partly infilled by ten short lines. The central element has two parallel lines running 9mm down from the break crossed by four short lines. The right hand element has two lines surviving for 13mm, converging but not joining and crossed by three short lines.

Face B also has two areas of decoration. The lower, on the broadest part of the pebble, is made up of a series of criss-cross lines which are incised, some very deeply, parallel to the pebble axis; second are a group of lines angling slightly down from left to right; and third are lines more sharply angled down from left to right. A few lines are strays, belonging to none of the groups. The upper motif on B extends c 20mm from the break. It consists of two curved parallel lines running down the pebble, with that on the right being a composite of two lines. At their base two short angled lines meet them. There are also four short cross

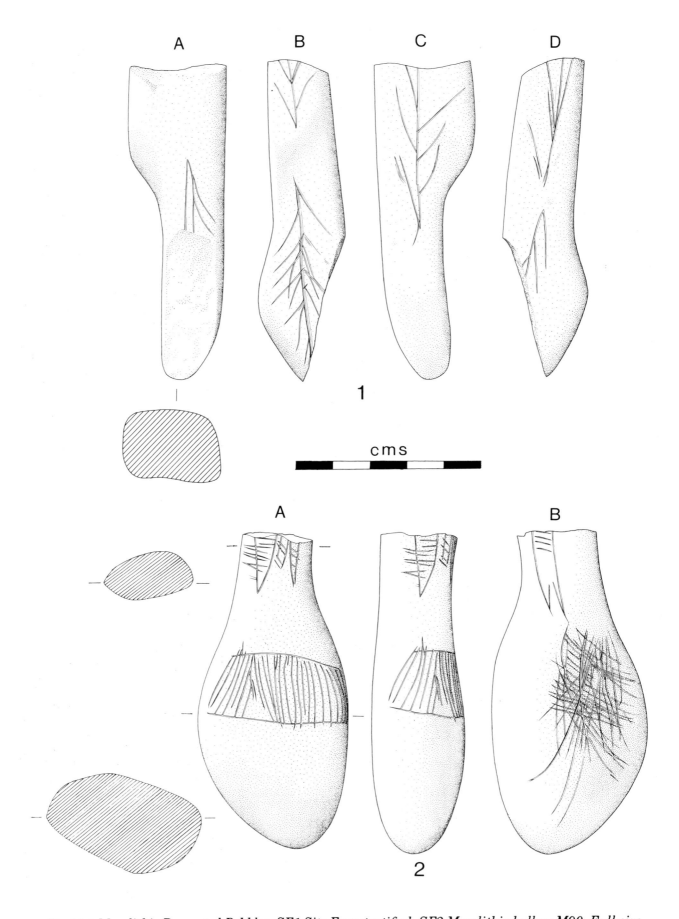

Fig 11.1 Mesolithic Decorated Pebbles. SF1 Site E unstratified. SF2 Mesolithic hollow M90. Full size.

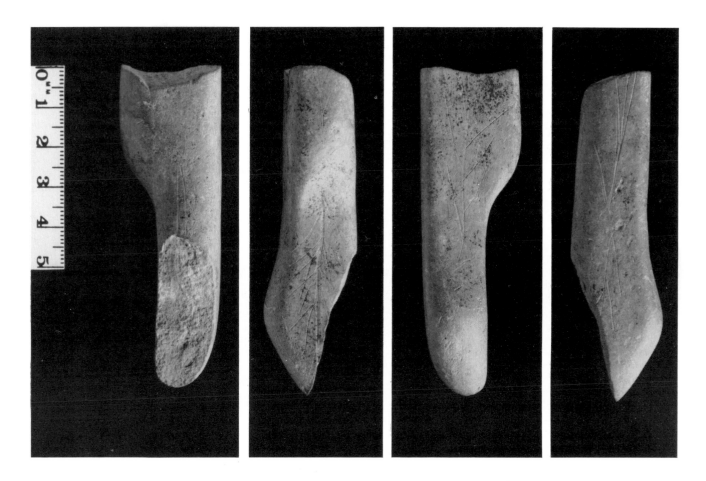

Pl 11.1–4 (l to r) SF1 Decorated Pebble Site E. Sides A, B, C, D. Photo: Total Publicity, Sidmouth

lines near the upper end of the motif.

SF3 (Fig 11.2)

SF3 from Romano-British soil, M64a, is of a slightly micaceous sandstone with far more silt, and therefore finer-grained, than the others. It is the broken end of a thin pebble decorated only on one of the broad faces with a series of criss-cross lines which roughly follow three main orientations. As the piece is fragmentary with some surface damage, analysis of the design and the identification of motifs is not possible.

SF4 (Fig 11.2)

SF4 from basal soil S31 is a slightly micaceous silty sandstone, elongated pebble, broken and eroded. At least 14 lines were incised on one face before breakage; erosion has made some very faint. No motif is discernible although the orientation of the lines falls into a restricted range with all lying within 30° either way of the longer axis of the pebble; all but one lies within 20°.

SF5 (Fig 11.2)

SF5 from topsoil, Site T, is an eroded fragment of a slightly micaceous silty sandstone pebble with 13 incised lines on one surface. Nine of the lines are roughly parallel and all but one lie 15° either side of the pebble's presumed long axis. The piece is too eroded for further interpretation.

SF6 (Fig 11.2, Plate 11.7)

SF6 from medieval soil 64, Site T, is of slightly micaceous sandstone, but with less silt than the other pebbles and therefore coarser grained. This is the only complete pebble, although now split into two along a natural bedding plane parallel with the decorated surface, and has the only complete design of the series. In addition to the main decoration on a flat surface, there are some relatively fresh marks on one side, probably of accidental recent origin (not shown on Fig 11.2, no 6). The piece is much worn. The design has two main elements. That drawn first ran up the pebble and consisted of eight roughly parallel and evenly spaced lines. The left three and the right two all curve inwards towards the top, and criss-cross with some additional branches. The outer right line also curves inwards at the base. The second element, cutting clearly across the first, comprises two groups of lines at right angles to the first set, at the top and bottom of the design. The bottom four

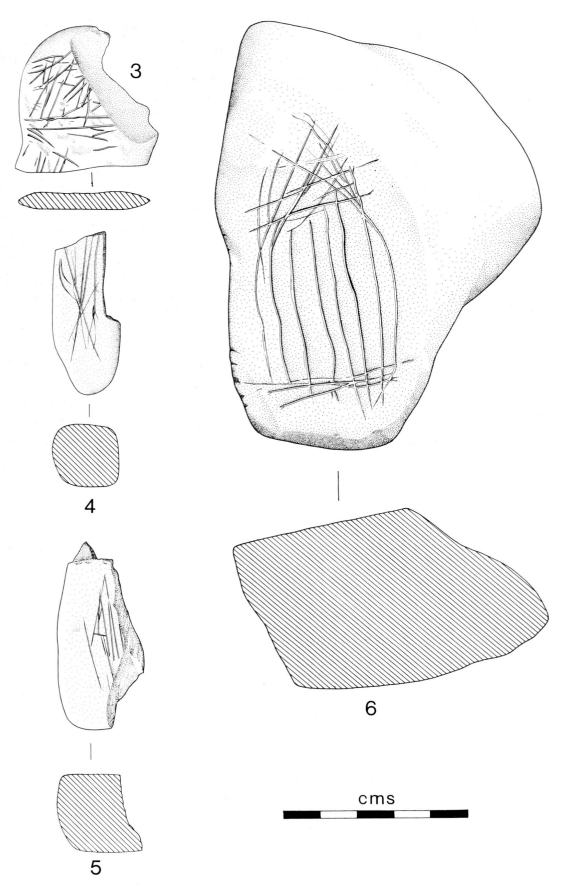

Fig 11.2 Mesolithic Decorated Pebbles. SF3 Romano-British soil M64a. SF4 soil S31. SF5 Site T topsoil. SF6 soil T64. Full size.

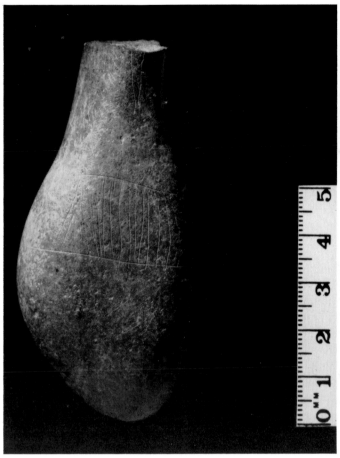

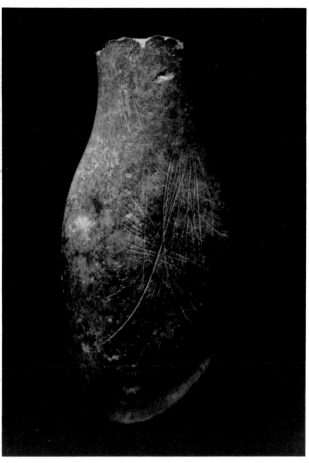

Pl 11.5 SF2 Decorated Pebble Mesolithic hollow M90. Side A. Photo: Total Publicity, Sidmouth

Pl 11.6 SF2 Decorated Pebble Mesolithic hollow M90. Side B. Photo: Total Publicity, Sidmouth

Pl 11.7 SF6 Decorated Pebble Site T soil T64. Photo: Total Publicity, Sidmouth

lines across overlap each other; at the top are six lines, some unclear because of wear damage. Many of the marks are deeply incised and were probably produced by several scorings, the divergent ends of which show faintly at the ends of some lines in both elements. There are at least eight nicks on the left hand edge, one of which definitely connects with a cross line of the second element in the design.

Dr R Taylor and Mr A J J Goode (British Geological Survey) comment: 'All the pieces are likely to be local fluvial pebbles, all of slightly micaceous silty sandstone, possibly with an ultimate origin in the Coal Measures. They differ only in the amount of silt components; those with more silt appear finer-grained. The narrow elongated shape of SF1 would have been unlikely to have survived in coastal conditions, suggesting the pebbles may have been selected from the bed of the Clwyd'.

11.1.2 The Scanning Electron Microscope Analysis of the Engraved Pebbles

Alison Roberts **(Plates 11.8–23)**
Introduction

The use of the Scanning Electron Microscope

(SEM) is a relatively new technique in the analysis of stone artefacts, but has a high potential in this field due to its wide and continuous range of magnification: the ability to change magnification without loss of orientation, good resolution at high magnification, and an exceptional depth of field. The microscope works by scanning a narrow beam of electrons over the surface of an object, collecting and processing the emitted electrons and displaying them on a monitor. The image is thus an accurate representation of the surface topography of that object. Details on the operation of Scanning Electron Microscopes can be found in Chapman (1986), and the advantages of using them in archaeological analysis in Cook (1986) and Olsen (1988). The engraved pebbles were submitted for SEM examination to determine if the marks on them were made by stone tools.

The pebbles were analysed under the ISI 60A at The Natural History Museum in 1986. This is the only SEM in the country currently fitted with a charge free anti-contamination system (CFAS), which enables uncoated specimens to be examined under a differential vacuum (Taylor, 1986; Claugher, 1988). Coating involves covering an object with a thin layer of carbon or gold palladium to increase conductivity, and is undesirable for archaeological objects. The machine also has an enviromental chamber able to take specimens of up to 10cm diameter, which allowed all the pebbles except SF6 to be viewed directly. Using this microscope it is possible to examine uncoated specimens at magnifications up to 800x, although most of this work was conducted at 25x–200x. Details of methodology are presented in Roberts (forthcoming).

Technology

As a control, the work was accompanied by a study of natural and taphonomic features, and replica engravings on pebbles of the same raw materials as the archaeological pieces. The archaeological engravings were experimentally reproduced using tools made from beach pebble flint, Gronant chert and metal. Details of the programme will be presented elsewhere (Roberts, forthcoming).

Analysis of the archaeological and experimental material showed that the engraved lines on the Rhuddlan pebbles were made by flint or chert artefacts, usually thin unretouched edges of bladelets but occasionally thicker edges such as burin facets or break surfaces. The distinctive features of metal tools (eg thin sharply defined V-shaped grooves with a high width to depth ratio) were not detected on any of the pieces. Lines incised by unretouched flint and chert artefacts are characterised by slightly parabolic U-shaped grooves and microscopic features that are similar in many respects to stone tool cutmarks on bone (Potts & Shipman, 1981; Shipman & Rose, 1983). The bottom of the experimental lines often show fine parallel microstriations caused by irregularities in the edge of the engraving tool (Pl 11.8). These latter features were not readily apparent on the archaeological engravings, and were probably removed by wear and post-depositional abrasion. Other characteristics of bladelet incisions were identified, in various combinations and in different conditions, on the archaeological pebbles.

Engraved lines tend to start abruptly, and taper in the width at the end. The direction in which they were made is indicated by the location of these sets of features, and in reverse by the orientation of 'chatter marks' and indentations in the grooves, in a similar manner to that described for cutmarks on bone by Bromage and Boyde (1984). Such details were often observed on the archaeological pieces.

The experimental engravings also showed irregularities and accidents related to the engraving process: eg overshooting, slipping of the cutting tool, accidental contact by other parts of the tool, and the irregular grooves typical of overcutting lines (Pl 11.9). Similar features were found on several pebbles, especially SF1 and SF2 which have clearly executed designs. The accidents are rarer on the other engravings where the decoration consists of multiple intersecting series of lines. It is possible these designs might result from using a pebble incidentally as a cutting surface rather than from intentional decorations.

Most of the engraved lines on the pebbles are between 0.25–0.5mm wide, and were made by bladelets. A few lines reach widths up to 1mm, either due to multiple cutting (as on SF2), or the use of broader working edges such as burin facets or break edges (as on SF1). The width of a line varies slightly over its course due to factors such as the texture of the engraving tool and material being engraved, the morphology of the tool edge and angle at which it was used, and the pressure applied while engraving. It is difficult to distinguish between lines made by chert as opposed to flint implements, except for marks made by tools with broad edge widths. Chert is a coarser material than flint and contains inclusions which affect the morphology of engraved lines, where the cutting edge width is >0.5mm, by producing sub-grooves within the main trough (Pl 11.18).

The experiments showed that thin bladelet edges were more effective tools for engraving quartzite pebbles than thicker edges. However, both bladelets and burins with thick edges were used successfully on softer stones. The tool edges used for engraving rapidly become ground down due to the abrasive nature of the stone (Pl 11.10). It is interesting to note that the Rhuddlan assemblage contains several bladelets with signs of heavy grinding on the edges (Pl 11.11).

Details of the pebbles

SF1 The pebble is of a very soft sedimentary rock and is decorated on four sides (Fig 11.1, no 1). Both

Pl 11.8 Experimental engraved line made with bladelet, showing characteristic features. ×200. Photo: Natural History Museum

Pl 11.9 Experimental engraving with bladelet, showing characteristic features and accidents associated with overcutting lines. ×25. Photo: Natural History Museum

Pl 11.10 Experimental chert bladelet with edge ground due to experimental use as engraving tool. ×50. Photo: Natural History Museum

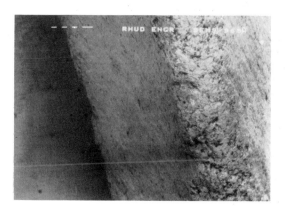

Pl 11.11 Heavily ground edge of chert bladelet from Rhuddlan. ×50. Photo: Natural History Museum

Pl 11.12 Detail of face B of SF 2, showing area of overcutting and intersecting engraved lines. ×17. Photo: Natural History Museum

Pl 11.13 Detail of face B of SF2, showing faint worn engraved lines cut by more clearly defined series. ×17. Photo: Natural History Museum

Pl 11.14 Detail of the edge of SF3, showing engraved lines being cut by the break surface, the start of a line, and a faint worn line underlying several others. ×16. Photo: Natural History Museum

Pl 11.15 Detail of SF5, showing the effects of erosion and abrasion on an engraved line. Apparent marks perpendicular to the engraved line are natural features. ×21. Photo: Natural History Museum

Pl 11.16 Detail of face A of SF1, showing the termination of the engraving and natural bedding features. ×19. Photo: Natural History Museum

Pl 11.17 Detail of face A of SF1, showing the main line and several intersecting lines. ×20. Photo: Natural History Museum

Pl 11.18 Experimental engraved lines made with a chert burin. × 25. Photo: Natural History Museum

Pl 11.19 Experimental engraved line made with a flint burin. × 25. Photo: Natural History Museum

the engraved lines and the natural surface of the pebble indicate very little post-depositional damage, unlike most of the other pieces. The engravings on sides A, C, and D are worn to a greater extent than those on side B. This was the only pebble where the use of chert tools could clearly be identified.

The thick (c 1mm) centre line on side B was made by a single wide irregular edge such as a chert burin facet or break surface. Most of the other lines, about half this width, also show the subgrooving indicative of chert engraving tools. Even the thinnest engraved lines could have been made with chert rather than flint bladelets, as shown by a 0.5mm wide chert-cut line at the bottom right which thins to half its original width at the edge of the pebble.

On side B, the thick centre line was engraved from the bottom of the piece up the long axis and terminating as the contour curves upwards and outwards. The actual starting point has been broken off. The line tapers at the finish with the end point obscured by an intersecting side line (Pl 11.16). In most cases the centre line is cut by the side lines branching off it, but a few at the top underlie it. Most of the side cuts start from the centre line and move out to the edges. There are two deep nicks in the centre line, which appear to have been the result of excess pressure in starting an incision. One nick was continued as a side line, although the engraving tool apparently 'slipped' c 0.5mm at the point that the line exited the centre groove. The morphology of the thicker (0.5–1.0mm) lines can be compared to those produced experimentally by thick burin facets of chert (Pl 11.18) as opposed to flint (Pl 11.19). It is interesting to note that the centre line is cut slightly deeper and at a sharper angle on the right side. This feature could indicate that the working edge was asymmetrical, or that the tool was held, or pressure applied slightly unevenly, favouring this side, perhaps by a right-handed person.

SF2 This hard rounded pebble is decorated on both sides. A 'ladder' design is carved on the curved side of the pebble (Fig 11.1, no 2A). The short lines were cut from top to bottom (as the piece is orientated in the illustration), and overcut the two longer lines wherever they intersect. Several short lines start below the upper longer line, and others cut the bottom one before they terminate. Therefore, it appears that the longer lines were made initially, and the shorter lines were then incised between them. Occasionally the start of a short line is marked by a dent in the surface of the pebble, presumably an effect of the initial pressure in engraving a particularly hard material as this feature was not recognised on softer stones. This side of the pebble is heavily worn and the edges of many of the lines are rubbed down. There are also several very faint engraved lines interspersed between the short lines and parallel to them.

The flatter side of the pebble is decorated by lines aligned along three separate axes (Fig 11.1, no 2B). From study of the intersections it appears that the lines perpendicular to each other were engraved some time before the obliquely orientated third set. The earlier lines are worn, whereas the third set are deeper and more distinct (Pl 11.13). The direction of manufacture could not be determined for the underlying perpendicular lines. The oblique lines were engraved from the upper left to the lower right, and the upper right to the lower left of the pebble. The oblique lines show overcutting and multiple cutting of lines with the resulting distorted width and curvature, and evidence of bladelet slippage (Pl 11.12).

Slightly worn lines relating to a third design appear around the broken top of the piece. These marks are truncated by the break showing that the pebble was broken after the engraving was made.

The variable condition of the lines on both sides of the pebble and the overcutting designs indicate that there were several stages in the decoration and wear of this object.

SF3 A small flat pebble of soft stone with engraved lines on one side (Fig 11.2, no 3). Much of the surface of the pebble is heavily abraded and pitted, removing features of some lines. The distinct engravings overlie a fainter series of stone tool incisions which are worn along the edges.

The break at the top right hand side of the illustration cuts several engraved lines, suggesting that the piece was broken after decoration. Several of the lines were made in a direction moving away from this break. The other break is rounded at the edges and two lines cut over it, suggesting that it predates the decoration. Pl 11.14 shows two lines truncated by the break, a worn line underlying several clearer ones, and the start of a line. The small hole is a natural feature common to several pebbles.

SF4 A small soft sedimentary pebble engraved on one side (Fig 11.2, no 4), and showing the effects of slight abrasion due to sediment movement. The lines are heavily worn and their edges rounded, especially close to the break which is very worn. It was imposible to determine if the piece was broken before or after decoration as the intersection between the break and any engraved lines has been worn away. In the few cases where it could be determined, the direction of movement was lengthways towards the unbroken end of the piece. Although all lines are worn, there do seem to be a few very faint lines undercutting the main design and perpendicular to each other as in SF2 and SF3.

SF5 A small soft sedimentary pebble with a heavily abraded surface and engraved lines on one side (Fig 11.2, no 5). A few of the lines are very eroded, but most are quite clear. Pl 11.15 shows the line in the centre of the pebble and illustrates the effects of the surface abrasion. Only the roughly parallel lines along the long axis of the piece near the break were deliberately engraved. Other marks visible on the surface are clearly natural features caused by accidental contact with other hard materials (Fiorillo, 1984; Andrews & Cook, 1985). The condition of the surface may be connected with the fact that the pebble was found in the topsoil.

Directionality was difficult to assess due to the pebble's surface condition but several lines seem to run in the direction of unbroken to broken end along the long axis. Chips in the edge of the pebble have removed any clear intersections between the engraved lines and the longer break, and therefore it is impossible to determine if the piece was broken before or after decoration. However, the relatively fresh condition of the break suggests that it is more recent than the engraving.

SF6 This large decorated sandstone pebble could not be viewed in the SEM because of its size. In such cases, small silicone rubber casts can be employed (as they have been in the analysis of large bone and metal artefacts), but since this pebble was very coarse and porous, such a procedure was not attempted because of the increased risk of damage to the surface of the object by exfoliation or the impregnation of chemicals. It is also unlikely that SEM study would have produced significant results as the surface was highly weathered.

The object was examined by hand lens and binocular microscope with limited results. The lines along the long axis are deeply incised and overcut, obscuring clear indications of the type of tool used to make them. However, the relative dimensions and morphology of the lines are more compatible with stone than metal tools. On the basis of the terminations, the lines appear to have been cut from the pointed to flat end. The cross-hatched series of shallower lines at the pointed end were less ambiguous and are likely to have been made by flint or chert bladelets. There were no features that were obviously attributable to metal engraving on the piece.

Conclusions

In summary the SEM analysis has shown two major important features about the engraved pebbles from Rhuddlan:
(1) Most of the engraved lines seem to have been made by unretouched edges of flint or chert bladelets. Thicker, irregular edges such as chert burin facets or break surfaces were probably also used on SF1. The tools used to do the engravings would rapidly have developed ground edges.
(2) On several of the pieces it was possible to see an underlying series of engraved lines that had

been heavily worn. This implies that the pebbles had more than one phase of decoration and use. A similar trait has been recognised in the Late Mesolithic engraving from Remouchamp, Belgium (Gob & Jacques, 1985). The overlaying of designs also occurs on some Azilian pebbles from South West France where painted lines may overlie engraved ones (Couraud, 1985).

The study has also shown features relating to the method of manufacture, wear, breakage and post-depositional damage on the individual pebbles.

11.1.3 Discussion Peter Berridge

It needs to be established that these decorated pebbles form a unified group, and if so, what date range is likely. SF2 is from Mesolithic hollow M90, SF4 is from a possible later prehistoric context, SF3 from a probable Romano-British context and SF6 was found in an old land surface with a possible *ante quem* of c AD 900 which sealed later prehistoric and Romano-British features. These contexts provide support for a pre-medieval date. SF1 and SF5 were unstratified. The context of SF2 makes it certain that this piece is Mesolithic, but as none of its motifs occur on the other pebbles, direct comparanda of decorative styles is of no help in dating the other examples. The study by Roberts has, however, shown a technological unity for the group in that the decorative lines were formed by the use of chert or flint tools. It therefore seems safe, despite the varied nature of the contexts, to regard all the pieces as Mesolithic.

Mesolithic artwork has as yet been only rarely recognised in Britain. Two dubious examples from Dorset have been put forward by Palmer (1970, 173–4; 1977, 132). That from Portland Site 1 is a stone with four scratched lines about which Palmer states that it is 'impossible to be certain that they are not accidental or co-incidental'. That from Culverwell, a surface find, 'a cylindrically shaped object of tufaceous limestone' with 'simple engraved lines on the convex base', is said to be similar to the Upper Palaeolithic 'figurine' claimed by Palmer from Hengistbury Head (Palmer, 1977, 132–2; 1984). It has, however, been convincingly argued that the latter is in fact a whetstone of historic date, a conclusion which casts doubt on the Culverwell piece (Cook, 1982: 1985).

Better candidates for Mesolithic art come from Nab Head, Pembs (Gordon-Williams, 1926; Jacobi, 1980, 159, Pls I–IV; David, 1989, 243–4). The well known Nab Head 'figurine' or 'phallus' is undoubtedly artificially shaped from a shale pebble, though it is a surface find. A second shale pebble has a single incised line, yet this could be natural or incidental to functional use of the piece. The claimed Mesolithic date for these pieces is reasonable given the abundant lithic remains of the period in the immediate vicinity.

Other examples of probable Mesolithic art have been discovered at Romsey and from the Thames

(Smith, 1934). These involve, respectively, a red deer antler tine engraved with rows of chevrons and an implement made on a bone of *bos*, also decorated with chevrons. Though these are good candidates for Mesolithic art, a later date, particularly Neolithic, cannot be excluded without radiocarbon dates.

Relatively large numbers of decorated Mesolithic artefacts, particularly of bone and antler, are known from Northern Europe (for some specific examples see Vebaek, 1938; Liversage, 1966; Larsson, 1978; general discussion Clark, 1975, 147–159). The artwork shows a complex interweaving of geometrical designs, perhaps seen at its peak on the wooden paddle from Tybrind Vig (Jensen, 1982, 50, Fig 18). Examples on stone are less well known (eg Althin, 1951; Petersen, 1971; Fischer, 1974; Gob and Jacques, 1985). Geometric designs comprise the most common motifs on all mediums, but anthropomorphic and zoomorphic representations occur such as the two human figures on the Olby Lyng antler shaft-hole axe (Liversage, 1966) and the two deer on a similar artefact from Ystad (Clark, 1975, Fig 34, Pl VI). Artefacts carved in the round are extremely rare and consist mainly of small amber objects including representations of

animals (see Clark, 1975, 157–8 for details and full references). With such a range of Mesolithic artwork in Northern Europe occasional pieces should be expected in Britain. The Rhuddlan examples fall within the European range, and the definite motifs on SF1 and SF2 have fairly close comparanda.

Interpretation of the Rhuddlan decorated pebbles is clearly difficult. There has been little work on the possible meanings of the European motifs, apart from the obvious human and animal representations. Clark's classification scheme (1975, Fig 37), despite its inadequacies, provides a more detailed definition of the various motifs than was previously available. More work is, however, needed on the relative frequency and combination of the motifs and on their associations and contexts.

Specific interpretions have previously been made of SF2 and SF6 which need review. SF2 was suggested by Miles (1972, 248) to be the lower part of anthropomorphic figurine, with the different motifs representing parts of the body and clothing. This interpretation relied heavily on the natural shape of the pebble, which is reminiscent of the 'figurine' from Nab Head. It may be supported by the layout of the motifs on face A which seem

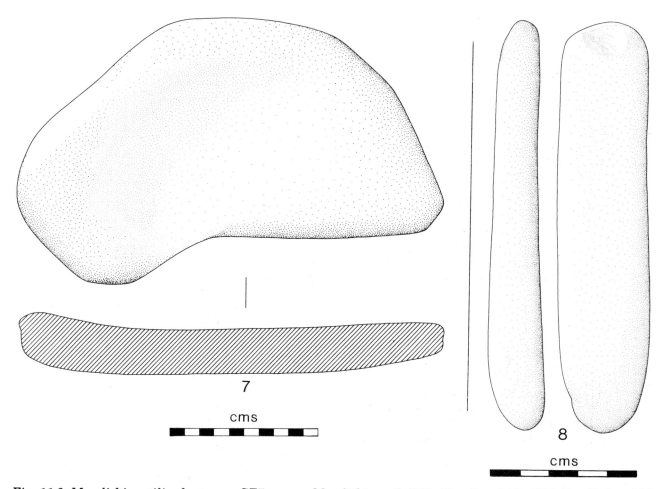

7

cms

8

cms

Fig 11.3 Mesolithic utilised stones. SF7 quern Mesolithic soil H39 Site E; ×2/5. SF8 Bevelled pebble residual Site E; ×4/5.

intended to be viewed as a group rather than individually. However in Northern Europe anthropomorphic representations normally consist of a single motif, not as a group designed to be seen together. Most Mesolithic art seems to have motifs designed to be seen two, not three, dimensionally, particularly human likenesses. If SF2 were accepted as a figurine, it would add a new element to the known range of Mesolithic human representations.

Jacobi (pers comm) suggested that SF6 represented a fish trap because of the similarity of the design to actual early post-glacial wheals such as those from Lille Knapstrup and Nidlose in the Holbaek district of Zealand (Clark, 1975, Pl II; Brinkhuizen, 1983).

The Rhuddlan decorated pebbles are an important addition to the range of material from the British Mesolithic. The sparsity of such decorated objects in Britain may partly be due to the scarcity of deposits which allow survival of the organic objects most frequently decorated in Northern Europe. However increasing numbers of pieces on non-organic materials such as flint and chert are being recognised as excavators become aware of the possibility of such items (eg Althin, 1951). Identification can sometimes be made more difficult by the fragmentary nature of the pieces. This was well illustrated by the ornamental flint nodule from Holmegård V (Fischer, 1974) which was subsequently used for raw material and ended up as three cores and more than 67 flakes. The first Rhuddlan pebble SF2 was found by chance, but the other five were retrieved through the strategy planned once such pebbles were realised as possible finds. It is hoped that the publication of the Rhuddlan pebbles will lead to improved awareness of the probability of such examples existing in Britain and that in consequence appropriate strategies will be adopted on excavations.

11.2 Utilised stones SF7–8

Peter Berridge (**Fig 11.3**)

Although large quantities of pebbles from prehistoric and later contexts were scrutinised only two were tentatively identified as utilised artefacts of prehistoric date.

SF7 from Mesolithic soil H39 Site E is a waterworn slab of local slightly silty and micaceous sandstone, measuring 285mm by 145mm with a maximum thickness of 30mm. The upper surface has been worn, through apparent use, into a smooth, dished depression. This wear deepened a natural depression and has removed various striations, presumably natural, which occur on the edge of the slab. The base of the slab has been a little rolled after a natural split. The worn hollow appears to be the result of grinding or rubbing, and may have been used in the processing of seeds and other plant foods. Such an artefact seems appropriate for a hunter-gatherer community. Its context

suggests a Mesolithic date, though the possibility of intrusion of a heavy stone into a soft sand soil cannot be ruled out.

SF8 from a medieval or later context on Site E is a waterworn elongated pebble of hard fine-grained slightly micaceous and silty sandstone; the elongated shape suggests a fluvial origin. It measures 135mm by 31mm by 18mm. One end has two opposing ground bevelled facets. A large flake has been removed, probably during some heavy percussive use, from the more pronounced of the two facets. The form, appearance and size of SF8 are similar to a group of tools found in Mesolithic contexts in South West Britain and South West Wales (Jacobi, 1980, 186–7). A Mesolithic date is probable although not certain. (Site E also produced over 2,500 pieces of Mesolithic flint and chert as residual material in later contexts.) The function of these bevelled pebbles is the subject of current research (Alison Roberts pers comm) which has so far shown the traditional nomenclature of 'limpet scoops' to be inappropriate.

11.3 General discussion of the Mesolithic at Rhuddlan Peter Berridge

11.3.1 Chronology

It is important to establish both the relative and absolute chronological position of the Rhuddlan sites, both in the Welsh and in the broader British Mesolithic. The change from broad blade assemblages, with comparatively large microliths and a high proportion of obliquely blunted points, in the first half of the Mesolithic, to narrow blade assemblages with smaller narrower microliths with fewer obliquely blunted points and many geometric forms, particularly micro-scalene triangles, in the Later Mesolithic is well attested both in Britain and Northern Europe (Jacobi, 1973; 1976). The dividing date, between the Early and Later Mesolithic, has been proposed at around 8750 BP (*ibid*). It is quite clear that the majority of the Rhuddlan microliths, particularly from Mesolithic contexts, group comfortably in the Early Mesolithic along with such Welsh sites as Trwyn Du (White, 1978), Daylight Rock (Lacaille & Grimes, 1955; Wainwright, 1963), and Nab Head I (Gordon-Williams 1926; Wainwright, 1963). The Early Mesolithic attribution for the bulk of the Rhuddlan material has already been extensively discussed (Jacobi, 1980).

Some metrical analysis was carried out in order to further confirm the Early Mesolithic dating. The measurements of waste flakes were of limited help due to the nature of the raw material and knapping technique, as discussed earlier. The dimensions of microliths are, however, also worth considering as their potential chronological value has been demonstrated (Pitts & Jacobi, 1979). From 35 Mesolithic sites in Southern Britain the average figures for length and breadth of complete obliquely blunted points were calculated and these showed a clear division between sites which would be considered, typologically, to belong to the Early and to the Later Mesolithic (*ibid*). The results convincingly revealed a marked reduction in size of obliquely blunted points from the Early Mesolithic to the Later Mesolithic. In the case of Rhuddlan similar figures were calculated for all complete obliquely blunted points from Mesolithic contexts H39 and J104. From a total of sixteen pieces (eight from each context) the average figures were 31.9mm, for length, and 10.8mm, for breadth; no other context produced a sufficient number of complete examples for a suitable sample. When placed alongside the results from the broader study the figures for Rhuddlan can be seen to fit firmly among the other Early Mesolithic assemblages.

In order to explore this aspect further the obliquely blunted points from the two contexts, H39 and J104, were considered separately. For H39 the average length was 37mm and for breadth 12.9mm. For J104 the similar figures were appreciably smaller at 29.1mm and 9mm. This is of some interest as pit J104 is stratigraphically later than soil H39. This would accord with a model of a progressive, gradual, reduction in size of obliquely blunted points through the Early to the Later Mesolithic. Such a progressive change has, however, not yet been established elsewhere and did not form part of the interpretation put forward by Pitts and Jacobi (*ibid*), whose results could argue for a sudden, rather than a gradual, size reduction. More metrical work of this kind is needed, supported by radiocarbon dating, to further explore this question.

It is interesting to note that there are additional variations between the microliths from the stratigraphically separated contexts H39 and J104. Triangular microliths were found in H39, five in all, nearly 15%, but none in the later J104. It has been suggested that, within the Welsh Early Mesolithic, an early group of sites may be recognized, as at Daylight Rock and Nab Head, typified by a relatively high percentage of large triangular microliths, and a later group, including Trwyn Du, with relatively low numbers of triangles (Jacobi, 1980, who also placed the whole of Rhuddlan Site E in this late group, based on a bulked sample from Site E, not contexts considered separately). It is tempting to see this proposed chronological difference reflected at Rhuddlan by the presence of triangles in the earlier context H39 and their absence from the later J104. This should still be approached with great caution due to the small sample involved and also, particularly, as David (1989) has tentatively suggested that the sequence should be reversed, sites with many broad triangles being later than those with only a few. The evidence at Rhuddlan cannot therefore be interpreted with certainty. Though H39 and J104 were stratigraphically separated other factors may be

involved, and any differences could be functional rather than chronological.

Two radiocarbon determinations were obtained from large features with abundant Mesolithic material; 8739 ± 86 BP (6789 BC) (BM-691) from pit J104, Site E, and 8528 ± 73 BP (6578 BC) (BM-822) from pit M90, Site M. The radiocarbon method has inherent uncertainties, especially where multiple dates cannot be obtained. At Rhuddlan neither sample was large enough for more than one date, and the possibility that one or both dates are incorrect cannot be checked. As well as problems with single determinations the question of sample integrity needs to be considered. In recent years doubts have been expressed, especially in regard to the British Mesolithic, about the validity of bulked samples (Jacobi, 1987). In particular, samples of charcoal obtained from diffuse contexts such as buried soils have been questioned. On this criterion two dates from another North Welsh site, Trwyn Du, have been queried: dates of 8640 ± 150 BP (6690 BC) and 8590 ± 90 BP (6640 BC) came from bulked samples of burnt hazelnut shells from a soil layer; (the third date from this site, 7980 ± 140 BP (6030 BC) was considered unreliable by the laboratory because of low carbon content).

The Rhuddlan dates have also been considered as unreliable because of their bulked sample origin (Jacobi, 1980; David, 1989). The nature of the samples and their contexts therefore need to be looked at more closely. BM-691 was a bulked sample of charred hazelnut shells from a discrete lens, maximum thickness 0.10m, of black sand midway down in the 0.50m fill of oval pit J104; the north edge of the pit was cut by medieval Ditch V but otherwise it was largely undisturbed. BM-822 came from charred hazelnut shells gathered throughout the fill of a large pit/hollow, M90. The feature was severely truncated by gully M82, of much later prehistoric date.

From these details it certainly seems to be correct to question the date from M90. Although the context was a pit and not a broad layer, the sample was collected from throughout its fill, and it is not known how long it took to become infilled; M90 was also extensively cut away by a later gully, which increases the possibility of contamination. The J104 date, on the other hand, is not open to so much doubt. Later disturbance was minimal and, more importantly, the sample came from a discrete context within the fill which is likely to represent a relatively short-lived, single episode of activity. Some of the hazelnut shells could be residual from soil H39 but the sample is unlikely to have been contaminated with younger material given its position within the pit. This is significant as the Rhuddlan dates have been criticised as being too young, rather than too old. The J104 date therefore seems reasonably secure and in fact may be one of the most secure from any Mesolithic site in Wales.

The Rhuddlan dates were, however, not only

criticised because of the nature of the samples but also because they appeared to be out of step with dates from other Mesolithic sites. As David (1989) has said 'they are amongst the latest dates for "early" assemblages from the British Isles'. It has been stressed that they overlap with dates for Later Mesolithic assemblages from North Britain and Ireland and therefore should be questioned (Jacobi, 1980). In the face of this criticism it is necessary to consider whether these other dates, from Later Mesolithic sites, are in fact secure. The North British dates are certainly open to doubt. Filpoke Beacon 8760 ± 140 BP (Q–1474) (Jacobi, 1976), Broomhead V 8570 ± 110 BP (Q–800) (Radley, Switsur & Tallis, 1974) and Stump Cross 8450 ± 310 BP (Q–141) (Godwin & Willis 1959; 1964) all came from bulked charcoal samples from generalised contexts, while Warcock Hill Site 3 8610 ± 110 BP (Q–789) was a sample collected from three separate contexts. Most archaeologists would now doubt the value of using such samples.

Similar doubts cannot, however, be expressed about the Irish dates. At Mount Sandel a date range of 8990 BP (7940 BC) to 7885 BP (5935 BC) was associated with a narrow blade assemblage; even though bulked samples of charcoal and hazelnuts were used they were from relatively discrete contexts (Woodman, 1985). However, some doubts have been raised as to whether the very early dates for narrow blade material from Ireland are relevant to the Mesolithic in North Wales at all (Jacobi, 1987, 167). Jacobi (ibid) has pointed out that the problem is not just with Wales as the 'dates for such a technology in Ireland, from Mount Sandel, seem, from a Northern European standpoint, anomalously early'. Jacobi (ibid) tentatively suggests a 'French Atlantic seaboard' link to explain Irish divergence from the general British and Northern European pattern. He also questions whether 'the pattern of dates (from Mount Sandel) is not a function of differing sample types and/or inter-laboratory variation'. It seems wise at present to exclude the Irish dates from any discussion of North Welsh material until further work is done.

With the validity of the North British dates questioned, and the Irish dates at present put to one side, the Rhuddlan date from J104, of 8739 ± 86 BP, need not be treated as so anomalous. Some support is provided by a date of 8779 ± 110 BP (6829 BC) (Q–973), associated with a typical Early assemblage, from Greenham Dairy Farm, Berks, though this was from a bulked sample of red deer bone (Sheridan, Sheridan & Hassey, 1967). A date, of 8760 ± 110 BP (6710 BC) (OxA–377), has also been obtained for Longmoor, Hants, which has an Early Mesolithic lithic assemblage (Jacobi, 1981; Gillespie et al, 1985).

In conclusion, it seems best to treat the date from M90 as unreliable and discard it and to use the same approach with dates from other sites, obtained from similar samples from diffuse con-texts. It is sobering to realise that this would in fact remove the majority of radiocarbon dates associated with the British Mesolithic. The date from J104 still seems reasonably secure and dates from other sites offer some corroboration. It is clear that the changes in lithic assemblages that undoubtedly happened in the ninth millennium BP can no longer be as closely dated as was once thought and that a date of 8750 BP separating the Early and the Later Mesolithic may no longer be appropriate.

11.3.2 The interpretation of excavated features

Excluding such contexts as the general 'soil' layers, the excavations produced fifteen features attributed to the Mesolithic. These range from possible stakeholes to large hollows or pits at Sites A, E, and M. The 'soil' layers are presumably entirely natural in origin, being made up of wind blown material, whereas, so far, it has been assumed that pits such as J104 and M90 resulted from human activity. The possibility that they might be of natural origin needs consideration. Man-made pits, postholes and stakeholes are of course well attested from Mesolithic sites, a good example being Mount Sandel (Woodman, 1985). This site had, however, a number of features which were interpreted as tree falls (ibid, 126). Such features have been widely recognised in Northern Europe (Newell, 1981). Tree fall holes can be suprisingly regular (eg F13, F29 and F52 at Mount Sandel; Woodman, 1985, Fig 4A & 9). Of the Rhuddlan features J104, J92 and J86 (Site E Fig 6.1) and C25, C38 and C77 (Site A Fig 3.1) fit within the known range of such features. The lens of black sand and quantities of artefacts from J104 need not argue against a natural origin. The hollow which a tree fall leaves will become an obvious repository of any human debris in the immediate vicinity. Such a hollow can become the focus of human activity, either because of the shelter it affords or because of its convenience for rubbish disposal. It is not suprising that when such features, containing occupation layers and artefacts have been excavated, they have been mistakenly thought to be of human origin (Newell, 1981).

It is difficult to decide, so long after their excavation, whether the Rhuddlan features were of natural or human origin. Simple pit-like features, including J104, could be of human origin but they could equally be natural. It seems difficult, however, to regard all the wide range of features on Site M as natural in origin. The features divide roughly into two phases. The lower group M52–M123 is covered by sand soil M26, while the upper M90–M127 cuts into it. Five of the first group could be postholes; their contemporaneity cannot be established but is not inconsistent with the limited stratigraphic evidence. They may form part of a structure, perhaps a hut or windbreak, extending beyond the trench. M52, M46 and M60 may have held some structure around or over the pit-like feature M50.

M90 seems, of the second phase of features, to have the most potential for interpretation. There were six smaller pits within this large flat-bottomed hole, of which five (a, b, c, e, f) had dark centres suggesting that they had been postholes; 'd' might also have been a posthole. 90a to 90d form a rough alignment (though 'b' seems to cut 'a'). Together with 'f' they might have been part of a curved structure. Alternatively 'a' to 'd' together with 'e' could link as part of a larger curve, the centre of which was cut away by the later gully M82; such a curve could represent a substantial windbreak or part of the wall of a hut set within the hollow M90.

11.3.3 Site location and economy

Major groups of Early Mesolithic lithic material came from Sites A, T, E and M and of the Later Mesolithic from adjacent Hendre (Manley & Healey, 1982). These are all areas with a sandy subsoil. Mellars and Reinhardt (1978) have suggested a correspondence between Mesolithic settlements and sandy soils. It has been questioned, at Rhuddlan, as to whether this correspondence is significant as so little was known of the non-sand areas (Manley & Healey 1982, 42; Manley, 1982b). Three areas, on boulder clay have, however, now been the subject of excavation and so perhaps the matter can now be further considered. Site D, on boulder clay, produced only 38 lithic pieces, and these are probably mainly post-Mesolithic. Excavations on the south side of the Town Ditch yielded only a handful of prehistoric lithic material (Manley, 1981; 1987). Work on the east side also produced similar results (Manley, 1982a). This, still limited, evidence from the three boulder clay sites is in sharp contrast to the sand areas and some equation with the latter areas and Mesolithic activity seems probable. The sand may have been chosen for its special vegetation cover and good drainage, but the position in which it occurs may also have been important. The sand forms a low promontory which provides both protection from flooding and good visibility over the neighbourhood – factors which were later appreciated by the builders of the various medieval defences.

Jochim (1976, 50) has suggested three major factors in the location of hunter-gatherer settlements: (1) proximity of economic resources; (2) shelter and protection from the elements; and (3) view for observation of game and strangers. Rhuddlan's topography fits well with (3) and good drainage and protection from floodwater relate to (2). Concerning (1), the economic potential for settlement of such river estuary areas as Rhuddlan has often been commented upon (eg Jacobi, 1973; Paludien-Muller, 1978). Manley (1982b) has attempted to reconstruct the environment and

subsistence potential of the Rhuddlan area for a number of periods including the Mesolithic. He pointed out 'that estuaries are among the most productive primary ecological zones' and that such areas 'may have carried the highest densities of populations during the Mesolithic'.

In assessing the potential for the area in regard to hunter-gatherer communities Manley (ibid) considered the question of seasonal occupation and pointed out the likely economic pull of the area during the winter, especially as at this time of year such an area is 'likely to have provided significant grazing areas for such animals as red deer, roe deer, wild boar and aurochs'. He also pointed out that such lowland sites as Rhuddlan, large and sprawling with multiple foci, are usually interpreted as winter base camps. This standard interpretation owes a lot to the seasonal model developed around Star Carr (Clark, 1954; 1972). The Star Carr model portrayed Early Mesolithic groups occupying relatively large lowland campsites during the winter while during the summer they broke up into smaller groups and moved into surrounding upland areas. This annual shift was seen as replicating the behaviour of red deer considered to be the main food source. Many Mesolithic sites, including Rhuddlan, have been interpreted using this classic model or variants of it. The Star Carr model has, however, in recent years been thoroughly reassessed and shown to be seriously flawed in many aspects, and the evidence for its seasonal use demonstrated to be incorrect (Pitts, 1979; Grigson, 1981; Legge & Rowley-Conwy, 1988). It is now realised that a far more balanced pattern of ungulate exploitation is reflected in the Star Carr evidence and that there was not such reliance on red deer as was thought (Pitts, 1979). This more balanced exploitation pattern accords well with the evidence for the Early Mesolithic of Northern Europe (eg Bay-Petersen, 1978). The ideas about the annual movements of red deer can now be seen to have been based on inappropriate field studies; the work of Ingebristen (1924) and Darling (1969) was unrepresentative because it dealt with extreme and peripheral environments not comparable with the pre-boreal conditions of the Vale of Pickering. It is now known that red deer are not primarily open country dwellers but well-adapted to woodland areas where they live in small stable groups throughout the year (Legge & Rowley-Conwy, 1988). It is also realised that hunter-gatherers can have a range of economic strategies which may involve varied annual patterns of movement (eg Dennell, 1983, 147–8).

The classic Star Carr model is therefore no longer relevant to the interpretation of a site like Rhuddlan. Hunter-gatherers in the Vale of Clwyd are unlikely to have subsisted primarily on a single ungulate species, red deer, but would have had a far more balanced exploitation strategy involving a mixture of resources such as roe deer, elk, auroch, wild pig, migrating fish, marsh birds, small mammals and a range of plants including hazelnuts (the only item for which there is direct evidence at Rhuddlan). Rhuddlan need not have been the winter base for a large scale annual migratory cycle from lowland to upland. Such an area may have had the subsistence potential for the whole year and could have been the permanent home for a community (as has been argued by Bonsall [1981]. Alternatively it may have been a major base with small specialist groups travelling to the uplands to hunt in summer and others dispersed to exploit resources in the lowlands.

11.3.5 Other Mesolithic sites in the Rhuddlan area

It can be reliably predicted that the major settlement at Rhuddlan will prove to be linked to a range of ancillary sites. It has been suggested that Star Carr may have been associated with specialised hunting sites and butchery sites (Jacobi, 1978, 316). This was based on the relatively small number of microburins and because certain elements were missing from the faunal assemblage. The concept of specialised hunting sites is certainly relevant to Rhuddlan which has a similar sparsity of microburins to Star Carr. Such sites would be typified by small quantities of lithics amongst which there would be relatively large numbers of microburins in relation to microliths. Sites for the procurement of raw materials may also exist in the Vale of Clwyd, on the valley edges near the scree slopes where Carboniferous chert could be collected. At such sites there might have been initial knapping which would yield distintive debitage. There should also be burial sites. Mesolithic burial sites in Britain are rare, but are now being dated from the specialised context of caves, such as Aveline's Hole and Gough's Cave, Paviland, Kent's Cavern and others (Housely, 1991). Caves occur in the limestone of North East Wales and have produced human skeletal material (Dawkins, 1874; 1901) These human remains have been assumed to be Neolithic but a possibility exists that some are Mesolithic; Gop Cave has produced Mesolithic material (see below) along with Neolithic artefacts and it cannot be certain which are associated with the human burials.

Though a range of sites can be predicted for the Rhuddlan area the actual evidence on the ground is extremely sparse. Within a 10 km circle around Rhuddlan only two sites of potentially Early Mesolithic date are known. Nant Hall Road, Prestatyn, has Early Mesolithic microliths among a large mixed lithic assemblage (Wainwright, 1963). Gop Cave, investigated and poorly recorded in the late 19th century, has produced Early material from the Cave itself and from the hillslope around (Dawkins 1901; personal observation of material at the National Museum of Wales). If the area searched is slightly more than doubled, the site at Aled reservoir is included from which Early Mesolithic material has been identified from amongst a mixed assemblage (White, 1978; Jacobi, 1980). Evidence for the Early Mesolithic is thus limited, though from varied locations, and indicates the use of the coastal plain, caves and uplands as well as the river valley location of Rhuddlan. This sparsity of information pertains to the whole of Wales, except for the coastal areas of the South and South West (David, 1989), and particularly affects our knowledge of inland and upland areas, despite an occasional site such as Gwernvale in the Usk valley (Britnell & Savory, 1984).

The 1969–73 excavations produced a small quantity of Later Mesolithic material which, together with nearby Hendre, shows that the Rhuddlan area continued to be a focus of activity. The Later Mesolithic site is not quite as isolated as that of the Early Mesolithic. Bryn Newydd, Prestatyn, a short distance from Rhuddlan, produced an assemblage in which micro-scalene triangles are the predominant microlith type; the site appears to have covered a large area (Clark, 1938; 1939). There was also activity around Gop Cave as the collections from it include several Later Mesolithic microliths, though none is recorded from the inside of the cave. An antler mattock found at Rhyl foreshore in 1910 is also relevant. It came from a 'hollow in the blue clay at a point where the tide had worn away the overlying forest bed stratum' (Davies, 1949, 327, Fig 143; Smith, 1989, Fig 5c). The mattock, now in the National Museum of Wales, has a radiocarbon date of 6560 ± 80 BP (4610 BC) (OxA–1009) (Hedges et al, 1988). Inland, a series of sites are well known at Brenig (Lynch et al, 1974; Lynch, 1975) and Later Mesolithic activity is attested at the Aled reservoir (Jacobi, 1980).

Future fieldwork should produce more sites and allow Rhuddlan to be better set in context. The extensive use of Carboniferous chert, used on all Mesolithic sites known so far in the Vale of Clwyd, should help distinguish surface scatters from those of the Neolithic and Bronze Age which are likely to be typified by the predominant use of flint. The recognition of Carboniferous chert in upland areas away from its source would establish wider links for Rhuddlan in the same way that studies of raw material types are making it possible to link upland sites in South Wales with areas on the coast (Barton & Berridge in prep).

Acknowledgments
We are grateful to Dr R Taylor and Mr A J J Goode of the British Geological Survey for comments on geology; to Sandy Morris for the drawings, and to Dr R Jacobi, Dr N Barton and Alison Roberts for constructive comments. Photographs are by David Garner (Total Publicity, Sidmouth). (Peter Berridge & Henrietta Quinnell)

Mrs Susan Barnes, Mr Don Claugher, and Mr John Spratt of the Microscope Unit of the Natural History Unit of the Natural History Museum are gratefully acknowledged for their invaluable technical advice and assistance. Nick Barton and Simon Collcutt provided geological specimens from North Wales for use in the experiments and provided stimulating commentary and discussion throughout the study. The plates were produced by the Photographic Department of the Natural History Department. (Alison Roberts)

12 Between the Mesolithic and the Iron Age, with a study of a Bronze Age pottery group in Pit C46   Peter Berridge

12.1 Bronze Age pottery

12.1.1 Introduction

Four sites, A, D, E and M, produced pottery of probable Bronze Age date. Prehistoric contexts with sherds were: C46, Site A, a pit with parts of at least fifteen vessels; J102, Site E, a pit with a small Early Bronze Age urn and cremation; a group of related features in soil H8 in the north east of Site E, postholes H16, H34, H37, H38, and pit H24. Sites D and M produced single sherds in residual contexts. E J Pieksma and Dr D F Williams (12.1.3) report that all the pottery was made of similar clay from a local source.

12.1.2 Descriptions

Site A (Figs 12.1–2)

Pit C46. Rim sherds represent a minimum of fifteen vessels, with the majority of all sherds from a single large vessel PP1. Three rimless sherds with cordons either relate to vessels among the fifteen, only represented by rim sherds, or to additional vessels. All the pottery is very similar in overall appearance, although individual sherds may show considerable colour variation across and between surfaces which derive from the vagaries of firing techniques. Most sherds show irregular finish with large grits frequently protruding; only the upper parts of some vessels have been smoothly finished. Rims typically are heavy flattened, T-shaped or bevelled.

The most frequent decoration, on at least ten vessels (eg PP6, PP8), is a single row of holes pierced, before firing, just below the rim. In six cases (eg PP8) the holes go right through the vessel wall and will be termed perforations. In four (eg PP6) they do not pierce the vessel wall and will be termed indentations. At least four vessels (PP15, 16, 17 and 18) had cordons, three decorated with slanting slashed lines and one (PP18) plain. PP5 and 6 have similar slashed lines slanting down from the top of their rims. PP14 has a more complex design of two horizontal rows of slashed lines slanted in opposite directions. Indentations and slashed lines are found together on PP6, 14 and 15. Only PP1 can be definitely said to be undecorated.

PP1 (Fig 12.1) Much of this vessel, particularly its upper part, has been reconstructed, involving the majority of sherds from the pit. Barrel-shaped but narrows sharply towards base; simply rounded rim, thick walled and undecorated. Rim diameter about 215mm, base 125mm.

PP2 (Fig 12.1) Rim of bucket shaped vessel. Rim has distinct internal bevel with externally a slight groove just below it. No trace of decoration. Rim diameter about 295mm.

PP3 (Fig 12.1) Rim similar to PP2, though with more pronounced interior bevel giving an almost T-shaped profile; no external groove. Rim diameter about 335mm.

PP4 (Fig 12.1) Small plain rim sherd with slight internal bevel.

PP5 (Fig 12.1) Two rim sherds of identical form, probably from the same vessel. Pronounced internal bevel. Decoration of short oblique slashed lines on the external rim angle.

PP6 (Fig 12.1) Rim sherd with pronounced internal bevel. External decoration of oblique slashed lines running a short way down from the rim. Below, about 30mm from the rim top, is a single circular deep indentation.

PP7 (Fig 12.1) Two rim sherds of nearly identical form, probably from the same vessel. Rim slightly expanded with an external groove below it. In the groove, c 18mm below the rim top, is a line of circular deep indentations. The four surviving holes are set about 25mm apart.

PP8 (Fig 12.1) Rim sherd with slight internal bevel. c 10mm below the rim top is a row of circular perforations 22–25mm apart.

PP9 (Fig 12.1) T-shaped rim sherd. 15–18mm below the rim top is an irregular row of perforations 15 and 24mm apart.

PP10 (Fig 12.1) Rim sherd with pronounced internal bevel. c 20mm below the rim top are two peforations 35mm apart, surviving on the edges of the sherd.

PP11a and **PP11b** (Fig 12.1) Two slightly expanded rim sherds with internal bevel or flattening. Both have part of a single large perforation set 20 and 25mm respectively below the rim top. Despite difference in profile probably from the same vessel.

PP12 (Fig 12.1) T-shaped rim sherd. Line of three circular perforations, 24 and 38mm apart, set

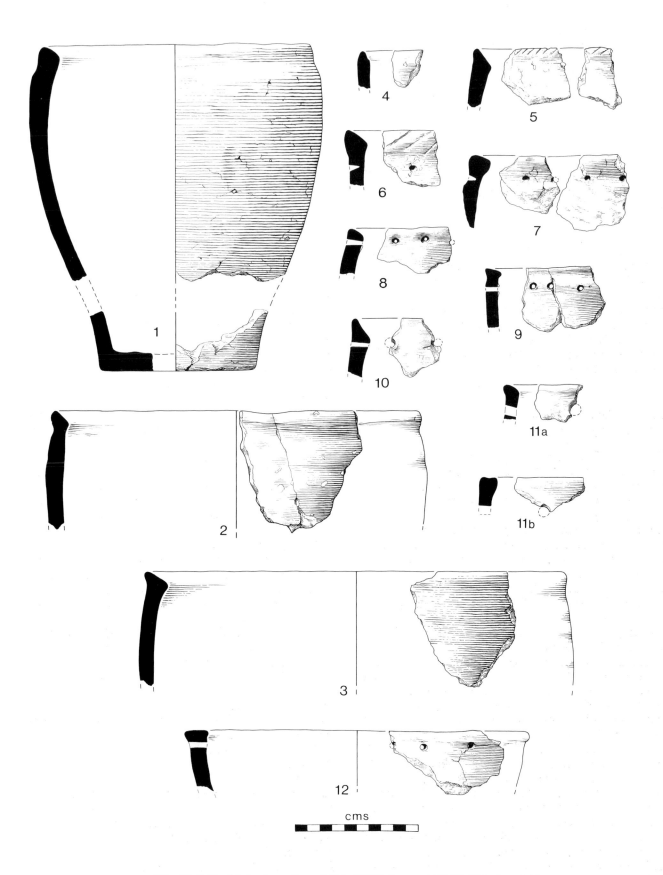

Fig 12.1 Prehistoric pottery PP1–PP12 from pit C46, Site A. ×1/3.

10–14mm below the rim top. Rim diameter about 280mm.

PP13 (Fig 12.2) Rim sherd from barrel shaped vessel. Rim rounded in profile and slightly everted. Circular perforation, and possible trace of a second, 27mm below rim top. Rim diameter about 300mm.

PP14 (Fig 12.2) T-shaped rim sherds from barrel-shaped vessel. Below the rim are two rows of slashed lines running in opposite directions to create a herring bone pattern. Set through this, 16–20mm below the rim top, is a row of circular indentations 20–30mm apart. One has been made by two overlapping holes. Rim diameter about 295mm.

PP15 (Fig 12.2) Large sherd from barrel shaped vessel with girth cordon. T-shaped rim. One indentation formed by two overlapping circular holes, and part of a second, c 18mm below rim top; the indentations are 55mm apart. Applied girth cordon decorated with angled slashed lines. Rim diameter about 300mm.

PP16 (Fig 12.2) Sherd with applied cordon decorated by slashed lines angled as on PP15.

PP17 (Fig 12.2) Sherd with applied cordon decorated by slashed lines angled in the opposite direction to those on PP15 and PP16.

PP18 (Fig 12.2) Sherd with a plain applied cordon.

Ditch I A52. Five plain residual sherds (not illus), similar in fabric and general appearance to those from pit C46; one sherd shows the beginnings of a base.

Site E

Pit J102 Small pit containing PP19 set upright containing human cremated bone. Top of vessel had been removed by disturbance in the overlying soil layer.

PP19 (Fig 12.2) Base, girth and neck of small vessel, surviving height about 105mm, diameter of girth 120mm. Fabric soft red and sandy with small and medium grits. Decoration by impressed single lines of twisted cord; surviving zone of decoration defined by a continuous line around the girth and a second, at the top of the zone, around the narrowest part of the neck; between are alternate blocks of five vertical and four horizontal rows. Because the amount and shape of the destroyed top are unknown, PP19 can not be certainly described either as a collared urn or a food vessel. The surviving part, though very small, could belong to either category.

H8 Soil layer associated with postholes H37 etc. Mostly small fragments but including PP20. These can be divided on fabric and general appearance into three groups. The first with ten sherds and PP20 is generally similar to the C46 pit group. The second group, of four sherds, is buff to reddish orange and has no visible grit. The third, a single sherd, is dark brown throughout, has very fine grit only, and a much finer external finish than the others.

PP20 (Fig 12.2) T-shaped rim sherd from undecorated bucket type vessel. Rim diameter about 245mm.

Pit H24 Two plain body sherds. Fabric as in C46.

Posthole H34 Four plain body sherds. Fabric as in C46.

Posthole H37 Single sherd from pot base. Fabric as in C46.

Posthole H38 Small body sherds, almost certainly from one vessel; one decorated by two short slashed angled lines. Fabric as in C46 pit.

Site D

PP21 (Fig 12.2) Rim sherd with slight internal bevel. Fabric as in C46. Residual in medieval context O14.

Site M

Single body sherd, fabric as in C46, residual in late prehistoric sand M55.

12.1.3 Petrological examination

E J Pieksma and D F Williams

Introduction

A number of plain and decorated sherds from the 1969–73 excavations were submitted for a detailed fabric examination in thin section under the petrological microscope. The main object of the analysis was twofold: (1) to characterise in detail the various fabrics involved and compare them with each other, and (2) if possible to suggest likely source areas for the pottery. The question of provenance is particularly important for the pit group, C46. Also provided from Rhuddlan was a sample of local boulder clay which was broken up and the coarser inclusions identified.

All the sherds submitted were initially studied macroscopically with the aid of a binocular microscope ($\times$ 20). Munsell colour charts are referred to together with free descriptive terms. The solid geology of the Rhuddlan area is made up of Bunter Sandstone, Pebble Beds and Basal Breccias, with Millstone Grit, Culm Measures and Carboniferous Limestone close by (Geol Survey of Gt Britain 1" series). The surface geology of the region is composed mainly of Boulder Clays bordered by Glacial Sands or Gravels and Marine or Estuarine Alluvium. The variety of rocks found in the drift deposits suggest that many come from extra-Welsh sources, such as the Southern Uplands of Scotland, the Lake District and North Eastern England (Smith & George, 1961).

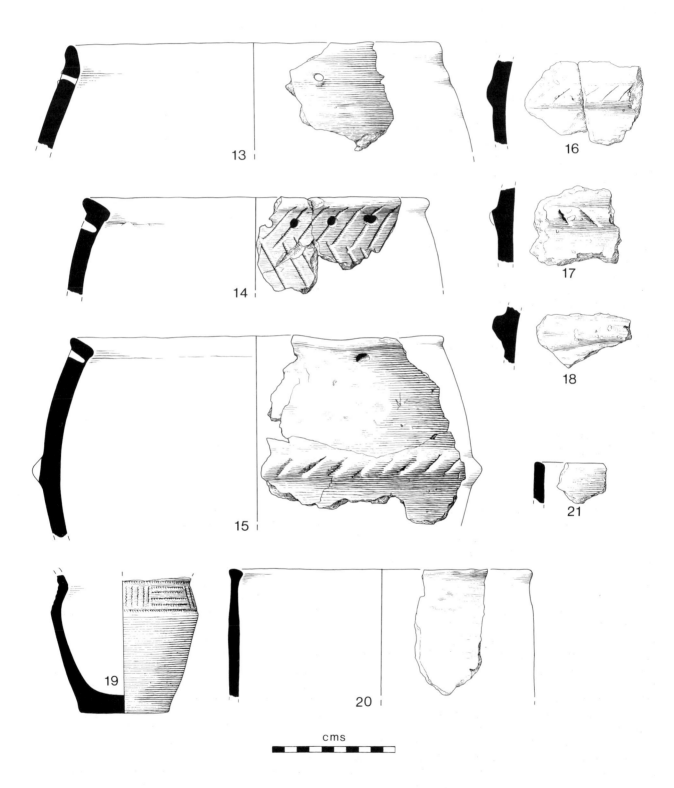

Fig 12.2 Prehistoric pottery PP13–PP18 from pit C46, Site A; PP19 pit J102, Site E; PP20 soil H8, Site E; PP21 residual, Site D. ×1/3.

Petrology and Fabric

The majority of sherds submitted are in a thick, fairly hard, rough fabric with frequent large inclusions of rock clearly visible. Surface colour varies from light reddish-brown (2.5YR 6/4) to very dark grey (5YR 3/1) or sometimes black (2.5YR N2.5), with a largely grey core. All of the vessels from the pit group C46, PP1–18, were thin-sectioned, as was the Early Bronze Age Vessel PP19 and a representative selection of the larger sherds from the remaining material. A number of sherds were rather small in size and thin sectioning of these would have left little if any of the sherd remaining.

The most commonly occurring non-plastic inclusions present in the pottery sampled are fragments of granite and microgranite, devitrified rhyolite, lava, fine-grained silica, sandstone and quartzite, and discrete grains of quartz, felspar, biotite, amphibole and clinopyroxene. The majority of the sherds contained 'mixed assemblages', that is more than one of the inclusion types listed. Quite a number of sherds in fact contained three or four different types, while very few had only one inclusion type present. In view of the overall results and taking into account the possible sampling error (Williams & Jenkins, 1976), it is not clear how significant, if at all, this may be.

Analysis of the boulder clay sample provided showed a similar range and texture of inclusions to those found in the pottery sampled. There did not appear, however, to be as many fragments of devitrified rhyolite in the clay as were found in the pottery. This may be explained for example if the clay is from a very heterogeneous deposit, with other local boulder clays richer in devitrified rhyolite. Certainly on this evidence there would seem to be no reason to suspect other than a fairly local origin for the Rhuddlan Bronze Age pottery. The materials utilized in the making of the pottery could come from the Boulder Clay and Drift deposits of the region, which are known to contain the range of inclusions sampled (Smith & George, 1961), rather than from clays derived from the solid geology of the area.

12.1.4 Discussion

Later Bronze Age ceramics, particularly pit groups of any size, are rare in Wales and the group from pit C46 is so far unique from the Principality. Because of its importance the Rhuddlan group has been briefly discussed in most accounts of the Welsh Later Bronze Age written since its excavation in 1969 (eg Savory, 1971a, 1976, 1980b; Burgess, 1976, 1980a, 1980b). It has been treated as an extension of Burgess's (1976, 94) 'wider Deverel-Rimbury' province. This was in line with the excavator's tentative suggestion that the vessels 'have their best parallels in Middle Bronze Age contexts from South and South West England' (Miles, 1972). The suggested Deverel-Rimbury connection can now be examinined by comparing

the Rhuddlan material with the geographically closest Deverel-Rimbury related groups (Bromfield, Shrops, and Ryton-on-Dunsmore, Warks; both sites are cremation cemeteries with radiocarbon dates) and any relevant Welsh material. It must be emphasised that the size of the pottery groups is small, except at Bromfield, and any conclusions must be tentative.

Bromfield has three radiocarbon dates ranging from the 16th to the 8th centuries BC (Stanford, 1982). Less than half the 150 cremation pits contained urns. Many of the 51 vessels, generally of bucket and barrel shapes, showed the classic Deverel-Rimbury traits of applied cordons, horseshoes and knob-shaped lugs, and of decoration by finger tip impressions; simple slashed decoration was less common. But the row of circular holes below the rim, found on 67% of the Rhuddlan vessels, is absent. Conversely finger-tip impressions, found on at least 30% of the much larger Bromfield group, are absent at Rhuddlan as are applied horseshoes and lugs.

Ryton-on-Dunsmore has two radiocarbon dates suggesting activity from at least the 10th to the 8th centuries BC (Bateman, 1976–77). Of 27 cremation pits, eight produced pottery representing at least eleven vessels; there were also some sherds from other contexts. Finger-tip decoration occurs on at least eight vessels, but simple slashed designs were, as at Bromfield, less common. There are several applied cordons and one instance of knob-shaped lugs but unlike Bromfield no horseshoes. The typical Rhuddlan decoration of the row of holes below the rim is doubtfully represented by one sherd with indentations. This sherd, F18, is not illustrated but its description mentions 'a series of impressions made with a broken bone or stick' set beneath the rim on the exterior (Longworth, 1976–7). The Ryton-on-Dunsmore pottery like that from Bromfield differs markedly in its decorative traits from the Rhuddlan group.

From Wales six sites have pottery groups which may be assigned broadly to the Middle Bronze Age, three from South Wales, Lesser Garth, Culver Hole and Ogof-yr-esgyrn, Four Crosses from mid-Wales, and Dyffryn Ardudwy and Llandegai from North Wales.

The three South Welsh sites have been discussed in detail by Savory (1958; 1976; 1980b). All are caves where deposits have been disturbed and so their pottery groups cannot strictly be regarded as closed assemblages. Culverhole, Glam, produced a maximum of eleven vessels (Savory, 1958, Fig 12, & p 166). Decoration is confined to simple slashed lines, rows of holes below the rim (on two vessels) and a single plain cordon. At Ogof-y-esgyrn, Brecks, five vessels may be represented (Savory, 1958, 45–6, Fig 4, Nos 1–5). The only decoration is a row of slashed slanting lines above the shoulder on one pot and an unperforated horizontal lug on a second. Lesser Garth, Glam, produced sherds of six or seven vessels (Savory, 1980b, 159, 220, Fig 72,

Nos 505: 1–6). The decoration consisted of knob-shaped lugs, simple lines of slanted slashes and finger-tipping along a rim top and on a cordon. Of the three groups that from Culverhole is most closely comparable to that from Rhuddlan in the rows of holes below the rim, the absence of finger-tipping and of lugs. The other two, particularly Lesser Garth with both lugs and finger tipping, appear more comparable with the West Midlands material than with Rhuddlan.

In mid-Wales the eight ring ditches at Four Crosses, Llandysilio, Mont, (Warillow, Owen & Britnell, 1986) produced Middle Bronze Age pottery from undated contexts; the material cannot be regarded as a closed assemblage. The most important group consists of three bucket shaped urns from site 1, one with traces of simple cord decoration, another with a single indentation below the rim, considered to be the remnant of a row of holes. Bucket shaped urns may also be represented by the plain body and base sherds and single rim with slashed decoration from site 5. The Four Crosses material is too fragmetary for reliable comparison with other groups, but its general nature – and in particular the possible row of holes – hint at links with the Rhuddlan pit groups.

The chambered tomb of Dyffryn Ardudwy, Merioneth, was excavated in 1963 (Powell, 1973). Sherds from several flat based, bucket shaped vessels were found in the eastern chamber and originally attributed variously to the Middle and Late Neolithic and the Early Bronze Age (*ibid*; Lynch, 1969). Savory (1980b, 86 & 153) later suggested that this pottery, Powell's vessels F, G, H, J, relates to a secondary deposit of the Middle Bronze Age. The deposit is not a closed assemblage as the eastern chamber was badly disturbed in recent times and only part of vessel J with cremated human bones seems likely to have been *in situ*. Vessels F and G are similar, plain except for a row of holes set below each rim. H, represented by body sherds only, is decorated with numerous finger nail impressions. J is more elaborately decorated with a groove around the shoulder, at least two rows of finger tip impressions, and, apparently, randomly distributed small oval impressions. F and G are closely comparable to the Rhuddlan group with their rows of holes; examination of the pieces shows that fabric and appearance are also comparable. H and J have decorative features not found at Rhuddlan. J is similar in general appearance, rim form and fabric to the Rhuddlan vessels but is distinctive because of the use of finger-tipping. It is worth confirming that finger-tipping is present on J as described by Powell (1973) since Savory's (1980b, 153) more recent account seems to cast doubt on this. The furrow on J is also confirmed though the published drawings overemphasise the slight and indistinct trace present. The use of random finger nail impressions, as opposed to finger-tip impressions, on H does not occur on much Welsh pottery and is absent from the West Midland sites. The decoration on H would find better parallels among late Neolithic and Early Bronze Age wares and so it may not belong with the other vessels.

The henge monuments at Llandegai, Caerns, excavated in 1967 but not yet fully published, produced a group of probable Middle Bronze Age pottery. The author has been shown unpublished drawings of pottery from the upper ditch levels of henge B associated with a hearth (briefly referred to in Houlder, 1968, 220). There are six rim sherds with flattened and slightly expanded profiles, of which four have single perforations just below the rim and could come from the same vessel. There are also larger sherds from one or two vessels with rounded, slightly inturned rims, rows of deep indentations just below, and lines of angled slashes extending down from the rim top. This pottery had been thought to be Iron Age but provides the closest parallel, in Wales, to the group from Rhuddlan.

Summarising the evidence presented so far, the Rhuddlan pottery shows affinities with that from Llandegai, Culver Hole, Four Crosses and Dyffryn Ardudwy, rows of holes below the rim, rows of angled slashes, absence of lugs or any applied decoration apart from cordons, and the rarity of finger-tipping. It is less similar to that from Bromfield, Ryton-on-Dunsmore, Lesser Garth, and perhaps Ogof-yr-esgyrn, where finger-tipping is frequent, lugs are present and rows of circular holes are virtually absent. It may be tentatively suggested that in the Middle Bronze Age much of Wales formed part of a broad ceramic zone typified by the Rhuddlan pit group. South East Wales lay outside this zone; its ceramics were more comparable to those of areas in the West Midlands and in Southern England. Occasional single finds seem to support this division. A barrel shaped vessel, plain except for a line of perforations below the rim, comes from a barrow at Llanarth, Cards (Savory, 1980b, 153, Fig 72 No 462). A vessel with a row of multiple perforations is reported, though not yet fully published, from St Govan's Head, Bosherton, Pembs (Savory, 1970). In contrast is the fragmentary vessel from Llanblethian, Glam, in South East Wales (Savory, 1980b, 156, Fig 72 No 478:17). This, from the upper fill of a barrow ditch, has a cordon decorated with finger tipping similar to some from Lesser Garth and Ryton-on-Dunsmore. These appear to be the only distinctive relevant single finds from Wales; the vessel from Llandegla, Denb (Savory 1980b, 153, Fig 72 No 461) is not distinctive as its relatively simple slashed decoration, not on the rim top, is common to both areas.

It is important to stress that the definition of the Rhuddlan group is based on a combination of decorative traits and their relative frequency or rarity but not on their exclusive presence or absence. Some overlapping of the main decorative traits into other groups is to be expected. Lines of circular holes below the rim top are not an exclusive feature of the Rhuddlan group. There is its occasional occurrence in the West Midlands, at Ryton-on-Dunsmore and perhaps on a single vessel from Barford, Warks (Smith, 1969, Fig 66 No 15). It is a rare feature of the Deverel-Rimbury wares from Southern England (Calkin, 1962, 30–3, Fig 12 No 6; Hawkes, 1935, Fig 1d) as it is of related wares in Northern England (McInness, 1968; Kinnes & Longworth, 1985, 42, No 27:5), in South West Scotland (Morrison, 1968, Fig 2, No 5, Fig 11, No 81) and in Ireland (Raftery, 1981, 177, Fig 31). These rows of holes are a far more significant decorative element in parts of the Thames valley, particularly Middlesex (eg Abercromby, 1912, Pl 95 No 470a; Barrett, 1973). They are also found in Essex among the Ardleigh group (Couchman, 1975) and in Norfolk (eg Lawson, 1980; Longworth, 1981). In all these areas this trait was used in combination with frequent finger tipping, applied horseshoes and lugs.

Savory (1958) originally suggested a Welsh ceramic zone defined by the occurrence of rows of holes as a decorative trait, which he later (1970; 1976) expanded as an 'Irish Sea ceramic zone'. Subsequently, as it became apparent that the Irish material was not contemporary with that from Wales and that rows of holes occurred very widely, he withdrew the suggestion (1980b). The negation of this zone was strongly supported by Burgess (1980b). Both authors, however, placed too much stress on this single decorative trait. It should be repeated that the Rhuddlan ceramic zone, suggested, is based on a combination of decorative traits and not on their exclusive presence or absence.

The close dating of the Rhuddlan group is difficult as there are no directly associated radiocarbon dates and so little of the material comes from closed contexts (it is presumed that the bucket and barrel forms and the general range of decorative traits place it somewhere in the middle of the Bronze Age). The Four Crosses barrow cemetery (Warillow, Owen & Britnell, 1986) gives possible *post quem* dating. Here the suggested Rhuddlan type pottery is stratigraphically late in the sequence. The relevant pottery from site 1 comes from contexts later than those associated with radiocarbon dates of 1470 BC ± 65 (CAR–666) and 1360 BC ± 70 (CAR–667).

Possible *ante quem* dating may come from the Breiddin, Mont, where the first hilltop defended enclosure is assigned on a series of radiocarbon dates to the 8th century BC (Musson, 1991, 28). The large associated ceramic assemblage (1677 sherds) was made up of simple forms, mostly from 'barrel-shaped, conical or situlate jars, though there are a few rims which probably belong to open bowls' (*ibid*, 119, Figs 52–3). Jars had round or internally bevelled rims, open bowls round or flattened rims. Only three sherds had definite decoration, cabling on the rim No 70, an impression circle No 79 and a plain horizontal cordon

No 76. The excavator considered that the Breiddin pottery should be regarded as 'a control sample of late Bronze Age pottery from a defended hilltop settlement in the central Welsh borderland in about the 8th century BC' (*ibid*, 119) and regarded comparisons with material, from Ivinghoe Beacon, Runneymede Bridge and Eldon's Seat as of 'tenuous value' although there are broad similarities. The Breiddin material, well dated, should postdate the Rhuddlan group. Radiocarbon dates 895 BC ± 95 (V–122) and 765 BC ± 95 (V–125) are also available for Late Bronze Age activity at Dinorben hillfort, but the associated pottery is too fragmentary to be of value for comparative purposes (Savory, 1971b).

On this limited evidence the Rhuddlan pottery might be tentatively placed between 1300 BC and 900 BC, with the possibility that its start may eventually be further backdated.

12.2 Discussion of Neolithic and Bronze Age activity
12.2.1 Lithics

Only three pieces, all of flint and residual, are demonstrably post-Mesolithic, leaf-shaped arrowheads 158–9, Site A and scale-flaked scraper 160, Site V. The arrowheads are probably Earlier Neolithic, the scraper Later Neolithic or Earlier Bronze Age. It is unlikely that these are isolated pieces but it is only possible to distinguish diagnostic later material from the mass of residual Mesolithic lithics. The percentage of flint to chert from different contexts may be a chronological indicator as both Neolithic and Earlier Bronze Age activity should show predominant use of flint with little or no Carboniferous chert. Table 10.2 shows a slight increase in the proportion of flint to chert in post-Mesolithic contexts. In the small Site D lithic group most of the 38 pieces were flint and sufficiently diagnostic to be assigned a post-Mesolithic date. Site D was not important in the Mesolithic and so later material is easily distinguished; similar amounts of later lithics may be present elsewhere, masked by the vast quantity of Mesolithic material.

12.2.2 Pottery and associated features

Prehistoric pottery was recovered from ten contexts but this cannot be taken as a reliable indicator of the scale of later prehistoric activity, as there was so much later human activity and erosion.

Features may be assigned to the Bronze Age on Sites A and E and, possibly, M. On Site E patchy soil H8 was associated with post-Mesolithic but prehistoric features, and on Site M some of the soil levels overlying Mesolithic M26 may be of later prehistoric date.

On Site A pit C46 produced a quantity of Middle Bronze Age pottery, and a small number of charred cereal grains (15.4). C58, a posthole cutting C46, and A51, truncated by the Norman Borough Ditch, produced no artefacts; they may be prehistoric because their sandy fills contrasted with the humic darker soils in later features. Bronze Age activity on the site apart from pit C46 is indicated by residual pottery in Ditch I (A52). The quantity of pottery from C46 suggests that the pit related to a substantial area of Middle Bronze Age activity, the remainder destroyed by later erosion and human activities.

Pit J102 (Fig 6.1), Site E, produced an Early Bronze Age urn and cremation (Fig 12.2, PP19). With so much later disturbance and erosion a small barrow mound over J102 could have been removed, although any ditch should have survived. In the north east corner of the site, a group of features close together was cut from within soil H8, which contained small sherds similar to the C46 material. Apart from scoop pit H24, these features were probably postholes (H16–18. 34, 37, 38, 42, 73), H42 with a ring of packing stones being the clearest example. Four of the postholes (H24, 34, 37, 38) produced Middle Bronze Age pottery. Some form of structure is obviously represented but so much of the area is eroded that no plan can be reconstructed. The structure may have been of some duration as H37 apppeared to replace H38.

12.2.3 The broader context

Excavations at Rhuddlan have taken place subsequent to 1973 (1.5, especially Manley & Healey, 1982; Manley, 1987) but none produced evidence for post-Mesolithic activity. Two Neolithic stray finds are recorded from the area. A ground stone axe found near Rhuddlan Vicarage has been identified by Professor F W Shotton as Group VII, Graig Llwyd (Clough & Cummins, 1988, 251 Flintshire No 12). A rim sherd of Peterborough pottery, probably Mortlake style, was reported as found in a 'drainage ditch' near Rhuddlan though the precise location is unclear (F Lynch pers comm). There is a possible barrow 2.5 km south east of Rhuddlan parish church, at Maes y Groes on Criccin Farm (at NGR SJ 043 539; Davies, 1949, 323); although recorded as a natural mound surmounted by a cross, its shape suggests a barrow.

There is a relatively dense concentration of Neolithic finds to the east of the Vale of Clwyd which includes the settlements of Gwaenysgor and Diserth (Savory, 1980a, 211, Fig 5.2). Tyddyn Bleiddin, the only recorded tomb (Savory, 1980a, Fig 5.4; Lynch, 1969), in the Elwy valley on the west of the Vale of Clwyd, appears to be a long cairn with at least two side chambers (Davies, 1929). Late 19th century excavations produced little result (Dawkins, 1874, 161–9). The two other tombs claimed for the Vale appear to be misidentified (Davies, 1929, 199-200, 398; Powell et al, 1969, 307-8). The sparsity of tombs in the Vale of Clwyd area, compared with those linked to the

other concentrations of Neolithic material in North Wales, may be due to a different burial style which exploits local geological features. Caves and fissures in the Carboniferous Limestone bordering the Vale of Clwyd contain a series of burials, some of which are almost certainly Neolithic. The best known examples are Gop, near Prestatyn (Dawkins, 1901; Glenn, 1935; Davies, 1949) and Rhos Ddigr (Dawkins, 1874, 156–7; Davies, 1929, 165–171; Glenn, 1935). A cave may be viewed as a natural alternative to the artificially constructed chambered tomb or timber mortuary house; cave burials around the Vale of Clwyd may represent a different expression of the practices shown in the chambered tomb groups further west in North Wales. The pattern of Neolithic activity around the mouth of the Vale of Clwyd suggests settlement concentrated in the river valley and low hills on either side with burial restricted to the upland fringe.

The cinerary urn PP19 remains the only Early Bronze Age material from the immediate Rhuddlan area, but, as for the Neolithic, it fits into the broader pattern for the period around the mouth of the Vale of Clwyd. On the Clwydian range to the west is the densest barrow concentration in Wales, and more scattered barrows occur among the hills to the east (Lynch, 1980, 240, Fig 6.4). It is likely the barrow distribution spread down into the river valley, but evidence has been removed by intense agricultural activity on its fertile soils. Ditched burial sites have been picked up as 'ring ditches' by aerial photography in for example the Severn Valley (Whimster, 1989, 16) and it seems highly probable that similar results can be expected in the Clwyd Valley.

For the Middle Bronze Age the 1969–73 excavations suggested a farming settlement which, based on the pottery, dates to between 1300 and 900 BC and has affinities with a contemporary group covering most of Wales except the south east. This settlement may have had one or more foci, not necessarily contemporary. It spread over a considerable area as shown by pottery from Sites D and M. There was a multi-period building of some form on Site E, while pit C46 on Site A, 200m south east, was perhaps originally a grain store reused as a rubbish dump. The soil and situation at Rhuddlan were eminently suitable for prehistoric agriculture and, comparing the Clwyd to river valleys in England, Rhuddlan may eventually be established as part of a large Middle Bronze Age landscape.

Acknowledgments
We are grateful to E J Pieksma and D F Williams of the HBMC Ceramic Petrology Unit, University of Southampton, for their contribution and to J Manley for providing samples of local clays. Frances Lynch was helpful in providing details of relevant chance finds from the area.

13 Iron Age and Romano-British artefacts and synthesis

13.1 Iron Age artefacts

13.1.1 Copper Alloy (Fig 13.1)

SF9 Ring-headed Pin. *T64 soil, date range later prehistoric to c AD 900.*

Length (surviving) 94mm, 3mm in diameter. The ring-head is decorated with incised transverse lines and crosses, badly corroded in part; the shaft has a pronounced shoulder and narrows toward the tip which is broken.

The only general discussion of the type is by Dunning (1934, 269–95). The type is probably to be dated from the 4th century BC onward (Hodson, 1964, 105). Decoration appears rare; an example was found in the Thames at Hammersmith (British Museum, 1905, 147; Dunning, 1934, Fig 3 No 5), and another at Woodeaton, Oxon (Dunning, 1934, Fig 4 No 11). In Clwyd ring-head pins have been found at Dinorben (Gardner & Savory, 1964, 131) and at Prestatyn (Blockley, 1989, Fig 42). The shaft and shoulder of the latter are almost identical to SF9 (the head has been broken off); the Prestatyn pin relates to Period I, the Iron Age occupation, probably dating to the 1st and 2nd centuries BC.

13.1.2 Stone (Fig 13.2)

SF10 Rotary Quern. *Site M posthole 73.* Part of an upper quernstone, around 350mm in diameter; broad groove and raised rim surround distinctly convex hopper with a small arc of the central eye surviving; parts very worn. The stone used (comments by M Owen) is buff quartzitic sandstone containing many quartz pebbles and the visible mould of a brachiopod (possibly Schizophoria). This is likely to have originated in the Cefn-Y-Fedw Sandstone of South Flintshire and Denbighshire.

The quern is of the type classified as 'Hunsbury' by Curwen (1941, 16-20, Figs 1–10) dating to the later pre-Roman Iron Age. Roman querns tend to be broader in relation to their height and to lack the distinctive decorative groove. Part of a similar quern, but in sandstone came from Period II at Prestatyn (Blockley, 1989, 125) where contexts of this Period, late 1st and early 2nd centuries AD, produced a number of 'Iron Age' finds such as VCP (see 13.1.4). The Hunsbury type is replaced in the full Roman period in Britain by simpler, flatter quern forms, but it is not known how late it remained in use and whether the examples from

Rhuddlan and Prestatyn should be regarded as residual. At Rhuddlan the earliest context with Roman material on Site M lies immediately over M73, the quern findspot.

13.1.3 ? Iron Age Pottery

Gully C43 Three sherds, fine grit, some vegetable temper, reduced, very uneven; dissimilar to all other material found.

Gully T127 Single sherd, fine, grey, sandy with occasional large grits, buff surfaces. It is macroscopically dissimilar to the Bronze Age fabrics (12.1.2), and may possibly compare to some of the few sherds found in Iron Age contexts at Dinorben (Gardner & Savory, 1964, 194).

13.1.4 Coarse ceramic salt containers or VCP

A number of small fragments of oxidised, handmade very coarse ceramic sherds were recovered from Sites T and V. This material has been described until recently as VCP (Very Coarse Pottery) (Gelling & Stanford, 1965), but Morris (1985) has recently shown it to be fragments of vessels used in the manufacture and distribution of salt.

The Rhuddlan fragments were generally oxidised, orange with buff tones especially on the outer surfaces; they contain large, angular rock fragments in a sandy clay matrix. Sherds were generally about 10mm thick and a few displayed the 'collar' features caused by the coarse coil construction of the vessels. The fabric corresponds in all respects to Morris's 'Cheshire Stony VCP' probably produced in the Nantwich area (1985, 366). A sherd from soil T322 had the characteristic white encrustation on its outer surface, formed during manufacture when calcareous clays are mixed with salt water from brine springs and allowed to dry before firing.

This salt ceramic can date from the 5th century BC; Rhuddlan is just on the edge of the 50km radius zone in which the Cheshire fabric has been demonstrated to have spread during the 5th and 4th centuries (Morris, 1985, 367). From the 3rd century BC until the 1st century AD it is widespread over much of North Wales. 68 fragments of Cheshire VCP came from Iron Age, 2nd to 1st centuries BC, levels at Prestatyn and was residual

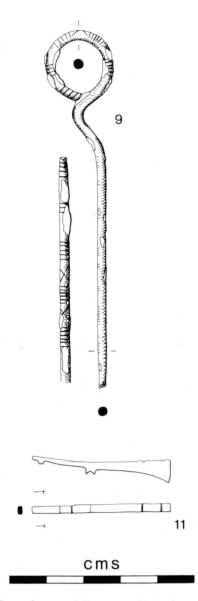

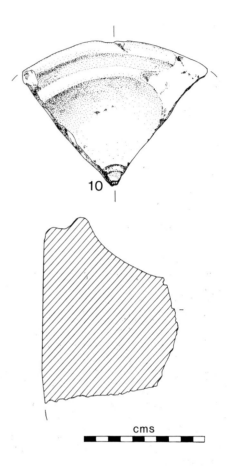

Fig 13.2 Rotary quern fragment SF10 from M73. ×1/3.

or from one closer in form to the cupped pedestals from Mucking, Essex (Jones, 1977, Pl LVI and pers comm).

T127 curved gully around house site: three sherds.

T326 posthole in four-post structure: two sherds.

T126 posthole pre-AD 900: two sherds.

T238 posthole as T126: one sherd 11mm thick.

T220 stakehole as T126: one sherd.

T64 soil (residual): two sherds 10mm thick.

T178 soil (residual): one sherd.

T80 industrial activity (residual): one sherd with both surfaces, 11mm thick, blocky structure with clay pellets.

T275 ditch (residual): one sherd.

T121 as T275: one sherd.

T55 in Ditch III (residual): one sherd.

Fig 13.1 Iron Age and Romano-British copper alloy objects. SF9 from soil T64 (detail shows decoration around ring head). SF10 from pit T151. Full size.

in Romano-British contexts (Blockley 1989, 166; M Blockley pers comm). Other local sites with this material, Iron Age but difficult to date closely, are the hillforts of Dinorben and Moel Hiraddug (Morris, 1985, Table 5).

Contexts with salt container ceramic (VCP)

(Most sherds are so crumbly and abraded that their original thickness cannot be measured.)

T322 soil: one sherd with both surfaces distinct, 14mm thick; one with salt encrustation on surface.

T222 gully: two sherds.

T142 gully: part of a rounded rim, either from a vessel of flared-cone shape (Morris, 1985, Figs 7–8),

V78 pit ? prehistoric: four sherds with clay pellets.

V64 gully ? prehistoric: three sherds.

V68 floor of Structure 5 (residual): two sherds.

V73 soil (residual): one sherd.

V24 hollow (residual): one sherd.

V20 soil (residual): one sherd.

V13 gully (residual): one sherd.

M99 gully, prehistoric: numerous comminuted sherds.

13.2 Romano-British artefacts

13.2.1 Metal (Figs 13.1, 13.3)

SF11 Part of a ? bronze steelyard arm (Fig 13.1). *T151 pit.* 37mm long rectangular sectioned bar, broken at one end. Appears to be calibrated on the upper surface by shallow grooves at 3–5mm intervals. The lower surface has a V-shaped projection which may have pivoted around a point or even have been a fixed point for a moving pointer, but was not a broken suspension ring. There is a trace of a second, broken, projection at the incomplete end of the object. No close parallels are known. A complete steelyard with similar calibrations was found at Marshfield, Glos (Blockley, 1985, 169–70 Fig 53), and another at Colchester (Crummy, 1983, 99 Fig 104).

SF12 Iron ? adze (Fig 13.3). *Gully T71.* 100mm long, maximum width 44mm, thickness 4mm. No exact comparison amongst material from the British Museum published by Manning (1985). B13 (Pl 8 & p 17) comes closest in form, though with a thicker butt. Most adzes are larger and have shaftholes. Most chisels (*ibid* Pl 11) are narrower and thicker. A somewhat similar but thicker tanged blade came from the Period II occupation at Prestatyn (Blockley, 1989, Fig 47).

13.2.2 Stone (not illus)

Worn fragments of Niedermendig lava probably from a quern, about 33mm by 30mm; no worked surface survives. *Soil M53.* Rhineland lava was often used for querns during the Roman period (A Welfare in Jarrett & Wrathmell, 1981, 224).

13.2.3 Pottery (Fig 13.4)

The assemblage is too small for numerical analysis to be valid. Most of the larger surviving sherds are either of mortaria from Mancetter/Hartshill or of black-burnished BB1 from Dorset. For the other fabrics, the lack of obvious comparanda from Cheshire, suggests, as with Prestatyn (Blockley,

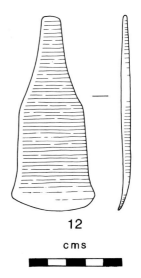

Fig 13.3 Iron ? adze SF 12 from gully T71. ×½

1989, 169), supplies from kiln sites as yet unidentified in North Wales.

Site A

Pit C44

RP1 Upper part of narrow-necked jar (many sherds); medium soft grey fabric, some slightly rounded grits mostly small but up to 4mm; slight soot blackening on exterior. Form possible copy of storage jars in Severn Valley Ware which date from mid-1st to mid-4th centuries (Webster, 1976, Fig 1 no 1) but no close parallels appear in the recently published groups from Prestatyn (Blockley, 1989), Pentre Farm, Flint (P V Webster in O'Leary, 1989) and Caersws (P V Webster in Britnell J, 1989).

Residual

Reeded out-turned rim; hard, fine, orange, virtually grit-free, eroded; from *C66 pit associated with Structure 1.*

Site T

Gully T71

RP2 Jar with out-turned rim and oblique lattice. Dorset BB1. Form later 3rd to later 4th centuries (Gillam, 1976, 63).

Also other BB1 sherds; body sherd from Malvern area (identified D F Williams); samian Dr 27 rim and scrap from Dr 33 cup; body sherd from Mancetter/Hartshill mortarium (identified P Booth); sherds from thin walled vessel, hard grey fine-gritted fabric.

RP2, in large chunks, suggests recent breakage and so deposition in T71 during the late 3rd or 4th centuries; other sherds such as the samian could

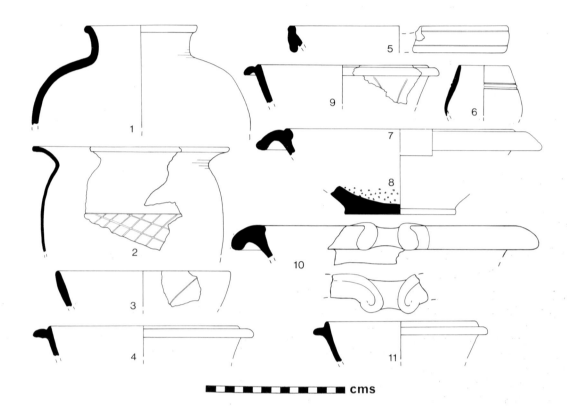

Fig 13.4 Romano-British pottery. RP1 Site A C44; RP2 T71, RP3 Site T residual; RP4, 5 Site E residual; RP6, 7, 8, M64a, RP9 M53, RP10, 11 Site M residual. × ¼.

either be residual or broken after a long period of use.

Posthole T305

Samian scrap.

Residual

About 36 sherds; most come from soil T64, medieval Ditch infills and features on the edge of the Ditches, and so could derive from the disturbed end of T71 or associated features.
RP3 Platter wall, with incised line, probably part arcading, on exterior. Dorset BB1. 3rd to mid-4th century (Gillam, 1976, 75–77).
Also five samian scraps; base sherd from New Forest beaker group III (Swan, 1973); orange body sherd with white external slip, ? from Mancetter/Hartshill flagon; body sherds from Mancetter/Hartshill mortarium and from orange mortarium with white trituration grits; hard fine grey sherds as in T71, sherd as RP1, and sherds of four other grey wares; sherds of four different buff-orange fabrics.

Given the association of a 2nd with a late 3rd/4th century form in T71, it is impossible to say whether

this material represents use of the site from the 2nd to the 4th centuries or for a shorter, late period.

Site V

Residual

Samian scrap, probably from the ovolo of a Dr 37; Dorset BB1 sherd; calcite-gritted sherd, from posthole V39 in Structure 5, produced sometime after AD 370 (comment Becky Wears) (cf Gardner & Savory, 1964, 200).

Site E

Residual

RP4 Flanged bowl. Dorset BB1. Late 3rd to mid-4th centuries (Gillam, 1976, 70–72).
RP5 Mortarium rim with deep collar and start of spout; buff-white Mancetter/Hartshill (comment P Booth), probably 4th century. Another similar rim in the same fabric.

Also three samian scraps; mortarium body sherd from Verulamium area (comment P Booth); grey ware sherd.

Site M

Soil M64a

RP6 Small beaker with incised horizontal lines, hard pink-buff fabric with grey core, much fine, rounded grit. Possibly from Cheshire or north part of Severn Basin. Form copies colour-coat beakers as Gillam (1970) types 78 & 81, late 2nd to mid-3rd centuries (comment P V Webster).

RP7 Mortarium rim Mancetter/Hartshill (comment P Booth), Antonine.

RP8 Mortarium base, cream-buff fabric with black trituration grit ? Wroxeter (comment P Booth).

Also samian footring from ? Dr 37; five sherds of fabric as RP6. A date in the late 2nd century would be feasible for soil M64a.

Soil M53

RP9 Flanged bowl with low bead and arcading incised on exterior. Dorset BB1. Form appropriate for 3rd century (Gillam, 1976, 70).

Also sherds from Dorset BB1 bowl late 2nd/early 3rd centuries (Gillam, *ibid*); three orange-buff and one grey ware sherd. Soil M53 could date to the early 3rd century.

Gully M62

Samian fragment.

Gully M91

Dorset BB1 sherd.

Residual

RP10 Mortarium spout, low-beaded rim, white-buff fabric, no grits surviving; second century type; ? Mancetter/Hartshill or Wroxeter (comment P Booth).

RP11 Flanged bowl with high bead. Dorset BB1. The classic late 3rd to late 4th century form (Gillam, 1976, 70–72).

Also two samian scraps; orange mortarium sherd with multi-coloured trituration grits, cf Prestatyn fabric R2 (Blockley, 1989, 158); two similar grey ware sherds; sherds of two different buff fabrics; sherd from heavily gritted storage jar. This material suggests activity continued on the site into the 4th century, though the original levels had been very much disturbed by the medieval graveyard.

Site D
Residual

Samian fragment, probably from dish in Dr 18/31 series; from R2 erosion of Edwardian Defences.

13.3 The Iron Age and Romano-British periods at Rhuddlan

Interpretation of material from these periods is hampered both by the difficulty of correlating the evidence from the different sites and by the scrappy survival of soil layers and features. No Iron Age material has been found so far on any other sites in Rhuddlan other than those excavated in 1969–73. Difficulties are compounded by the notorious dearth of datable artefacts from the first millennium BC in North Wales.

The longest stratigraphic sequence occurred on Site T in a flattish area defined on the west by lynchet T196 and preserved beneath the line of the Norman Borough Defences. The earliest features predated an agricultural episode with ploughmarks T319. Curved gully T127 produced sherds of salt container fabric, possibly dating as early as the 5th century BC; there were no surviving traces of structural features – door postholes or wall line. T127 had been eroded by later agricultural activity; it is not possible to say whether this gully had surrounded a house or some less substantial feature like a storage area. Even with erosion some trace of door postholes might have been expected to have survived.

Marks from cross-ploughing with an ard such as T319 are being recognised with increasing frequency where conditions are right for their preservation (cf Stackpole Warren, Dyfed, Benson, Evans & Williams, 1990). The Rhuddlan marks appear to have formed at the bottom of a soil profile, and would be appropriate traces from a 'rip ard' suggested by Reynolds (1981, 104) as an implement for breaking in land which had not been in agricultural use for some time. (Marks R97 on Site D may have been produced in a similar way but are probably post-Roman [8.3].) The length of the agricultural episode cannot be estimated, but this part of Site T had another change of use while salt container fragments were still being discarded.

The suggested four-post structure T237-326-325-116 produced salt container ceramic from one of its postholes; its size, c 2m by 2.5m, is typical of these structures which are now generally recognized as standard Iron Age multi-purpose storage units (Gent, 1983). The second possible four-poster T396-399-398-397 has smaller postholes and is suggested only tentatively; it has no dating material. The hillforts closest to Rhuddlan, Dinorben and Moel Hiraddug, both have four-post structures, but the open settlement at Prestatyn of the 2nd or 1st centuries BC did not (Blockley, 1989), at least in the area excavated. Four-post structures of later, Roman, date, are known in Wales, at Collfryn (Powys), Dinorben and elsewhere (Britnell, 1989, 121), and a Roman date for those at Rhuddlan cannot be ruled out (see below). Other structures must be represented by postholes in the area of the Site T four-posters; postholes T324 and 316, 2m apart, both replacing similar, smaller holes, could have held the door frame of a circular house. Presumably the structures postdating the agricultural episode date late within the Iron Age, and before the appearance of Roman pottery in the area around AD 70/80.

Some form of activity of Iron Age date is probably indicated by gullies such as C9 on Site A. Of these only C43 produced a few sherds which could be pre-Roman. (The ambiguous relationship of the gully system to pit C44, with many sherds from vessel RP1, is commented upon above. If the gullies were later than this pit, some residual material might be expected in their contents. On balance the gullies are best regarded as late Iron Age.) The Site A gullies, like gully T127, do not have related post-holes or evidence for wall structure. They are therefore best interpreted as drainage around structures such as like lightly built storage units rather than houses. Such gullies were found at Collfryn, particularly in the south west part of the site (Britnell, 1989, Fig 37), where they were clearly distinguished from those gullies associated with structural elements interpreted as round houses, as were those at Prestatyn (Blockley, 1989). On Site M posthole M73 containing a quern fragment suggests some structure of later Iron Age date.

The other features which need to be considered in regard to the Iron Age at Rhuddlan are the gully groups M82 etc and V69 etc. Of these M99, the latest of the long series on Site M, produced salt container sherds, as did V64, the earliest of the gully sequence on Site V. Both groups seem best interpreted as field or plot boundaries, recut frequently in the soft sandy soil. At simplest they suggest that there was a spread of fields beyond the foci of activity identified on Sites T and A; the undated, possibly later, boundary/ploughmark evidence from Site D may indicate such fields spread at least 500m to the north. The long sequence of recuts in M could indicate a boundary roughly parallel to the Clwyd maintained over a long period; the low position in the soil build-up from which the initial boundary was cut suggests that this boundary was laid out first during the Bronze Age. Its importance is demonstrated by its recutting, after a sand-blow (see below), during the Roman period.

The Site V boundaries run on a line approximately at right-angles to the Clwyd. From the plans it might be expected that these were originally continuous with those on Site T (T175 etc). T143, early in the Site T boundary sequence cut Structure 2, possibly Roman but more likely later in date; the Saxo-Norman sherd from T222, early in the sequence, is probably intrusive and therefore irrelevant to the current argument. The Site T gullies seem to run across the lynchetted area containing prehistoric settlement, ploughmarks etc. It is just possible that the Site V gullies are post-prehistoric, the salt container ceramic being residual, but they occur right at the bottom of soil build-up below a building, Structure 5, likely to date somewhere between the 9th and 12th centuries. A more likely explanation is that both the V and T gullies were cut alongside a natural demarcation line, the projection inwards from the Clwyd of the ravine which was utilised eventually as the south side of the Edwardian Castle. Our knowledge is too scrappy at present for further discussion to be useful.

Evidence for Iron Age settlement at Rhuddlan shows concentration on the sand soils around an eminence overlooking the Clwyd; field systems may be extended more widely. The excavations should be regarded as a keyhole into an extensive prehistoric landscape, one which may well have extended on more suitable soils the whole way up the Vale of Clwyd and linked the hillforts of Moel Hiraddug and Dinorben. A univallate enclosure has been located by aerial photography at SJ 033 799 about 2km to the north east of Rhuddlan. Whimster's (1989) correlation of recent aerial photography in the upper Severn Valley has indicated a dense pattern of sites and there is no reason why the Vale of Clwyd should not produce similar evidence eventually.

It is worth noting that no feature at Rhuddlan (except in contexts of later, medieval, date) has produced both salt container ceramic and pottery of Roman date. This is the converse of the situation at Prestatyn where much VCP was found residually in early Roman period features (Blockley, 1989, 166). It may indicate, at least in the areas excavated, that there was something of a hiatus in activity during the later 1st and early 2nd centuries AD.

Chronological development may be approached with the stratified sequence on Site M, where there appears to have been a gradual build-up of soil through the Iron Age and Romano-British periods; this may be the result of down-hill lynchetting. Boundary M99, with salt container ceramic, appears to have been largely infilled by soil M64a, leaving only a slight depression; soil M64a contained pottery of 2nd century AD date. This soil passed upwards into the more humic M53 for which an early 3rd century date is suggested. There were no structural features associated with either soil but the quantity of pottery from the comparatively small area excavated suggests domestic activity in the vicinity. Soil M53 was covered by a sand-blow M58 – presumably during the 3rd century, after which the line of boundary M99 was recut as M62. Pottery from the soil M27 which formed over the sand-blow, and from graves cut through it, indicates the suggested nearby domestic activity continuing well into the 4th century AD. The only feature on Site T which can be definitely assigned to the Roman period is gully T71 of the late 3rd or 4th centuries.

It is unclear whether any structures located during the 1969–73 excavations could be of Romano-British date. The post-built Structure 2 on

Site T could be Roman in date (see 4.5) but as the concentration of Roman pottery on Site T occurs at the other end of the Site an alterative, later date is more probable; there is no Roman pottery even from residual contexts in its area. It is quite possible that postholes under soil T64, in the area where Roman pottery was most common, may relate to buildings of this date; posthole T305 produced a samian sherd. However the partial survival of posthole patterns, due to later activity, defies any attempt at the reconstruction of plans; it is possible that the four-poster T327-326-325-116 could be of Roman date. On Site A it is argued above that gullies such as C9 are more likely to be Iron Age than Roman in date. The only definite feature is therefore pit C44 with vessel RP1. Sites V and E produced only residual material, which confirms the continuance of activity into the later 4th century, indicated by that from Site M, and indeed by residual pottery from Site T.

Scattered material of Romano-British date has now been found at Rhuddlan over an area stretching at least 1200m along the east bank of the Clwyd, from Site D (a single samian sherd) on the north to the 1979–81 excavations (Fig 1.2) in the south, which produced gullies, a few samian sherds, a first century AD brooch and two coins of the 3rd and 4th centuries (Manley, 1987, 16). Most of the artefactual material has no real association, while most of the contexts relating to it appear to be either gullies/ditches or soil levels. The earliest group of artefacts found so far is that of the late 1st and early 2nd centuries from a small ditch at Lôn Hylas (Fig 1.2; Manley, 1985c); the quality of this material has lead Manley to hint at the possibility of military activity somewhere in the Rhuddlan area. It is apparent from recent work at Prestatyn that Roman pottery was reaching the area by AD 70/80 (Blockley, 1989, passim). Despite lack of understanding of how trade and distribution networks operated locally at this date, it would seem reasonable to expect any domestic settlement occupied by around AD 100 to have used some Roman pottery, and on this basis to regard Iron Age and Roman artefacts as indicating continuity of settlement. There were so few features producing material of either date that the lack of

association of the two may not be meaningful. While a hiatus at the end of the Iron Age cannot be ruled out, this seems unlikely in an area as suitable for settlement as the Vale of Clwyd. If any hiatus occurred it may have been localised in the small area tested by excavation and no deductions should be drawn from this about occupation of the lower part of the Vale.

As with the Iron Age, the Roman period settlement at Rhuddlan appears to have been dispersed and agricultural, with major foci still to be identified. It should be remembered that sea-level was locally high at this period (Manley, 1982b, 14), and that the ridge of high land at Rhuddlan may actually have overlooked the sea covering what is now Morfa Rhuddlan west of the Clwyd. Indeed it is possible that the sand-blow M58 derived from nearby dunes, which appear to have been forming along the contemporary coastline from around 2000 BC (Manley, 1982b, 9). It is probable that activity in the Rhuddlan area formed part of a landscape incorporating much of the Vale of Clwyd. Diserth, 4km to the east, is the nearest site to have produced Roman material (Davies, 1949, 119–24). Blockley (1989, 4–10) has recently produced a useful review of Roman sites in Flintshire, part of territory occupied by the Deceangli, identifying Rhuddlan as the only lowland rural site on which buildings of distinctive Roman type have not yet been located. There are no indicators such as tile fragments for the existence of masonry buildings. While the area concerned is large and definitive statements would be unwise, it seems best to regard Rhuddlan as a glimpse into the Roman rural landscape of north east Wales, which would be best followed up at later date by investigation of protected deposits in the area around Twt Hill.

Acknowledgements
We are grateful to M Owen for petrological identifications of the querns, M U Jones for comments on salt container ceramic, and to Paul Booth, Becky Wears, Peter Webster and David F Williams for assistance with the pottery. Drawings are by Kathy Holland (bronze), Diann Timms (stone), Lesley Simpson (pottery).

14 The vertebrate remains   Bruce Levitan (1986)

14.1 Introduction

The bones from Rhuddlan submitted for analysis were selected on the basis of their provenance and potential interest archaeologically. The excavations were carried out more than a decade ago, before the importance of sieving was generally recognised, so the sample is hand picked and must be regarded as biased to the detriment of small bones such as those from birds and fish and from small mammals.

The sample totals 3893 fragments of which 2621 (67.3%) are identifiable to species level. The unidentifiable portion has been divided into six groups: bird bones, fish bones and four groups of mammal bones – large ungulates ('cattle-size'), small ungulates ('sheep-size'), small mammals, other mammal. Ribs have been assigned cattle-size or sheep-size status, and have been included under cattle and sheep in the analyses below on the assumption that the majority of ribs were, in fact, from cattle and sheep.

A wide time span is represented, and the bones have been divided into eleven temporal groups:

period 1 – Bronze Age, 3 contexts, 25 bones;
period 2 – Iron Age, 4 contexts, 6 bones;
period 3 – Romano-British, 9 contexts, 39 bones;
period 4 – probably 10th century, 7 contexts, 179 bones;
period 5 – 10th–11th centuries, 13 contexts, 300 bones;
period 6 – 11th–12th centuries, 11 contexts, 297 bones;
period 7 – 12th–13th centuries, 18 contexts, 403 bones;
period 8 – late 13th century, 24 contexts, 2170 bones;
period 9 – late 13th–14th centuries, 5 contexts, 37 bones;
period 10 – 14th century, 2 contexts, 431 bones;
period 11 – post-medieval, 2 contexts, 6 bones.

There is a degree of uncertainty in the dating of contexts grouped in periods 4–7 and 9–10; the most probable dates are presented here.

All but period 8 have small samples, and those with less than 100 bones are clearly too small to warrant analysis. Species represented are summarised for each period in Table 14.1. In order to provide larger samples and to simplify the temporal divisions, the following analysis is based upon the following period groups (PG):

PG 1: pre-Norman (periods 1–3), 70 bones;
PG 2: 10th and 11th centuries (periods 4–5), 479 bones;
PG 3: 12th & early-mid 13th centuries (periods 6–7), 700 bones;
PG 4: late 13th century (period 8), 2170 bones;
PG 5: late 13th–14th centuries (periods 9–10), 468 bones;
PG 6: post-medieval (period 11), 6 bones.

The bones have been packed in plastic bags, each labelled with context code and bone analysis code. The latter was employed since the former are alphanumeric and do not easily transfer to the computer. The bone archive contains a list of site contexts and their bone analysis equivalent, together with the period designations. The computer archive (two copies) with the main site archive, is in the care of the author. The bones have been deposited with the rest of the finds. The following analysis employs a number a fairly standard techniques, most of which have been published – these are referenced in the report, but not described. Descriptions of techniques employed are given only where they have not been published, or where the method departs in some way from the published original.

The analysis is divided into a series of topics and is concluded with a general summary. The topics are: 1) Taphonomic evidence, 2) Quantification of the major species, 3) Exploitation of cattle, 4) Exploitation of sheep and goat, 5) Exploitation of pig, 6) Exploitation of minor mammals, 7) Bird remains, 8) Fish remains.

Tabulated data are in summary version since listings of untransformed data are unrealistic in terms of publication. These listings may be obtained, upon request, from the author. A charge may be made to cover postage and packing.

14.2 Analysis

14.2.1 Taphonomic evidence

The manner of bones recording employed (Jones et al 1981) limits the detail concerning taphonomy, so this topic is considered under the following general headings: chewing and gnawing, weathering and erosion, fragmentation (fresh and ancient), burning.

Chewing and gnawing

Table 14.2a summarises the incidence of chewing and gnawing. These data are possibly an underestimate since some evidence may have been obscured by weathering and modern damage. The

Table 14.1 Summary of vertebrate species represented

Column groups: Period Group 1 (P1, P2, P3, Total); Period Group 2 (P4, P5, Total); Period Group 3 (P6, P7, Total); Period Group 4 (P8); Period Group 5 (P9, P10, Total); Period Group 6 (P11); Total.

Species	P1		P2		P3		Total		P4		P5		Total		P6		P7		Total		P8		P9		P10		Total		P11		Total	
	N	%	N	%	N	%	N	%	N	%	N	%	N	%	N	%	N	%	N	%	N	%	N	%	N	%	N	%	N	%	N	%
Cattle (*Bos taurus*)	4	28.6	4	80.0	15	65.2	23	54.8	66	58.4	96	53.9	162	55.7	146	61.9	124	51.7	270	56.7	759	54.1	7	29.2	188	60.5	195	58.2	2	50.0	1411	55.3
Sheep/Goat [a]	1	7.1	1	20.0	6	26.1	8	19.0	14	12.4	33	18.6	47	16.2	22	9.3	80	33.3	102	21.4	374	26.7	5	20.8	79	25.4	84	25.1	1	25.0	616	24.2
Pig (*Sus domesticus*)					2	8.7	2	4.8	19	16.8	17	9.6	36	12.4	17	7.2	21	8.8	38	8.0	140	10.0	2	8.3	28	9.0	30	9.0			246	9.6
Horse (*Equus caballus*)									13	11.5	10	5.6	23	7.9	24	10.2	6	2.5	30	6.3	53	3.8	10	41.7	12	3.9	22	6.6			128	5.0
Dog/Cat [b]											3	1.7	3	1.0	23	9.7	4	1.7	27	5.7	69	4.9			3	1.0	3	0.9	1	25.0	103	4.0
Deer [c]															4	1.7	4	1.7	8	1.7	7	0.5									16	0.6
Other mammal [d]	9	64.3					9	21.4	1	0.9	19	10.7	19	6.5			1	0.4	1	0.2					1	0.3	1	0.3			30	1.2
Σ mammal	14	56.0	5	83.3	23	59.0	42	60.0	113	63.1	178	59.3	291	60.8	236	79.5	240	59.6	476	68.0	1402	64.6	24	64.9	311	72.2	335	71.6	4	75.0	2550	65.5
Domestic fowl (*Gallus gallus*)									3	60.0			3	42.9			5	50.0	5	45.4	29	51.8			1	6.7	1	6.3			38	42.2
Goose (*Anser* sp.)			1	100.0							1	50.0	1	14.3			5	50.0	5	45.4	10	17.6	1	100.0	1	6.7	2	12.5			18	20.0
Other bird [e]									2	40.0	1	50.0	3	42.9	1	100.0			1	9.1	17	30.4			13	86.7	13	81.3			34	37.7
Σ bird									5	2.8	2	0.7	7	1.5	1	0.3	10	2.5	11	1.6	56	2.6	1	2.7	15	3.5	16	3.4			90	2.3
Fish [f]											3	1.0	3	0.6			2	0.5	2	0.3	11	0.5			1	0.2	1	0.2			17	0.4
Cattle-size	7	63.6			14	87.5	21	75.0	56	91.8	81	69.2	137	77.0	55	91.6	110	72.8	165	78.2	507	72.3	11	91.7	78	75.0	89	76.7	2	100.0	921	74.3
Sheep-size	4	36.4	1	100.0	2	12.5	7	25.0	5	8.2	36	30.8	41	23.0	5	8.4	38	25.2	43	20.4	194	27.7	1	8.3	25	24.0	26	22.4			311	25.2
Other Indeterminate																	3	2.0	3	1.4					1	1.0	1	0.9			4	0.3
Σ Indeterminate	11	44.0	1	16.7	16	41.0	28	40.0	61	34.1	117	39.0	178	37.2	60	20.2	151	37.5	211	30.1	701	32.3	12	32.4	104	24.1	116	24.8	2	25.0	1236	31.7
Species total	25	35.7	6	8.5	39	55.7	70	1.8	179	37.4	300	62.6	479	12.3	297	42.4	403	57.6	700	18.0	2170	55.7	37	7.9	431	92.1	468	12.0	6	0.1	3893	

Notes: a = Sheep (*Ovis aries*) and goat (*Capra hircus*) identifications – P5 = 8:1, P6 = 6:0, P8 = 80:3, P9 = 0:1, P10 = 20:1. b = Dog (*Canis familiaris*) and Cat (*Felix domesticus*) identifications – P5 = 2:1, P6 = 23:0, P7 = 1:3, P8 = 52:17, P10 = 3:0, P11 = 1:0. c = Red deer (*Cervus elaphas*) – P6, P7, P8 = 5; roe deer (*Capreolus capreolus*) – P8 = 2; fallow deer (*Dama dama*) – P4. d = Mole (*Talpa europaea*) P5 = 1; rabbit (*Oryctolagus cuniculus*) – P1 = 9, P5 = 18, P10 = 1; whale (*Cetacea*) – P7 = 1. e = 1 Woodcock (*Scolopax rusticola*) – P4; 1 Crow (*Corvus* cf *corone*) – P6; 1 rook (*Corvus frugilegus*) – P8; 1 raven (*Corvus corax*) – P10; 1 buzzard (*Butes butes*); remainder not identified to species. f = 2 spurdog (*Squalus acanthias*) – P5, P8; 2 roker (*Raja clavata*) – P7, P8; 1 Salmonid (*Salmo* sp) – P5; 3 cod (*Gadus morhuea*) – P8 = 2, P10; 1 tub gurnard (*Trigla lucerna*) – P8; 1 bass (*Dicentrarchus labrax*) – P8; remainder not identifiable.

% calculations – for individual species: % based on phylum totals; for individual phyla: % based on column totals; Period total % based on Period – Group totals; Group total % based on site total.

Table 14.2 Summary of taphonomic factors

Species	Period – Group 1		2		3		4		5	
	N	%	N	%	N	%	N	%	N	%
a) chewing										
Cattle	3	13.0	14	8.6	21	7.8	54	7.1	8	4.1
Sheep/Goat	–		4	8.5	5	4.9	23	6.1	4	4.8
Pig	–		3	8.3	2	5.3	11	7.9	1	3.3
Horse	–		2	8.7	1	3.3	2	3.8	1	4.5
Red deer	–		–		–		1	20.0	–	
Goose	–		–		–		1	10.0	–	
b) weathering										
Cattle	7	30.4	29	17.9	25	9.3	43	5.7	28	14.3
Sheep/Goat	1	12.5	10	21.3	2	2.0	17	4.5	6	7.1
Pig	–		2	5.6	5	13.2	3	2.1	2	6.7
Horse	–		3	13.0	5	16.7	5	9.4	3	13.6
Red deer	–		–		5	62.5	2	40.0	–	
Domestic fowl	–		–		1	20.0	–		–	
Cattle-size	2	9.5	7	5.1	11	6.7	–		–	
Sheep-size	–		4	9.8	1	4.7	–		–	
c) Burning										
Cattle	–		1	0.6	2	0.7	7	0.9	–	
Sheep/Goat	–		1	2.1	–		1	0.3	–	
Pig	–		–		1	2.6	1	0.7	1	4.5
Horse	–		–		2	6.7	–		–	
Cattle-size	3	14.3	1	0.7	3	1.8	6	3.1	2	2.2
Sheep-size	–		–		1	2.3	2	3.8	1	3.8
d) Fresh breakage										
Cattle	5	38.5	78	56.1	97	39.4	250	38.4	64	41.0
Sheep/Goat	5	62.5	10	52.6	32	35.2	124	40.1	24	38.7
Pig	1	50.0	28	32.1	12	41.4	37	31.4	13	54.2
Horse	–		12	80.0	13	54.2	21	44.7	5	26.3
Red deer	–		–		1	12.5	1	20.0	–	
Dog	–		–		15	71.4	37	74.0	1	33.3
Goose	–		1	33.3	2	40.0	2	6.9	–	
Cattle-size	8	36.4	101	73.7	102	61.8	288	56.8	66	72.4
Sheep-size	–		8	19.5	2	4.7	77	39.7	15	57.6

table indicates that chewing may not have been an important factor in bone destruction since proportions of damage are generally below 10%. The highest general level is in PG 2, 10th–11th centuries, and the very similar proportions may indicate that all the bones were subject to similar deposition treatment. The proportions are a little lower in PG 4 (late 13th century), but similarly consistent, so perhaps similar conditions pertained.

Weathering and erosion

This is a difficult factor to assess because scoring for weathering damage is rather subjective. Almost all bone from archaeological sites has undergone some damage of this kind, but it is often only when bone is very degraded that the condition is commented upon. An attempt has been made here to score for damage which is greater than the background 'noise' described above. The scoring has erred on the conservative side, and the proportions given in Table 14.2b are probably minima. There does not appear to be any temporal or species related patterns among these data. Weathering damage is at its peak for sheep/goat and cattle in PG 2 (10th–11th centuries), but for pigs, horses and red deer the peak is during PG 3 (12th–13th centuries). It is interesting to note that weathering damage is relatively little for cattle- and sheep-size fragments, indicating that this factor probably does not account for fragmentation at this level.

Burning

Table 14.2c summarises incidence of burnt bones (this includes all degrees of burning from slight blackening through to calcination) – generally burning can be seen to be insignificant.

Fragmentation

The fragmentation status of the bone was recorded in nine size classes ranging from less than a quarter complete to complete. Although incidence of fresh breakage was also recorded, no attempt has been made to separate freshly broken bones from ancient fragmentation. (This is due to the computer recording programme used which does not allow for such separation in the records).

Fresh Breakage

Table 14.2d gives a summary of the fresh breakage, proportions based on counts which exclude loose teeth and unfused epiphyses. The larger and more common species all suffered large proportions of damage: never less than 30% for cattle, sheep/goat and pig, and such high proportions obviously will have a biasing effect on the analysis of species quantity and body part distribution.

A more detailed analysis of fresh breakage, by body part, is in the archive. Cattle suffered the most wide ranging and consistent damage, with all long bones and cranial elements affected, and often bones such as tarsals and phalanges also damaged. In some cases elements have less than 20% damage, but the general picture is of greater damage. Sheep/goat and pig are similar in that not all the long bones are damaged, and the pattern of damage is not consistent from period to period. Both have high proportions for most long bones,

Table 14.3 Summary of anatomical indices for species representation

| | Period – Group | | | | |
	1	2	3	4	5
Cattle					
Index	0.30	11.50	27.45	52.65	15.25
%	17.8	54.1	53.2	39.0	46.4
<¼	88	74	65	65	69
Sheep/Goat					
Index	1.22	5.29	17.90	59.76	12.78
%	72.2	24.9	34.7	44.3	38.9
<¼	40	60	31	32	47
Pig					
Index	0.17	4.46	6.28	22.51	4.81
%	10.1	21.0	12.2	16.7	14.6
<¼	50	58	58	36	43

Index: see text for method – higher values = greater representation
<¼: Proportion of fragments less than ¼ complete (%)

however, and although this may be less than cattle generally, it is nevertheless very high.

Ancient Fragmentation

The nine size classes have been compressed into four for this analysis: a quarter or less complete, greater than a quarter and up to half complete, greater than half and up to three quarters complete, and over three quarters complete. The analysis has been carried out only where samples are over 100, excluding loose teeth and unfused epiphyses. The results are illustrated in Figs 14.1 (cattle), 14.2 (sheep/goat) and 14.3 (pig), though sheep/goat and pig suffer from small samples from most period groups. The most striking result for all the species is the considerable degree of fragmentation in all elements. Those which have survived more or less intact are small, compact bones such as carpals and tarsals, phalanges and patellae, but even among these elements there is sometimes much fragmentation (eg cattle tarsals from PG 3).

These results may be compared with (the less detailed analysis from) Middleton Stoney castle, Oxfordshire (Levitan, 1984a, 141). At the latter site, during the medieval period, fragmentation in cattle is broadly similar to Rhuddlan, though metapodials and small bones are rather less fragmented at Middleton Stoney. Similar points of comparison can be made for sheep and pig: at both sites the fragmentation is less severe than for cattle, but fragmentation is higher at Rhuddlan (Levitan 1984a, 143, 145). A site where the same method of analysis was used is that of St Katherine's Priory, Exeter (Levitan, 1989a). Although this is of the same time span, it is not an urban site adjacent to a castle, so the comparison may be less valid. Results here are very much more similar for cattle and pig; the Rhuddlan bones are only a little more fragmented: and in the case of sheep/goat, Rhuddlan is perhaps less fragmented. The bones from Rhuddlan, then, can be seen as generally more fragmentary than those from other medieval sites, but following the same general patterning within the skeleton. The high proportion of fresh breakage, described above, may account for the higher degree of fragmentation, but this may not have affected the ancient patterning referred to above.

Summary

The above discussion underlines the difficulty of assessing taphonomy and related factors. Generally aspects such as chewing and burning appear to be unimportant at Rhuddlan, though weathering is possibly a more serious damaging factor. The degree of ancient fragmentation may be obscured by modern damage, which is fairly considerable, but comparisons with other sites (where modern damage was less severe) indicate that the patterns of fragmentation may be unaffected.

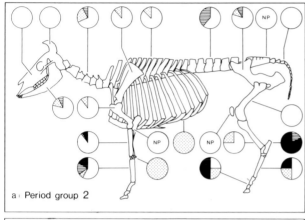

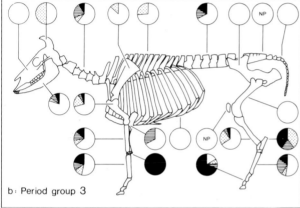

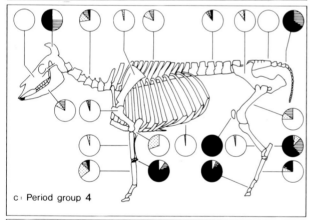

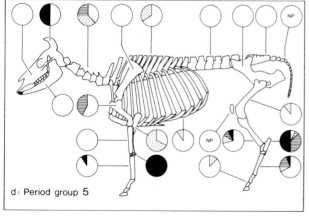

Fragmentation of bone

NP = not present

CATTLE

percentage complete

≤ 25 % 51-75 %

26-50 % > 76 %

14.2.2 *Quantification of the major species*

There are various methods of quantifying species, and there is still much controversy as to the most appropriate method (eg Uerpmann, 1973; Fieller and Turner, 1982; O'Connor, 1985a). Those methods which rely on complex transformation of data are not favoured here because the results do not allow the reader to assess the raw data, and the statistical complexity involved serves only to alienate the lay reader from the data (eg Gilbert and Singer, 1982). Three familiar methods are fragment counts, minimum number of individuals (MNI, Chaplin, 1971) and meat weight estimates. For various reasons the last two may be inappropriate for samples such as Rhuddlan, one major factor being that the animals are often slaughtered and processed in specialist locations and then prepared for domestic consumption in another location, thus the remains of single individuals may be widely dispersed. MNI, and meat weights (which are consequent upon them) also suffer from the problem of recognising pairs of elements, this not being as simple as at first sight (O'Connor, 1985a, 27–28).

Here, therefore, the basic method of quantification employed will be fragment counts. There are several problems with this method, the most important being that some animals (typically cattle) are over represented due to the higher degree of fragmentation which results from butchery processes. Thus, for the purposes of comparison the method recommended by O'Connor (1985a) will also be used, and also an 'index' of representation calculated from anatomical indices (see below).

The fragment counts are summarised in Table 14.1, the indices in Table 14.3 and the relative frequencies in Table 14.4. Results from these tables are illustrated in Fig 14.4 for the major species, with percentages in Fig 14.4a and 14.4b calculated from totals of those species and not the mammal totals as in the tables. In the figure PGs 1 (periods 1–3) and 6 (period 11) are not illustrated because samples are so small (it is clearly ridiculous to draw inferences about the species for a 2400 year period based upon a sample of 33 bones from PG 1; the same is true of PG 6 where only three bones represent up to 500 years).

As might be expected from two sets of results based upon fragment counts, Figs 14.4a and 14.4b show similar overall patterning, differences being in the degree of change and the relative status of the species. The general pattern is one of decrease in proportions of cattle and pig, and increase in proportions of sheep/goat. In cattle and sheep/goat the trends are slightly reversed after the late 13th century, and in pigs there is a slight reversal in the late 13th century. Fig 4a emphasises the importance of cattle overall, with proportions around twice those of sheep/goat and three times those of pigs. This may, however, be influenced by higher

Fig 14.1 Fragmentation of cattle bones.

Table 14.4 Summary of relative frequences

Species	Period Group 1				Period Group 2			Period Group 3			PG 4	Period Group 5			PG 6
	P1	P2	P3	Total	P4	P5	Total	P6	P7	Total	P8	P9	P10	Total	P11
Cattle	0.33	0.75	0.78	0.69	0.86	0.92	0.90	0.73	0.39	0.52	0.83	0.80	1.00	0.86	0.50
Sheep/Goat	0.33	0.25	0.44	0.38	0.71	0.62	0.65	0.55	0.61	0.59	0.75	0.40	1.00	0.57	0.50
Pig			0.22	0.13	0.57	0.15	0.30	0.55	0.11	0.28	0.54	0.20	1.00	0.43	
Horse					0.71	0.23	0.40	0.45	0.11	0.24	0.50	0.40	0.50	0.57	0.50
Dog/Cat						0.23	0.15	0.27	0.17	0.21	0.25		0.50	0.14	
Deer					0.14		0.05	0.27	0.06	0.14	0.12				
Other mammal	0.33			0.06		0.15	0.10		0.06	0.03	0.18		0.50	0.14	
Domestic fowl					0.14		0.05		0.11	0.03	0.04		0.50	0.14	
Goose						0.08	0.05		0.17	0.10	0.12	0.20	0.50	0.29	
Other bird					0.29	0.08	0.20	0.18		0.03	0.21		1.00	0.29	
Fish						0.23	0.15		0.11	0.07	0.38		0.50	0.14	

Method from O'Connor (1985)

Table 14.5 Epiphyseal fusion summary, late 13th century

a) CATTLE:

Age	Element	Fused	Not Fused
Infant	Scapula D	15	0
	Humerus D	24	1
	Radius P	18	0
	Metacarpal P	19	1
	Pelvis	13	0
	Metatarsal P	23	1
	Phalanx 1 P	16	0
	Phalanx 2 P	16	0
		N 144	N 3
		%F 97.96	%NF 2.04
Juvenile	Metacarpal D	8	2
	Tibia D	12	2
	Metatarsal D	7	5
	Calcaneum P	5	5
		N 32	N 14
		%F 69.57	%NF 30.43
Adult	Humerus P	4	1
	Radius D	5	4
	Ulna P	1	1
	Femur P	2	4
	Femur D	7	6
	Tibia P	6	4
		N 25	N 20
		%F 55.56	%NF 44.44
Old Adult	Cervical	4	6
	Thoracic	4	13
	Lumbar	8	5
	Sacrum P	1	2
	Caudal	2	1
		N 19	N 27
		%F 41.30	%NF 58.70

b) SHEEP/GOAT:

Age	Element	Fused	Not Fused
Infant	Scapula D	9	0
	Humerus D	10	2
	Radius P	8	3
	Metacarpal P	6	0
	Pelvis	17	0
	Metatarsal P	8	1
		N 58	N 6
		%F 90.63	%NF 9.38
Juvenile	Metacarpal D	7	1
	Tibia D	17	2
	Metatarsal D	5	2
	Phalanx 1 P	4	0
	Phalanx 2 P	0	0
		N 33	N 5
		%F 86.84	%NF 13.16
Adult	Humerus P	3	0
	Radius D	1	1
	Ulna P	2	1
	Femur P	2	1
	Femur D	5	2
	Tibia P	6	2
	Calcaneum P	3	2
		N 22	N 9
		%F 70.97	%NF 29.03
Old Adult	Cervical	6	5
	Thorasic	0	7
	Lumbar	1	9
	Sacrum P	3	2
	Caudal	0	0
		N 10	N 23
		%F 30.30	%NF 69.70

c) PIG

Age	Element	Fused	Not Fused
Infant	Scapula D	2	1
	Metacarpal P	3	0
	Pelvis	4	2
	Metatarsal P	0	0
		N 9	N 3
		%F 75.00	%NF 25.00
Juvenile	Humerus D	1	0
	Radius P	1	0
	Metacarpal D	0	2
	Tibia D	3	5
	Metatarsal D	0	2
	Calcaneum P	0	1
	Phalanx 1 P	0	0
	Phalanx 2 P	1	0
		N 6	N 10
		%F 37.50	%NF 62.50
Adult	Humerus P	1	0
	Radius D	0	2
	Ulna P	1	2
	Ulna D	0	1
	Femur P	0	5
	Femur D	2	4
	Tibia P	0	2
	Fibula P/D	0	1
		N 4	N 17
		%F 19.05	%NF 80.95
Old Adult	Cervical	1	2
	Thoracic	0	0
	Lumbar	0	4
	Sacrum P	0	0
	Caudal	0	0
		N 1	N 6
		%F 14.29	%NF 85.71

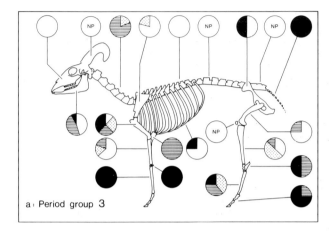

a: Period group 3

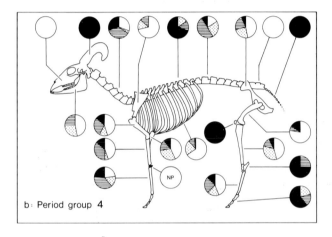

b: Period group 4

Fragmentation of bone		percentage complete
	NP = not present ≤25% ☐	51-75% ▤
SHEEP/GOAT	26-50% ▨	>76% ■

Fig 14.2 Fragmentation of sheep/goat bones.

fragmentation in cattle.

The fragmentation pattern is partly overcome by weighting the fragments according to completeness, and further weighting may be carried out according to skeletal part (see below). The index obtained, however, does not use fragments less than a quarter complete, so the bias in Fig 14.4b may be the opposite to 14.4a, an emphasis on less fragmented species, and indeed sheep/goat and pig are much more common relative to cattle, with sheep/goat proportions even higher than cattle in PG 4. The patterns remain the same, but cattle are apparently much less important using this method.

Fig 14.4c is based upon relative frequency in terms of occurrence rather than quantity, ie 'If one phase of a site has yielded 200 separate context groups of bone fragments, and brown hare is represented in ten of them, hare can be said to have a relative frequency of 10/200 = 5%' (O'Connor 1985a, 29). The results are rather different from the above. The species cannot be said to follow obvious patterns (other than 'down-up-down'

reversals). Cattle, in PGs 2, 4 and 5, occur in over 80% of contexts, falling to less than 60% in PG 3 (influenced by period 7 – Table 14.4). Sheep/goat frequencies are around 65%, with the exception of PG 4 where they rise to 75%. Pig frequencies are about 35% in PGs 2 and 3 and then rise to approximately 55% in PGs 4 and 5. Thus the changes do not appear to be related to other species.

The following analyses of cattle, sheep/goat and pig deal only with PG 4, the late 13th century because this is the only period which produced large enough samples (Table 14.1).

14.2.3 Exploitation of cattle
Ageing

Epiphysial fusion data are summarised in Table 14.5a. This indicates fairly convincingly that only a small minority of cattle were killed as infants, 2% of the 147 bones being unfused. About 30% of bones from the juvenile fusing group are not fused, and about 44% from the adult fusing group are not fused. Eighteen mandibles provided ageing results consistent with the above: about 16% are 2 years old or less, 24% are 2–3.5 years old, 23% are 3.5–4 years old, and the remainder (37%) over 4 years. Thus it would appear that more than half the cattle killed were at least adults, and perhaps as many as 40% were old adults. Such results are inconsistent with a beef-rearing economy, since it would be expected to have a higher proportion of earlier deaths. Rhuddlan, therefore, may not have been a buyer of prime beef.

Sexing

Alternative economies are those based upon dairying and/or traction, and obviously information about population sex structures would be required. Unfortunately, only relatively crude estimates are possible, based upon measurements, and these are often open to alternative interpretation. A plot of distal humerus dimensions (measurements 5 and 6 in Jones *et al*, 1981) shows a loose 'group' of five bones with a much larger 'outlier'. Possibly the larger specimen is a bull or an ox, and the others are cows, but this is too small a sample to make positive assertions (plot in archive). A plot of metacarpal proximal breadth and depth also produces two groups, a smaller bone group of five specimens (females ?) and a larger bone group of two (males – bulls or castrates ?). Perhaps more convincing are nine astragali of which eight have greatest lengths between 56.0 and 60.3mm and one is 65mm. A plot of six proximal metatarsals (archive) has a group of three smaller ones, two intermediate and one large (possibly three cows, two oxen and one bull ?). None of these are particularly convincing, but they are, at least, consistent, indicating a majority of females. Tentatively, then, the cattle were mainly adult females with a few males (possibly oxen).

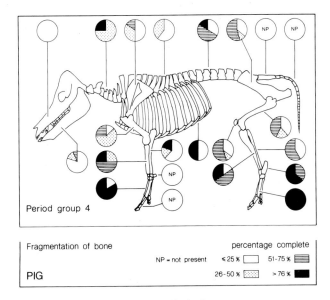

Fig 14.3 Fragmentation of pig bones.

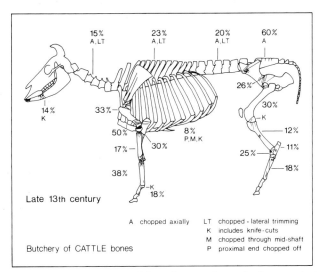

Fig 14.4 Summary of butchery of cattle bones, late 13th century.

Measurements

Metrical analysis of the cattle bones was limited by the fragmentary nature of the remains. Some of the measurements are summarised in Table 14.6a which illustrates that the size of the cattle was similar to other sites of this period (eg Taunton – Levitan 1984b; Bath – Grant 1979; Hereford – Noddle 1985).

Butchery

The evidence above relates to the selection of cattle for consumption; evidence from butchery can provide clues about methods of carcass processing. Fig 14.4 illustrates the zones of butchery and gives the proportions of bones with butchery evidence. The carcass was probably split axially since most vertebrae have been chopped through axially; and perhaps were delivered as sides of beef to the site. Butchery is then clearly concentrated around joints, particularly those of the upper limb indicating disjointing at the shoulder/hip, elbow/knee and wrist/ankle. Butchery of the metapodia is mainly in the form of longitudinal splitting, presumably for later bone working, and some butchery of phalanges is evidence of skinning. There is no evidence of butchery of the skull (mainly because of high fragmentation) though some frontals had the appearance of having been poleaxed. Mandibles were chopped through at the diastema and the articulation with the skull to facilitate removal of tongue and masseter muscles.

Anatomical representation

Finally, analysis of the body parts represented can provide clues about the nature of the deposits (eg whether they are slaughter waste, domestic waste, etc). Certain body parts occur in greater numbers in the skeleton than others (eg eight first phalanges versus one atlas vertebra in cattle), so simple counts will over-emphasise the former. This can be weighted by dividing the bone counts by the number of the body part in the skeleton (see O'Connor, 1985b for a full discussion). A further problem is fragmentation, since some body parts are more fragmented than others, either due to butchery (see Fig 14.5) or robusticity. This factor can be weighted by dividing by a number which adjusts for the degree of fragmentation, eg fragments which are half complete are divided by two, and those which are a quarter complete divided by four. Unfortunately fragments less than a quarter complete cannot be weighted in this way since the division factor is not known. (This method is fully described in Levitan, 1989b).

Fig 14.6a illustrates the body part representation after weighting for both the above factors (data in archive). The figure is clearly dominated by the astragalus and calcaneum, and by the metapodia, remaining tarsals, and carpals. It should be noted that the exclusion of fragments less than a quarter complete biases the results in favour of these bones (for instance only 3% of astragalus/calcaneum are less than a quarter complete, but all skull are less than a quarter complete, and 71% of femur/tibia/patella are less than a quarter complete). Even if an arbitrary weighting factor of ten for the fragmentation of bones less than a quarter complete is used, however, (and this assumes the fragments were a tenth complete), the adjustment to the data, shown as broken lines in the figure, does not alter the predominance of metapodia and tarsals/carpals. Indeed, the body parts which are greatly increased (skull/mandibles) confirm the impression of butchery waste bones. The relative paucity of horncores and phalanges might indicate that hides were removed with horncores and phalanges still intact, and sent elsewhere.

Table 14.6 Summary of selected measurements of major mammals, late 13th century

Bone	Measurement[a]	N	Range	Mean	s.d.[b]	c.v.[c]	Hereford[d]
a) CATTLE							
Horn core	GLC	2	109.0 – 135.0	–	–	–	–
Scapula	GLP	4	58.2 – 67.0	61.1	4.0	6.6	–
Humerus	Bd	5	66.5 – 80.7	74.9	6.8	9.2	–
Radius	Bp	6	70.2 – 84.0	76.2	4.6	6.1	–
Metacarpal	Bp	7	42.6 – 50.5	46.6	2.8	6.1	52.4
	Bd	7	49.8 – 57.4	54.3	3.1	5.8	48.8
Tibia	Bd	4	48.0 – 54.5	51.3	2.8	5.5	–
Calcaneum	GL	3	118.5 – 133.0	124.2	–	–	–
Astragalus	GL	10	55.8 – 65.0	58.7	2.8	4.7	–
	Bd	12	31.2 – 43.2	36.3	3.0	8.2	–
Metatarsal	Bp	8	34.2 – 49.3	40.9	4.6	11.3	–
	Bd	3	46.0 – 46.5	46.2	–	–	–
b) SHEEP[e]							
Scapula	GLC	6	28.2 – 31.2	29.4	1.3	4.5	–
Humerus	GL	2	127.3 – 130.8	–	–	–	127.0
	Bd	9	24.5 – 30.9	28.2	2.3	8.2	27.0
Radius	Bp	4	28.4 – 32.0	30.5	1.5	5.0	28.3
Metacarpal	GL	1	117.8	–	–	–	115.0
	GL[f]	1	110.0	–	–	–	106.0
Femur	GL	2	153.5 – 154.0	–	–	–	–
	Bd	4	33.7 – 35.5	34.2	0.9	2.7	–
Tibia[g]	GL	2	183.3 – 184.0	–	–	–	–
	Bd	14	22.4 – 26.7	24.7	1.3	5.4	–
Metatarsal	GL	2	112.3 – 135.5	–	–	–	119.0

a – all measurements from Jones *et al*, 1981 and van den Dreisch, 1976, in mm
b – standard deviation
c – coefficient of variation (%)
d – Hereford mean figures calculated from data in Noddle, 1985
e – all sheep unless shown
f – goat
g – sheep/goat

14.2.4 Exploitation of sheep

The sheep/goat remains were identified to species level where possible, and this indicated that sheep outnumbered goats in the order of 27:1. Thus, although goats were undoubtedly present, they were in the minority, so the sheep/goat remains will be considered as 'sheep' below.

Ageing

The ageing evidence from epiphysial fusion is rather similar to cattle (Table 14.5b), though with a slightly larger proportion of infant deaths (about 9%) and a peak in kill-off between adult and old adult: about 30% did not reach adulthood and about 30% survived as old adults. The ageing evidence from mandibles, using the method of Grant (1982), indicates that about 34% were killed by two years old and a further 9% at about two years. Approximately 28% were killed between two and three years old, and the remaining 20% surviv-

ing beyond three years (the sample is only thirteen mandibles). These results are not inconsistent with the epiphysial fusion data, though more juveniles and fewer old adults are indicated. Such patterns indicate that wool production may have been important with most sheep surviving into early adulthood at least, but an important minority being killed as juveniles for their meat (these, presumably, being mostly males).

Sexing

Sex designation, however, is problematic since measured specimens are few, and distributions of measured bones do not show any clear bimodality (ie sex dimorphism). The largest sample of measurements is of fifteen distal tibiae, but a plot of distal breadth and distal depth does not show any clear grouping, and similarly a plot of nine distal humeri which might be expected to show sex dimorphism more clearly. One interpretation is that the sexes overlap in size; another is that only one sex is represented.

Measurements

There are too few measurable bones for a detailed analysis. Some measurements are summarised in Table 14.6b. The few complete bones can be used to give withers heights estimates: the nine estimates are in the range 51–61cm with a mean of 56cm (coefficient of variation = 5.3%). These heights and measurements are similar to sheep from other medieval sites.

Butchery

The sheep bones are characterised by much less butchery than the cattle, probably a result of the fact that the smaller body size requires less preparation, and many bones are left in the joint. Like cattle, vertebrae were split axially indicating that the sheep were cut into halves. Butchery of other bones included chops at the shoulder (scapula) and hip (pelvis), at the elbow (humerus and radius) and ankle (tibia).

Anatomical representation

The body part distribution is also in contrast to cattle, with girdles and upper limbs predominating (Fig 14.6b). Fragmentation is less severe than cattle, so adjusting the results in the same manner makes little difference. 'Waste' bones, such as metapodia and skull/mandibles, are quite well represented, so this deposit cannot be said to be entirely domestic in nature. It is typical of many medieval rubbish deposits which are of a generally mixed nature.

14.2.5 Exploitation of pig
Ageing

Ageing evidence from pig mandibles is too limited for analysis: only four mandibles could be aged, one at Grant stage 14, two at 29–31 (estimate) and one at 47 (estimate). Thus only one fully adult pig is represented, with two young adults and one infant/juvenile. The epiphysial fusion evidence is also rather limited (Table 14.5c). This indicates that the majority of pigs were killed before reaching adulthood, but those which survived generally lived into old adulthood. This reflects the classic pig raising economy of killing most pigs as soon as possible, economically (ie at round 12–18 months), and keeping only a few females into old age as breeders.

Sexing

Sexing cannot be carried out using measurements since there are too few measurable bones. Sexing of mandibles (using canine teeth) reflected the sex of mainly younger individuals (see above), with two males (both juveniles) and one female (an adult).

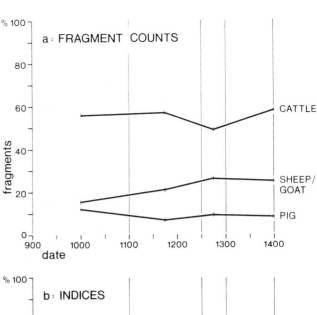
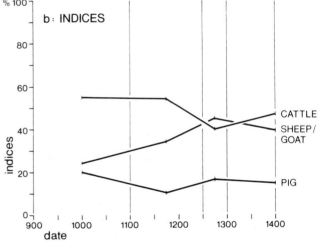
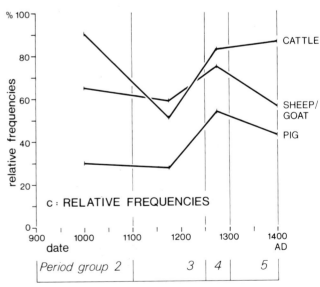

Fig 14.5 Proportions of major species varying through time.

Butchery

Only five bones have evidence of butchery: an axially chopped cervical vertebra, two pelves

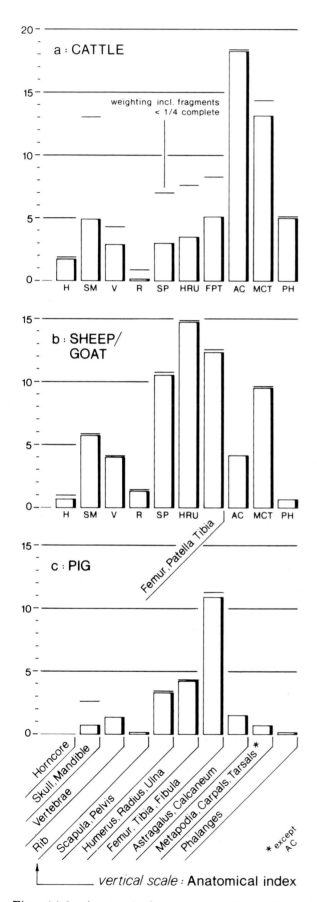

Fig 14.6 Anatomical representation of major species, late 13th century.

(chopped halfway along the ilium, and at the distal end, axially) and two femora (one with proximal articulation removed, and one chopped at the distal end). This is too scant for any analysis, though splitting of the carcass into sides is indicated.

Anatomical representation

Anatomical representation (Fig 14.6c) shows a predominance of upper hindlimb, and a lesser peak of girdles and upper forelimb. The pattern is essentially similar to that of sheep, described above.

14.2.6 Exploitation of minor mammals

Table 14.1 summarises the occurrence of the remaining mammals. Domestic mammals are represented by horse, dog and cat. Horse is the most common of the three, both in terms of fragment counts (Table 14.1) and frequency (Table 14.4). Dog is the next most common/frequent, with cat occurring only in periods 5, 7 and 8. Numbers of bones are too small for detailed analysis of any of the species.

Horse

The horse remains present a consistent pattern throughout the site, with bones from all periods fused (only one exception from period 6, a femur with proximal not fused, distal fused). There is no evidence for butchery, and this is backed-up by the lesser degree of fragmentation compared with cattle. Some groups of articulated bones were recovered, including the tarsals and metatarsal III of a hind limb from period 8 and metacarpals II, III and IV, and carpals of a forelimb from period 9. Some measurements are summarised in Table 14.7a).

Dog

All the dog bones represent adult individuals. Two partial skeletons are present, one from period 6 comprising eleven bones, and one from period 8 with eighteen bones. Two bones, also from period 8, represent large dogs, but the majority are medium sized (Table 14.7b).

Cat

The few cat bones all represent adults. Cats may have been truly less common than dogs, or possibly they are under represented due to the lack of sieving. Measurements are given in Table 14.7c.

Deer

Three species of deer are represented, with red deer predominant. The single fallow deer is not a certain identification: it might alternatively be a

Table 14.7 Summary of selected greatest length measurements, minor mammals and birds

a) *Horse*

Metacarpal III	P5: 223.3
Tibia	P7: 321.9; P8: 351.9, 355.8
Astragalus	P5: 65.2; P8: 51.0
Calcaneum	P6: 108.1
Metatarsal III	P5: 240.5; P6: 283.1, 282.8, 261.0; P8: 269.0

b) *Dog*

Mandible	P8: 119.0
Humerus	P6: 237.0; P8: 137.3
Radius	P6: 235.5; P8: 140.8, 159.0
Femur	P8: 173.2
Tibia	P6: 263.9; 174.0
Calcaneum	P6: 61.1

c) *Cat*

Humerus	P8: 95.0
Radius	P8: 80.0
Tibia	P7: 89.3

d) *Birds*

Domestic fowl:	
Coracoid	P8: 47.3
Ulna	P8: 62.2, 62.0, 71.0
Carpometacarpus	P7: 38.5
Femur	P8: 77.4
Tibiotarsus	P8: 90.7, 115.5
Goose:	
Coracoid	P8: 74.5, 71.6
Femur	P7: 79.0, P8: 79.1
Woodcock:	
Humerus	P4: 52.8
Crow:	
Femur	P6: 55.7

small red deer. The limited representation of deer (Table 14.4) may indicate that they did not form a major part of the diet (contrasted with Okehampton, Maltby, 1982 and Middleton Stoney, Levitan, 1984a). Alternatively, remains of deer might have been disposed of elsewhere.

Other mammals

The other wild mammals represented are rabbit, mole and whale. The rabbit may be intrusive (the prehistoric occurrences certainly so), as may be the mole bone. A fragment of whale vertebra is present from period 7. Such finds are not infrequent, and whale bones sometimes end up at sites far inland.

14.2.7 Bird remains

The very poor representation of birds (Table 14.1) may be a reflection of the lack of sieving, and it is interesting to note that the largest species represented, goose, is also the most common after domestic fowl (which is ubiquitous on medieval sites) (Table 14.1). The wild birds are mainly corvids: crow, rook and raven – all possibly scavengers here. The woodcock could represent wildfowling, and the buzzard might have been a captive bird, or possibly just a chance occurrence. With such small numbers of bones, the frequency table (Table 14.4) probably gives a truer picture of their status. It is intriguing to note, therefore, that goose is better represented than fowl using this method, the greater number of fowl bones being concentrated in fewer contexts. Selected measurements are given in Table 14.7d.

14.2.8 Fish remains

The comments about sieving (above) are even more relevant in the case of fish, and the site would almost certainly have had a greater number of species than the six listed in Table 14.1. The spurdog is common in the coastal and offshore waters of northern Europe. It has only been exploited commercially in relatively recent times for its liver oil and as fish meal; formerly it was regarded as a nuisance due to the damage it caused in nets. Roker, or thornback ray, is the commonest ray of shallow water, mainly living on muddy, sandy or gravelly bottoms. It is the principal constituent of the 'skate' catch landed by bottom trawling, inshore fishing vessels. The salmonid is probably either salmon (*Salmo salar*) or trout (*Salmo trutta*). Both are valuable food fish, and are also popular sporting (ie angling) catches. The cod is a widely distributed fish and has been exploited since prehistory. When salted or dried, it can be kept for many months, and thus transported for inland trading. The tub gurnard is relatively common in inshore waters, it is exploited both commercially and by anglers. Finally, the bass is common in the sea around England and Wales, and is another popular, commercially exploited fish. The above comments on the fishing and habitats are based on Wheeler (1978). All the fish could represent fairly local, inshore catches, or possibly some angling.

14.3 Conclusions

Analysis of the whole temporal range represented at this site is hampered by small samples for all the periods except period 8, the late 13th century. This period is when the Edwardian Castle was built, and the main bone bearing context (G4, Site E, 57) contained the largest number of bones of any of the contexts from the site. Selected comparisons with two other castles of similar periods, Okehampton,

Devon and Middleton Stoney, Oxfordshire, indicates a number of similarities and differences. The main difference is in the exploitation of deer, these being very important at both English sites. The absence of large numbers of deer bones here need not indicate that deer were not important, but there is no positive evidence to show that they were. Since this context is outside the castle itself, it probably contained a mixture of urban and castle rubbish; this might explain the paucity of deer bones.

Cattle were the most important species exploited, though in period 8 they were less common in terms of fragment counts than periods before and after (Table 14.1), though in terms of frequencies, they were more common (Table 14.4). It would appear that prime beef was not generally consumed, most of the cattle being adults or old adults, with sex structures indicating that the main reason for this was a dairying economy, a result which is broadly similar to both Okehampton and Middleton Stoney. In contrast to both sites, however, is the anatomical representation which indicates mainly primary butchery waste at Rhuddlan.

Okehampton had no evidence of any goat, and at Middleton Stoney there was only one goat bone present. Thus, although goats are uncommon at Rhuddlan, they do appear to be better represented than the other sites. Sheep remains are similar to the other sites, with mainly kitchen/food refuse being represented, the samples being dominated by girdle and upper limb bones. Ageing results are also similar, implying that sheep were probably mainly reared for wool, and were slaughtered as adults.

Pigs were an important minority species at both Okehampton and Middleton Stoney, but at Rhuddlan they were present in smaller proportions: 11% of fragments, compared with 31% from Okehampton and 21% from Middleton Stoney. In other respects, however, the evidence from pigs was similar.

The Rhuddlan assemblage is an important and welcome addition to the small corpus of Welsh sites.

15 Botanical Remains

15.1 Introduction

Samples were taken on site from contexts which appeared rich in charcoal or in charred grain. There was no programme of sieving. Because of the lack of a systematic on-site sampling programme and with the time-lapse in the preparation of the report, samples for analysis were selected from a few contexts for which understanding of the plant remains appeared useful for their interpretation.

15.2 Charred plant remains from T50 and T61 T G Holden (1989)

Pits T50 and T61 contained layers rich in charred plant remains. Samples from these layers (samples k1 from T61E, the basal deposit in T61, k2 from T61F, the deposit immediately above the base of T61 and the sample from 333A, the basal deposit in T50) were floated and subjected to detailed analysis. The full report formed the subject of a dissertation submitted as part of the requirements of a MSc in Bioarchaeology of the University of London in 1984. This, together with details of other analyses, is filed with the archive. The overall aim of this dissertation was to attempt to throw light on the possible function of the pits and also upon crop husbandry practices employed in and around 13th century Rhuddlan.

15.2.1 The plant remains
Cereals

Although both pits contained remains of barley (*Hordeum sativum*), bread wheat (*Triticum aestivum*) and rye (*Secale cereale*), it was the grains and chaff fragments of oats (*Avena* sp) that were found clearly to dominate the samples. Once separated, it could be seen that a number of oat grains were substantially larger than the majority. It was felt that because of this striking difference and the lack of intermediate forms that the larger ones could be safely put into the *Avena sativa* category whereas the majority fell into an *Avena strigosa/brevis* category. Of the oat chaff fragments, large numbers of the lemma/palea bases and fragments of awns, lemmas and paleas were recovered.

The other cereals were represented mainly by the grains, but the occasional rachis fragment of rye and rachilla or awn fragment of barley was also recorded. Numerically, barley proved to be the second most abundant crop. However, the low numbers of this, together with cereals other than

oats, make any meaningful comments on relative abundance difficult.

It seems fairly certain that the barley was of a hulled variety. The twisted grains characteristic of a six row variety were well represented but this does not exclude the possibility that a two row variety was also present.

Pulses

The only traces of pulses from the samples were several fragments of either pea (*Pisum sativum*) or bean (*Vicia faba*). The poor condition of these did not allow for any more accurate identification.

Remains other than crops

Large numbers of seeds of non-crop plants were recovered. The majority of these are to be found in field environments (ie segetals) and are indeed dominated by common agricultural weeds *Anthemis cotula* (stinking mayweed), *Chrysanthemum segetum* (corn marigold) and *Chenopodium/Atriplex* type (goosefoot family). Several of the species recovered, notably *Polygonum hydropiper* (water pepper), *Rumex palustris* (marsh dock), *Filipendula* sp (meadow sweet) and members of the Cyperaceae are, however, more commonly associated with wet or marshy conditions.

Finally as well as the seed component, quantities of rush stems (*Juncus cf maritimus*) were recovered from T61, and samples from T50 revealed substantial numbers of small soil accretions. These were of a mixed composition, containing both mineral and charred organic material. This, together with their cylindrical and constricted shape, gives rise to the supposition that they were possibly insect droppings.

15.2.2 Second phase deposit in T50

A preliminary examination of a sample from 333, the secondary use deposit in T50 was prepared by G Hillman in 1978. The sample was not available in 1984. The following is taken from Hillman's preliminary report (filed with the archive).

'Sample 333 has a composition very similar to that of 333A except that there is an abundance of straw nodes and oat inflorescence fragments. The ratio of primary to secondary (and tertiary) grains is also much lower. All this suggests that much of the grain and weed seeds in this sample came from chaff and straw burned on the fire. Another component of the fuel is perhaps represented by the very large number of charred fragments of twigs. However it seems probable that tail grain from the chaff was supplemented by prime grain from the kilning chamber as well, in which case it must be assumed that it was being kilned prior to storage or prior to dehusking, though it is not altogether impossible that whole sheaves were being dried'.

15.2.3 Discussion

The charred assemblages and their implications for the interpretation of the function of pits T61 and T50

The high ratio of oat grains to all other classes of debris suggests that the assemblage does not represent a waste fraction discarded during crop processing. It would seem more likely that it represents a part-cleaned fraction of a crop in which oats were by far the dominant cereal. The absence of many of the larger items, such as straw fragments, culm nodes or weed seed-heads that might be expected to be present during crop processing, suggests that the crop had been winnowed and probably coarse sieved prior to deposition. The presence of many of the smaller segetal type weed seeds such as *Anthemis cotula* (stinking mayweed) however would imply that the crop had not yet been, or had only partially been, fine sieved, this being a process that would normally remove seeds smaller than the cereal grains. Hillman (1981) has pointed out that minimal processing is often carried out by traditional agricultural communities living in wet climates. This would inevitably leave substantial numbers of weed seeds in with the prime-product. He also suggests (per comm) that with a small grained crop such as *Avena strigosa* the smaller mesh sieves required would not eliminate many of the weed seeds that might have been removed had a wheat sieve been employed. Either way, all three samples, having similar composition, fit into a category equivalent to Hillman's (1981; 1984) description of semi-clean prime grain ready for storage.

A relatively high proportion of the grains are still enclosed within their lemmas, suggesting that the crop had not yet been dehusked. Hillman (1981), using ethnographic models taken from modern Turkey, points out that it is in this partially cleaned and hulled state that one might expect to find both glume wheats and the hulled free-threshing cereals such as barley or oats being stored until they could be processed in a piecemeal fashion throughout the year as they were required for food. This is a practice that is apparently more common in areas where wet summers are the norm and so preclude the large scale processing of crops out-of-doors. It would seem likely then that the local crops of oats, given the nature of the climate in North Wales, would have been stored in this semi-cleaned state.

The possibility of such an assemblage becoming charred relates to the general form of pits T61 and T50 and their similarity to structures identified elsewhere as drying kilns. The use of drying kilns for both parching cereals prior to dehusking, and for drying prior to storage or milling has been recorded both archaeologically and ethnographically from Northern Europe (see eg Fenton, 1978 or Monk, 1981). Fenton, using examples from Orkney and Shetland, points out that the risk of accidents during this process was relatively high. Such accidents must be assumed to result in the charring of quantities of cereal fragments.

The fraction that is represented by the charred samples is of a class that could be expected to have been put into a drying kiln prior to dehusking or storage; it is therefore not improbable that they could be the result of the kind of accident described by Fenton. It would be quite feasible for the floor supporting the drying crop to catch fire, thus charring the crop but leaving the main structure of the kiln intact. Since Fenton (1978) also records that in kilns from the Northern Isles 'the bed on which the grain was laid to dry was made of drawn straw' the charred rush stems might be interpreted as part of the drying floor or a less permanent part of the kiln's structure. If the material was the result of a drying kiln accident, the two separate layers of charred material from T61 indicate that such an event occurred at least twice during the working life of this kiln.

The sample from T50 was found to contain small soil accretions similar to those produced by certain species of insect. If these can be proved to be of this origin it might indicate that the sample represented the disposal of grain by burning because it had for some reason spoiled. As Hillman (1982b) points out, drying kilns can be used to dispose of infested crops as one of their regular functions.

Crop husbandry

Although oats were evidently the major crop represented in all the samples, there were traces of the cereals barley, bread wheat and rye together with either peas or beans. In this respect Rhuddlan fits into a pattern already set for medieval North Wales. Similar combinations are known both historically (see Thomas, 1968 who identifies oats, 'corn', barley and peas as the major crop complex) and archaeologically from medieval Cefn Greanog (Hillman, 1982a) and 13th century Conwy (unpublished work by author). Hillman notes that as yet there is no basis for inferring that rye was grown as a crop in its own right and suggests that its presence may merely have been tolerated as a contaminant in one of the more common crops.

It is impossible to tell whether the mixture of crops in the assemblages represented by the Rhuddlan samples was the result of untidy crop processing, in which crops, although grown separately, became mixed on the threshing floor, in the drying kiln or storage room, or whether more than

Table 15.1 Charcoal analysis

Context	Species	dia mm	rings	est age	growth
H39 Mesolithic soil	Oak *Quercus* spec	5	5	5	–
	Oak *Quercus* spec	40	7	7	fast
	Oak *Quercus* spec	60+	9	9+	fast
	Oak *Quercus* spec	60	18	20	–
	Oak *Quercus* spec	80	23	25	–
	Oak *Quercus* spec	80	13	13	fast
	worm eaten oak bark, 20 mm thick				
	Hazel nut shells				
J92 Mesolithic pit	Oak fragment				v fast
M90b Mesolithic pit	Hazel nut shells				
M90d Mesolithic pit	Hazel nut shells				
M90f Mesolithic pit	Hazel nut shells				
M122 Mesolithic hollow	Hazel nut shells				
M120 Later prehistoric pit	Oak	60?	frags	–	fast
T400 Stakeholes pre-AD 900	Oak	40	26	26	–
T145 *Grubenhaus*	Elm *Ulmus* spec	80	10	10	fast
	Unidentifiable bark fragment				
V4 mid-13th century pottery kiln	Oak	50?	frags	–	fast
	Oak	150	20	30	fast
	Oak	150+	20	30+	fast
	Oak	60+	35	40+	slow
	Hazel *Corylus avellana*	50	15	15	slow
	Hazel knot	60	10	10	fast
	Hazel	70	10	10	fast
J68 pit pre-AD *c* 1280 (ironworking)	Oak	60	28	30	–
	Oak	80	21	25	–
	Oak	100	26	36	–
	iron-replaced oak fragments	80+	12	15+	fast
T50 late 13th corn dryer	Oak (not listed)	60+	25	50+	slow
T349 pit with whetstone	Hazel	5	2	2	–
	Hazel	10	3	3	–
T80 industrial activity	Oak	60	11	11	fast
14th century	Oak	40	45	50	v slow
	Oak	80+	20	30	fast
T115 pit assoc T80	Oak	25	19	19	–

one crop was being harvested together from the same fields. The latter does seem to have been deliberate policy in some places. This is illustrated by Keil (1965, 236) who shows that oats and barley were grown together as a mixed crop known as 'drage' in parts of England during the medieval period. The low frequency of crops other than oats does, however, suggest that if they were present in the field they were more likely to have been tolerated contaminants than part of a deliberate mixed crop.

It is notable that the seeds of several species of plants showing an affinity for damp conditions are represented. The most probable explanation is that they too were harvested as weeds with the main crop. Oats are, to a certain extent, tolerant of damp conditions and it would not be suprising to find some of these damp loving species in the wetter margins of fields on the low lying marine or estuarine clays that surround Rhuddlan.

15.2.4 Summary

Each of the samples seems to represent a partially cleaned crop of oats containing minor contamination from other crops, either the result of pre- or post-depositional activities. The presence of seeds of certain water-loving species suggests that the fields may have been somewhat waterlogged for at least part of the year. The composition of the assemblage indicates that it was charred at a stage in the processing sequence appropriate for placing in a drying kiln to facilitate drying prior to storage, or parching prior to dehusking. This supports the identification of both T61 and T50 as drying kilns.

15.3 Sample with charred grain from infill of drying kiln C3

T Holden (1986)

Context C3D, an infill layer in the suggested kiln, contained mainly charcoal, with one or two cereal grains and grass caryopses. Three grains of *Triticum aestivo-compactum* (bread wheat) together with two which could be *Avena* (oats) were the only identifications. The small number prevents any interpretation of the assemblage as a whole.

15.4 Sample with charred grain from pit with Bronze Age pottery C46 T Holden (1986)

The most significant identifications were of cereal grains, two of *Hordeum* (unref) and seven of *Triticum aestivo-compactum* (bread wheat). This wheat is often thought to have been brought into this country at a later date than the Bronze Age but earlier finds are now being reported such as that from Abingdon, Oxon (Jones, 1978). The assemblage also contained several types of weed seed: *Chenopodium/Atriplex* spp (ten), *Vicia/Lathyrus* (medium-sized) (one), *Plantago lanceolata (maritima)* (one), *Galium aperine* (probable) (one), *Bromus* spp (one).

The assemblage as a whole could have been the product of various types of processes but the number of items is so small that no definitive suggestions can be made.

15.5 Sample with charred grain from pit B7

This sample, from a pit which was filled with material black with charred material, was floated by T Holden in 1984, and shown to contain 'considerable quantities of grain and weed seeds'. It was decided, with the limited resources available, not to work on this further as there was no dating evidence for the pit.

15.6 Charcoal G Morgan (1988)

Samples were selected to cover (a) all Mesolithic contexts producing this material (b) charcoal-rich contexts of other dates where, in most cases, information might relate to activities such as metalworking.

The sample is too small to make any particular comments but in general the presence of fast growing oak and hazel would fit in with the Mesolithic dates. It is interesting that larger oaks were used in the industrial processes. This would be as charcoal for metalworking but not for the pottery kiln where a fast burning fuel is usually required. In this case it may represent offcuts or waste from other uses.

While elm is known from the Mesolithic (Godwin, 1975), personal research suggest that it is more commonly found in Roman and Medieval contexts.

15.7 Pollen

Samples from Site E Mesolithic pit J104 were submitted to Dr P Moore of the Botany Department, School of Biological Sciences, King's College, University of London in 1971. Dr Moore was able to identify 'two grass pollen grains and a few derived spores' but considered that conditions must have been too aerobic on deposition for sufficient pollen to have survived for analysis. In retrospect it is unfortunate that negative results from an early and possibly atypical context caused no further samples to be collected for study.

Acknowledgments
We are grateful to Gordon Hillman for all his initial help as well as to the authors for their contributions.

16 Coins and medieval small finds

16.1 The coins George C Boon

The seven medieval coins were originally identified in 1978 by the late Michael Dolley. They are now in the National Museum of Wales (except No 3).

1 Edward the Confessor

'Sovereign/Eagles' type (BMC ix, North, *English Hammered Coinage*, 827), *c* 1056–9. Rev. + [B]RVNNIC. ON LEG. – Chester mint, moneyer Bruning, cf Pirie, 1964, nos 333–4, same rev. die. Broken, with a fragment missing. *From mechanical clearance of topsoil, Site A.* A very similar piece was found on the beach at Meols, near Hoylake (Wirral) last century (Gibson, 1977, 64).

2 William II

'Cross Voided' type (*BMC* iii, North 853), *c* 1093–6. Rev. +BAT ON LVNDN – London mint, moneyer 'Bat' (?Bartelme), cf Dolley 1969, Stockholm no 225, same rev. die, perhaps same obv. Broken and repaired. For provenance see next.

3 William II

Same type, known only from a transparency taken by the excavator; the coin disintegrated during conservation. Mint and moneyer uncertain. *From the groin area of burial M117*, together with Coin No 2, a small rock crystal fragment and some very decayed leather, possibly from a purse. The fact that both were of the one type argues strongly that the grave belongs to the period of their formal currency and was thus one of the earliest, just postdating the construction of the Norman Church mentioned in Domesday.

4 Edward I

London farthing, Class IIIc (North 1053/1), *c* 1280–1, very little worn: Loss even as late as 1285 seems unlikely. *Unstratified, Site A.*

5 Edward I

Bristol farthing, Class IIIg (North 1053/1), marginally later than Coin No 4; less well preserved. *Site E, plot boundary gully H4*, from a field system imposed on soil build-up over a lightly metalled roadway and working area associated with the construction of the Edwardian Castle *c* 1280.

6 Edward I

London penny, Class IIb (North 1015), spring 1280. *Site T, level of deliberate dumping superimposed on the infill of the Ditch of the Norman Borough T59.*

7 Edward I

Bristol penny, Class IIId (North 1019), *c* 1281. *Site T, top of filling of a large timber structure postdating the levelling of the Norman Borough Ditch T34.* Somewhat corroded, as is Coin No 6.

Comment

It was, of course, hoped that there might have been some numismatic support from these excavations for the identification of Rhuddlan with the *burh* 'aet Cledemuthan' ('at the mouth of the Clwyd'), but the fort may not have been long enough occupied for a mint to be sited there. By the time of the Bryn Maelgwyn (Llandudno) Cnut hoard, buried in the mid 1020s (Boon, 1986, 1–35), it must in any case have faded. Alternative locations for the *aet Cledemuthan* of the annal are discussed in Chapter 19.

Of the Confessor's penny, as of any single find, the circumstances of loss must remain obscure. I am not aware of any other Welsh find of the reign, but stray Saxon pennies from Offa onward are well known, though still uncommon (Boon, 1986, 14, 18 note; some others since). In general they illustrate frequent references in the Welsh Laws to payments in (English) pence: some elements in that body of material must certainly go back to pre-Conquest times, though many are demonstrably later.

More sanguine hopes attended the attested mint of the Norman Borough, its profits (based perhaps on local silver from the argentiferous lead of Halkyn Mountain) shared between Robert of Rhuddlan and Hugh of Avranches, Earl of Chester: the rare pieces 'sign' RVDILI, where the D must stand for Đ and the final I for the the first stroke of an A, as in other instances about this period. But it was not to be. Likewise there was no sign of the more prolific, though longer and periodic, coinage in the 'Short Cross' period running from the latter years of Henry II down to 1240 or 1245; Dolley's is the best account (1963, 226–7) of this coinage, 'signed' RVLA and on one die RVLAN, obviously a syncopated form of the placename; doubts as to the ascription are stilled by finds of such pennies at Holywell and also in Anglesey. It will be remembered that Giraldus Cambrensis (ii, 10) refers in 1188 to a 'silver mine' encountered in the journey from St Asaph to Basingwerk.

Work on the construction of the defences of the Castle and Edwardian Borough is believed to have been substantially complete by 1282. Dolley in his original comment notes that this fact may help to explain the absence from these excavations of English pennies struck from the mid 1280s until the end of the 1320s, and of their counterparts struck in quantity in Dublin and Waterford in the early 1280s, of which even *Segontium* has yielded a specimen dropped by stone-robbers (Boon, 1976, 79 no 81 – a Waterford halfpenny). Also to be remarked is a parallel absence from these Rhuddlan sites of jetons or so-called 'wardrobe counters', which are finds characteristic of royal castles.

16.2 Objects of copper alloy (Fig 16.1)

MSF 1 Cast rectangular loop buckle 23mm by 15mm with decorative cast internal projections. The square-sectioned bar would have carried the pin which is missing. There are no close parallels for this buckle shape in Fingerlin (1971). Date later than 12th century? *T84 posthole, context ? 10th–12th centuries.*

MSF 2 Cast buckle with flat back and curved upper surface: pin broken. Single piece of sheet metal buckle plate doubled back around the bar and originally fixed to the strap with two rivets, hammered through from the underside to raise, but not pierce, the upper plate in two small bosses. The buckle and buckle plate are a total of 35mm long. The upper surface of the strap end is edged with rocked graver lines (Lowery, Savage & Wilkins, 1971) executed from the outer edge of the plate inward to a common line and then from the interior back to the same point to leave a raised line running through the decoration. There is a repoussé central boss. The cast decorative projections are paralleled by Fingerlin (1971, 73 & 85, Cat No 461), a type dated by her to between 1250 and 1300. *A48 upper fill of Ditch III.*

MSF 3 Buckle and buckle-plate. Cast D-shaped buckle with attached buckle plate, total length 34mm, pin missing. The buckle loop is decorated with raised cast decoration, possibly devolved snakes' heads. The buckle was subsequently decorated with rocked graver lines in the same manner as buckle MSF 2 to leave a raised line. The buckle plate was formed by a single sheet of metal wrapped around the bar and fixed to the strap with two rivets which pierce the top plate and are hammered over. The top surface of the buckle plate has a corrosion product which preserved traces of fibres. There are traces of tinning or silvering on the lower edge of the buckle plate which was presumably originally gilded. There are no close parallels for the decoration of the buckle loop in Fingerlin

(1971), but the general shape is dated by her to between 1250 and 1350. *Site A, B5 pit or oven.*

MSF 4 Small strap end cast buckle 13mm long with decoratively moulded ends. Some of the buckle plate survives around the bar; the pin is missing. Possibly a shoe buckle from Smithfield (London Museum, 1967, 272, Pl LXXVI) and from St Peter's Street, Northampton (Williams, 1979, 253, Fig 108) are close parallels for size and shape. See Fingerlin (1971, 73, 86 Cat No 224, 89 Cat No 288), suggesting dating to between 1250–1300. *T22 pebble horizon over Ditches.*

MSF 5 Buckle plate, tinned or silvered on upper surface, made out of sheet metal 23mm by 32mm folded double around a rectangular-sectioned bar (broken). Cut out in centre of plate for brooch pin; plate is pierced with holes for rivets, part of one rivet surviving. A groove in the upper plate adjacent to the cut out marks the position of the brooch pin (cf Beresford 1975, 91, Fig 43 No 8). *T22 pebble horizon over Ditches.*

MSF 6 Belt fitting ? Fragment of sheet metal 29mm long, bent double, 10mm wide. The sheet is pierced with two holes and has an elongated hole at the broken end. Decorated with incised lines using a graver. Possibly some form of belt fitting. *T65 slot for compound.*

MSF 7 Buckle or brooch pin; cast, 33mm long. Originally cast as a T, the loop has been formed by bending round the flat arms of the T, and clenching at the base of the loop. *Site E G5 base of c 1280 surface.*

MSF 8 Ewer or skillet leg and fragments. Cast foot and tubular leg 62mm long, very heavy, possibly a lead/copper alloy. The leg is too small to have supported a cauldron and may have been from a three-legged jug, ewer or skillet. Some of the body fragments had tight curvature which might suggest a spout from a ewer. The vessel is likely to have been late 13th or early 14th century. The London Museum Catalogue illustrates a 14th–15th century bronze three-legged ewer (1967, 200–1, Pl LIII), a bronze three-legged skillet (Pl LV) and a bronze three-legged cooking vessel (Pl LVI). A small cauldron from excavations in Southampton had a similar leg 90mm long (Platt & Coleman-Smith, 1975, 260, Fig 243). Date? *C31 void left by rotting wood in House 2 walltrench, body fragments also from floor C32.*

MSF 9 Needle 40mm long, made from drawn wire; eye is 4mm long. *T 59 upper fill Ditch III.*

MSF 10 Needle 61mm long made from drawn wire; eye 4mm long set in countersunk groove. *Site E G5 base of c 1280 surface.*

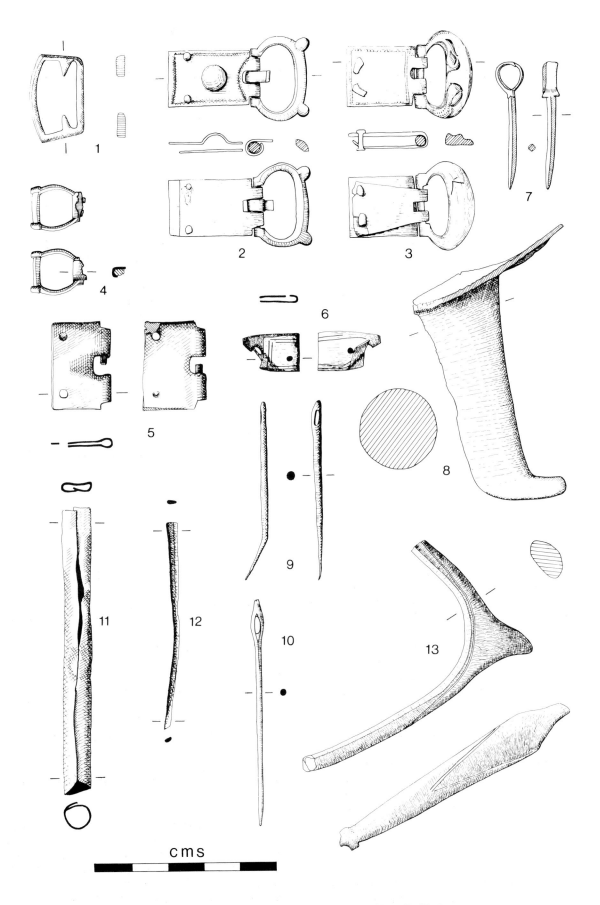

Fig 16.1 MSF 1–13 Objects of copper alloy. Full size.

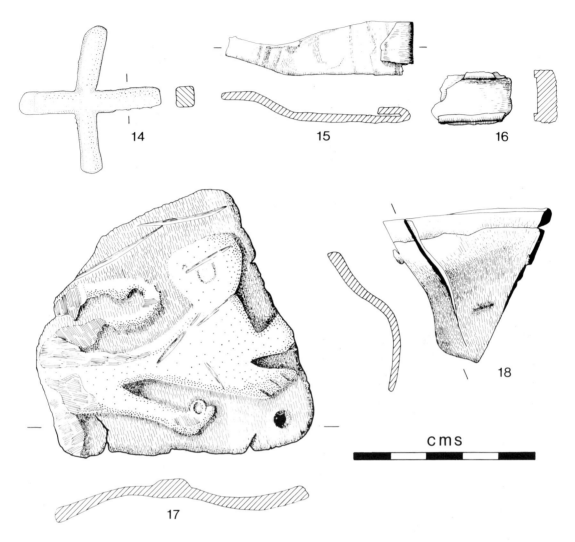

Fig 16.2 MSF 14–18 Objects of lead. Full size.

MSF 11 Tube of metal 76mm long, made from sheet rolled into a tube *c* 7mm in diameter and flattened at one end. Possibly a large lace tag (cf Rahtz, 1969, Fig 49, 87). *T59 Ditch III upper fill.*

MSF 12 Lace tag 54mm long, made from curved sheet metal; conforms to G E Oakley (in Williams, 1979, 262) type 1 from Northampton, although longer than examples found. *T65 slot for compound.*

MSF 13 Part of a small bronze rowel spur 56mm long from heel to terminal. Blanche Ellis comments: 'The sides evenly taper from behind the heel to narrow near the terminals. The incised horizontal V-shape on the sides and the small size are all features typical of early 17th or late 18th century spurs.' *Topsoil Site T.*

Not illustrated

(a) Small fragment of sheet bronze vessel with repair. *Edwardian bank O18.* (b) Fragment of oval-sectioned bracelet. *G86 boundary trench.* (c)

Heavily corroded mass of tightly twisted wire 1mm thick. *T231 gully date between the Iron Age and c AD 900.* Also about fifteen fragments, mainly of sheet metal, from various contexts (see archive).

16.3 Lead (Fig 16.2)

MSF 14 Cast cross 40mm by 40mm, no recesses on sides. *C2 Grubenhaus infill.*

MSF 15 Sheet offcut, 58mm long from sheet 2mm thick, end bent over. *T145 Grubenhaus infill.*

MSF 16 Fragment of window came 24mm long, recessed on one side only, internal width 8mm. *A82 upper fill Ditch III.*

MSF 17 Triangular plaque cast with figure of a lion. Originally at least 70mm by 70mm, 3–5mm thick; 200g in weight. Several old slashes across the lion as well as more recent damage. Rivet hole in bottom right hand corner. Heraldic lion in relief facing right. *T115 pit associated with industrial activity.*

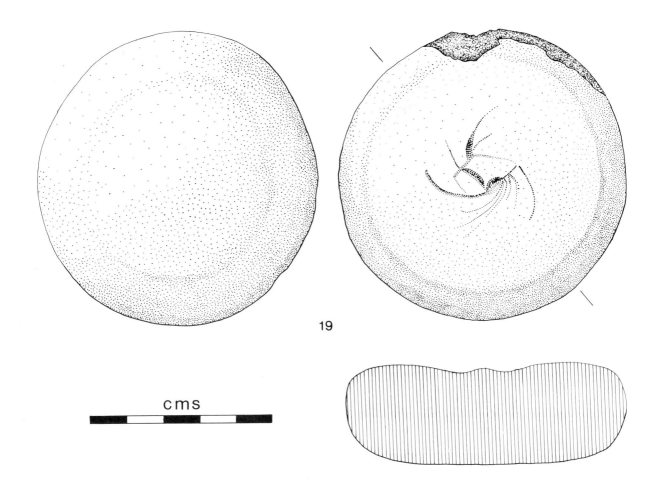

19

cms

Fig 16.3 MSF 19 Glass linen smoother. Full size.

MSF 18 Offcut, equilateral triangle 45mm by 45mm, cut from piece of lead sheet 3mm thick. Slash 40mm long down one side. *T59 Ditch III upper fill.*

Not illustrated

Lead, mostly very small fragments, was found in about 20 contexts (see archive). This included about 5kg poured around a piece of wood in *pit T349*, 0.5kg of molten lead in runs and dribbles on *C32 floor of House 2*, and runs of lead from the Site M Church in *soils M8 and M27* and in *burial M77*.

16.4 Glass (Fig 16.3)

MSF 19 Glass linen smoother. Opaque dark blue glass, 78mm in diameter. Dished base with swirling creases and central scar where handle or pontil was removed. A frequent find in Saxon, Viking and medieval contexts. A short discussion on examples from Northampton by G E Oakley (in Williams, 1979, 296–7 Fig 130) gives parallels and suggests a tendency for later examples to be larger. The late 13th century date for the context of MSF 19 fits well with the Northampton sequence. *Site E J65*

upper infill Ditch III.

Not illustrated

MSF 19 Two joining fragments of opaque dark green medieval window glass 2.5mm thick, forming half of a diamond-shaped quarry at least 30mm by 40mm. It has two grozed edges, trimmed to leave conchoidal scars at an angle. It is likely to have come either from an ecclesiastical context or perhaps from apartments at the castle. (cf G E Oakley in Williams, 1979, 296, Fig 130). *Site EG6 c 1280 surface.*

16.5 Fired clay (Fig 16.4)

MSF 20 Approximately one third of a fired clay loomweight *c* 150mm in diameter. The fabric is of hard sandy clay, possibly the local boulder clay, fired on the exterior to pinkish red, the core reduced to light grey. There are sparse inclusions ranging from rounded grits of 1mm to sub-angular pebbles of 10mm, with traces of burnt-out vegetable temper. The object fits into the category of bun-shaped loomweights, albeit with a slightly larger hole, discussed by Hurst (1959, 23–5, Fig 6);

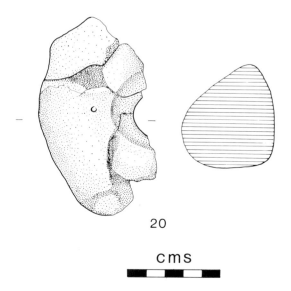

20

cms

Fig 16.4 MSF 20 Part of clay loom weight. ×½.

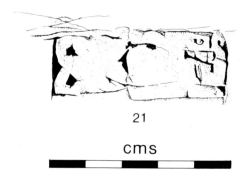

21

cms

Fig 16.5 MSF 21 detail of carving on bone trial piece. Full size.

bun-shaped loomweights are suggested to date between the 9th and 12th centuries (Shoesmith, 1985, 70, Fig 64). The Clwyd Archaeological Record No 2139 lists stray finds in a garden at Bryn Llithnig, Cwm Diserth 'bun-shaped, flattened clay discs; loomweights. One whole specimen and fragments of others'; these appear never to have been published and are now in St Asaph Chapter House Museum. *T97 posthole south of Ditches.*

16.6 Bone objects (Fig 16.5–6)

MSF 21 Bone trial piece on the right radial bone of a calf (250mm long) (Pl 16.1). The incised design is enclosed in a panel 43mm long by 14–17mm wide. The decoration appears to consist of a beast facing right with its foreleg raised up against the frame and its hindquarter developing with interlace. There may be a nostril above its jaw or perhaps an eye set rather forward. The design is roughly executed and unfinished; it may have been a 'practice piece'.

Dominic Tweddle considers that MSF 21 shows similarities with some of the Jellinge style sculpture at York (pers comm). It could be 10th century or earlier in date. Bone trial pieces including motifs of similar crudity are known from London (Pritchard, 1991, Figs 3.57–64) 1985, 12, plate). Two very fine 11th century bone trial pieces are known from Dublin in Ringerike style (O'Riordain, 1971, Pl VIII A,B) and in Borre style (O'Riordain, 1971, Fig 21). Trial pieces are also known from 10th century Viking levels in York (Hall, 1984, Figs 56, 57). *A78 middle fill of Ditch I.*

MSF 22 Fragment of bone comb fixing plate with five lines of incised decoration down its length and notches along its edge. The decorated upper surface is curved, the back flat. Probably part of the fixing plate of a (?Saxon) bone comb. Several examples of

this type of decoration are known from West Stow, Suffolk (West, 1985, Figs 216, 218). The fragment is too small for certainty and might be of much later medieval date. A ? medieval composite bone comb No 15/248/1 is among the material in the National Museum of Wales excavated from Diserth Castle by T A Glenn. *V14 pit, context ? 13th century.*

MSF 23 Bone handle, made from long bone, surviving length 75mm; broken at one end with the interior hollowed out, at the other a carefully finished chisel point with two facets. Each face bears two grooves 1mm deep. *T29 soil, context probably late 13th/14th centuries.*

MSF 24 One half of a bi-partite bone handle 77mm long with three small rivet holes. Probably for a small iron knife (see Good & Tabraham, 1981, Fig 11 for a similar handle in wood). *Site E soil G143, a pre-Norman context.*

Not Illustrated

Four other bone fragments with some evidence for working came from different contexts (see archive).

16.7 Antler objects and waste

(Fig 16.7)

The concentration of waste antler and objects on Site A, especially in *C2 Grubenhaus infill*, suggests that working of antler took place in that area. It cannot be determined whether or not this took place in C2, the disused hollow of which could have been used for dumping waste. The waste contained only tines and two burrs, but no part of a beam. The identifications of antler type and species are by Melvyn Davies who states that the burrs can be positively identified as from shed antlers of red deer. The tines are probably from red deer, but can assume a variety of shapes depending on feeding conditions. Two pieces, apart from those individually described, had facets suggesting unfinished artefacts. The small number of deer bones from the excavations is consistent with the use of shed

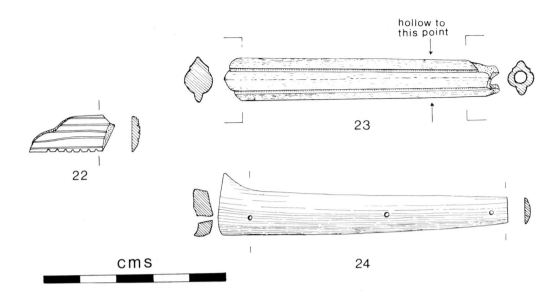

Fig 16.6 MSF 22-24 Bone objects. Full size.

Pl 16.1 MSF 21 Trial piece on calf radial bone.

antlers rather than those from animals culled for food.

Manufacture of antler and bone objects was common in early medieval centres. At West Stow (West, 1985, 96, 177) sawn antler objects are common, more frequent than those of bone. 11th to 13th century levels at Dublin (O'Riordain, 1971, 75) evidenced intensive bone and antler working, shed red deer antler being the principal material

used. Antler and bone working was also prominant among the crafts of Anglo-Danish York (Radley, 1971, 51–2) and of Saxon Southampton (Holdsworth, 1976, 45).

16.7.1 Antler waste (Not illus)

(a) Burr from the shed antler of a red deer, probably an animal at least four years old. Diameter

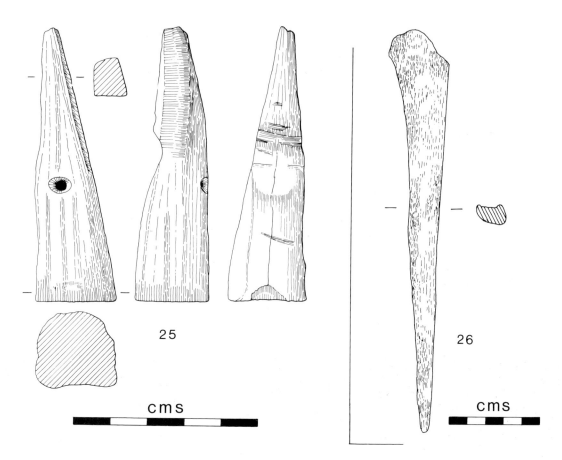

Fig 16.7 MSF 25–26 Antler objects. MSF 25 full size, 26 ½.

75–80mm, with five saw cuts parallel to the face and two at right angles, which suggests very thorough use of every fragment of material that could be utilized from the antler. *C2 infill.*

(b) A brow tine 237mm long, complete with whole but damaged burr. The burr is only 67mm diameter maximum, so it was not shed at the same time as (a). It may be from another animal or the same animal a year or two earlier. The beam was sawn straight across, so there is only one saw mark. *C2 infill.*

(c) A 110mm piece neatly cut from a (?) terminal tine furthest from the skull. To have a terminal tine the animal must have been at least five years old. *C2 infill.*

(d) Antler tine fragment 111mm long, tip partly sawn through and then snapped off; base hacked. Size suggests a brow tine and it is compatible with burr (a) above, but does not quite fit onto it. The hacking is crude in this piece. *C2 infill.*

(e) A rather straight tine, 101mm long. Hacked four or five times to chop it off from the beam - possibly a trez tine. *C2 infill.*

(f) A large tine 215mm long with very corrugated surface. The cut end bears one major saw mark, one minor saw mark and a saw cut 6mm deep. There are also a series of about seven shallow saw marks covering about 11mm halfway along the tine. The tine is too large for a terminal tine, and

may have been a brow or trez tine. *A80 upper fill Ditch I.*

(g) Tine 110mm long, almost straight with very corrugated surface. Slender, only 170–190mm wide at the cut. The striations on the cut surface suggest sawing, the final 3mm snapped off by pulling the cut apart. *T65 compound slot.*

16.7.2 Antler Objects

MSF 25 Roughly cut red deer tine 73mm long, maximum diameter 26mm, cleanly sliced down both sides to form a point; roughly cut notch in centre. On the opposite face is a tapering oval hole 5mm deep. No trace of any wear.

The closest parallel, from Romano-British levels at Colchester (Crummy, 1983, 105 Fig 109, 2538), has been interpreted as an antler cheek piece; the author cites Britnell (1976) among other sources. However, the Bronze Age cheek pieces described by Britnell are fundamentally different, having a diagnostic central rectangular perforation to hold the mouthpiece flanked by five or more holes at either end of the cheekpiece (Britnell, 1976, 24 figs 1 & 3a). The Rhuddlan and Colchester objects are not types recognized by Britnell (pers comm) as harness fittings. Use of the Rhuddlan object may have involved wrapping a strap or cord round the notch, which was held in place with a peg set in the

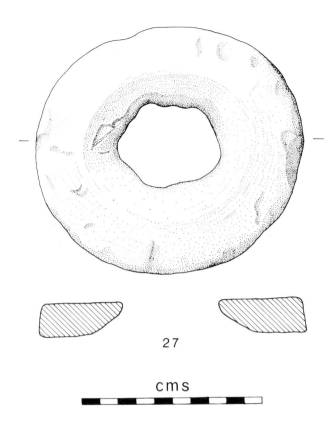

Fig 16.8 MSF 27 Stone weight. ×¹/₂.

hole, an arrangement which would not withstand much strain. *C2 Grubenhaus infill.*

MSF 26 Point 105mm long, quite straight and probably from one of the terminal tines, unless it had been cut from a beam. The tip is smooth and worn. Probably for use in weaving. See G E Oakley (in Williams 1979, 312–3). *A82 dump in top of Ditch III.*

16.8 Stone objects (except bakestones & whetstones) (Figs 16.8–9)

MSF 27 Perforated disc made from a waterworn pebble 142mm by 130mm, 20mm thick. The centre has been perforated to form a rough hole approximately 26mm by 2mm. Possibly a weight or net sinker. The pebble is too hard to show wear through suspension. *T145 Grubenhaus infill.*

MSF 28 Sandstone spindle whorl 40mm in diameter, 12mm thick, with hole 10–12mm across slightly off centre. Fine-grained sandstone, light grey and soft, showing frequent small file marks. *Soil M8.*

MSF 29 Globular spindle whorl in hard, coarse grey sandstone, diameter 28mm, hole 12mm across, well finished. Appears to fit within the mean range of whorl size and weight to be effective in the hand spinning of yarn (G E Oakley and A D Hall in Williams, 1979, 286–9, Figs 125, 126,

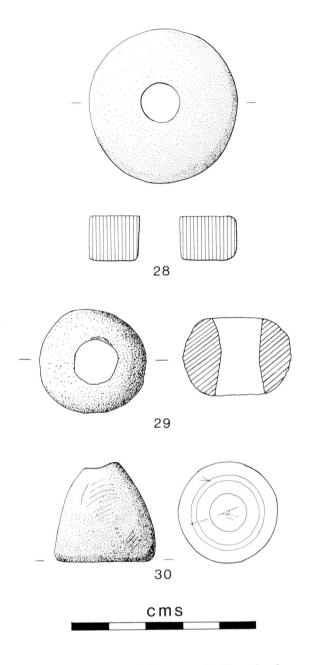

Fig 16.9 MSF 28-30 Stone spindle whorls and gaming counter. Full size.

Tables 28, 29). The globular spindle whorl in stone is a frequent find in early medieval contexts (Clarke & Carter, 1977, 315–7). *Soil M8.*

MSF 30 Small dome-shaped siltstone gaming piece, 24mm diameter, top broken. Base has been ground flat and bears three incised concentric circles and a central compass point. On the side of the dome, part of a series of nine lightly incised concentric circles is visible. *T61A in top of drying kiln.*

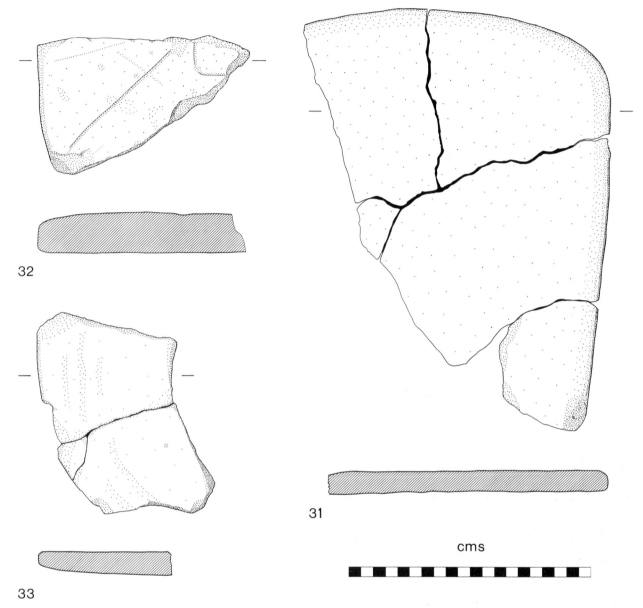

Fig 16.10 MSF 31-3 Bakestones. ×1/3.

16.9 Bakestones (Fig 16.10)

Parts of three bakestones were found, all of the same purple coarse-grained sandstone with some mica flakes, possibly from the Upper Coal Measures near Flint. Though differing in shape and thickness, they were all carefully made, with smooth, flat surfaces and rounded edges; they had been heavily burnt. Their lower surfaces were blackened and sooty, and they had started cracking during use as soot and blackening had spread partway up the sides of broken edges. It is likely they were used for baking bread or cakes over an open fire, a practice traditional in Wales (Peake, 1946, 111). Comparandum from 13th/14th century rural context at Barry (Thomas & Dowdell, 1987, 132). The stone used would be suitable because its even-grained texture would have assisted even

distribution of heat. The thickness of the bake-stones may have been determined by the way in which the stone split naturally into slabs. Even so considerable skill was used in the dressing of the two thinner examples 31 and 33. They may have been artefacts of high value in their time; all three are almost certainly of 13th century date.

MSF 31 Part of bakestone, 15mm thick, originally rectangular in shape and over 300mm by 300mm in size. *Site A, C24 pit in House 1.*

MSF 32 Part of bakestone, probably of rectangular shape but 35mm thick, much more durable than MSF 31. The upper, baking, surface has been decorated with a lightly incised geometric design reminiscent of the patterns used on gaming boards (see Merrills boards from Treworld, Cornwall, and

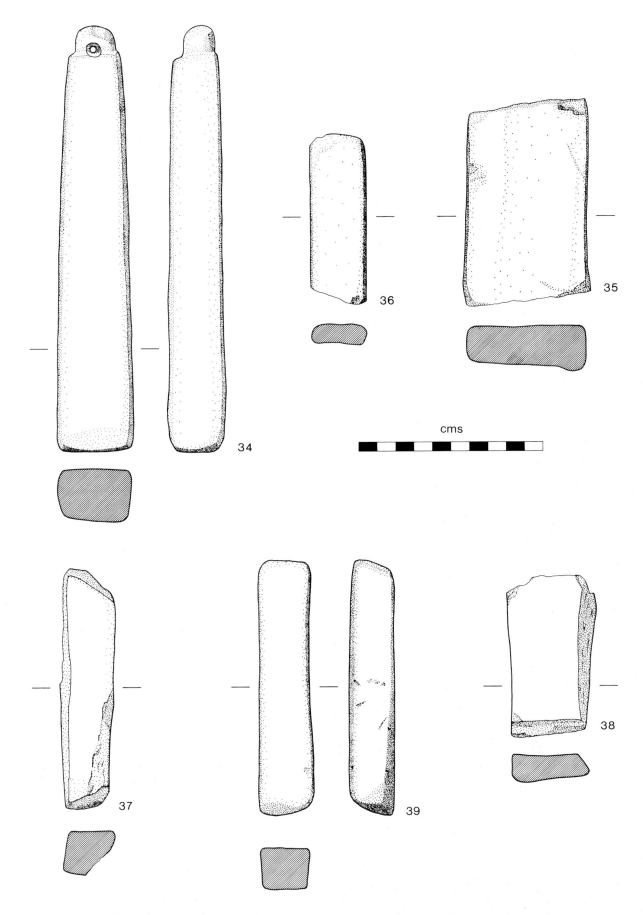

Fig 16.11 MSF 34-9 Whetstones. ×¹/₂.

Pl 16.2 MSF 34 Whetstone from pit T349.

references, Dudley & Minter, 1966, 56, Fig 17). *Site A. C3a fill of ? drying kiln.*

MSF 33 Part of bakestone, oval or round in shape with a radius of at least 110mm. 20mm thick. A marked chamfer on its lower edge, and slight grooves, ground almost flat, showing remnants of the dressing of the upper, baking, surface. A small fragment possibly of MSF 33 from *G16. Site E. G26 pit before* c *1280.*

16.10 Whetstones (Figs 16.11–12)

Only two were of the few rock types used for medieval whetstones with a wide distribution (Moore, 1978, 72), MSF 37 of Norwegian Ragstone (Ellis, 1969, type 1A(1)), and MSF 39 (Ellis, 1969, Type III) of Pennant rocks, with increasing archaeological evidence for a source in the Bristol Coalfields (Moore, 1978, 65). All other Rhuddlan examples were probably from North Wales, and quite local in origin.

MSF 34 (Pl 16.2) Large well-shaped whetstone with a carefully shaped suspension loop; 226mm long overall, with a slightly rounded rectangular section tapering towards the loop. The surface has been finished to almost a polish all over, and there are no signs of use. Made out of a flaggy, grey, impure quartzose sandstone, common in Upper Carboniferous or Lower Palaeozoic rocks in North Wales. Its size, finish and condition suggest that it was a status object, an interpretation which the circumstances of its deposition, in the late 13th century, supports (see 4.8.1). Possible comparandum from Southampton in a context dated 1250–75 (Platt & Coleman-Smith, 1975, 311, Fig 270). *Pit T349.*

MSF 35 Fragment of rectangular whetstone 65mm wide. A ferruginous feldspathic quartzose sandstone. Resembles Millstone Grit. Possibly local. *T341 Ditch III upper fill.*

MSF 36 Fragment of whetstone with thin rounded rectinlinear section. A grey fissile muddy siltstone. *Hollow V24.*

MSF 37 Whetstone, damaged, of pale grey fine-grained quartz-muscovite-calcite-chlorite schist. This rock is closely comparable to the honestone rock from Eidsberg in Southern Norway. *Soil V2.*

MSF 38 Whetstone, dark grey, fine-grained impure sandstone. *Site E pit J21 with postholes.*

MSF 39 Whetstone of finely laminated subgreywacke of Coal Measure type (Pennant). Similar rocks occur in the Flintshire Coalfields, as well as the South Wales and Bristol area, so its allocation to the Bristol Coalfields can not be certain. *Site E J16 soil build-up.*

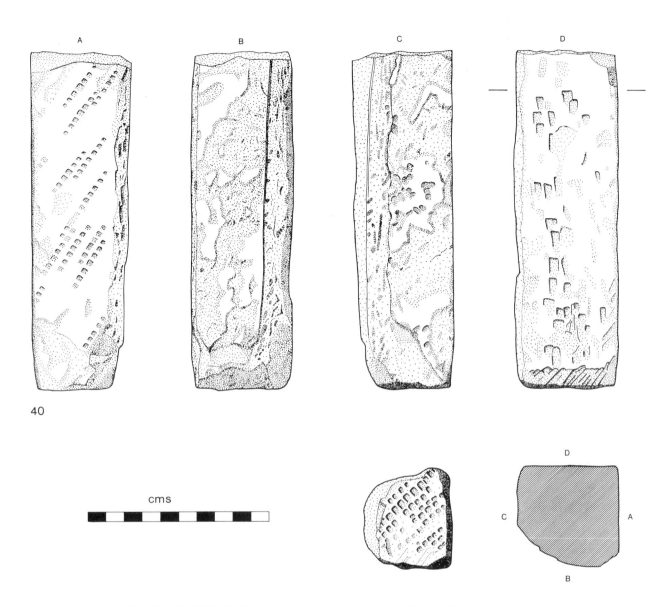

40

cms

Fig 16.12 MSF 40 Whetstone used as a mason's 'trial piece'. ×¹/₂.

MSF 40 Substantial whetstone, at least 175mm long, of rectangular cross-section 55mm by 50mm. Fine grained greenish buff sandstone, Carboniferous Gwespyr Sandstone from Gwespyr on the Dee Estuary (the main building stone of the Edwardian Castle). Side A subsequently marked by a seven-toothed claw chisel used vertically; sides B and C have punch marks but oblique chisel working at their junction has resulted in a distinct very straight edge to side B; side D has marks of a 6mm wide chisel used obliquely. The surviving end, E, has been dressed all over with a claw chisel, giving an effect similar to that on much surviving 13th century masonry, for example on the church of the Holy Trinty at York (RCHME, 1972, Pl 20.5). It would seem as though this whetstone had been subsequently used as some kind of mason's trial or demonstration piece. On side A some of the claw chisel marks have been partly obscured by further use as whetstone. Although a variety of medieval punches and straight edged chisels are known (Goodall, 1980b, 44–5, Fig 38) claw chisels do not survive nor are there documentary references to them although they often occur in medieval illustrations (Salzman, 1967, 334). A traditional (1946) claw chisel, incidentally with seven teeth, is illustrated by Arkell (1947, Fig 20). *Site E. Pit J68 immediately preceding c 1280 surface.*

16.11 Dressed stone (not illus)

MSF 41 Fragment, 150mm by 100mm by 100mm, of purple Carboniferous Sandstone (the second building stone used in the Castle). Heavily burnt after breakage. Three adjacent facets worked smooth, the first flat, the second concave, and the third flat; the latter two form a depression with a pointed end. The remainder of the piece is not dressed, suggesting that it was designed to be inset in a masonry structure. No definite structural purpose can be suggested for the piece, which would need consideration in any study of the minor decorative stone details used in Edward's North Welsh Castles. *T59 upper levelling in Ditch III*.

Acknowledgements
We are grateful for advice on the artefacts from Dominic Tweddle, Blanch Ellis, Ian Goodall, John Allan and Stuart Blaylock; for comments on the antler to Melvyn Davies; for geological identifications from Martyn Owen and R W Sanderson; for drawings by Kathy Holland, Sarah Noble and Diann Timms.

17 Ironwork and Metallurgy

17.1 Iron objects by Ian H. Goodall,
Spurs by Blanche Ellis

17.1.1 Tools

1 Axe with burred poll, pointed lugs above and below the hafting eye, and a blade which flares to the cutting edge. Weight 2lb 10oz (1.2kg). Sturdy woodman's axes of this type, mounted on a wooden handle, would have been used to fell trees and to cut and split trunks in the manner shown in the Bayeux Tapestry (Stenton, 1957, 109, Pl 38). The lugs enabled the handle to be securely hafted, and the poll or thickened butt also made the axe-head steadier to handle and easier to direct. The burring of the poll shows that the axe, in addition to being used to cut wood, had also been used as a hammer, probably driving splitting wedges into a log, or had itself been hammered to achieve a similar result.

Axes of this basic type have a long history through to the present day, but the distinctive pointed lugs fit a period either side of the Conquest. Similar lugs occur on an axe of probable 11th or 12th century date from Parliament Street, York (Tweddle, 1986, 188–90, Fig 90 No 961). Axes of similar form and date, but with more rounded lugs, include those from a late 10th, early 11th century context at Exeter (Goodall, 1983, 337, Fig 189 No 1) and from the construction deposit of Baile Hill, York (Addyman and Priestley, 1977, 139, 143, Fig 10 No 5). *C2 (Site A) Grubenhaus fill 10th century.*

2 Flaring tip from axe blade similar to 1. *J16 (Site E) Soil build-up over c 1280 surface 14th–15th centuries.*

3 Terminal and part of stem from a substantial auger bit, perhaps an incomplete forging, similar in size to examples from Cheddar, Somerset (Goodall, 1979, 267, Fig 90 No 146) and Clough Castle, Co. Down (Waterman, 1954, 135–7, Fig 11 Nos 1,2). The auger blade, once complete, would have been of a size appropriate for drilling pegholes in major structural and roof timbers. *G4 (Site E) Soil on c 1280 surface late 13th–early 14th centuries.*

4 Claw hammer head with incomplete flat claws, rounded face and an eye developing into a partly-open socket for the lost wooden handle. The nail driven through the top of the eye was intended to secure a haft which had worked loose; wedges were sometimes used for this purpose, but the smallness of the eye here dictated the use of a nail instead. Claw hammers were general purpose hammers used by craftsmen such as woodworkers, blacksmiths and farriers to drive in and extract nails. The medieval claw was generally flat or gently curved, and in an attempt to counteract the loosening of the handle caused by constant levering, eyes sometimes had lugs, side straps or shallow sockets. Deep sockets similar to that on this claw hammer are unusual and the eventual need for a nail indicates that it was not fully effective. *C18 (Site A) Feature associated drying kiln C3 13th century.*

5 Part of the flat claw from a claw hammer head. *J48 (Site E) Soil below c 1280 surface just pre 1280.*

6–8 Wedges with heads burred to one side. No 7 is the most slender and the most likely to have been a tool handle wedge in an axe, hammer or pick, as in the pick from Lydford Castle, Devon (Goodall, 1980a, 165, Fig 18 No 2). 6 and 8 are stouter and could equally as well be from the structure of buildings as from tools.
6 *G40 (Site E) Pit pre 1280, probably post c 1100.*
7 *A28 (Site A) Industrial phase on Ditch edge late 13th century.*
8 *E Topsoil* Not illus.

9–11 Teeth from wool or flax combs used in the preparation of fibres for spinning. No 9 is complete and has a distinctive bearded head; 10 and 11 are broken. Complete combs had one or more rows of iron teeth set in a wooden handle which was sometimes strengthened with iron binding, and it is these components which usually survive. Late Saxon and post-Conquest seem to have had wooden handles with rectangular backplates (Goodall, 1984, 79, Fig 119 Nos 20–30; Goodall, 1980b, 51–3, D1–43, Fig 40), but by the late medieval period a different type with a semicircular backplate was in use (Goodall, 1985, 62, Fig 46 Nos 80–2).
9 *A48 (Site A) Upper silts Ditch III) 13th century–?earlier.*
10 *G4 (Site E) Soil on c 1280 surface late 13th-early 14th centuries.*
11 *K2 Layer over major ditch post-medieval* Not illus.

12 Hook, both arms broken. Small hooks of this type had several uses. As tenterhooks they were set in timber rails in frames which were used to dry

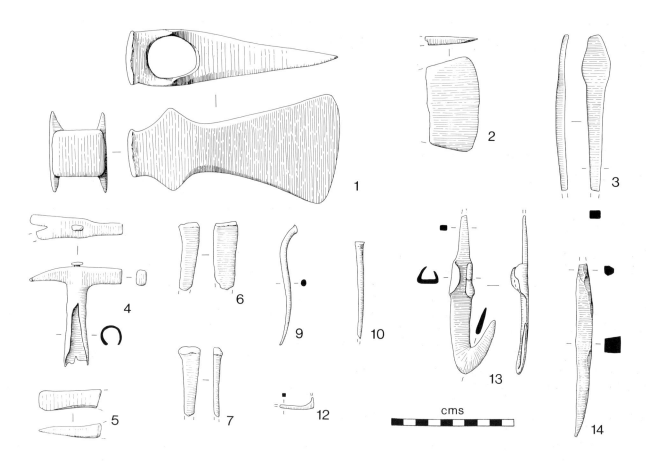

Fig 17.1 Medieval Iron Objects. Tools nos 1–14. ×1/3.

and stretch cloth (compare a series of more than eighty from medieval Winchester (Goodall, 1990, 234–9, Fig 50)). Similar hooks were also used to support cloth hangings in rooms, and they may on occasions also have supported roof tiles. *J64 (Site E) Soil immediately below* c *1280 surface.*

13 Weedhook with a strongly recurved crescent-shaped blade and a pair of flanges at the base of the broken tang. Weedhooks hafted on plain wooden handles were often used in conjunction with a crotch, a long wooden stick forked at one end, to weed crops. The tanged weedhook was the most common medieval type but the flanged tang, which served to bind the tool more firmly to its handle, became increasingly popular in the late medieval period. *J16 (Site E) Soil build-up over* c *1280 surface 14th–15th centuries.*

14 Pick or harrow tooth, rectangular in section, distorted and with an asymmetrically-set top. *T390 Pit 10th–12th centuries?*

17.1.2 Knives, shears and scissors (Fig 17.2)

15–29 Knives with whittle tangs. The blades are of three different shapes: 15–17 have straight horizontal backs which angle down to the cutting edge close to the tip, 18–22 have back and edge parallel before both taper to the tip, and 23–29 have back

and edge tapering evenly from tang to tip. These three blade shapes are among the commonest found among medieval whittle-tang knives, and all are continuations of established pre-Conquest forms. They equate with three of the four types found in the Saxo-Norman town of Thetford, Norfolk (Goodall, 1984, 81–3, Figs 122–5); the absent type, a characteristic pre-Conquest type with a rising angled back, is restricted to early post-Conquest contexts, a period not well represented at Rhuddlan. The various other less common types of medieval whittle-tang knife which, during and after the 13th century co-existed with the scale-tang knife, are also absent from the total Rhuddlan assemblage. The uses of the knives cannot be individually identified but they were probably mostly general purpose tools capable of being used for craft work, for food preparation and in its consumption. None has a cutler's mark or any form of decoration, nor was any trace of organic handles observed.

15 *T266 Grubenhaus fill 10th century.*

16 *J16 (Site E) Soil build-up over* c *1280 surface 14th–15th centuries.*

17 *V37 Boundary ditch ?17th century.* Not illus.

18 *J24 (Site E)* c *1280 surface* Not illus.

19 *T153 Posthole in compound T65 ?late 13th–early 14th centuries.*

20 *T80 Industrial activity 14th–15th centuries.*

21 *T80 Industrial activity 14th–15th centuries.*

180

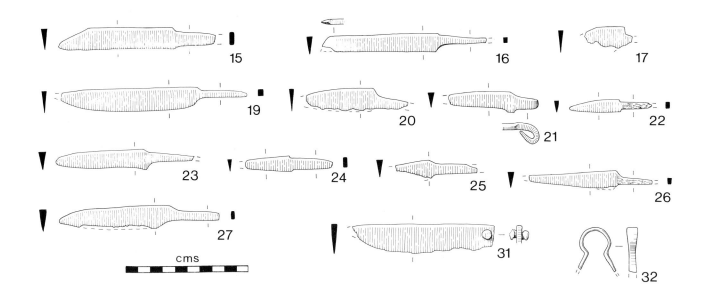

Fig 17.2 Medieval Iron Objects. Knives, shears nos 15–32. × 1/3.

22 *V2 Soil build-up 13th–17th centuries.*
23 *J21 Pit/posthole structure any date pre-1280*
24 *M94 Burial of first phase ?late 11th century.*
25 *T56 Infill of corn dryer 50 ?late 13th century.*
26, 27 *J16 (Site E) Soil build-up on c 1280 surface 14th–15th centuries.*
28 *H26 (Site E) Foundation trench 15th-18th centuries.* Not illus.
29 *E Topsoil.* Not illus.

30 Knife blade, tang and tip missing. 51mm long, 12mm deep. *G34 (Site E) Pit ?11th–12th centuries.*

31 Folding knife, blade tip missing, handle lost. The pivoting rivet has domed heads. Medieval folding knives are rare finds, but two others, one retaining its handle, and from contexts of slightly later date, are known from London (Cowgill, de Neergaard and Griffiths 1987, 106, 169, Fig 69). *J87 (Site E) Ditch III upper silt early 13th century.*

32 Shears. Plain looped bow and top of arms. The looped bow, the most efficient form of spring, developed in the immediately pre-Conquest perod and became the usual bow of medieval and later shears (Goodall 1984, 87, Fig 126). *G5 (Site E) Silt on surface immediately pre c 1280.*

33 Scissors with centrally-set finger loops, moulded stems and narrow blades. 140mm long. Typologically post-medieval. *V50 Boundary ditch ?17th century.* Not illus.

17.1.3 Building ironwork and fittings
Fig 17.3
34–40 Staples, 34–38 U-shaped, 39–40 looped.

Both types were driven into timber to secure fittings such as chains.
34 *V20 Soil mid 13th century?* Not illus.
35 *C3 (Site A) Drying kiln 13th century.* Not illus.
36 *G4 (Site E) Soil on c 1280 surface late 13th-early 14th century.* Not illus.
37 *T80 Industrial activity 14th–15th centuries.*
38–40 *J16 (Site E) Soil build-up over c 1280 surface 14th–15th centuries.* Not illus.

41–43 Hinge pivots, 41–2 not very complete but evidently of the commonest type with tapering tangs which were driven into timber or even joints in masonry. 43 is recent, as its condition and context imply.
41 *G6 (Site E) c 1280 surface.*
42 *G86 (Site E) Slot 14th–15th centuries.*
43 *E Topsoil.* Not illus.

44–51 Hinge and strap fragments. 44 is part of the rear arm of the nailed U-shaped eye of a hinge. 45–50 are strap fragments which may be from hinges, from strengthening straps on such items of furniture as chests, or from carts or wagons. 51 is one shaped leaf from a pinned hinge. Its elaborate shape suggests that it may be from furniture.
44 *J24 (Site E) c 1280 surface.*
45 *C2 (Site A) Grubenhaus fill 10th century.*
46 *A4 (Site A) Industrial activity late 13th century.*
47, 48 *G6 (Site E) c 1280 surface*
49 *J24 (Site E) c 1280 surface.* Not illus.
50 *T80 Industrial activity 14th–15th centuries.*
51 *V50 Boundary slot ?17th century.*

52–58 Lengths of binding strip, all flat in side view, the smaller and more delicately-shaped pieces like 52-7 probably from caskets or boxes. 55-7 have a

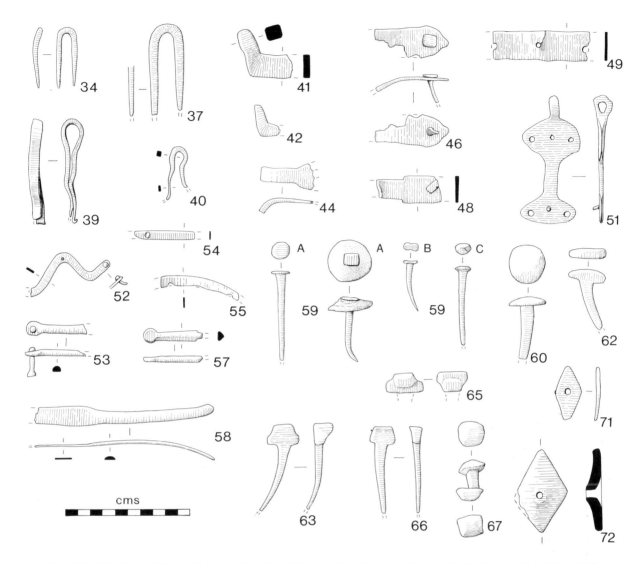

Fig 17.3 Medieval Iron Objects. Staples, hinges, bindings, nails, studs, bolts nos 34–72. ×1/3.

non-ferrous coating which served to protect them from rusting as well as to give them a more noble appearance. 58 is a larger example of uncertain use and date. Decorative binding strip was frequently of copper alloy, particularly in the 12th and 13th centuries (Goodall, A R, 1987, 173–6, Figs 154–55 Nos 17–65), although carefully crafted iron equivalents were in use both before and after the Conquest (Goodall, 1984, 89, Fig 130 Nos 160–1; Goodall, 1982, 228, Fig 39 Nos 59–61).

52 *T266 Grubenhaus fill 10th century.*
53 *T81 Palisade posthole 10th–12th centuries.*
54 *J68 (Site E) Pit mid–late 13th century (pre 1280).*
55 *G6 (Site E) c 1280 surface.*
56 *T22 Surface over Ditches later 13th century.*
57 *E Topsoil.*
58 *J16 (Site E) Soil build-up over c 1280 surface 14th–15th centuries.*

59 Timber nails. Three types were recognised, A–C, all of them with square or rectangular-sectioned shanks. Type A has a flat head which is square, rectangular or rounded in shape, the precise shape often obscured by corrosion; Type B has a flat head which is figure-eight shaped; Type C has a raised and faceted head which is oval in shape. The range of timber nail types is limited in comparison with that from other sites, including Waltham Abbey (Goodall 1973, 175, Fig 13, Nos 1–6) and Ospringe, Kent (Mold 1979, 149, Fig 30, Nos 1–9).

The date bands cover contexts with the following date ranges: 1: any date up to c 900; 2: any date up to 1300; 3: 10th and 11th centuries; 4: 11th to early 13th century; 5: 13th century, pre c 1280; 6: c 1280–c 1300; 7: 14th and 15th centuries; 8: contexts into the post-medieval period.

60–66 Studs. 60 and 61, both with domed heads, 60 circular and 61 sub-rectangular in shape, and the T-shaped 62, are types not uncommon in the medieval period. The eared heads of 63–5, and of the related 66, seem derived from those of a type of horseshoe nail (see 134B below) current in the second half of the 13th century and early 14th century. 60–2 may have been set in doors, but 63–6

182

Table 17.1 Timber nails

Date band	1	2	3	4	5	6	7	8
Type A	1	7	3	2	15	18	42	33
Type B	1	4	–	1	9	16	14	9
Type C	–	–	–	–	–	–	1	1

are probably strake nails which were driven into cart wheels, their function, like that of the projecting heads of horseshoe nails, being to give grip. Wheels set with such nails are occasionally depicted in medieval manuscripts (Hartley and Elliot 1928, Pl 33b).

60 *J43 (Site E) Gully 13th century, pre 1280.*
61 *P10 (Site D) Pit ?16th century.* Not illus.
62–4 *J24 (Site E) c 1280 surface.* 64 Not illus.
65 *J22 (Site E) Surface just pre-1280.*
66 *E unstratified.*

67–72 Clench bolts and roves. The clench bolts, 67–9, formed by nails whose tips were clenched over a rove to stop them pulling through timber, were used in ship construction and that of doors, shutters and hatches. Simply-shaped roves like 70–2 were already in use in the Viking period, and they continued in use throughout the medieval period, for a time alongside more elaborately shaped examples (Bersu and Wilson, 1966, 13–14,

Fig 4, Pl III; Geddes, 1982, 313–5; Goodall, 1987, 181–2, Fig 158 Nos 86–7).
67–8 *T266 Grubenhaus fill 10th century.*
69 *R2 (Site D) Erosion of Inner bank 14th–15th centuries?* Not illus.
70–1 *J24 (Site E) c 1280 surface.*
72 *T34 Slot for compound late 13th–14th centuries.*

73–4 Candlesticks (Fig 17.4). 73 is socketed with a cranked stem, while 74 has two arms, both developing from an angled stem, one an upright pricket spike, the other angled and with a socket. A wide range of different types of iron candlestick developed during the late medieval period, some with prickets on which the candle was impaled, some with sockets into which the candle was inserted, others with a combination of the two (Goodall 1981, 60, Fig 58 No 6-10). 73-4 are slightly unusual types of candlestick. 73 has a cranked stem rather than the straight or angled stem more usually found on medieval candlesticks, while 74 has just a single socket rather than one either side of a central pricket. The few candlesticks of this last type come mainly from ecclesiastical sites, including Rievaulx Abbey, Yorkshire and the monastic grange of South Witham in Lincolnshire (Goodall, 1980, 164, J119–28, Figs 115–16).
73 *G4 (Site E) Soil on c 1280 surface.*
74 *J16 (Site E) Soil build-up over c 1280 surface.*

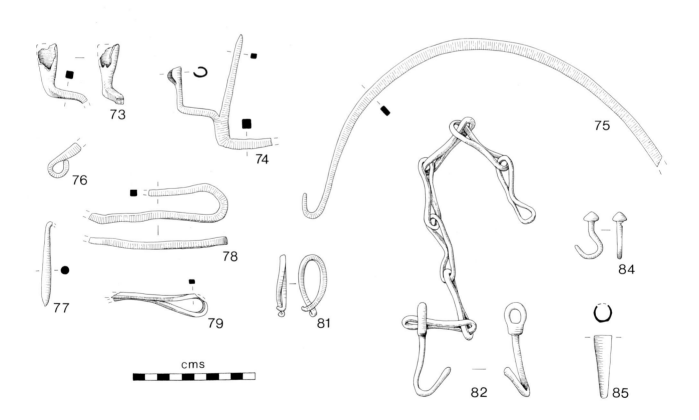

Fig 17.4 Medieval Iron Objects. Candlesticks, handles, chains, ferrule nos 73–85. ×1/3.

14th–15th centuries.

75 Handle of plain rectangular section, one end hooked, the other broken and distorted. The handle may be from a bucket or cauldron or some other vessel. Actual medieval timber buckets with similar handles include those from Taunton Castle, Duffield Castle and Castell-y-Bere (Butler, 1974, 100–6, Figs 10–13, Pl XXIV). *T349 Pit mid–late 13th century.*

76 Terminal from handle. *T80 Industrial activity 14th–15th centuries.*

77 Clapper from bell, 67mm long, with swollen stem and broken suspension loop. *H7 (Site E) Boundary ditch 17th century onwards.*

78–84 Chains and associated fittings. 78–81 are chain links, 78 and 79 figure-eight shaped, 80 distorted but originally with parallel sides, 73mm long by 17mm wide, and 81 oval. 82 is a chain of seven figure-eight shaped links with a terminal hook with a shaped head, its form not certainly medieval. 83 is a swivel ring and loop from a late context, 84 a swivel ring with non-ferrous plating. **78** *J64 (Site E) Surface just pre-1280.* **79** *G4 (Site E) Soil on c 1280 surface.* **80** *J16 (Site E) Soil build-up over* c *1280 surface 14th–15th centuries.* **81** *T349 Pit mid–late 13th century.* **82** *G4 (Site E) Soil on* c *1280 surface 14th–15th centuries.* **83** *H26 (Site E) Foundation trench 15th–18th centuries.* Not illus. **84** *V50 Boundary ditch ?17th century.*

85 Ferrule. *V20 Soil ?12th–13th centuries.*

17.1.4 Locks and keys Fig 17.5

86 Barrel padlock case and bolt. The case consists of a plain, oval-sectioned sheet-iron cylinder with an attached tube, both set between pear-shaped end-plates and reinforced by six plain rods and by upper and lower triangular-shaped pivoting fins with scrolled ends. The U-shaped padlock bolt, which has a circular closing plate with two decorative scrolls, has a spring arm with a single spine and one leaf spring; the free arm is held in the small tube attached to the main part of the case. The keyhole has corroded over, but must be a rectangular slot in the closing plate near the top of the spring arm. Barrel padlocks of this type have a pre-Conquest ancestry, and although they continued in use for a century or two after the Conquest, they were never a particularly common type. They were eclipsed by other types of barrel padlock, particularly the related type with a fin and tube, and that with a shackle (Goodall 1981, 60, Fig 57 Nos 2–6). Post-Conquest examples of barrel padlocks similar to that from Rhuddlan include one

from a context of *c* 1110 at Winchester, Hants. (Goodall 1990, 1001, 1008, Fig 311 No 3643) and another from Christchurch, Hants. (Goodall 1983b, 77, Fig 34 No 46). *T349 Pit mid–late 13th century.*

87 Barrel padlock (Fig 17.6). Fragment of plain case with end-strap. *J16 (Site E) Soil build-up over* c *1280 surface 14th–15th centuries.*

88–93 Padlock bolts, 88–91 U-shaped or originally so, 92–3 T-shaped. The U-shaped bolts are of two types, 88 and 90 with closing plates, now incomplete, which closed against the end-plate of the padlock case (see 86, above), and 89 and 91 each with an expanded stop which prevented the bolt passing too far into the case. 91 has a shaped stop on its free arm. U-shaped padlock bolts of the type represented by 88 and 90 were used with both box and barrel padlocks. Box padlocks such as those from Thetford, Norfolk (Goodall, 1984, 89, Fig 131 No 169) and Goltho Manor, Lincolnshire (Goodall, 1987, 100–1, Fig 158 No 100) were little used after the Conquest, when barrel padlocks finally superseded them in popularity, and the date and form of 88 and 90 indicate that they come from barrel padlocks. 88, which has lost almost all of its closing plate, is the head of a padlock bolt which must, when complete, have closely resembled one from a context of *c* 1200–30 at Weoley Castle, Warwicks (Oswald, 1962–3, 129, Fig. 51 No 2). The scrolls were partly intended for decorative effect but they could, as on the Weoley Castle example, give support to an independent spine which held leaf-springs. Scrolls are found on padlock bolts throughout the medieval period, although they were generally used in a more restrained way than on 88, and in the manner of those on the complete barrel padlock from Rhuddlan, 86. 90, which has lost its head and free arm and retains most of its rounded closing plate, is unusual in having copper-alloy leaf springs and one of an original pair of lugged iron arms whose purpose was to provide extra barriers for the key to pass and so enhance security. Padlock bolts like 89 and 91, with an expansion at the head of the spring arm and an equivalent change of size on the free arm where this survives, are far less common than those with closing plates. In addition to 89 and 91 from Rhuddlan, one from a late 14th century context at Lochmaben Castle, Dumfries and Galloway (Macdonald and Laing, 1974–5, 148, Fig 11 No 21), and a related type of bolt from Hen Caerwys, Clwyd, in a probable late 15th to early 16th century context (excavated by G B Leach), suggest a late medieval date for the type.

92 and 93 are T-shaped padlock bolts from barrel padlocks with shackles which were particularly suitable for securing and restraining limbs, both human and animal, as well as being capable of other uses. The bolts fitted into cases like that from Greyfriars, Oxford (Goodall, 1989, 228, Fig 64 No 143) and some from Winchester (Goodall, 1990,

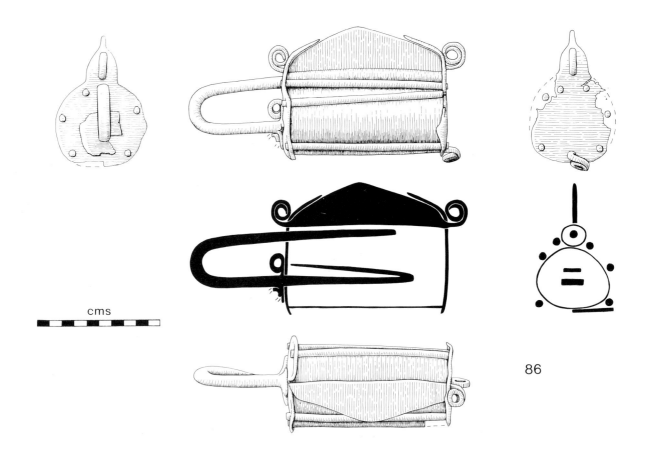

cms

86

Fig 17.5 Medieval Iron Objects. Barrel padlock no 86. ×1/3.

1001–5, 1011–12, Figs 314–6). 92 is a short bolt with a single spine now without leaf springs, whereas 93 is complete and has two spines, each with a pair of leaf springs. One of the spines on 93 projects through the head and forms a loop to assist its withdrawal from and insertion into the padlock.

The various padlock bolts show signs both on the X-radiographs and in the green corrosion on their surfaces of the copper-base brazing spelter used to assemble them and in some cases to plate them. All the sufficiently complete spines have evidence of the iron rivets used to fix the springs in place, including the copper alloy springs on 89. This feature has been metallurgically studied on some iron padlock bolts from Goltho, Lincs (Tylecote 1975).

88 *T24 Slot late 13th century.*
89 *J64 (Site E) Metalling just pre-1280.*
90 *G4 (Site E) Soil on c 1280 surface late 13th–14th centuries.*
91 *J16 (Site E) Soil build-up on c 1280 surface 14th–15th centuries.*
92 *G5 (Site E) Soil just pre 1280.* Not illus.
93 *V50 Boundary ditch ?17th century.*

94 Hasp from an embossed padlock. Embossed padlocks, of which those from Goltho, Lincs and North Elmham Park, Norfolk (Goodall, 1975, 84, Fig 39 No 65; Goodall, 1980c, 509–10, Fig 265 No

10) are good examples, have flanged and dished cases attached to rectangular backplates. Their stapled hasps were of either a rounded or squared U-shape with either a staple or a stop to engage the lock bolt. The Rhuddlan hasp is of squared U-shape with a staple, and in use its lost arm passed through the padlock case and acted as a pivot for the arm with the staple, which is shaped to fit against the outside of a dished case. The staple entered the case and a toothed sliding bolt, similar to that in the Goltho embossed padlock, was thrown by a key and so engaged in it and secured it. Embossed padlocks are of late medieval and post-medieval date. *G3 (Site E) Soil build-up on c 1280 surface 14th–15th centuries.*

95–7 Fittings from locks, 95 a lock bolt, 96 a tumbler, 97 a stapled hasp. Locks fixed to the doors and gates of buildings, or to items of furniture, had mechanisms attached to lockplates which were either flat or dished. These mechanisms, well illustrated by that on a lock of late or post-medieval date from Oxford Castle (Goodall, 1976, 300, Fig 28 No 59), generally consisted of a mount set behind the keyhole in which the key tip located, collars and wards to add complexity to the lock, and a toothed sliding bolt held in place by a sprung tumbler. The bolt engaged in the staple of the stapled hasp as it passed through the lockplate (some locks had two stapled hasps and a bolt with a

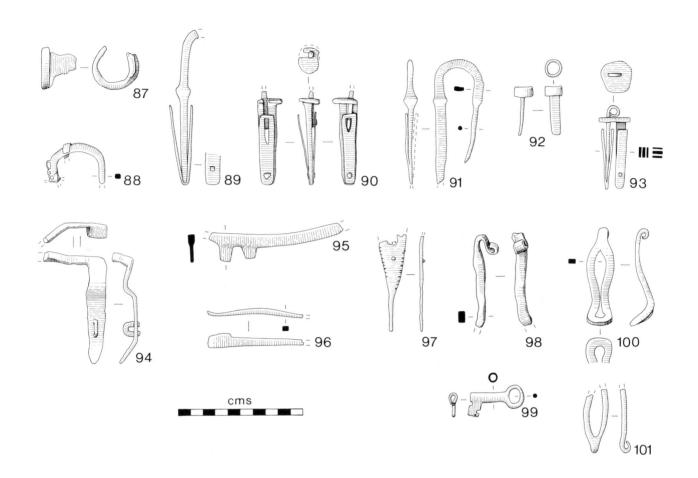

Fig 17.6 Medieval Iron Objects. Locks and keys nos 87–101. × 1/3.

recurved end). 95–7 are three of these components. 95 is a broken and distorted lock bolt with a pair of teeth: the key bit struck the inner face of one tooth in opening the lock and of the other in closing it. The Rhuddlan bolt most closely resembles others from Joydens Wood, Kent and Southampton, Hants (Tester and Caiger, 1958, 30–1, Fig 4 No 30); Harvey, 1975, 285, Fig 255 No 2077) which were used in conjunction with stapled hasps; bolts of more substantial form engaged in keepers outside the case. 96 is the lower end of a tumbler with a shaped and curved tip but without the expanded terminal through which it was riveted to the case. In use the tip, held taught by the spring action of the fixed terminal, rested on the back of the lock bolt causing it to be held firm. On some lock bolts, such as that from Joydens Wood just noted, it rested against a stop on the upper edge of the bolt which served to hold it closed. The Rhuddlan bolt and some other bolts have no such shaping. 97 is the tip of a stapled hasp retaining the stub of the staple which the lock bolt passsed through. The edge has decorative incisions which retain non-ferrous plating; the tip is long and straight to assist its being lifted, an alternative to the thickened tip of some other hasps.
95 *G86 (Site E) Slot 14th–15th centuries.*

96 *V20 Soil 12th–13th centuries.*
97 *E Topsoil.*

98 Terminal and distorted shank from a padlock key. *C66 (Site A) Feature connected with Gruben-haus 10th century.*

99 Key with a ring bow, its bit rolled in one with the hollow stem. A common type of medieval key, here in a residual context. *H4 (Site E) Slot 15th–18th centuries.*

100–1 Figure-of-eight shaped hasps, 100 angled in side view, 101 broken. Both have hooked tips to ease their use, for example in conjunction with staples and padlocks in securing gates, doors or chests.
100 *C7A (Site A) House 2 soil on floor late 13th–early 14th centuries.*
101 *J14 (Site E) Soil 16th–18th centuries.*

17.1.5 Buckles Fig 17.7

102 T-shaped buckle frame with non-ferrous plating. The shape is particularly well-related to joining straps of different widths which formed part of harness, one of them being fixed to the frame and the other capable of adjustment with a now-lost buckle pin. *G6 (Site E) c 1280 surface.*

103 Swivelling bar from a buckle, one terminal lost. Such bars, found on medieval buckles which are rectangular, trapezoidal and T-shaped, were probably from harness since they allowed straps to move freely without chafing. *T59 Dump in Ditch III 13th century.*

104–5 Buckle pins, 104 incomplete but with non-ferrous plating.
104 *T24 Slot late 13th century.*
105 *G4 (Site E) Soil on c 1280 surface late 13th–14th century.*

17.1.6 Horse equipment

106–32 Horseshoes. Horseshoes from 9th to mid to late 11th-century contexts on sites such as Thetford, Norfolk (Goodall, 1984, 104–5, Figs 142–3), London (Clark, 1986) and Winchester (Goodall, 1990, 1054–7, Fig 340) were almost invariably forged from comparatively wide but thin iron, with rectangular countersinkings for the nail head and a round hole for the nail shank. 106 is of this type, having a web (arm width) some 23mm wide, but it is just an arm tip. During the mid to late 11th century, horseshoes forged from narrower, thicker iron were introduced and continued in use into the first half of the 13th century. Like the earlier horseshoes, they have countersunk nailholes, the holes sometimes rounded but increasingly rectangular, and because of the narrow but thick webs, the punching of these nailholes often created a distinctive wavy outer edge. 107–10 are of this type, all but 107 being residual. The webs are between 18 and 20mm wide, and 108 and 109 have calkins. None of these first two types of horseshoe has other than three nailholes in a complete arm; inner profiles are U-shaped, and 108 and 109 have fiddle-key horseshoe nails (see 134A, below) whose heads are no thicker in side view than their shanks.

The second half of the 13th century saw a return to broader-webbed horseshoes which continued in use into the early 14th century. These horseshoes still had countersunk nailholes, and the edges were consequently either smooth or only very slightly wavy. The webs were generally between 20 and 30mm in width, and the tips sometimes had calkins, sometimes not. 111–23 are examples of this type, 111–15 in contemporary contexts, 116–18 residual unless from early in their period, and 119–123 residual. Three of these horseshoes (113, 117 and 120) retain nails, all of the eared type (see 134B, below) which succeeded the fiddle-key horseshoe nail.

124–7 are examples of horseshoes of the succeeding type with rectangular nailholes which was introduced in the mid 14th century. All are arm fragments which retain their tips, that of 125

thickened, the others up-turned. 124–5 are probably of late medieval date, but 126–7, which have their nailholes set in a fullered groove, must be post-medieval.

128–32 are horseshoe tips, 130 and 131 broken across countersunk nailholes, the others less complete.
106 *C2 (Site A) Grubenhaus fill 10th century.*
107 *T246 Pit 13th century or later.*
108–10 *T200 Soil 14th–17th centuries.*
109–10. Not illus.
111 *J65 (Site E) Ditch III upper fill 13th century, pre-1280.*
112 *J64 (Site E) Industrial activity 13th century, pre-c 1280.* Not illus.
113 *J36 (Site E) Bedding for c 1280 surface*
114 *J24 (Site E) c 1280 surface* Not illus.
115 *T24 Slot late 13th century.*
116 *J16 (Site E) Soil build-up on c 1280 surface 14th–15th century.*
117–18 *G4 (Site E) Soil on c 1280 surface late 13th–14th centuries.*
118. Not illus.
119 *J16 (Site E) Soil build-up on c 1280 surface 14th–15th centuries.* Not illus.
120–22 *E unstratified.* Not illus.
123 *E Topsoil.* Not illus.
124 *P2 (Site D) Disturbed levals outer bank 14th–15th centuries.*
125 *D Topsoil.* Not illus.
126 *O4 (Site D) Erosion outer bank 14th–15th centuries.* Not illus.
127 *D Topsoil.* Not illus.
128 *C2 (Site A) Grubenhaus fill 10th century.* Not illus.
129 *G5 (Site E) Silt immediately pre-1280.* Not illus.
130–32 *J16 (Site E) Soil build-up on c 1280 surface 14th–15th centuries.* Not illus.

133 Oxshoe arm with distinctive broadened tip and closely-set nailholes. The other end is broken and the clip lost. The cloven feet of oxen had to be shod with pairs of shoes; an oxshoe from Eynsford Castle, Kent (Rigold and Fleming, 1973, 105, Fig 9 No 11) retains its clip. *P9 (Site D) In outer bank Ante quem c 1280.*

134 Horseshoe nails. Two types, A and B, were recognised. Type A are fiddle-key nails whose heads, which were never thicker in side view than the shank, were originally semicircular in shape or had straight sides and a rounded top, and might ultimately be worn down to T-shape. Type B has an eared head which expands in side view to a broad top; the ears are sometimes pronounced, but where not the head is more trapezoidal in outline. Both these types of nail were used in horseshoes with countersunk nailholes, for which their shape was designed, Type A with horseshoes like 106–10, Type B with those like 111–23. The eared Type B seems to have developed for use with this last type

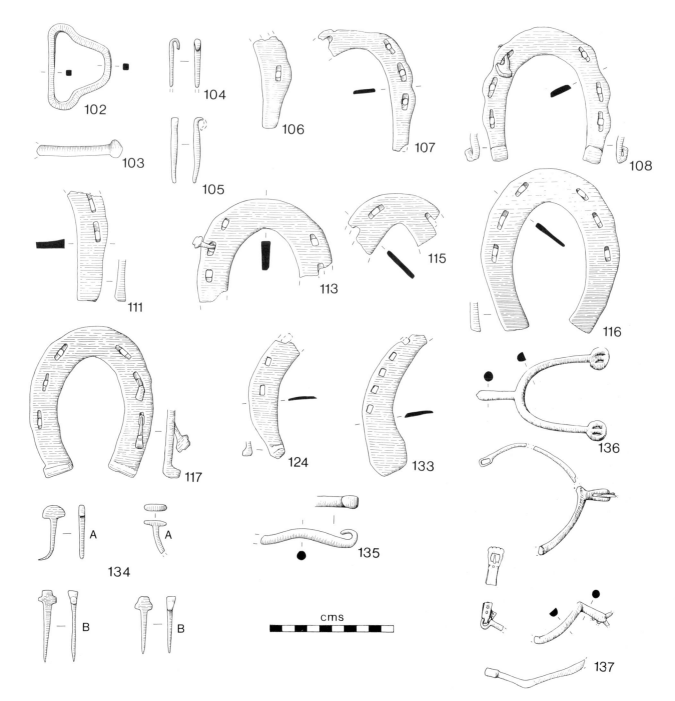

Fig 17.7 Medieval Iron Objects. Buckles, horseshoes, spurs nos 102–137. ×1/3.

of horseshoe, but whether fiddle-key nails continued in use into the 14th century, or are merely residual when found in such contexts, is uncertain (see Goodall, 1973, 173–5, Fig Nos 13A–D, Goodall,

Table 17.2 Horseshoe nails

Date band	1	2	3	4	5	6	7	8
Type A	–	–	2	3	1	2	–	1
Type B	–	1	1	1	9	49	52	8

For explanation of Date Bands, see Table 17.1

1980b, 181–3, Fig 22, and Clark, 1986 for further evidence and details of subsequent nail types not found at Rhuddlan).

135 Mouthpiece link from a bridle bit of a simple form of medieval or later date. *J16 (Site E) Soil build-up on* c *1280 surface 14th–15th century.*

17.1.7 *Spurs* by Blanche Ellis

Fig 17.7

136 Prick spur. The straight, D-section sides have large, round terminals each pierced with two horizontal slots. The round neck swells towards the back where its flattened end has a tiny pointed goad projecting from the centre. Overall length 107mm. Length of neck 33mm. Span (between terminals) 75mm. Typologically 10th century. *C2 (Site A) Grubenhaus fill 10th century.*

137 Rowel spur. This early rowel spur, of slender proportions, is of iron with a copper alloy buckle and attachments for the leathers. It is broken into several fragments, the largest of which consists of a short, straight, round section neck with a damaged rowel, and part of one side of the spur. The small rowel rusted into the rowel box originally had five or six points, only one of which is still complete. The D-section spur side plunges downwards from its junction with the neck and is broken where it appears to have bent sharply under the wearer's ankle. Its detached single ring terminal survives. Two rivet attachments for the spur leather are looped through this terminal; they are each formed as a narrow strip of copper alloy, bent into a U-shape into which the end of the spur leather was inserted and held by two rivets. One attachment would have held the end of a very short leather, with its other end inserted into the base of a narrow copper alloy buckle which is now separate. The buckle, which retains its pin, has a little frame, decoratively moulded at one end, beneath which its long, narrow body is bevelled, its lower edge slit to accommodate the end of the leather. A small stump of the second side of the spur is on the main fragment, the rest is in two parts. As far as can be told in its present condition, it appears to have been less strongly curved under the ankles than the more complete side. Its terminal is a vertically-pierced slot through which the spur leather would have passed freely as it encircled the foot. The X-radiograph suggests possible traces of non-ferrous plating on this side.

Overall length of main fragment 80mm. Length of neck 25mm. Length of one complete rowel point about 10mm. Length of broken side fragments (together) about 90mm. Length of buckle 31mm. Length of attachments approximately 20mm. Typologically 13th century.

This is the earliest type of rowel spur. This form continued into the early 14th century but the slender proportions of 137 and the rivet attachments for the leathers are early features. A similar, undamaged, iron rowel spur is known from London (Ward-Perkins, 1940, 105, 112, Fig 30 No 6). Small spurs with short necks and inner slot terminals are incised on the monumental slab of Sir Johan le Botiler in St Bride's Major church, Glamorgan (Greenhill, 1976, II, Pl 46b) which Claude Blair dates by its armour c 1330. The slot terminal was always worn to the inside of the foot, with the buckle attached to the outer ring terminal, so 137 was worn on the left foot. Spur leathers were generally made of leather, but sometimes of fabric. Copper alloy was sometimes used for the

attachments of iron spurs to reduce wear and to avoid rusting together of moving parts. Iron spurs were frequently enhanced and protected from rust by a thin plating of tin (Jope, 1956). *J16 (Site E) Soil build-up on* c *1280 surface 14th–15th centuries.*

17.1.8 Arrowheads Fig 17.8

138–52 The arrowheads, where sufficiently complete, are all socketed. All could have had a military use, although 138 and 139 in particular, having barbed and triangular blades respectively, might as appropriately have been used in hunting. 140 is a short pointed arrowhead, whereas 141–52 are long slender points, only 141 and 150 complete. All have blades of square or diamond section; in some the blade develops evenly out of the socket, but in most there is a perceptible swelling. Most of the arrowheads (138–9, 141–6) are from mid or late 13th century contexts, many of them evidently relating to activity associated with the Edwardian Castle, the others (140, 147–52) probably being residual. These arrowheads are of similar types to those from other Welsh castles with Edwardian connections, including Diserth Castle (Glenn, 1915, Fig 90), Criccieth Castle (O'Neil, 1944–45, 40–1, Pl VIII) and Castell-y-Bere (Butler, 1974, 95, Fig 8 Nos 2–6).

138 *A82 (Site A) Ditch III upper levels 13th century, ?earlier.*

139 *T61 Infill of corn drying kiln late 13th century.*

140 *J16 (Site E) Soil build-up on* c *1280 surface 14th–15th centuries.*

141–2 *T59 Ditch III upper levels 13th century, ?earlier. Not illus.*

143 *J87 (Site E) Ditch III upper levels 13th century, pre c 1280.*

144 *G5 (Site E) Silt immediately pre* c *1280. Not illus.*

145 *G6 c 1280.*

146 *J24 c 1280 surface.*

147 *J16 (Site E) Soil build-up on* c *1280 surface 14th–15th centuries.*

148 *H4 (Site E) Slot 15th–18th centuries. Not illus.*

149 *J14 (Site E) Soil 16th–18th centuries. Not illus.*

150–2 *E Topsoil.*

154 Iron shot, 4cm in diameter. *M Topsoil. Not illus.*

17.2 Slags and metalworking

A large number of contexts produced slags of various kinds, most of which appeared to be connected with ironworking. The nearest source of iron ore is probably around Moel Hiraddug about 4 km east of Rhuddlan; here haematite occurs in veins in the limestone and contains about 50% metallic iron (Strahan, 1885, 53). The reference to iron mines in Domesday Book is relevant (Tait, 1925).

Tap slag, smithing hearth bottoms and some

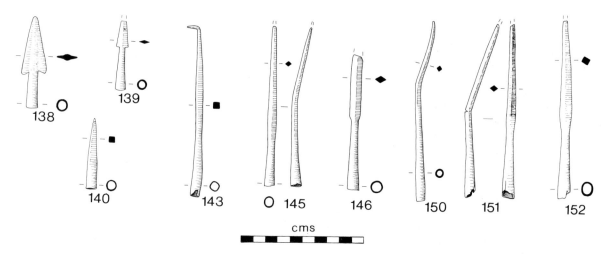

Fig 17.8 Medieval Iron Objects. Arrowheads nos 137–152. ×1/3.

hammer scale were distinguishable. Most smaller scraps were very rusted and not distinctive. The only specialist work was the analyses presented in Table 17.3. A selection by both context and type was made for future reference; a full list of contexts and weights is filed with the archive, annotated according to whether material has been kept or discarded.

The major prehistoric context to produce slag was Bronze Age pit C46; this slag differed in appearance from all others found, being glassy and greenish black with a weight of *c* 50 g. The analysis (Table 17.3) was not conclusive. Other prehistoric contexts with apparent iron slag scraps were Iron Age features T170, T375 and T322, and V64.

The major contexts with tap slag were the Church foundation trenches M4 and M5. Mixed with the tap slag was small quantities of iron ore in small lumps, identified by M Owen as 'massive haematite – Fe_2O_3', which has been mined in the recent past from Carboniferous rocks between Prestatyn and Abergele. Other tap slag contexts for Site M, mainly burials, are given in Chapter 7. Contexts on other sites with more than 500 g of tap slag were A83 in Ditch III, drying kiln C3, and *Grubenhaus* fill T145. Only shaft furnaces, producing tap slag, are documented for the Anglo-Saxon period (Wilson, 1976, 262). The quantities of tap slag present in the Norman Church foundations suggest a flourishing industry in the area by the 1080s.

Hammerscale was noted in soils T178 and T200 (which overlaid each other in places) and T115, a pit associated with ?14th century industrial activity.

Smithing hearth bottoms weighing between 1.5 and 2 kg came from A91 in Ditch II, A47 and A82 in Ditch III, pits A5 and A82, pit T227 (two), upper levels in Ditch III Site T (five), T34 compound slot and pits J79 and G135 on Site E.

Contexts with large quantities of scrappy slag, apparently from smithing, were the dump levels in the top of Ditch III on Sites A, T and E, the 'industrial activity' T80, and layers on Site E above the Ditch fills but below the *c* AD 1280 surface. Pit J68 produced a 2 kg lump of iron as well as lumps of slag.

No material was identified as iron ore, apart from that in the Church foundations. It would appear that all the ironworking activities carried out on the sites excavated related to stages after smelting, from working on blooms smelted elsewhere to smithing and the production of iron objects. There appears to have been some ironworking from at least the 10th century onward; there was slag in the fill of *Grubenhaus* C2. All the major sites excavated in the Norman town, except the Church Site M, were on its perimeter. There is evidence to suggest that in some Saxon and Norman towns certain industries were concentrated in restricted zones (eg Thetford, Davison, 1967). In a small town like Rhuddlan they may have been conveniently restricted to the perimeter, behind the defences and even on their line when they were not being maintained.

Most of the ironworking is probably to be related to the presence of Edward I's work teams, in dump levels in the top of the Ditches and in contexts immediately below the *c* AD 1280 surface on Site E. These contexts produced the only significant amounts of 'furnace lining', in burnt clay with slag adhering. They also produced most of the coal from the excavations (17.3). Pits such as J68 may relate to metalworking activity as their fills contained so much relevant detritus. There was also concentrated ironworking activity on Site T in the 14th century, suggesting that this area, just outside the Edwardian Borough, continued to be used for craft activities which were perhaps thought unsuitable for the interior of the town.

Sample E was presumed to relate to bronze/copper because of its context in Bronze Age pit C46; it had a blue-green glassy appearance to which sample F from *Grubenhaus* infill C2 was

Table 17.3

Sample	Fe	FeO	SiO$_2$	Al$_2$O$_3$	CaO	MgO	S	P$_2$O$_5$	MnO	Cu	CO$_2$	H$_2$O
A *Pit A5*	44.1	40.8	33.6	1.82	2.40	0.65	0.011	0.86	0.13	0.008	0.21	0.60
B *A82 Ditch III*	37.2	40.1	44.9	2.72	1.20	0.58	0.023	0.45	0.13	0.013	0.12	0.67
C *Pit J68*	61.0†	22.2	24.9	2.48	2.00	0.79	0.094	1.47	0.20	<.005	0.21	0.56
D *Pit J79*	47.8	52.3	28.4	3.56	2.82	0.72	0.020	0.86	0.46	<.005	0.09	0.75
E *Pit C46*	50.3	57.3	20.8	6.05	4.90	0.79	0.003	0.29	0.59	0.025	0.20	0.43
F *C2 Grubenhaus*	46.2	34.3	22.4	5.55	7.82	0.86	0.044	0.36	0.85	0.034	0.07	0.67

Analyses provided by I O Penberthy, British Steel Corporation: method (described in archive) and components chosen because samples A to D submitted considered to be from ironworking and samples E and F from bronze/copper working. † indicates magnetite present in quantity.

similar, but which seemed dissimilar to the majority of slags from the excavations. I O Penberthy comments on these analyses 'From the results, the samples do not appear to be very dissimilar in composition but more or less seem to cover a range of concentrations with no distinct gaps. Samples E and F nevertheless occupy positions at the higher extremity ranges for CaO, Al$_2$O$_3$, and Cu although the latter does not approach the levels quoted in the Cyprus bronze slags. Samples E and F were reprepared and the Cu determined again. The results confirm precisely the figures in the table'.

A sample of tap slag from Church foundation trench M4 was also analysed by I O Penberthy (details of methods/components searched for in archive). The results were Fe$_2$O$_3$ – 68.39%: SiO$_2$ – 23.44%: Al$_2$O$_3$ – 2.74%: CaO – 5.09%: MgO – 1.23%: P$_2$O$_5$ – 1.15%: MnO – 0.06%: Ti – 0.131%: Cr – –%: V – –%: Cu – 0.007%: Ni – 0.011%: Zn – 0.004%: Sn – –%.

17.3 Use of coal

Small pieces of coal were found in contexts on Site E: *J45 upper fill Ditch V* (one), *J58 pit 13th century before* c *1280* (one), *J43 gully 13th century before* c *1280* (one), *J36 base of* c *1280 surface* (four), *G6 c 1280 surface* (five), *G4 soil on* c *1280 surface* (seven), *J16 soil build-up over* c *1280 surface* (six), *G11, G12, G88 14th/15th century boundary slots* nine in total, contexts dating from the 15th century onward – ten. On other Sites small pieces were only found infrequently in post-medieval contexts. This is significant in view of the documentary evidence for coal production, for use in iron forging and in the making of lime for mortar, towards the establishment of Edward I's castles (Lloyd Gruffydd, 1981–2, 111). The nearest documented coal production site to Rhuddlan is at Mostyn, about 11 km south east, but coal-bearing deposits lay only seven km away (Lloyd Gruffydd, 1981–2, 108).

Acknowledgements
Drawings of the iron objects by Jean Stokes. The authors are grateful to all who assisted in initial study and X-rays of the artefacts. M Owen (British Geololgical Survey) commented upon ore samples. R F Tylecote provided advice after the initial discovery of the tap slag foundations. Especial thanks are due to I O Penberthy and the British Steel Corporation (Welsh Division, Llanwern) for all the care with analyses.

18 Medieval and post-medieval pottery

Wendy Owen (1991)

18.1 Introduction

The following report presents only a summary of the medieval and post-medieval pottery from the excavations at Rhuddlan between 1969 and 1973. Finances and time have severely limited its scope, restricting work to concentrate on the assemblage from the kiln (V4). The report is based on the illustrations prepared in 1976, which remain in their original somewhat unsatisfactory state. The archive contains a fuller description of the pottery, ordered by context number. Apart from the kiln pottery, the illustrations were originally selected to cover a wide range of contexts of which only two can be securely dated on historical evidence.

a) G6, J24 and associated levels. Dumped layers of gravel and sand, the base for a metalled track approaching the Edwardian Castle from the East. Dated 1277–82 (see 6.8).

b) Site D. Incorporated in the Edwardian defences, possibly mid 13th century date pottery which had been redeposited (see 8.4).

It was decided to include new illustrations of a few extra sherds which help to illustrate more fully the range of vessel forms and decoration occurring at Rhuddlan, particularly the examples of the early medieval pottery and imported vessels. No attempt has been made to deal fully with the entire range of pottery from the site. A series of tables present those contexts containing post-Roman pottery, both illustrated and unillustrated. These are intended both to provide an overall picture of the amount of pottery found, and to demonstrate which contexts were aceramic, which ceramic. In these tables single sherds are identified '1'; '+' indicates a small group of sherds (about two to five); larger quantities are given to the nearest multiple of five. 'w' indicates a definite waster, (i) indicates the probability of intrusion. The identification and quantification of the V kiln type, medieval and post-medieval material has been prepared by H Quinnell. The excavations produced a total of 166165g of pottery (excluding the weight of the Rhuddlan kiln pottery restored and now in the care of the National Museum of Wales), of which 124150g (again this figure excludes the weight of the Rhuddlan kiln material in the National Museum of Wales) (83%) came from the kiln [context V4]. The assemblage was subdivided macroscopically into 11 fabric groups on the basis of petrological inclusions, as identified through a ×8 hand lens and with the aid of selective thin sections. With the exception of the foreign imports, the fabrics have been coded according to the Clwyd-Powys Archaeological Trust Pottery Fabric Series (Courtney and Jones, 1988). The report on thin section work prepared by Dr D F Williams is filed with the archive; sherds thin sectioned are coded DFW.

18.2 The fabrics

18.2.1 Saxo-Norman wares

MB21 Sandy Micaceous ware

Hard, slightly rough, sandy fabric, dark grey on the outer surface and inside the top of the rim, light grey elsewhere. Thin sectioning shows a groundmass of small quartz grains (normally up to 0.05mm with a scatter of frequent larger subangular grains up to 0.6mm across). Also present are flecks of mica, a little sandstone, quartzite, iron ore, siltstone and an odd grain of pyroxene. There are similarities between this fabric and late Saxon Chester ware, which has a broad dating of early 10th–mid 11th century (J A Rutter in Mason, 1985, 55) but the inclusions are common and may simply indicate a source in the same general area of the Triassic sandstones of the West Midlands. (P3 thin sectioned by DFW). Chester-type ware from Hereford was found in well stratified layers dated between AD 910 and 916, and is assumed to go out of use by the mid 11th century (Vince, 1985, 62–3).

MK Shelly ware

Hard, rough shelly fabric, with reddish brown surfaces and a dark grey core. A large amount of shell is present, much of which is fossiliferous. The fabric has much in common with St Neots type ware and may also have affinities with the 'Shelly Vesicular ware' from Lower Bridge Street, Chester (Mason, 1985, 41). Possibly of Saxo-Norman date. (P4 thin sectioned by D F Williams).

ML Calcite Tempered ware

Hard, rough dark grey fabric containing angular pieces of calcite, with grains of quartz, sandstone and some flecks of mica. One sherd (P1) has a smoothed, burnished suface, another (P2) has evidence of knife trimming. No likely source for the calcite can be suggested as yet, but the fabric seems unlikely to be of local origin. (P1 and P2 thin sectioned by D F Williams).

18.2.2 Medieval wares
MA Sandy red wares

A variety of hard, sandy, usually orange-buff (but occasionally reduced) fabrics, rough to the feel. The amount and grain size of quartz present varies, but is generally frequent. This group also includes some finer and smoother fabrics. Olive-green glazes are usual on the exterior surface of jugs. This fabric group includes products of the Rhuddlan kiln (Fabric MA2, described in more detail below) now dated to the Henry III period by the excavator, and is also typical of fabrics of 13th and 14th century date found over a large part of Cheshire and North East Wales, derived from glacial or post-glacial clays. The decoration too is in typical Cheshire style, paralleled for example at Beeston, Ashton, Chester and Audlem (Webster, 1960). It is impossible to say whether or not these wares were produced locally (except in the case of vessels from the Rhuddlan kiln group, context V4) – stylistically and petrologically, they could have been manufactured over a wide area of Cheshire and North East Wales (cf Manley's fabrics B–D). It may be, however, that there are other kilns to be found at Rhuddlan, perhaps some of Edwardian date. This might explain the presence of a quantity of the pottery in contexts associated with Edward I.

Pottery from the kiln group has been classified as fabric MA2. Several sherds have been thin sectioned by D F Williams (see Archive for further details). A hard sandy fabric, slightly roughish to the feel. There is very little variation in the fabric, though it ranges in colour from reddish-yellow to dark grey. The non-plastic inclusions are generally made up of a groundmass of numerous sub-angular quartz grains, mostly under 0.1mm (but also a few larger grains up to 0.8mm), mica flecks, some quartzite, iron ore and occasionally small pieces of sandstone, fine grained silica, altered igneous rock and discrete grains of feldspar and pyroxene. There is often a patchy olive-green or yellowish-brown glaze on the exterior surface.

P73 and 75 are of generally similar fabric to the kiln group, but have atypical decoration. This may suggest that they are either from elsewhere, or from a contemporary kiln in Rhuddlan producing different wares - including more highly decorated smaller pieces.

MD Coal Measures

Fine wares. Hard, white or off-white fabric, slightly rough to the feel, derived from fine iron-free clay. The fabric contains a moderate amount of fine quartz, and some occasional rock inclusions up to 1mm. Vessels usually have dark streaked green glazes externally. These fabrics are very common over a large area of the West Midlands and the Welsh borders, but this does not mean that they could not have been produced more locally in Flintshire where very similar clay was available. Vessels in this fabric do not seem to have been very common at Rhuddlan, since only thirteen sherds were recovered.

Ewloe type wares. Hard, rough, gritty white or pinkish white fabrics with frequent quartz inclusions, sometimes rounded. The surface is often dark or reddish, which may be the result of applying an iron-rich slip, or may simply be an oxidation effect. One vessel has a yellowish glaze externally. Petrologically they are similar to Coal Measures Fine wares fabric (see above), but have distinctive late medieval forms (eg baluster jugs) and different potting and firing characteristics. It has been suggested that, like the fine wares above, these fabrics are derived from Coal Measures clays (some wasters are known from Ewloe in Clwyd, approximately 20 miles from Rhuddlan). There is a suggestion that the earliest Ewloes may have been produced in the 14th century, by analogy with material from other North Western sites (Harrison and Davey, 1977).

18.2.3 Foreign Imports
Saintonge ware

Hard, smooth, fine, cream coloured fabric, with only occasional mica and haematite inclusions. Bright green speckled glaze on the exterior surface.

Alkaline-glazed bowl (P34)

Hard, smooth, slightly sandy buff fabric with a clear alkaline glaze inside and out. Evidently contaminated (in manufacture): inside, blue flecks; outside, red and brown spots/flecks. The vessel is typical of Mediterranean wares of the 14th century. Alkaline-glazed wares were made both in North Africa and the Middle East. (Report by J G Hurst, L Biek, R King and J Bayley filed with archive)

Maiolica (P46)

Very thin fine sandy pinkish fabric with buff surfaces. Inside is unglazed. Outside has a very thin white lead glaze and dark purplish-brown stripes applied over-glaze. This vessel too is typical of Mediterranean wares of the 14th century (report by J G Hurst *et al* filed with archive), but is unusual in being unglazed inside.

18.2.4 Post-medieval wares
LA Buckley-type wares

A hard, smooth pinkish-brown fabric with cream streaks, occasional fairly hard red-brown inclusions and some fine quartz. Decorated with a dark brown shiny glaze on both surfaces, and with a creamy-

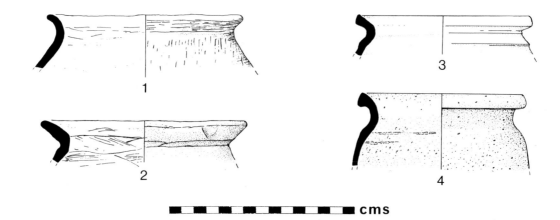

Fig 18.1 P1-4 Saxo-Norman pottery. ×1/3.

yellow trailed slip. The wares are of post-medieval date, probably of the 17th and 18th centuries (pers comm P Courtney).

LB Mottled ware

Very hard, dense, pale buff coloured fabric with no visible inclusions. There is a shiny, mottled brown glaze on interior and exterior surfaces. The only vessel form at Rhuddlan was a reeded tankard. These wares were produced between about 1680 and 1760 (pers comm P Courtney).

LC Slipware

A hard smooth, fine fabric, pinkish-cream in colour with inclusions of occasional rounded quartzite and red-orange iron ore and a sparse amount of fine quartz. A white slip is applied to both surfaces and the interior is decorated with light and dark brown slips and then glazed. The only form found at Rhuddlan is a press-moulded dish, probably a product of Buckley or other kilns in the Mersey region (pers comm P Courtney).

18.3 Saxo-Norman wares (Fig 18.1)

P1 Cooking pot. Fabric ML, dark grey to black, with burnished surface. *T178 soil* (sectioned DFW)
P2 Cooking pot/jar. Fabric ML, dark grey to black. Knife-trimmed internally. *T29/200 soil* (sectioned DFW)
P3 Cooking pot/jar. Fabric MB21, light to mid-grey, similar to late Saxon Chester ware. *C69 associated with drying kiln C3* (sectioned DFW)
P4 Cooking pot/jar. Fabric MK, a shelly ware, red-brown to dark grey. *T7 soil* (sectioned DFW)
For other findspots see Tables of site contexts.

18.4 The Site V Kiln group

The kiln had three phases, V51, 4a and d–f, 4c and g–h. A Henrician date of 1241–63, initially suggested for the kilns by the excavator (Miles, 1977b) still seems the most probable although a date anywhere in the 13th century pre *c* 1280 is possible. After its final use the superstructure appears to have been dismantled and backfilled with material including a large quantity of wasters (ie pots which have broken in the firing, and their glaze run across the break; also pots fused together); virtually all the material described and illustrated comes from deposit 4h.

This fabric falls within the broader grouping of Sandy wares (MA), described above, but only the pottery known to have been produced in the kiln, ie recovered from contexts V4, V51 associated with a large number of wasters, kiln props etc, has been included in the kiln fabric type MA2. It is almost certain that a proportion of the pottery assigned to Fabric MA was also produced in the Rhuddlan kiln, but due to the great similarity in fabric and in decorative style of pottery produced over a large area of Cheshire and North Wales, it is extremely difficult to identify the source of vessels or to say whether a vessel was produced in the Rhuddlan kiln rather than imported from another kiln in the same general area.

The assemblage of material from the kiln has been classified into different types of vessels, which have been quantified by weight and number of sherds (see Table 18.1); the surviving rim percentages have been calculated, but no attempt has been made to estimate the minimum number of vessels by looking for joining sherds. About 70% of the kiln products appear to have been jugs, with cooking pots, pipkins, large bowls and kiln props in much smaller quantities. In dealing with the kiln material no difference was observed in that from the three phases. The small amounts from Phase 2 V51 and Phase 2 Vc, 4g–h, could not be distinguished from the large quantity in the infill of Phase 3 (mainly 4h). The group has therefore been dealt with quantitatively as a single unit.

Examination of the drips of glaze, particularly on jug P10 and the kiln props, P21–22, provides some evidence of kiln stacking. From the way the glaze has dripped and the fused remnants of another pot on its base, the jug would appear to have been fired standing on its rim. The kiln props also appear to

Table 18.1 Quantification of the kiln group [context V4]
(weight in g, percentages given in brackets)

	weight		no sherds		rim%	
Jug	85632	(68.97%)	2471	(55.26%)	3320	(73.77)
Cooking pot	2647	(2.13%)	55	(11.23%)	511	(11.35)
Pipkin	467	(0.37%)	18	(0.40%)	124	(2.75%)
Bowl	2197	(1.76%)	1	(0.02%)	74	(1.64%)
Curfew	?		?		?	
Kiln prop	4773	(3.84%)	43	(0.96%)	471	(10.46%)
Unidentified	28434	(22.9%)	1868	(41.78%)	0	(0%)
TOTAL	124150		4471		4500	

Jugs are typically ovoid shaped with a simple pinched spout, a thumb frilled base and a simple strap handle (eg P5). Some, however, are more globular in shape (eg P7), and around a third by weight have plain bases. The bodies often show quite pronounced rilling and are glazed externally, mostly a dark olive-green, but the colour varies a great deal. Some jugs have no further decoration, but brown painted vertical stripes, or applied thumbed vertical strips (also painted brown), are common. Handles tend to be plain straps, with a simple thumbed groove running down the length. Several have a thumbed strip applied in the groove. Out of the large number of jugs from the kiln group there are only two bridged spouts (P8–9), both of which are frilled externally where they are attached to the body; both have simply modelled arms supporting the tip of the spout. One spout has a face mask beneath it.

Cooking pots all have simple out-turned, more or less squared rims, and a sparse light yellow-brown glaze externally (eg P17–20).

Pipkins have a rolled rim and a horizontal handle with a deep thumb groove along the top (eg P16). They are decorated with rilling on the body and a light brown external glaze similar to that on the cooking pots.

Large bowls have a simple out-turned rim and a sagging base (P23). They are decorated with a sparse light brown glaze externally.

Curfew. A single curfew, glazed externally, was present (P24).

Kiln props. A minimum of eleven of these small, thick-walled kiln supports were found (P21–22).

NB Table does not include figures for the vessels which have been restored and are on display in the National Museum of Wales.

have been positioned standing on their rims, probably supporting jugs – since the circular drips of glaze on them have diameters which correspond closely with those of the jugs.

Illustrated sherds from V kiln group

(Fig 18.2–4)

P5 Jug. Fabric MA2. It has a simple pinched spout and a strap handle with a deep groove. The base is thumb frilled. The body is decorated with vertical dark brown painted stripes and glazed externally. *V4*

P6 Jug with simple pinched lip a strap handle and thumb-frilled base, sagging slightly. Fabric MA2, pinkish-orange coloured. Greenish-brown to golden-brown glaze externally. Rilling on the middle to upper part of the body. *V4*

P7 Jug with wide mouth and simple strap handle. Fabric MA2, orange coloured. Honey-yellow to dark olive green glaze externally. The body is

decorated with vertical applied thumb-pressed, dark painted strips. *V4*

P8 Jug with bridged frilled spout. Fabric MA2. Decorated with a face mask below the spout. Scars indicate that a pair of arms once supported the tip of the spout. The incised fingers still remain. *V4*

P9 Jug with bridged frilled spout, and arms supporting the tip of the spout. Fabric MA2, orange-coloured. Yellow-green glaze externally. *V4*

P10 Plain, slightly sagging jug base. Fabric MA2, orange-coloured. Light yellow to olive-green glaze externally. On the exterior surface of the base are drips of glaze together with the fused remnants of the rim of another pot; this appears to suggest that the pot was fired standing on its rim. *V4*

P11 Jug with pinched lip and a strap handle. Fabric MA2, orange-coloured. Glazed all over externally; the colour varies from dark to light olive green. There is rilling on the middle to

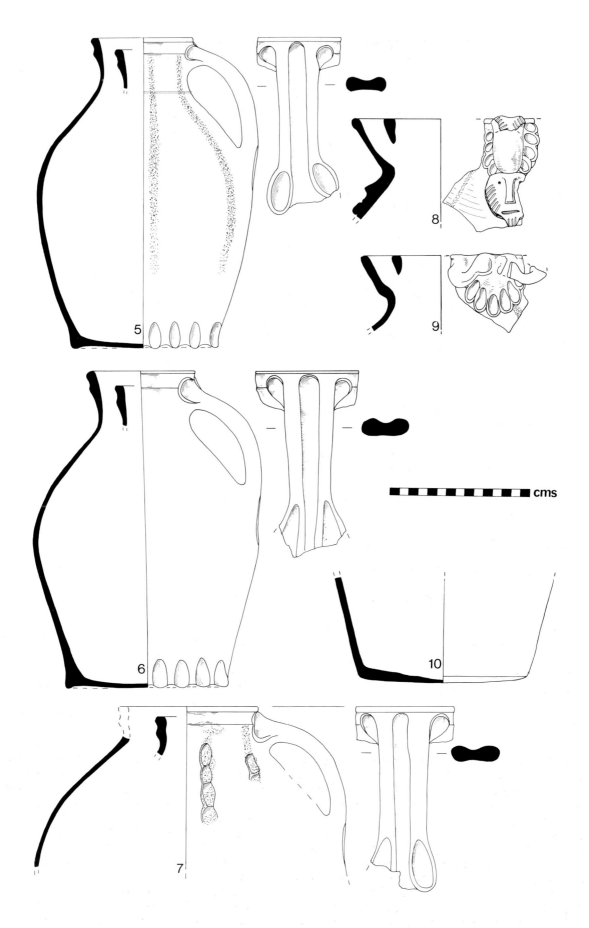

Fig 18.2 P5–P10 V4 Kiln Products. ×¼.

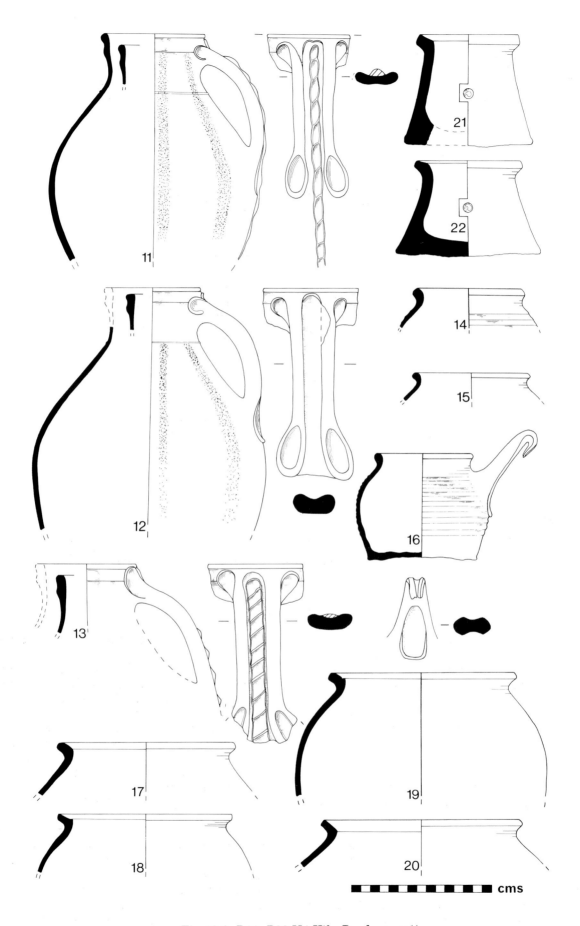

Fig 18.3 P11–P22 V4 Kiln Products. ×¹/₄.

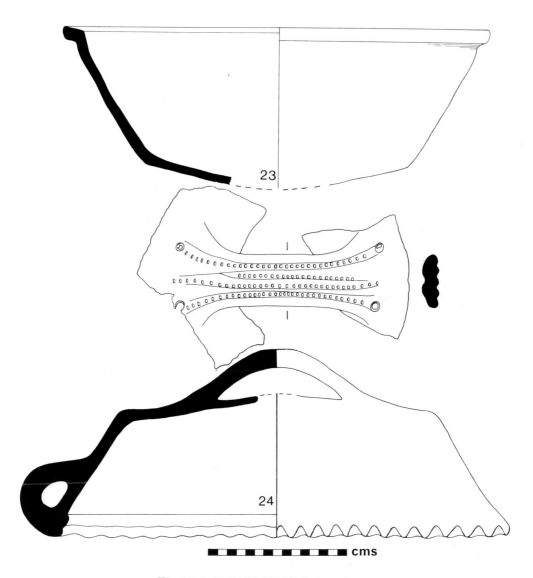

Fig 18.4 P23–P24 V4 Kiln Products. ×¹⁄₄.

upper part of the body which is decorated with vertical painted dark brown stripes at intervals around the body. The handle has an applied thumb-pressed strip in the groove, which extends onto the body of the pot. *V4*

P12 Jug with simple strap handle. Fabric MA2, orange-coloured. Yellow-green glaze externally. Rilling over most of the surface. Decorated with vertical dark brown painted stripes at intervals around the body. *V4*

P13 Jug with strap handle. Fabric MA2, pale orange. Light olive-green to golden glaze externally. Handle has an applied thumb-pressed strip in the groove. *V4*

P14 Pipkin. Fabric MA2, orange throughout. Glazed a light brownish-green colour externally. The body is rilled. *V4*

P15 Pipkin. Fabric MA2, orange-coloured. *V4*

P16 Pipkin with handle intact. Fabric MA2. Light brown glaze externally. The body is rilled. The handle has a deep thumb groove in its upper

surface, and a short impress where the handle joins the body. *V4*

P17–20 Cooking pots. All have simple out-turned, more or less squared rims. Fabric MA2, orange wth a grey core, though they have a varying degree of grittiness, and P18 is reduced. Sparse light yellow-brown glaze on exterior, similar to that of the pipkins. There is rilling on the body, just below the neck. Some of the flat, unthumbed bases may in fact belong to cooking pots rather than jugs. *V4*

P21–22 Kiln props. Fabric MA2, orange coloured. These two drawings are representative of several more very similar props. They all have a single pierced hole in the side. Evidence that they have been used in the kiln to support jug mouths is provided in the form of drips of glaze in rings on the exterior of all their bases as well as in patches on their sides. *V4*

P23 Bowl with simple out-turned rim and a sagging base. Fabric MA2, orange-buff. Sparse light brown glaze splashed onto exterior surface. *V4*

P24 Curfew. Fabric MA2. The rim is frilled and one small rod handle survives, springing from the rim. On the top is a broad strap handle, decorated with rows of incisions deeply stabbed. There are four holes pierced through the top of the curfew, two at either end of the handle. Sparse yellowish brown glaze externally. *V4*

18.5 Site A Catalogue (Fig 18.5–6)

P25 Large pipkin handle with thumb groove on top. Fabric MA, medium-hard sandy orange-red fabric with grey core. Sparse yellow-green glaze. Sherd not securely stratified. Similar to/possible Rhuddlan kiln product. *A91 Ditch II middle silts*

P26 Jug sherd with thumb-frilled rim. Fabric MA, hard fairly rough sandy orange-red fabric with a grey core. Yellowish-green glaze externally. *A58*

Ditch III middle silts

P27 Thumb-frilled base sherd of a jug. Fabric MA, a hard orange fabric, burnt dark grey in places. Overfired whitish external glaze, appears to have been heavily burnt after breakage. Decorated with vertical applied notch-stamped strips. *A82 dump in top of Ditch III*

P28 Rim and strap handle of a jug with bridge spout. Fabric MA, very hard, medium sandy dark red fabric with a grey core. Fabric has fired redder than the usual Rhuddlan kiln fabric. Brownish-yellow glaze externally. Body is decorated with frilling where the spout is attached. Handle has slashed decoration. NB The angle of the spout is in fact more upward- pointing than in the illustration. *A82 dump in top of Ditch III*

P29 Rod handle. Fabric MA, medium-hard, slightly sandy, buff-coloured with a grey core. Unglazed. *C18 associated with drying kiln C3*

P30 Sherd from a jug neck. Fabric MA, Very hard fired sandy fabric, reddish-brown with a dark

Table 18.2 Site A: contexts with medieval and post-medieval pottery

Site A Context	Saxo-Norman	Saintonge	V kiln type	Medieval	Post-Med
A91 Ditch II middle silts	–	–	–	P25(i)	–
A98 Ditch III middle silts	–	–	–	1	–
A58 Ditch III middle silts	–	–	–	P26	–
A48 Ditch III upper silts	–	–	+	+	–
A47 Ditch III upper fill	–	–	+	+	–
A43 Ditch III upper fill	–	–	+	+	–
A82 Ditch III upper fill	–	–	5P27P28	15	(i)
C66 Hollow associated C2	–	–	–	(i)?	(i)
C3 Drying kiln	–	–	–	+	–
C69 associated C3	P4	–	–	P36	–
C18 associated C3	–	–	–	P29 +	–
C24 pit in House 1	–	–	–	+	–
House 1 slot packing	–	–	1	+	–
House 2 C7 on floor	–	–	–	P34 15	–
House 2 C31 void	–	–	–	1	–
C85 Posthole by House 2	–	–	–	1	–
A33 Industrial activity	–	–	1	–	–
A28 Industrial activity	–	–	1	–	–
A4 Industrial activity	–	–	–	1	–
A106 Industrial activity	–	–	1	P30	–
A105 Industrial activity	–	1	–	P31 1	–
A104 Industrial activity	–	–	–	1	–
A5 Industrial activity	1	–	20	P32 20	–
A11 Industrial activity	1	–	–	–	–
A7 Slot	–	–	–	P33 1	–
A14 Slot	–	–	–	1	–
A34 Slot	–	–	1	–	–
A35 Gully	–	–	–	1	–
C15 Pit	–	–	+	–	–
B9 Pit	–	–	–	–	+
B8 Pit	–	–	–	–	+
C26 Pit	–	–	–	–	+
A2 Pit	–	–	–	–	+
C50 Pit	–	–	–	–	+

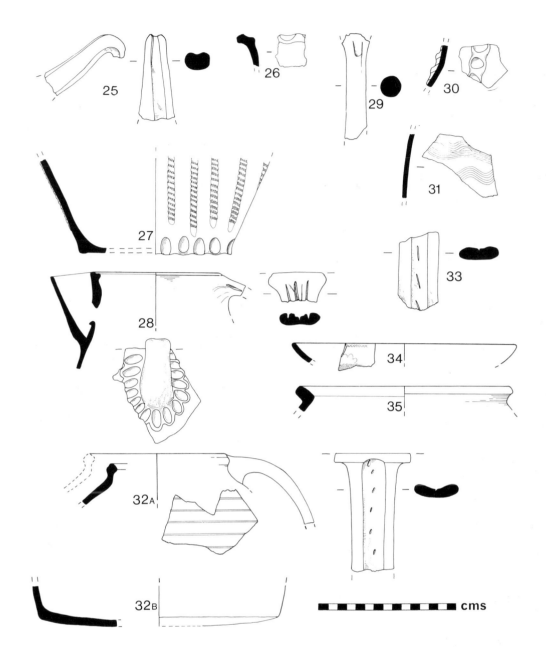

Fig 18.5 P25–P35 Pottery from Site A contexts. ×¼.

grey core. Dark green-brown glaze externally. Decorated with applied strip, thumbed or pinched. *A106 industrial phase post-dating Ditches*

P31 Jug sherds. Fabric MD (fine ware), very hard, quite fine, grey-white, with some fine sand. Mottled bright green glaze externally. Combed decoration. *A105 industrial phase post-dating Ditches*

P32 Rim and sagging base, almost certainly of the same jug. Fabric MA, medium-hard slightly sandy, mostly overfired to grey. Dark green glaze externally has run into the cracks (could be a waster, but fabric is not quite identical to MA2). The body is decorated with shallow

parallel grooves. The strap handle has stabbed decoration. *A5 industrial phase post-dating Ditches*

P33 Strap handle of a jug. Fabric MA, hard sandy, quite gritty, orange-buff coloured. Yellow-brown glaze externally. Slashed decoration along the groove of the handle. Similar to/possible Rhuddlan kiln product. *A7 boundary slot*

P34 Small, simple rim sherd from an alkaline glazed bowl. A Mediterranean import. *C7A soil on floor of House 2*

P35 Simple out-turned cooking pot rim. Fabric MA, hard buff fabric with grey core. Unglazed. *A topsoil*

P36 Jug rim with spout. Fabric MA, very hard,

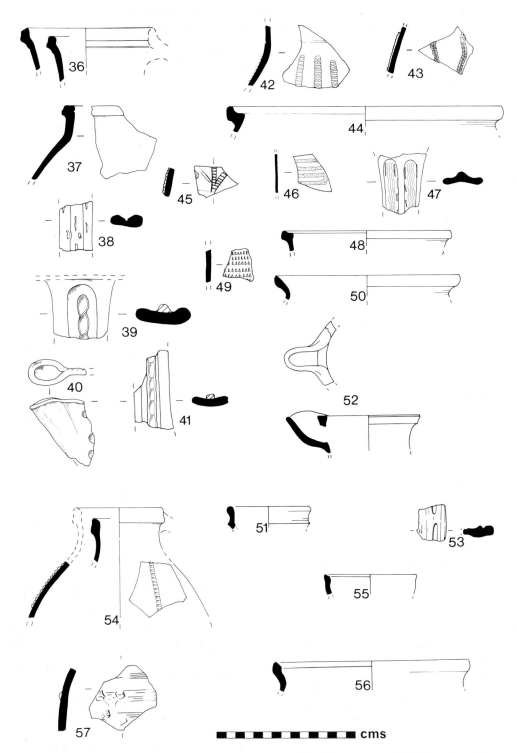

Fig 18.6 P36 Site A; P37–P56 Pottery from Site T contexts; P57 Site V. × ¼.

slightly sandy orange-buff throughout. Brownish glaze externally. Similar to/possible Rhuddlan kiln product. *C69 associated with drying kiln C3*

18.6 Site T Catalogue (Fig 18.6)

P37 Jug rim. Fabric MA, slightly porous and sandy, red-orange with a grey core. Lustrous olive-green glaze externally. Similar to/possible Rhuddlan kiln product. *T55 Ditch III upper fill*

P38 Jug handle. Fabric MA, hard and gritty, reddish-orange. Light greenish glaze externally. Stabbed decoration. Similar to/possible Rhuddlan kiln product. *T55 Ditch II upper fill*

P39 Jug handle. Fabric MA, orange coloured, rather porous and sandy. Olive green glaze externally. Decorated with an applied thumbed

Table 18.3 Site T: contexts with medieval and post-medieval pottery

Site T Context	Saxo-Norman	Saintonge	V kiln type	Ewloe	Medieval	Post-Med
T370 Ditch II upper silts	–	–	–	–	(i)	–
T341 Ditch III middle silts	–	–	5	–	1	–
T55 Ditch III upper silts	–	–	10	–	P45 P37 + P38 P39	–
T59 Ditch III dumps	–	–	20	P44 5	P40 P41 P42 P43 30	–
T14 Ditch III sand over	–	–	1	–	P46	–
T222 Gully	1	–	–	–	–	–
T227 Pit	1	–	–	–	–	–
T64 Soil beneath rampart	1	–	(i)	–	–	(i)
T178 Soil	P1	1	+	2	P47 + 2(i)?	(i)
T81 Palisade	–	–	–	–		–
T24 Ditch surface	–	–	+	–	+	–
T52 Slot in Ditch top	–	–	–	–	1	–
T57 Slot in Ditch top	–	–	+	–	–	–
T61 Corn Dryer	–	–	+	–	P48 P49 +	–
T50 Corn Dryer	–	–	1	–	–	–
T22 Surface over Ditch	–	–	1	–	+	(i)
T29/200 Soil	P2	5	60 P50 P55	P51 P56	+	(i)
T34 Compound slot	–	–	+	–	2	–
T65 Compound slot	–	P52	+	–	+	–
T21 Industrial activity	–	–	–	–	1	–
T80 Industrial activity	–	–	40	P53	25	(i)?
T243 Industrial activity	–	–	–	–	1	–
T268 Soil	–	–	P54 +	–	1	(i)?
T275 Boundary Ditch	1	–	1	–	5	–
T121 Boundary Ditch	–	–	–	–	1	1
T15 Pit	–	–	1	–	–	1
T132 Pit	–	–	1	–	–	1
T7 Soil	P4	–	+	–	50	100

strip in the groove. Similar to/possible Rhuddlan kiln product. *T55 Ditch III upper fill*

P40 Jug spout, bridged by pinching rim together on either side. Fabric MA, but rather porous and sandy, orange-red with a grey core. Brownish-green glaze externally. The spout is frilled externally. Similar to/possible Rhuddlan kiln product. *T59 Ditch III dump in top*

P41 Jug handle. Fabric MA, hard, but less rough than most of the sandy wares, with buff surfaces and a dark grey core. Olive-green glaze. Decorated with applied thumb-pressed strip in the groove. *T59 Ditch III dump in top*

P42 Jug sherd. Fabric MA, very hard, sandy orange coloured. Brownish glaze on exterior. Decorated with almost vertical, applied heavily stamped strips. Similar to/possible Rhuddlan kiln product. *T59 Ditch III dump in top*

P43 Jug sherd. Fabric MA, hard slightly sandy, dark grey, but less rough than most of the sandy wares. Dark green glaze externally. Decorated with applied stamped strips. *T59 Ditch III dump in top*

P44 Rim of jar. Fabric MD (Ewloe), hard pink gritty, with darker orange-brown surfaces. Splashes of honey-coloured glaze on the tip of the rim. *T59 Ditch III dump in top*

P45 Jug sherd. Fabric MA, orange with a grey core. Light yellow-green glaze externally. Decorated with applied stamped strips. *T55 Ditch II upper fill*

P46 Body sherd from a straight-sided vessel of uncertain shape. A Mediterranean maiolica import. The inside is unglazed, the exterior has a very thin white lead glaze. *T14 sand over Ditch III*

P47 Strap handle of a jug. Fabric MD (fine ware), hard, white, slightly sandy. Bright green to brown glaze externally. Stabbed and combed decoration. *T178 soil*

P48 Rim sherd of cooking pot. Fabric MA, medium hard, fine sandy, orange-pink with a grey core. Similar to/possible Rhuddlan kiln product. *T61 Corndryer infill*

P49 Jug sherd. Fabric MA, medium-hard, very sandy, grey with buff inner surface. Greenish glaze externally. Decorated with horizontal rows of rouletting. *T61 Corndryer infill*

P50 Cooking pot rim. Fabric MD (Ewloe), hard pinkish fabric, almost white just beneath a dark red surface (possibly a slip?). *T29 soil*

P51 Rim sherd, probably from a jug. Fabric MD (Ewloe), cream-coloured. *T29 soil*

P52 Saintonge jug rim with parrot beak-shaped spout. The exterior surface has a bright green mottled glaze. *T65 compound slot*

P53 Strap handle of a jug. Fabric MD (Ewloe), pinkish-white with a light grey core. Glazed a mustard-yellow colour. Slashed decoration. *T80 industrial activity*

P54 Jug sherd. Fabric MA, hard sandy with orange surfaces and grey core. Greenish glaze externally. Decorated with vertically applied rouletted strips. *T268 soil*

P55 Rim sherd. Fabric MD (Ewloe), Orange-buff coloured with redder surfaces. *T200 soil*

P56 Rim sherd. Fabric MD (Ewloe), creamy white with orange-red surfaces. *T200 soil*

18.7 Site V Catalogue (Fig 18.6)

P57 Body sherd, probably of a jug. Fabric MA, orange with a grey core. Olive-green glaze externally. Decorated with horizontal combing and applied roughly square-shaped blobs. *V24 hollow*

18.8 Site E Catalogue (Fig 18.7)

P58 Jug of unusual form. Fabric MA, fine medium-hard grit-free grey, with pink inner surface. Decorated with stamped applied blobs and vertical strips. Greenish-brown glaze externally. Possibly a 13th century vessel, though the unusual form may indicate a later date. *From both pit J79 and silt G5*

P59 Strap handle, its edges pinched lightly giving a frilled effect. Fabric MA, orange with a grey core. Olive-green to golden glaze externally. Decorated with an applied impressed strip in the groove. Similar to/possible Rhuddlan kiln product. *G5 silt immediately below c 1280 surface*

P60 Cooking pot. Fabric MA, orange with a dark grey core. Similar to/possible Rhuddlan kiln product. *G5 silt immediately below 1280 surface*

P61 Cooking pot. Fabric MD (Ewloe), pinkish-orange with a grey core. *G4 soil on c 1280 surface*

P62 Jug with strap handle. Fabric MA, light orange with an almost black core. Sparse dull olive-green glaze externally. Slashed decoration along the groove. The body is decorated with horizontal incised wavy lines. *J16 soil build-up over c 1280 surface*

P63 Strap handle of a jug. Fabric MD (Ewloe), pinkish white. Brownish green glaze on external surface. Slashed and grooved decoration. *J16 soil build-up over c 1280 surface*

P64 Pipkin. Fabric MA, reddish-orange. Brownish glaze externally. Rilling on the body below the neck. *J16 soil build-up over c 1280 surface*

P65 Jar rim. Fabric MA, orange-buff. On top of the rim is a splash of green glaze. *J16 soil build-up over c 1280 surface*

P66 Saintonge jug handle, import from South West France. Bright green mottled glaze. *G125 pit*

P67 Strap handle of a jug. Fabric MA, orange with a grey core. Brownish green glaze. Slashed decoration. *G130 pit*

P68 Jug rimsherd. Fabric MD (Ewloe), hard white and gritty with orange- brown surfaces. Horizontal rouletted decoration and traces of yellowish glaze below. *H5 pit*

18.9 Site M

See Table 18.6.

18.10 Site D Catalogue (Fig 18.8)

P69 Strap handle of a jug. Fabric MA, orange with

Table 18.4 Site V: contexts with medieval and post-medieval pottery

Site V Context	Saxo-Norman	Saintonge	V kiln type	Medieval	Post-Med
V73 Soil	–	–	–	–	(i)
V24 Hollow	–	–	20 (w)	P57 +	–
V71 Pit	–	–	+	–	–
V34 Pit	1	–	–	–	–
V20 Soil	–	–	50 (w)	+	(i)
V51 Kiln	–	–	20 (w)	+	(i)
V4 Kiln	–	1	P5–P24 Table 18.1	–	–
V5 Clay associated kiln	–	–	+	–	(i)
V82 Boundary Ditch	–	–	+	+	–
V37 Boundary Ditch	–	–	+	+	–
V50 Boundary Ditch	–	–	+	+	+
V2 Soil	–	–	+	+	+

Table 18.5 Site E: contexts with medieval and post-medieval pottery

Site E Context	Saintonge	V kiln type	Ewloe	Medieval	Post-Med
G112 Ditch III primary silts	–	–	–	+	–
J94 Ditch III middle silts	–	1	–	+	–
J89 Ditch III upper silts	1	1	1	2	–
J65 Ditch III upper silts	–	1	–	–	–
J50 Ditch IV upper silt	–	–	–	1	–
H47 Ditch IV upper silt	–	1	2(i)?	3	–
J88 Ditch V primary silt	–	–	–	1	–
J45 Ditch V upper fill	–	10	–	+	–
G143 Pit	–	1	–	+	–
H32 Pit	–	1	–	–	–
G26 Pit	–	1	–	–	–
G103 Pit	–	+	–	–	–
G101 Pit	–	+	–	1	–
G89 Pit	–	–	–	1	–
J79 Pit	1	+	–	P58	–
J58 Pit	–	+	–	+	–
J60 Gully	–	+	–	–	–
J43 Gully	–	+	1	+	–
J71 Gully	–	1	–	1	–
H9 Gully	–	–	–	1	–
J68 Pit – metalworking	–	–	–	1	–
J64 Industrial/metalworking levels	–	–	–	1	–
J49 Base of early lane	–	+	–	+	–
G5 Layer under c 1280 lane	–	P59 P60 +	–	+	–
J36 Base of c 1280 surface	–	+	–	+	–
G6 c 1280 lane	–	+	–	P64 +	–
G4 Silt on G6	2	+	P61	50	+(i)
J16 Soil build-up	2	+	P63	P62 P64 P65 50	+(i)
G11 Slot	–	–	–	+	–
G12 Slot	–	–	–	+	–
G86 Slot	–	–	–	+	–
G125 Pit	P66	–	–	+	+
G130 Pit	–	–	–	P67 +	+
G131 Pit	–	–	–	5	–
G113 Pit	–	–	–	+	–
G13 Pit	–	–	–	+	–
G87 Pit	–	–	–	1	–
H4 Slot	1	+	–	+	+
H26 Foundation trench	–	–	1	+	+
H5 Pit	–	–	P68 +	+	–
J14 Soil	1	–	–	20	+
G16 Boundary ditch	–	–	2	+	+

a grey core. Olive green glaze in the groove. Slashed decoration. *R63 gully post-dating inner bank*

P70 Jug sherd. Fabric MA, grey throughout. Olive-green glaze externally. Close rouletted decoration. Possibly a late medieval sherd. *R64 gully post-dating inner bank*

P71 Cooking pot. Fabric MD (Ewloe), light buff with reddish-brown surfaces. *R64 gully post-dating inner bank*

P72 Jug sherd with scar from handle. Fabric probably MA2, orange-buff with a grey core. Green glaze surviving in patches externally.

Horizontal lines of rouletted decoration. *R36 posthole post-dating inner bank*

P73 Fragment of a strap handle of a jug. Fabric MA, pale buff. Decorated with an applied vertical strip. *O14 outer bank*

P74 Body sherd, probably of a jug. Fabric MA, pale orange with a light grey core. Decorated with lines of horizontal rouletting. Similar to possible Rhuddlan kiln product. *O14 outer bank*

P75 Body sherd, probably of a jug. Fabric MA, similar to that of P94. Light olive-green glaze externally. Decorated with an incised lattice pattern. *O14 outer bank*

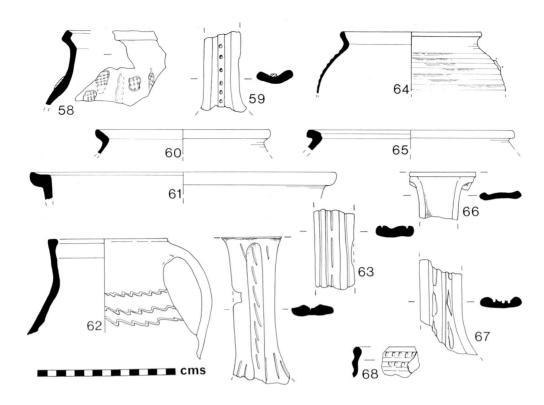

Fig 18.7 P58–P68 Pottery from Site E contexts. ×¼.

P76 Storage vessel. Fabric MA, pale orange with a grey core. Unglazed. *O14 outer bank*

P77 Jug rim. Fabric MA, pale buff with a dark grey core. Traces of yellow-green glaze externally. Similar to possible Rhuddlan kiln products. *O8 outer bank*

P78 Sagging thumbed base, probably of a jug. Fabric MA, orange with a grey core. *O17 outer bank*

P79 Body sherd, probably of a jug. Fabric MA, orange with a grey core. Decorated with vertical applied strip. *O46 inner bank*

P80 Body sherd, probably of a jug. Fabric MA2, orange coloured. External glaze varies from honey-coloured to dark brown. Similar to/possible Rhuddlan kiln product. *P12 inner bank*

Table 18.6 Site M: contexts with medieval and post-medieval pottery

Site M Context	V kiln type	Medieval	Post-Med
M27 Soil	–	+	(i)
M8 Soil	15 (w)	5	20(i)?
M93 Phase 1 burial	–	1	–
M88 Phase 2 burial	1	–	–
M71 Phase 2 burial	1	+	–
M72 Phase 3 burial	1	–	(i)
M37 Phase 3 burial	–	1	–
M40 Phase 3 burial	–	1	(i)
M31 Phase 3 burial	–	–	(i)
M30 Phase 3 burial	–	1	–
M67 Phase 3 burial	1	+	–
M16 Phase 3 burial	1	–	–
M32 Phase 3 burial	1	1	–
M36 Phase 4 burial	1	1	(i)
M23 Phase 4 burial	1	–	–
M24 Phase 4 burial	1	1	–
M2 Soil	1	+	20

Table 18.7 Site D: contexts with medieval and post-medieval pottery

Site D Context	V kiln type	Ewloe	Medieval	Post-Med
O14 Outer Edwardian bank	P74 15	–	P76 P73 P75 20	–
O8 Outer Edwardian bank	P77	–	+	–
O17 Outer Edwardian bank	–	–	P78	–
P9 Outer Edwardian bank	+	–	+	–
P8 Outer Edwardian bank	+	–	+	–
O27 Inner Edwardian bank	+	–	–	–
O46 Inner Edwardian bank	+	–	P79 15	–
P12 Inner Edwardian bank	P80	–	–	–
P16 Inner Edwardian bank	P81	–	P82 25	–
O29 Primary ditch silt	–	P83	+	–
P45 Primary ditch silt	–	P84	–	–
P44 Middle ditch silt	P85 +	1	+	–
O28 Gully post-outer bank	1	–	+	–
O50 Erosion outer bank	–	–	+	–
R63 Gully post-inner bank	–	–	P69	–
R64 Gully post-inner bank	+	P71	P70 15	–
R36 Posthole post-inner bank	+	–	P72	–
R2 Erosion post-inner bank	–	–	100	(i)?
O49 Gully post-outer bank	–	–	1	–
O11 Upper ditch silt	–	–	P89	P86-8 50
P43 Upper ditch silt	–	–	–	1
Q8/9 Upper ditch silt	–	P90	P91	+
P10 Posthole post-outer bank erosion	–	–	–	+
P21 Gully post-inner bank	–	P92	10	P93+
O2 Gully post-inner bank	–	–	–	+
R7 Gully post-inner bank	–	–	–	+
P3 Gully post-outer bank	–	–	1	–
P6 Gully post-outer bank	–	–	–	1
R38 Gully post-inner bank	–	–	–	20

P81 Body sherd, probably from a jug. Fabric MA2, pale buff. Olive-green to brown external glaze. Decorated with horizontal rows of rouletting. Similar to possible Rhuddlan kiln products. *P16 inner bank*

P82 Part of a flat lid. Fabric MA, pale pinkish-orange. Splashes of olive- green glaze on both surfaces. *P16 inner bank*

P83 Jug with rod handle. Fabric MD (Ewloe), orange with a grey core. Thick olive-green glaze. *O29 primary ditch silt*

P84 Body sherd, probably from the neck of a jug. Fabric MD (Ewloe), cream throughout. Traces of a dull green glaze splashed all over. Brown painted decoration on exterior. *O45 primary ditch silt*

P85 Rim, probably of a cooking pot. Sherd is now missing; preliminary description 'gritty and highly fired, dark grey, brown surface, splashes of dark green glaze'. Similar to possible Rhuddlan kiln products. *P44 middle ditch silt*

P86 Body sherd, probably of a shallow bowl. Fabric LC, fine, hard, smooth pinkish-cream. Both surfaces have a white slip, but the inner surface is decorated with dark and light brown slips and a glaze. The result is a pattern of patches of creamy-yellow, light and dark brown, sometimes overlapping. *O11 upper ditch silt*

P87 Rim, probably of a jar. Fabric LA, is typical of post-medieval Buckley ware; dark, red-brown fabric containing creamy-yellow streaks where the clay is not perfectly blended. Dark brown glaze on both the interior and exterior surfaces. *O11 upper ditch silt*

P88 Body sherd. Fabric LA, late Buckley slip ware; a hard pinkish-brown colour with creamy-yellow inclusions. Thick dark brown glaze on interior and exterior surfaces. Decorated with a creamy-yellow slip, trailed and in spots. *O11 upper ditch silt*

P89 Rim, probably of a jug. Fabric MA, pale orange. Olive-green glaze surviving on the exterior suface of the neck. *O11 upper ditch silt*

P90 Handle of a pipkin or skillet. Fabric MD (Ewloe), but not very gritty, orange-red surface with a pale orange core. *Q8/9 upper ditch silts*

P91 Jug rim. Fabric MA, a hard micaceous pinkish-red with a grey core (frequent quartz inclusions). Light green glaze on exterior surface. *Q8/9 upper ditch silts*

P92 Bung hole. Fabric MD (Ewloe), pinkish white with red-brown surfaces. Similar to examples

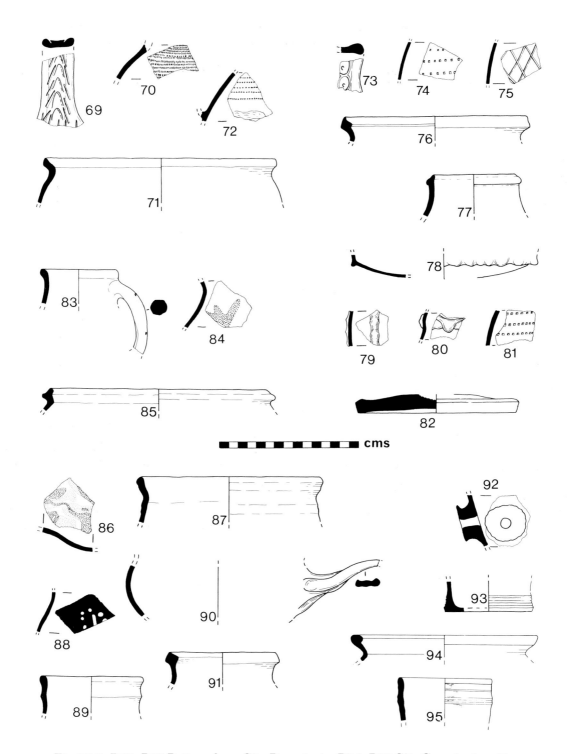

Fig 18.8 *P69–P93 Pottery from Site D contexts; P94–P95 Site S contexts.* ×¹⁄₄

found at Hen Blas (Davey and Morgan, 1977, 47, nos 26–7). Possibly of 16th century date. *P21 gully cutting bank*

P93 Base of a cup. Fabric LB, fine, very hard light buff. A shiny mid-brown mottled glaze on interior and exterior surfaces. *P21 gully cutting bank*

18.8 Site S Catalogue (Fig 18.8)

P94 Jar/cooking pot rim. Fabric MA, hard rough grey fabric with buff surfaces, possibly burnt. *S25 soil*

P95 Rim, probably of a storage vessel. Fabric MD (Ewloe), very hard, gritty buff-coloured. Unglazed. *S3 soil*

Discussion

The collection of pottery excavated at Rhuddlan is particularly valuable to pottery studies as so few

Table 18.8 Site S: contexts with medieval and post-medieval pottery

Site S Context	Saintonge	Ewloe	Medieval	Post-Med
S25 Soil	–	–	P94	–
S21 Soil	–	–	–	+
S3 Soil	–	P95	+	+
S19 Pit	–	–	1	+
S29 Pit	–	–	–	1
S28 Pit	–	–	–	1
S28A Posthole	1	–	+	+
S4 Posthole	–	–	–	+
S6 Gully	–	–	–	1
S27 Gully	–	–	–	+
S9 Soil	–	–	–	50

medieval kiln sites have been excavated in North Wales. Here we have a sizeable group containing a range of different vessels, known to have been produced in the same kiln. The majority of the pottery recovered was of local or Cheshire manufacture, consisting of sandy red wares; the fabrics and the decoration being typical of the Cheshire and North East Wales area. Only a few sherds of imported foreign vessels were found. These were all from green glazed Saintonge jugs (it is worth noting the complete lack of late 13th century Saintonge polychrome imports) with the exception of two Mediterranean imports – an alkaline-glazed bowl and a vessel in Mediterranean maiolica. The low number of French imports (0.87%) by weight of non-kiln medieval pottery would tend to argue against Rhuddlan having much, if any, direct overseas trade. This can be compared with the medieval pottery from the 76–78 trenches at the Dominican Friary, Chester, where French imports form a more noticeable proportion (1.39% by weight) of the pottery (Rutter, 1990). These imported vessels may well have reached Rhuddlan overland, or perhaps by secondary coastal trading, most likely from Chester (P Courtney, pers comm).

Acknowledgements
Thanks are due to Marion Blockley for general assistance and preparatory work; Paul Courtney on fabric series; Janet Rutter; D F Williams on thin sectioning some sherds; J G Hurst, L Biek, R King, J Bayley on foreign imports; Brian Hart for quantification of kiln group; Henrietta Quinnell for identification of the Rhuddlan kiln products. Pottery illustrations are by Lesley Simpson; nos 1–4 are by Marion Blockley.

19 Rhuddlan during the early Medieval period and the location of Cledemutha

19.1 The post-Roman period until the 8th century AD

No artefacts can be dated to this period; material from Welsh sites of this period tends to be sparse. Imported B amphora is attested from Deganwy but it is unclear whether Rhuddlan lies within the zone into which it was imported. Rhuddlan is certainly east of the general distribution of the rather later Class E ware (Thomas, 1981). It is unlikely that Rhuddlan would have been under the control of Gwynedd throughout this period. Davies (1982, 98) argues persuasively for the existence of minor kingdoms which were not documented and which later were absorbed by major units; she points to a minor kingdom of Rhos (*ibid*, 102, & Fig 38) around the Conwy valley recorded from the 6th century and possibly later. There are also the problems of the line of Cynddylan, his realm of Dogfeiling (Davies, 1982, 100 & Fig 37) in North East Wales, and the extent of the kingdom of Powys during the 7th century. It seems clear however that by the time of the conflicts with Mercia which cumulated in the construction of Offa's Dyke in the 780s (2.1) Gwynedd would have been in overall control of the area. The complex interactions probable between the various kingdoms, major and minor, in the area between the Clwyd and the Dee – the cantref of Tegeingl, make a settlement and strong point at Rhuddlan likely, quite possibly on several different occasions; it would also have been a suitable site for the home base for the control of units smaller than kingdoms, such as would later be recorded as *cwmydau* or commotes.

Soil build-up continued on Site M after the Roman period with layers M27 and the truncated M8. It seems likely that these originated in sand-blows. As with the Roman period sand-blow M58, these layers, though later much disturbed by the overlying graveyard, may have derived from sand dunes along a coastline which was close in below Rhuddlan through these centuries (Manley, 1982b, 14). 'Morfa Rhuddlan' (Rhuddlan marshes) were in existence by the time of the battle of 796, suggesting that the sea had retreated by the later 8th century. Another possibility for this soil build-up would be lynchetting, perhaps unlikely in view of

the short distance of Site M from the Clwyd. A final alternative would be erosion from some disturbance such as the construction of an earthwork along the cliff overlooking the Clwyd. The likely historical contexts for a defensive earthwork have already been commented upon. The soil build-up in M may be continued by V30, but it will be argued below that this was of later date. The build-up did not continue into Site E nor was it found further from the Clwyd in T or A.

The only possible construction which might date to this period is Structure 2, Site T (Fig 4.1), although the large number of pits and postholes on A, T, E and D which can not be dated should be borne in mind. Structure 2, a complex rectilinear building of post-in-trench construction, has no associated Roman pottery despite its occurrence in other areas of Site T. Further it is cut through by gully T143, one of a sequence which seems to postdate the Iron Age-Romano-British use of the area and may (19.2) be of 8th to 9th century date. Until recently the 'aisled' post-Roman building at Dinorben (Gardner & Savory, 1964, Fig 14) might have been considered as a parallel, but this is now considered more likely to be of late Roman date (Edwards & Lane, 1988, 66). Structure 2 should be borne in mind as a possible building dating somewhere between the 4th and 8th centuries. In view of the lack of Welsh buildings known for this period (Edwards & Lane, 1988, passim), the matter must remain open until possible comparanda are found in the future.

19.2 The expansion of Gwynedd and the struggle with Mercia: 8th to 9th centuries

This long period of complex military campaigns allows numerous occasions for the use of Rhuddlan as a strong point, apart from the probability of the continuance of some form of agricultural settlement. Welsh fortifications of this probable date are now being recognised, as at Cwrt Llechrhyd, Powys (Musson & Spurgeon [1988] includes a discussion of possible sites). Mercia was also adopting a strategy of urban foundations, especially under Offa (757–796), designed both as market centres and as fortresses usually commanding river crossings (Haslam, 1987).

It will be argued below (19.3) that the most likely context for Ditch I at Rhuddlan is the later 10th century. As the data used is not conclusive, it needs emphasizing that this, the most likely date in the authors' opinion, should not be accepted as final, and a wide range of other dates and contexts are possible. Among these would be a foundation by Offa in advance, chronologically and geographically, of the frontier line established by his Dyke in the 780s.

A scatter of artefacts could date to the 9th century. The bone trial piece MSF 21 (16.6) from Ditch I infill could be this early as could the loomweight MSF 20 from posthole T97 (16.5). The few fragments of 'shelly ware' (Fabric MK 18.2.1) may relate to the 'Shelley Vesicular Ware' from Chester (J A A Rutter in Mason, 1985, 41); this has been suggested to be an East Midlands product only differing slightly from St Neots ware, itself not yet demonstrated to date before the late 9th century (Hurst, 1976, 323).

The gully group on Site T, T175, T143 etc, appeared to be sealed by the old land surface T64 beneath the only surviving rampart material possibly connected with Ditch I. One gully, T222, and an interconnected pit, T227, both produced sherds of shelly MK fabric. Assuming these comparatively small pieces are not intrusive, they would suggest the gully group, at least in part, could belong to the 9th century. The group *may* be a continuation of that on Site V containing features such as V67. If so, they were here cut directly into natural sand, but their tops and higher related deposits may have been eroded. A major boundary, many times recut in soft sand soil, is indicated, but, from the scale of the gullies, one more likely to relate to agricultural, or possibly urban, plot division than defence. It is possible that the gullies and ploughmarks on Site D (Fig 8.2) may relate to agriculture of this period, given their similarity to features from Chester dated within the range AD 40–850 (Mason, 1985, 2).

Pit J21 on Site E (6.5; Fig 6.1) is likely to be of 8th or 9th century date. Its distinctive timber lining suggests Saxon comparanda; it was cut into (probably eroded) prehistoric soil levels and covered by soil G143 into which the earliest Ditches were cut. Its position beyond Ditch II, suggested (19.3) to be 10th century, may indicate a date before the establishment of this defensive system.

Returning to Site T, soil T64 over the gullies appears to have been left undisturbed, except possibly by agriculture, before the construction of a rampart connected with the Ditches. Yet posthole T97 (Fig 4.2), which contained loomweight MSF 20, cut into its top; it was in an area unsealed by surviving rampart material and could have been cut during a period when the defences were out of use and eroded. Yet it opens the prospect of gullies such as T175 being rather earlier than the dating

assigned from the shell fabric sherds. So little is known about the sparse ceramics from this area that there is the possibility that these and the gullies predate the 9th–early 10th century by some time. The undisturbed soil T64, perhaps like G143 on Site E and V30 – assuming the gullies beneath correlate with those on Site T, may indicate a period of quiet agricultural/pastoral use or even total disuse between two periods of activity.

Assigning structures to the 8th and 9th century is difficult; again the undated and unstratified features on the various sites should be borne in mind. Structure 2 on Site T could be contemporary with the gullies and 8th or 9th centuries. Such a Structure could well have an English background (Rahtz, 1976, passim), though no precise parallels are forthcoming. Postbuilt Structure 6 Site V can only be dated to a period substantially before the 13th century. Structure 5 Site V postdates gullies V67 and overlying soil V30 and predates the 13th century. It could be of any date from perhaps the 8th to the 12th centuries.

The above discussion is inconclusive, based on scrappy evidence from eroded and ill-dated contexts. It does however underline the potential for multi-phase settlement at Rhuddlan before the tenth century.

19.3 The 10th century and the location of *Cledemutha*

The earlier phases of the Norman Borough Defence Ditches and Structures 1, 3 and 4, together with their associated finds, are relevant here. The discussion also considers Manley's identification of the Town Ditch (Fig 1.2) as the defences of *Cledemutha* (Manley, 1987).

Taylor (1984) has reviewed the siting of *Cledemutha* using a 14th century document in which the place name 'Cloudesmouth', assumed in the transliteration of *Cledemutha*, occurs for the first time. The document links 'Cloudesmouth' to the name 'Birchloyt', which is known to have lain on the coast on the east bank of the Clwyd near Rhuddlan but which is not recorded as a medieval settlement. Taylor (*ibid*), suggesting that 'Birchloyt' derives from '*burh*' and 'Clwyd', proposes a fortified site on the coast now beneath the west part of Rhyl or even beneath the sea. He strengthens his argument by stressing that Rhuddlan was already an established place in the 10th century, and its name might be expected to have been used for a *burh* sited there. *Cledemutha* on a different site, at the very end of the Clwyd estuary, would be an appropriate interpretation for a small fort set up to provide a military response to Viking incursions. This siting would not be appropriate for a *burh*, intended as a market and mint centre with, preferably, control of a river crossing, which the authors have accepted as the intended role for *Cledemutha*; it may be that future reviews of the subject will accept Taylor's pragmatic military interpretation for *Cledemutha* and that they are in error in rejecting it.

It is expecting too much from the archaeological data, which comprises imprecisely dated artefacts, radiocarbon dating and general assumptions, that it should provide an indisputable location for *Cledemutha*, which almost certainly was short lived, but there is now sufficient data from Rhuddlan for two different circuits for *Cledemutha* to be proposed.

The Norman Borough Defences excavated 1969–73

The circuit encloses some 8 ha including the 'knoll' of sand soil overlooking the Clwyd. It is presumed here that Ditches I, II and III represent the same defensive sequence on Sites A, T and E, as fills and dimensions – as far as these were ascertainable – were similar; this presumption could only be proved by continuous excavation between the Sites. Ditch I appears to have been *c* 3m deep and 10m wide, V-shaped with a cleaning slot in places, on all three sites; its clean sand fill may represent fairly rapid silting, possibly from the collapse of a revetted rampart, almost up to its top. The only datable artefact is MSF 21, the bone trial piece of the 10th century or earlier. The line of the rampart related to the Defences as a whole is indicated by the ridge of eroded but compacted natural sand 8m wide with a possible 2m berm on Site A. On Site T a 10m strip of buried soil T64 lay below a remnant of bank material T69 6m wide, with no indication of a berm; soil T64 appeared to be truncated, probably by turf-stripping, and in it were the run of postholes T81. The T81 postholes may be described as a palisade as they run parallel to the Ditches and along the approximate centre of the buried soil; they do not run up through remnant bank T64. No rampart area was available for excavation on Site E. The simplest interpretation for the rampart in Site T is that the bank complementing Ditch I (or possibly II) contained timbering, that this bank became almost totally eroded and its site was then stripped of turf before a later rampart to which T69 belonged was constructed. The palisade T81 may have fronted its bank, leaving a 6m berm, or may have been central to it, with perhaps a turf revetment at the front.

On Site E Ditch IV, 5m wide and 2m deep, lay 6m beyond the assumed outer edge of Ditch I; it again appeared to have silted quickly with clean sand and contained no datable artefacts. There is no reason why IV should not be contemporary with I (or II). If so, and assuming it continued around the defensive circuit, it swung out to at least 18m beyond the outer edge of I on Site A where it was not found.

There is no indication of where any entrance might have been. Site A is close to the suggested centre of the circuit.

The dimensions of Ditch I, and of Ditch IV if accepted as part of the same system, are not inappropriate for those of a *burh*. *Burh* fortifications vary widely and more is probably known about ramparts than ditches, more about Wessex than Mercia (Radford, 1978; Biddle, 1976). Wide berms seem to be usual and spaced double or triple ditches are known (eg Cricklade, Haslam, 1984b; Lydford, Haslam, 1984c). Timbering was used in ramparts. Tamworth is the only Mercian *burh* in which the defences have been reasonably fully investigated (summarised Biddle, 1976). This had an elaborate timber framed rampart 9m wide, a 6m berm and a ditch 4m wide and 2m deep. Given the wide variety of topographical situations, some on new sites, some on former urban foundations, a variety of defensive arrangements is likely in Mercia. The most unusual feature at Rhuddlan is the apparent lack of a berm, which could be met by accepting palisade T81 as a front rampart revetment.

On size the Rhuddlan Ditch I circuit might be most usefully compared to those of the Northern frontier of Mercia, of which *Cledemutha* formed the Western end: Manchester–Thelwall–Runcorn–Eddisbury–Chester–*Cledmutha*. These varied very much in size from Runcorn and Eddisbury which were under 4 ha (Hill, 1981) to Chester which may have enclosed 52 ha reusing the former Roman circuit (Mason, 1985, 38). Hill (1981, 143) has suggested that there was an intended division between those under 7 ha which were only planned as forts and those of 9 ha and over which were intended to become full market and urban centres.

The Town Ditch – Manley's excavations 1979–82

The excavations on the south side 1979–81 showed this to have comprised a flat-bottomed ditch 15m wide with an inner bank 11m wide and an outer of 13m; there were no berms nor any evidence of timbering (Manley, 1987). The 1982 excavation on the east side of the Town Ditch, designed to test for an entrance, was inconclusive. The only datable find from the old ground surface and the banks was a decorated link from a bit of probable 10th or 11th century date; this came from a deposit sealed by the inner bank on the south of the Town Ditch (P Ottoway in Manley, 1987, 33). Nine radiocarbon dates from seven of ten fires on the old land surface beneath the inner bank were obtained (R L Otlet & A J Walker in Manley, 1985b; Q Dresser, R L Otlet, A J Walker in Manley, 1987). Seven dates from six of the hearths were combined into a single uncalibrated date of AD 870 ± 35; two further dates from hearth ten combined to give AD 1145 ± 55. Material in the fires comprised charred oats and other grain, legumes and weed seeds, as well as charcoal, and were interpreted as discarded following processing (D Williams in Manley, 1985b. Fig 5 (Manley, 1987) shows one of the hearths beneath the bank as in a slight depression. There were further dates, uncalibrated; AD 1440 ± 60 from the basal ditch infill and four dates, between AD 830 ± 100 and 1160 ± 70 from a gully at the back of the inner bank which also contained 13th/14th century pottery.

The combined date from hearths beneath the inner bank was calibrated by R L Otlet & A J Walker (in Manley, 1985b, 109–10) following Stuiver (1982) to AD 955 ± 35, which they considered statistically consistent with the historical date of AD 921 for the foundation of *Cledemutha*. None of the other dates were calibrated, and they considered that some other archaeological explanation should be sought for the later date for hearth 10 of AD 1145 ± 55. Manley accepted the consistency of the calibrated AD 955 ± 35 with the historical date of AD 921, and considered the uncalibrated date of AD 1145 ± 55, after critical review, as an example of the acceptably anomalous dates which appear to occur on many sites (1985b, 114). (The AD 1440 ± 60 (uncalibrated) date [from a small sample of cattle and sheep bones and teeth in the basal ditch infill] was interpreted as from material pushed in deliberately long after construction.)

Sunken-floored buildings or Grubenhäuser Structures 1, 3 and 4

These, the only sunken-floored features located, were set 9m, 4m and 4m respectively behind the suggested bank line. Given the comparatively small areas of the interior excavated and that none was situated on the bank line, the siting of the Structures may be significant and they may be regarded as contemporary with the bank or its remnants as represented by T64, the posthole line T81 and the sand ridge on Site A.

'Classic *Grubenhäuser*' with an evenly-shaped pit and a regular arrangement of postholes at each end appear to become uncommon in Britain after the 8th century, although they may continue for specialised usage, particularly on urban sites, and in some rural areas of Northern Europe (Chapelot & Fossier, 1985, 126). The Phase III, probably 9th century, sunken hut from Lower Bridge Street, Chester (Mason, 1985, 6–7), appears typical of such structures in urban contexts of this date; the sunken area was large and evenly shaped, rectilinear with rounded corners, the timberwork probably set outside its edge. The 10th century sunken-floored or cellared structures from this site, probably in part contemporary with the *burh*, are built in large shallow rectilinear excavations, around the base of which timbering is set at regular intervals. These structures have many parallels, for example at Coppergate, York (Hall, 1984b). Compared with these 10th century examples the Rhuddlan Structures, of which S1 and S3 had single postholes at either end, appear earlier; it should be noted that their outlines are unusually irregular.

The fill of Structure 1 contained a spur (No 136)

of 10th century date, and that of Structure 4 a Saxo-Norman knife (No 15). It is presumed that the sunken areas in each case formed underfloor areas to buildings, most structural traces of which do not survive. Artefacts were scattered through the fill of the depressions, with no concentrations on the sub-floors which might have been associated with the use of the Structures themselves. It is likely that the depressions of S1 and S3 were subsequently used, with lightweight structures represented by the stake-holes. For S1 the contemporary pit and gullies C66 etc may belong to this re-use phase. The artefacts in the fill may relate to this re-occupation or may derive from a third phase, being refuse dumped in a convenient hollow. In S1 this includes debris from antler working. The degree of secondary re-use relates neatly to the irregularity of outline in the soft sand subsoil, S4 having the most regular outline and the fewest subsidiary features such as stakeholes. The only stratigraphic relationship is the cutting of S4 through the phase of gullies T143 suggested as being of 9th century or earlier date. It is difficult to estimate how long a time may have elapsed between the construction of the initial sunken-floored buildings and their final fill. Only S1 contains closely datable, 10th century, material. All phases of use of the Structures could be within the 10th century; it is unlikely that the hollows would have remained open for long once the initial structures had gone in such soft sand subsoil. This means that the building in Structure 1 would have gone out of use within the 10th century; it is quite likely that the building had a life of only a few decades. If such buildings are regarded as an anachronism in the 10th century, this could be because of adaptation of structures with underfloor space to soft sand subsoil.

The Structures appear to have been located with special reference to the Defences (unless they were built in the lee of an eroded bank). The interior of the Defences may have been very extensively occupied, forcing space immediately behind the bank into use, or there may have been some form of zoning, with sunken-floored structures associated with specialised activities, grouped immediately behind the bank. Post-built, ground-set Structures 5 and 6 on Site V could be contemporary examples of the other building types to be expected in a 10th century *burh*.

All the Saxo-Norman pottery, including P1–P4 (Fig 18.1 and Tables 18.1–3) came from residual contexts on Sites A, T, and V (with the exception of the shelly MK fabric body sherds from gullies T222 etc); this material is likely to have a date span of early 10th to mid 11th centuries (J A A Rutter in Mason, 1985, 53–5). Thus it occurs on all the sites excavated inside the suggested *burh* with the exception of the narrow trench M. There was also a sherd of possible Chester ware (P Courtney in Manley, 1987, 28) and some possible Saxon metal artefacts (*ibid* 33) from the Town Ditch excavations.

The location of Cledemutha

The 10th century iron work, associated structures and pottery, make it clear that there was a substantial contemporary settlement at Rhuddlan. If this is accepted as part of the *burh* of *Cledemutha*, a church (a minster, within the see of Lichfield), a bridge and mint might be expected. The earliest burials support a Norman foundation for the church located in M, but there may be another church site to be located. While *burhs* are usually associated with bridged crossing points (Haslam, 1987), *Cledemutha* was effectively a frontier post, and the construction of a bridge would have depended on how much trade and contact was envisaged with Gwynedd to the west. A bridge would have lain within the confines of the defences, south of the present one. The absence of coins from the mint at *Cledemutha* is commented upon in 16.1.

Any 10th century settlement at Rhuddlan is likely to have focussed on the higher sandy ground in the vicinity of the later Castles; the location of the structures and artefacts discussed above are of only slight help in determining where the line of the defences of *Cledemutha* ran. There are three possible alternatives: (1) a line as yet unlocated: (2) the Town Ditch: (3) the earliest components of the Norman Borough Defence line.

(1) A defence line as yet unlocated is possible because the archaeology of Rhuddlan has proved, in the very small sample excavated, far more complex than was suspected at the start of the series of excavations published here – for example there was no surface indication of the line of Ditches I–V. It would be wise to assume that there will be new data forthcoming.

(2) The Town Ditch defences, consisting of a flat bottomed ditch 15m wide between two broad banks, appear to have no parallel at any other *burh*. The 30 ha enclosed is far larger than any of the northern Mercian frontier *burhs*, except Chester which appears to re-use the Roman circuit. The Mercian *burhs*, again excepting Chester, appear to have defensive circuits which are curved rather than composed of long linear elements. The large foundations in Wessex relate to a different historical context from that in which Edward and Aethelflaeda were operating. If *Cledemutha* was intended as the major commercial centre for North East Wales, in addition to the end fort of a frontier line, a large size might be explained. *Burhs* in both Mercia and Wessex were often planned with room for expansion inside their defences (see Mason, 1985, 38; Haslam, 1984a *passim*).

The excavation of the Town Ditch (Manley, 1987) provided no evidence for recutting or cleaning and had accumulated only about 0.5m of silt. Manley suggests that the overlying deposits were deliberate infill and attributes them to activity by Edward I (1987, 20). It seems unlikely that a 10th century ditch should accumulate so little silt in 350 years.

The radiocarbon date from the silt CAR–239 AD 1440 ± 60 calibrates at one σ to AD 1410–1460 (Stuiver & Pearson, 1986, who state that there are no significant differences between the calibration they present and that of Stuiver (1982) used by Otlet & Walker in Manley, 1985b). It would be easier to accept this date as anomalous if there were not the date from hearth 10 beneath the outer bank AD 1145 ± 55 (Otlet & Walker in Manley, 1985b, 109), which calibrates (Stuiver & Pearson, 1986) to AD 1180–1280 at one σ. (The general difficulties in the use of radiocarbon dating are highlighted by the range of four dates AD 830 ± 100 to 1020 ± 80 (uncalibrated) from gully 240, behind the inner bank, which also contained 13th/ 14th century pottery.) The dates could accord with a post-10th century date for the Town Ditch, explored further in Chapter 21. If the Ditch remained open until the 13th century, some material might be expected in its fill from the nearby Dominican Friary founded in the 1250s; (of course an alternative non-Edwardian context for the infill remains a possibility).

Manley himself comments (1987, 41) on the differences between the the Town Ditch system and features normally found in excavated *burh* defences and highlights the lack of modification to the inner bank, the absence of a turf or timber revetment, the lack of a mutliple ditch system, and the absence of an intra-mural street. He does not comment on the only other two defensive circuits known comparable to the Town Ditch with a broad ditch flanked by broad inner and outer banks without berms; these are the Edwardian defences of Rhuddlan and Flint (Chapter 21).

Alternative contexts for the Town Ditch will be explored in Chapter 21. The main difficulty in rejecting the *Cledemutha* interpretation lies in otherwise accounting for such a substantial earthwork. One other difficulty involves the apparent lack of disturbance to the fires beneath the bank if they had been left uncovered for over three hundred years; a solution might relate to the siting of some of these fires in hollows which silted over (Manley, 1987, Fig 5). Another is the absence of 13th century pottery in the banks as well as the ditch, though this might be countered by stressing the general sparcity of pottery at Rhuddlan before the late 13th century.

(3) The earliest elements of the Norman Borough Defences are Ditch I, and possibly its aceramic recut II, Ditch IV and associated remnant rampart levels and timbering on Site T. This remnant rampart line consists of two elements, the palisade line T81, and rampart material T69 which lay over the palisade line. If these two elements are accepted as related to two different defensive episodes, the earlier, the T81 palisade, should relate to the earliest Ditch system. The various alternatives for the T81 palisade have been set out above (p 211). If the palisade fronted a rampart, there would have been a berm, but the rampart

could only have been about 8m wide if Structures S3 and S4 were built in its lee. If the palisade were central to a rampart, there would have been little room for a berm but more space behind between it and the structures.

Ditches I, II and IV predate the 13th century but cannot be dated at all closely. The palisade T81 sealed by remnant rampart T69 again only has a general pre-13th century date. Only two artefacts, loomweight MSF 20 and bone trial piece MSF 21, provide tenuous chronological indications. The loomweight, 9th or 10th century in date, comes from posthole T97 cut in soil T64, truncated and sealed by remnant rampart material T69. The bone trial piece, 10th century or earlier in date, comes from the middle level silts of Ditch I. The clustering of probable 10th century structures and finds just inside the rampart line may be considered as support for the date of that line.

Ditch I, or II, with IV parallel is the kind of multiple ditch layout common in Wessex, and probably to be expected in Mercian *burhs*. Palisade T81 provides evidence of timbering. In these two respects, and with the presence of a berm, the early elements of the Norman Borough Defence line fit current perceived ideas of *burh* construction better than the inner bank of the Town Ditch. The other two features emphasised by Manley (1987, 41) as absent from the Town Ditch but to be expected in *burh* defences, modification of the rampart and an intramural road, are not found on the Norman Borough Defence line; any evidence for modification would have been removed with the rampart material related to T81.

Ditch I seems to have almost silted up, leaving only a slight depression, before Ditch II was cut, and the same appears to have happened with Ditches II and III. This might suggest a time interval of the same order between I and II and between II and III. A reasonable interval between two defensive episodes would fit the situation on the rampart line. If Ditch I related to *Cledemdutha*, Ditch II to the Norman Borough and Ditch III to the re-occupation by Henry III (Chapter 20), the intervals would both have been about 160 years. There should be some reason for two recuttings of the Ditch I line. It may simply have represented the best position for a small defensive enclosure. Alternatively the line itself may have been remembered and regarded as a significant boundary. This would be in accord with the evidence put forward above, which the present authors believe presents a stronger case for the circuit of the *Cledemutha* defences being on the line of the Norman Borough Defences than on that of the Town Ditch.

The publication of two contrasting arguments for the location of the *Cledemutha* defences at Rhuddlan itself underlines the caution with which such arguments need to be accepted and highlights the need for further extensive exploration; to this extent differing views may be regarded as positive. The authors are aware that they have ignored the possibility, as has Manley, that any of the defensive episodes may relate to Welsh activity and that the English historical record may not be comprehensive in its references to military activity at Rhuddlan.

19.4 The later 10th century and the 11th century before the Norman incursions

Towards the middle of the 10th century Welsh power had become much more organised under Hywel Dda (died AD 949/50). Viking raids continued to cause a problem, and the death of Edgar in AD 975 weakened English rule and worsened the breakdown in co-operation between the Welsh princes and England. The survival of *Cledemutha* into the second half of the 10th century is unlikely, and much of Tegeingl may have passed back to Welsh control before AD 1000. In AD 1015 Llywelyn ap Seisyll constructed a *palatium* at Rhuddlan, and by the 1050s Rhuddlan formed the centre of operations for Gruffudd ap Llywelyn, who between 1039 and 1063 increased the power of Gwynedd and kept the Viking threat at bay. The archaeological evidence currently available is of no help, either in determining the end of English *Cledemutha* or of the presence of these Welsh kings. It may be that the unusual platform bailey of Twt Hill was a Welsh stronghold. It has parallels with platform raths in Ireland, and some Irish influence on North Wales at this date is possible (Davies, 1982, 117). A larger area than Twt Hill would presumably have been needed, and a Welsh context for some elements of the Norman Borough Defences is a possibility. The survey by Musson and Spurgeon (1988) suggests, against a background of very limited knowledge, that the possible Welsh defended sites so far identified are likely to have been of three ha or less. Any Welsh occupation is perhaps to be expected in the area immediately around Twt Hill.

The only artefact relevant to this period is the coin, from Site A, of Edward the Confessor, issued in the autumn of AD 1056 (16.1). This may have been lost during the period of Welsh ascendency, or relate to Harold Godwinson's raid on Rhuddlan in 1062 which successfully removed Gruffudd.

20 Rhuddlan between AD 1070 and 1277

20.1 The Norman occupation and Borough between the 1070s and 1140

It is generally assumed that the motte of Twt Hill represents the castle built by Hugh of Chester about 1073, and then held by his cousin Robert of Rhuddlan as the base for his attempted conquest of North West Wales. The Twt Hill bailey may have reused earthworks of the earlier Welsh rulers. Twt Hill overlooks a fording point across the Clwyd and the broad ditch on its south side perhaps functioned as a route down to the river and broadened as a hollow way. The first (and only) mention of the Norman Borough occurs in Domesday Book, where it is described as 'new' (Tait, 1925). The relevant entries after Tait (1925) are

(1) 'EARL HUGH holds of the king ROELEND. To it belonged ENGELFELD T.R.E. and the whole was waste. Earl Eadwine held (it). When earl Hugh received (it) it was likewise waste. Now he has in demesne half of the castle which is called ROELENT and is the caput of the district. He has there eight burgesses, and half the church and mint, and half of every iron-mine wherever discovered in this manor, and of the river Clwyd and of the mills and fisheries which shall be made there, that is to say, in that part of the river which belongs to the earl's fief, and half of the forests which did not belong to any vill of this manor, and half the toll, and half of the vill which is called BREN (Bryn)... It is worth 3 pounds.'

(2) 'ROBERT DE RHUDDLAN (Roelent) holds of earl Hugh half of the same castle and borough, in which the said Robert has 10 burgesses, and half of the church and mint, and of (any) mine of iron found there, and half of the river Clwyd and of the fisheries and mills made or to be made there, and half of the toll, and of the forests which do not belong to any vill of the aforesaid manor, and half of the vill which is called BREN.... It is worth 3 pounds.'

(3) 'In this same manor of ROELEND a castle, likewise called ROELENT, has lately been made. There is a new borough and in it 18 burgesses (divided) between the earl and Robert, as has been said above. To these burgesses they granted the laws and customs which are (enjoyed) in Hereford and Breteuil.......In the year of this inquest the toll of this borough was let to farm at 3 shillings.'

(Details of BREN have been ommitted because of uncertainties about the precise locations involved). The church was portionary; two rectors, one appointed by the Earl of Chester, the other by the holder of Rhuddlan, divided the income of the living.

When the Ditch sequence was discovered during the first season's excavation on Site A in 1969, it was immediately considered as potentially relevant to the Norman Borough. While little was, and still is, known about borough defences in the March in the Norman period, it was thought more likely that these would have been of earth and timber than of stone, and that the area enclosed would have been comparatively small. So far the only Norman foundation in Wales to have earth and timber defences established is Abergavenny (Radcliffe & Knight, 1972–3), among the dozen or so established in the initial conquest period. There is common agreement that these early boroughs would be small (Soulsby, 1983, 7) with a simple street layout around a market place. In many cases, such as Cardiff, there are topographical indications of a small early town within the later stone defences (*ibid*, 96); it is most unlikely that a borough in a forward and vunerable position such as Rhuddlan would have been left undefended.

The line of what has been here termed the Norman Borough Defences encloses about 7 ha, excluding the steep cliffs along the Clwyd; of this nearly 1 ha is occupied by Twt Hill. Some confirmation of the size of the original borough may be found in an extent of 1428 (Jones, 1915) when land listed as situated in 'le Oldtowne' totals some 16 acres (about 6 ha). The north end of the Defences was clearly established across Sites T and E. The south end is more difficult to reconstruct. In two small cuts south of Site A (Fig 1.2) the ditch showed no sign of turning, and its most likely course is fairly straight south and then turning above the line of a slight dip with a small stream. This circuit would include Twt Hill entirely, rather than positioning it on one corner as is usual in Norman towns; to position Twt Hill on the south west corner the defences would have to turn very sharply beyond the point to which they have been traced and the area enclosed would be restricted to about 4 ha. It is probable that the situations of the castle and the town were influenced by the former

Welsh defences and *burh* respectively, so the layout might not be standard but adapted to make the most of local topographic features.

If it is accepted that the Norman Borough is likely to have had defences, and that there had previously been a *burh* on the site, they are probably represented by Ditch II. (This again leaves aside the possibility of defence lines which have not yet been found). Ditch II was about 3m deep and about 6m wide. It was more irregular in profile and depth than I and III, and might be accounted for by a prolonged period of maintainence in subsoils of variable softness. On Site A there was a pronounced slot in part of its base (by section CD, Fig 3.3) which looked more like an emplacement for a timber than a cleaning slot. A groove similar to a cleaning slot was found in section EF on Site T (Fig 4.4). The fills on Sites A and E were mixed, and suggested some deliberate infilling with wadges of clay; the fill in T was of cleaner silts. It is possible that the associated bank, of which T69 may contain the remnants, had a front revetment of turf. On Site T soil T64 was truncated, after the positioning of the palisade line T81 tentatively linked with Ditch I; this would have provided turf for revetment. The rather messy nature of the fill in places could be due to the collapse of a turf-revetted rampart. There is no real indication of an entrance, unless the basal slot found on Site A had held a timber bridge; there was no indication of any connected track.

Ditch II was aceramic; (the intrusive sherds shown in Tables 18.2 & 18.3 were found at the junction of II with the later III). There were no other datable finds. On Site E II predated the extensive area of scarping at the east end of the Site (6.1). In broader terms II predates III, by at least the time necessary for it to silt up almost completely; III, it is argued below, belonged to the mid 13th century. It is suggested that Ditch II, with an associated turf-revetted rampart, is the defence of the Norman foundation. The silting of the upper levels of Ditch II would have occurred in the period of Welsh occupation initiated by Owain Gwynedd in 1140.

The boundary of a borough had significance; those living inside were controlled by a different set of rules from those in the countryside beyond. Moreover the actual boundary acted as a tax point; a borough had a market and certain goods brought within it were taxable. It was natural for the borough boundary to be marked in some way even when there was no immediate threat and there must always have been considerations of defence at Rhuddlan. Many Norman boroughs had simple earth and timber defences, and Bond (1987), in his discussion of these, points out the varied functions that town defences might fulfill.

Within the Norman Borough the best attested structure is the church (7.7). The coincidence of the reference in Domesday Book and the two coins of William Rufus with the earliest burial located,

M117, is one not often met with archaeological data. It has already been pointed out that this provides high probability, but not proof, that the church located in Site M is that mentioned in Domesday Book. It should be emphasised that these coins were minted in London, not Rhuddlan, despite the Domesday reference to a mint at the latter. The William II coins are nevertheless the only artefacts from the excavations that can be assigned with confidence to either the 11th or 12th centuries. Grave M117 was also lined with specimens of all building materials known to have been used in the church – limestone, lime, mortar, and wood in a charred form; could this indicate that this burial was specially distinguished, either because it was the first on the new site or the interment of a personage connected with the construction of the church?

Amongst the dozen or so Norman foundations of the late 11th and early 12th centuries in Wales, about half have churches placed close to the castle as at Rhuddlan (Soulsby, 1983; Bridgend p 84, Haverfordwest p 140, Kenfig p 150, Monmouth p 184 and Pembroke p 215); information is lacking for some, eg Abergavenny.

The church appears to have been a simple structure 27m long internally with a nave 9m wide. The work involved in the construction was substantial. The foundations would have incorporated about 75 cubic metres of tap slag. Presumably this was brought from smelting sites (the mines mentioned in Domesday Book) near the iron ore outcrops about 4km to the east, as was the limestone used for building. Lime for mortar could also be made in the limestone hills on the east of the Vale of Clwyd and transported. There is no parallel known to the authors for the use of slag as foundation material. The size of the church seems large for the 18 burgesses referred to in Domesday Book, and may have been planned for a larger congregation with continued growth envisaged for the town. This seems in keeping with Robert of Rhuddlan's optimistic attitude towards the control of all Gwynedd. The church would have formed part of the See of Chester, to which Lichfield was transferred in the 1070s.

The Normans regarded their urban foundations as means of controlling more than just markets and strongpoints. Land for cultivation was allotted to the burgesses, and this may have marked the start of the strip fields which became a major feature of the Flintshire landscape (Sylvester, 1955). The undated ploughmarks and boundaries found on Site D could be of this date. While there must have been displacement of Welsh occupants, some Welsh presumably continued to live in the vicinity, and it may have been intended, by the provision of a spacious church, to provide an alternative focus to Llanelwy (St Asaph).

Within the Norman town no domestic buildings can be assigned to this period with certainty. There is no reason why Structure 5 and 6 should not be of this date, rather than earlier. The amount of erosion, particularly on Site A, has affected the survival of slight timber features and precluded interpretation of building plans. Iron slag, including smithing hearth bottoms, was contained in the fill of Ditch II, and suggests the working of blooms of iron within, or just outside, the town, as well as smithing.

The mint of Domesday Book produced a few coins of William I with the mint mark 'Rudili'. Moneyers Aelfwine and Hrveov are recorded (Mack, 1963, 143). None of these coins have been found at Rhuddlan.

20.2 Welsh and Norman interaction between AD 1140 and 1241

The initial confident Norman advance into North Wales had many set-backs, and it is unclear how far Rhuddlan prospered as a town in the early 12th century. Owain Gwynedd took advantage of the English Anarchy to seize control of Rhuddlan and Tegeingl from 1140. There is no direct evidence linking him to Rhuddlan, but the foundation of the See of St Asaph, responsible to Canterbury, in 1143, suggests that he was taking an interest in the area. As the 12th and 13th centuries were marked by almost continuous friction between the Welsh and the English, it seems unlikely that Owain would have neglected the strongpoint of Rhuddlan Castle. It has been thought that Welsh rulers would not have presided over centres of population, and that therefore a town like Rhuddlan would have ceased to function. Soulsby (1985, 17) has, however, demonstrated the encouragement by Welsh rulers of urban foundations from the 13th century onward, and there seems no reason why, allowing for poorer documentation, this trend should not have started in the 12th century. It is likely that the church at Rhuddlan remained in unbroken use, the phasing of burials representing a cyclical use of the graveyard which in itself argues for continuity of management.

Butler (1987) has argued that by c AD 1200 data derived from the Welsh law codes about buildings can legitimately be applied to settlements, and may be considered in a general way for the preceding century. The area excavated at Rhuddlan was inappropriate for a broad application of this data. Two points are perhaps relevant. The term castell is used and 'from every bond township the king has a man and a horse with axes for constructing his strongholds' (ibid, 49). This is in flat contradiction to Giraldus Cambrensis' assertion that the Welsh 'do not live in towns or villages or in defended enclosures (castris)'. Butler is undoubtedly correct as seeing Norman influence in the provisions of the law codes. The second point is the great range of buildings allowed for a prince, and the substantial range allowed for a lord; both include provision for agriculture especially a barn. It would seem unlikely that there would be sufficient room in a fortified site like Twt Hill for all princely or lordly buildings, and that therefore, in any period of Welsh occupation some structures should be expected beyond this. At some aceramic stage, the features on Site D, some structural, postdating the ploughing episode but predating the Edwardian Borough Defences, must be fitted in. They could represent a long period of use, during which this area of land was not directly farmed.

Henry II reasserted the English position in North Wales with an expedition in 1157. He took the castle at Rhuddlan directly into Royal control and held it until 1167. In 1165 he was in the area for a few days looking to its defences (Lloyd, 1939, 516) and put further resources into the maintainence of the castles of Rhuddlan, Prestatyn and Basingwerk in 1165 (ibid, 518 note 123). Owain was pressing to re-establish his position, and in 1167 took and destroyed Rhuddlan Castle after a three month siege. The situation at Rhuddlan during this decade appears to have been precarious and there is no mention of the borough but it seems an unlikely occasion for the redigging of any of the Norman Borough Defence line.

The castle at Rhuddlan, despite the destruction by Owain, appears to have been rebuilt under Welsh rule as in 1188 Dafydd of Gwynedd entertained there Archbishop Baldwin and his companion Giraldus Cambrensis. It may well have provided a focus of occupation in the area for some time. With the exception of the brief excursion by John 1211–1213, Rhuddlan was to remain in Welsh hands until 1241. The scarping across the line of the Defences located in Site E should date to some stage during the period 1147 to 1241. This produced a flattened area across the east end of Ditch II on that Site (Fig 6.1), and may be linked to the hollow way (pre 13th century) V24, the two together providing access into the area within the defences. The flattened area had a long sequence of pits upon it, some of which may have been structural. The majority, stratigraphically early, were aceramic, but a few contained 13th century sherds. The area of scarping and any structures within it are unlikely to have continued in use after the renovation of the Defences with Ditch III, suggested below to have been dug around 1241. If so, some pottery would appear to have been reaching Rhuddlan before Henry III's re-occupation in the mid 13th century. This would allow some features with a few 13th century sherds to belong to the Welsh period prior to AD 1241. The only distinctive feature, apart from the odd small pit, which might be of this period is drying kiln C3 on Site A. Kilns are given as appurtenances of both lordly and princely establishments, and were held in common by groups of bondsmen (Butler, 1987). Kiln C3 is very similar in construction to kilns T61 and T50, stratigraphicallly late 13th century, which appear to be structurally more like English than Welsh corndryers (4.9.3), but the possibility that C3 is Welsh and early 13th century cannot be entirely ruled out.

The church on Site M must be presumed to have continued to function, both as a place of worship and a burial ground, throughout this period. The burials represent, from the foundation onward, a mixed range of sex and age, and would seem appropriate for the burial ground of a community rather than than as one used occasionally in military emergencies.

Coins minted at Rhuddlan during the Short Cross currency of 1180 to *c* 1245 present a problem (16.1). During this period Rhuddlan is only recorded as under English control during 1211-13 and after 1241. But a group of coins of the moneyer Halli are contained in the Aston hoard deposited *c* 1195 (Dolley, 1959, 307), and one of the moneyer Simon(d) formed part of the Newry hoard deposited before 1210 (North, 1963, 165). Dolley (1963) summarises the situation; he considers that Halli was striking at Rhuddlan very late in the reign of Henry II, followed by Tomas soon after 1190, and by Simon(d) between *c* 1205 and 1215. (Henricus was working under Henry III). Dolley obviously considers the historical record for the period to be incomplete; in discussing the apparent intermission in the Rhuddlan mint between *c* 1215 and 1240 he says 'it would be dangerous to infer from this that the fortress at any given time was in the hands of the Welsh' (*ibid*, 227). For the coins which predate John's occupation, the historical record *must be* inadequate, for they imply relationships between English and Welsh more complex than the occasional stark references of conquest and reconquest would imply. There is evidence for an increased use of money in Wales at this time (Davies, 1987, 163), and for English moves to promote accord with the Welsh by other than military means.

20.3 Henry III AD 1241-1256

Henry III took advantage of the power struggles within Gwynedd caused by the death in 1240 of Llywelyn ap Iorwerth, the predominent Welsh leader of the early 13th century, to re-establish English power in much of Wales. After a campaign launched from Chester in 1241 Llywelyn's son Dafydd yielded Tegeingl in perpetuity to Henry and paid homage for Gwynedd. Henry re-occupied Rhuddlan, but planned to consolidate the new position by new stone castles at Diserth and Degannwy. Diserth was evidently intended as the main fortification for the Vale of Clwyd and an attempt was made to establish a small borough (Soulsby, 1983, 130). Deganwy was intended as a forward control base for Gwynedd. There are no references to the re-establishment of a borough at Rhuddlan, but moneys were paid for the repair of wooden works at its castle and for the construction of a chapel in the bailey during 1241-2 (Taylor, 1956, 4). Henry was at Rhuddlan with his army between about 25th August and 1st September 1241.

It seems reasonable to propose that Henry reinforced Rhuddlan Castle to act as his base of operations in North Wales; its position on the Clwyd would allow for some support from the sea. The agreement of 1241 was not maintained and Henry was back in the Conwy area in the summer of 1245 to subdue a serious Welsh revolt which was only terminated by the death of its instigator Dafydd in February 1246. It seems doubtful whether Diserth would have been sufficiently complete to have provide much defence during this revolt.

A range of 13th century activities at Rhuddlan is best explained on the assumption that Henry planned his main supply base there for the early 1240s. The principal features are Ditches III and V and the pottery kiln V4. Ditch III was a broad V shape on each Site, with its dimensions varying between 5 and 6m across and between 2 and 3m deep. The irregularity of the profile in places may represent some cleaning out and the presence of clay lenses low in the primary silt might indicate a turf-revetted rampart that had collapsed after a comparatively short space of time. Its fill generally was darker with more organic material than those of I and II. There was the occasional sherd of pottery, even in the primary silt (Table 18.5), and a Type B horseshoe nail (Table 17.3) extremely unlikely to have been current before the mid 13th century. More pottery, and another Type B horseshoe nail occurred in the middle silts; this included material from the V4 kiln. The pottery and ironwork together make a date for Ditch III in the 1240s appropriate. Ditch V may well be contemporary; there is pottery in its primary silt (Table 18.5), and its fill was at least as dark and organic as that of Ditch III. There are no indications as to its bank. If V formed a second line of defence to III, either it was only dug in the more vulnerable section close to the Clwyd or it swung well out from III around the circuit as it was not located in Site A. It seems a reasonable hypothesis that Henry would have provided a fortified base for his army by digging these Ditches, and its simple earthen form meant that it could have been rapidly constructed.

The precise dating of the V4 pottery kiln, and its precursor V51 (5.7.2) is difficult. The odd sherds, apparently of its products, from low levels in Ditch III, could have come from another kiln not yet located. The general dating makes a 13th century date likely, as does the presence of a Saintonge sherd within the kiln infill (Table 18.4). It has been suggested above that some pottery was circulating at Rhuddlan before Henry III's occupation, but the kiln or kilns imply the introduction of a master potter from the Cheshire area, *cf* Audlem (Webster, 1966) and the new kiln located at Chester (Rutter, 1980). Such an introduction, along with others which must have been made both to supply the army and possibly to provide products for an area now regarded as part of England, would be appropriately ascribed to Henry III. The C3 Site A drying kiln, of English type, might also date to this period. Manley's excavation on the west of the Town Ditch produced a single penny minted in London 1248–50 (P Courtney in Manley, 1987, 37). The limited areas excavated within the Defences provide no further evidence for activity of this period.

The V4 kiln was constructed on top of soil V20. Links with soils on Site T are not clear, despite the short distance (undug) between them. It seems likely that V20 would continue down into Site T to form part of soil T178 and that the surface layer T207, loosely assigned to the 13th century, might be the continuation of the surface on which the kiln was built. Until some date in the 14th century there was no soil build-up on Site T, although this had formed V20 on the slope west of T. The difference may be accounted for by some disturbance at the top of the slope above V and overlooking the Clwyd, but this would not explain why the build-up did not continue down into T.

20.4 AD 1256–1277 The ascendency of Llywelyn ap Gruffudd

Llywelyn emerged as the predominant Welsh leader during 1255 and with swift campaigns in 1256 had retaken North Wales to the Dee, with the exception of the castles of Deganwy and Diserth, which held out with some attempts made at their relief, until 1263. From 1256 Rhuddlan and Tegeingl were under Llywelyn's control. There appears no direct evidence linking Llywelyn and Rhuddlan though the founding of the Dominican Priory around AD 1258 might be taken as evidence of Llywelyn's interest.

Despite the Treaty of Montgomery of 1267 which was intended to stabilize relations between England and Wales, the situation remained tense. Since it is known that Diserth Castle was razed after its capture it seems probable that Rhuddlan Castle would have been retained as a centre of control for Tegeingl. Its site could be viewed as rightfully Welsh since the days of Llywelyn ap Seisyll in 1015. The outer fortification line may have been given different treatment, particularly if it had a tradition of association with English occupation. The use of a borough defence line as the perimeter of a market area within which taxes could be charged (Bond, 1987, 112) may have caused it to have been viewed unfavourably. Ditches III and V silted up half-full fairly rapidly, the silting containing possible turf revetment material. There could be a case here for deliberate slighting. There was virtually no rampart material left in position by 1277, and the line appeared even eroded by that time. Was this the work of Llywelyn or levelling by Edward I's forces? Much of the land could have been returned to agriculture.

21 Rhuddlan under Edward I and after

21.1 The impact of Edward's army and workmen

Edward's campaign against Llywelyn ap Gruffudd, whom he had proclaimed a rebel in November 1276, was swift and effective. By July 1277 all areas had been subdued except Gwynedd. In that month Edward arrived at Chester ready to lead in person the attack on North Wales. He had already (Taylor, 1963, 309) arranged for large groups of masons, carpenters, woodmen and diggers to assemble from many parts of the country at Chester by the time he arrived there. Edward already had some knowledge of the terrain; at the age of 17, after being granted lordship of holdings in Wales in 1254 by Henry III in a period of ascendency, he made a personal tour of North East Wales (Davies, 1987, 310). On about 21st July Edward moved his whole force forward to the site which was to become Flint. Having started defence construction at Flint, Edward arrived at Rhuddlan on 19th August and visited intermittently until a three month stay between 27th September and 18/19th November when he lodged at the Dominican Friary. Edward is known to have been paying an army of 15,600 men in August 1277; a good proportion presumably moved forward with him to Rhuddlan. He was also employing during that month 1,800 axemen to clear a road through wooded territory between Flint and Rhuddlan, and by September at Rhuddlan 968 *fossatores* or diggers. In August 1277 when the main army was there Rhuddlan must have been occupied by many thousand men, more than at any time in its previous history. Much of this army moved forward into Gwynedd and by November 1277 had sufficiently harassed Llywelyn for the latter to agree to the Treaty of Aberconway, in which he held Gwynedd in homage to Edward. Edward continued with the fortification of Flint and Rhuddlan to hold North East Wales under his direct control, and his initial plans were followed until Llywelyn's revolt of March 1282. These plans involved the accomodation at Rhuddlan through these years of several thousand men.

Such a force must have left a considerable mark on the local landscape. If Edward was staying at the Friary, Twt Hill was probably out of commission, its materials salvaged for the new works; in any case the shelter it provided was negligible compared to the numbers involved who would mostly have been accommodated in tents or temporary shelters. The amount both of food debris and of excrement to be disposed of was large. Ditch III, in all three Sites A, T and E, had an upper fill clearly distinguished from that beneath. On Site T the division was marked by an iron pan 340. The rows of 'slots' T387 etc in the iron pan on the outer edge of the Ditch in T resemble individual shovel marks and may be interpreted as temporary steps to facilate dumping of rubbish and possibly latrine use. On Site A levels A48 upward are relevant, on Site E J94 and above. Something similar happened with level J45 in Ditch V on Site E. All these upper layers were extremely organic in places, contained large quantities of animal bones, sea shells and ash, and also pottery and iron slag. (A penny of Edward minted in the spring of 1280 was found trampled into the very top of T59, the darkened surface showing in section GH Fig 4.4). On Site A this material seemed to have mounded up above the actual Ditch top. A reasonable interpretation of these upper layers would be that the open top of Ditch III had been used as a rubbish dump, and also latrine area, in the late summer and autumn of 1277. On all three Sites the top of this infill is cleaner than the underpart and may represent a period of trample and rainwash after the actual infill. The total absence of rampart (except patch T69) may be better explained by its having been shovelled in over rubbish and excrement than any slighting by Llywelyn; its absence in areas such as the depression later occupied by House 2 Site A is remarkable. This interpretation fits the archaeological facts. If accepted, it would offer the largest medieval military latrine/rubbish area so far detected and a deposit datable to within a year.

It is probably to the year 1277 that we should look for a possible 13th century context for the 30 ha enclosure of the Town Ditch. Its arrangement of a flat-bottomed ditch 15m wide between two broad banks is closely paralleled by the Edwardian Borough Defences on both Site D and at Flint

Table 21.1 Comparative Dimensions of Edwardian Defences at Rhuddlan and Flint with the Town Ditch

Site	Inner bank	Ditch	Outer bank
Town ditch	10m	15m wide – 3m deep	13m
Site D	13m	14m wide – 2.75m deep	12–13m
Flint	19m	16m wide – 2.75m deep	not excavated

(Cherry, 1971, 192; personal observation by H Quinnell).

It was argued in Chapter 19 that aspects of the Town Ditch as excavated made a Saxon date inappropriate. Two further points may be considered. Viewed on plan (Fig 1.2) the Town Ditch and the Edwardian Borough have a similar relationship with Edward's castle, the castle projecting by most of its area beyond both enceintes. The relationship would be a remarkable coincidence if a three hundred-year old earthwork were involved. Secondly, if the Town Ditch were Saxon some effect might have been expected on Site E. The edge of this Site was within 20m of the continuation of the Ditch recorded by Pennant and substantiated by excavation in Site K. The inner bank of the Town Ditch must have lain between Sites E and K. The ground rises from the edge of Site E up towards the Clwyd cliff and the subsoil is soft. Erosion of a bank might be expected to have caused some build-up of soil in E. Yet the only distinguishable early medieval soil in E, G143, was remarkable for its evenness both of level and of organic content. Soil layers over the horizons connected with the Edwardian Castle construction do, by contrast, seem to have accumulated rapidly (see below). The clean sand layer J98 over the top of Ditch V could be the tail of the inner bank itself.

The Town Ditch *could* have been constructed by Edward I in 1277 starting on his arrival there in August. The bank-ditch-bank format, unknown apparently elsewhere in England – indeed in Europe, was already under construction at Flint in the early part of August (see absence of parallels in Turner 1971). Taylor (1963, 310) suggests that the primacy given to this work at Flint and the urgency with which it appears to have been pursued indicate its importance as a protection for the army and workforce. Edward must have viewed Rhuddlan as his main forward base for his final confrontation with Llwyelyn. He may have remembered its geography from an earlier visit, and have had in mind the predominant position that the site had held for English control of North East Wales for at least the last two centuries. He intended to make Rhuddlan both a cathedral city and a shire town (Taylor, 1955). (Rhuddlan, within its present Edwardian circuit, was smaller than Flint, 10 as opposed to 13.5 ha.) A large simple enceinte could have been laid out quickly in August 1277, with the site of the castle already selected and positioned suitably to work with the enceinte/Town Ditch as a defensive unit. It would have afforded a provident fortification for the main forward base, protecting both the army if necessary and the workforce for the castle and other works, and presumably was intended to be fully developed as the Borough in due course. The sum of £300 was expended at Rhuddlan between 29th August and 15th November. Details are given of the numbers of various workmen employed but not, as later, on what they were working. The 968 diggers could

have made a substantial impact even on an enclosure of 30 ha. It is also possible that troops could have been used at this early stage.

The final decision on the Borough site may have been taken about the time of the Treaty of Aberconwy in November. Further experience of conditions in North Wales may have helped Edward to decide what was feasible in both building and maintaining a town. Edward was at Rhuddlan from late September until mid-November, during the period when expenditure remained modest. It is likely that much of this time was spent on planning the details of the canalisation of the Clwyd, for which considerable detailed survey work would have been necessary. A decision on the length of the Clwyd to be canalised would effect the position of the Borough. On this scenario Edward would have left Rhuddlan in November with detailed arrangements worked out for the Clwyd, the castle and most probably the Borough. The first references to the Borough at Rhuddlan come in February 1278, and after this there are no indications in the records of any change in plan.

Pit T349 deserves special comment. It appeared to have been dug through the final infill of Ditch III, ascribed above to the summer of 1277. The collection of objects it contained is remarkable. The barrel padlock No 86, with a possible date range within the 11th and 12th centuries, was found with bucket handle No 75 and chain No 80 and the finely worked, unused whetstone MSF 32 above a layer of lead which had been poured into the pit around some wooden object. If the collection were prehistoric it would undoubtedly be labelled 'ritual'. Even around 1277 its deposition suggests some deliberate act connected with changes in control and perhaps the moving of the castle and Borough sites.

Immediately over the infill of Ditch III on Sites E and A were levels and features with quantities of iron slag, charcoal and even coal. The whole suggested all stages of ironworking from the treatment of blooms to the smithing of finished objects. On Site E this episode is covered by a surface dated to c 1280 (see below). On Site A it cannot be so precisely dated; the episode may have lasted longer or have been of a slightly different date. On Site T there was less iron slag, but at this stage a series of small slots were cut, of which T24 at least had held a fence, perhaps evidence for the division of the area close to the new castle into plots for different activities.

Work on the castle definitely started with ordering of stone on November 11th 1277 (Taylor, 1963, 321), and proceeded fast in the fifteen months to March 1289 during which time £2746 was expended. Between March 1289 and November 1280 costs were £4216. Thereafter expenditure dropped sharply and the main building effort moved back to Flint (Taylor, 1963, 321). The amount for the *Fossa maris* or Clwyd canal was £755, which was probably substantially complete by November 1280 as no further moneys are recorded as being spent on it. The working surface J24 and lane from the castle eastward G6 on Site E (6.8) were composed of chippings from the various stones used in the castle and would fit best as a surface organised during the summer of 1278, when sufficient stone would have been worked to provide the chippings but the need both for a track and a good working area remained. The clean yellow clay and sand J98 and J36 found over the very top of Ditch V might be explained as the levelling of the now obsolete inner bank of the Town Ditch enceinte to provide a large working surface around the castle. Sand layers below the lane itself may have derived from material dug from the Ditches around the castle. The surface was worn and rutted with a scattering of horseshoe nails and even horseshoes. No more ironworking was carried out. Smithing may have been transferred to a different area, perhaps even to Site A.

The horizon G6/J24 is important if the arguments for its dating are accepted. It provides a *terminus ante quem* for all the stratigraphy beneath it, a point prominent in much of the discussion concerning these lower levels and of help with the dating of artefacts. There is a lot of pottery identical to that made in the V4 kiln in the upper Ditch III levels and in the metalworking deposits sealed by the G6 lane. It is unlikely that it survived from the Henrician period, more likely that pottery-making was reintroduced at Rhuddlan. Given the general similarity of jug forms, which make up the bulk of the material, throughout the 13th century, no great differences might be expected between pottery made by Cheshire-trained craftsmen in the 1240s/50s and the late 1270s. More kilns are evidently to be found at Rhuddlan.

21.2 The Edwardian Borough

References exist from February 1278 to Edward's Borough at Rhuddlan and in March 1279 the 'king's men were erecting burgages near the Castle' (Taylor, 1963, 322). No specific reference to expenditure on the Borough occurs until that recorded in the Pipe Roll started in March 1279. Between that date and March 1282 a total of £1276 is recorded as spent on the town (Taylor, 1963, 322); of which £538 was for payment to diggers at 3d a day, £548 for carpenters and £191 for cartage (Edwards,1946, 69). £1025 of the total was spent before November 1280.

In July 1279 the king sent to Rhuddlan his clerk William of Louth to 'view the void sites and other sites in that town, and to assess and rent burgages in the same plots and to demise the burgages at the king's will and to (blank in original) the king's ditches about the town and the king's port as shall seem expedient' (Taylor, 1963, 322). In August 1279 the men of Rhuddlan were granted the fee farm of the town at £80 a year for seven years. By November 1280 it was reported to the king that the burgesses 'are now building the town and are expending......great costs about making the town, building and improving it, as they promised to him', in consequence of which the fee farm was deferred until 1286. References to the *Clausturum villa* include diggers and carpenters but not masons, indicating an earth and timber defence (Taylor, 1963, 322).

The regularity of the street plan of present day Rhuddlan indicates its origins as a planned town, carefully related both to the castle and the Clwyd Bridge which Edward built. The Borough was subdivided by the principal road, the High Street, running east–west, and intersected by Gwindy, Church, Parliament and Castle Streets. An extent of 1428 (Jones, 1915, 45–90) reveals that, apart from High Street and Castle Street, the streets were named differently from today – Peperstrete, Hardingstrete, Pyloristrete, Briggestrete. Assuming Briggestrete was the bottom end of the High Street, the three medieval names substitute neatly for the modern Gwindy, Church and Parliament Streets, though it would take further research to establish which was which.

The complete length of the ditch survived on the north of the town into the 1960s (Taylor, 1956, endpiece: information from inhabitants of Rhuddlan) and was aligned with the slightly skewed arrangement of street plan; by 1970 only the north east Gwindy Street corner, Site D, survived. The excavations showed that the inner and outer banks of the defences contained a similar range of pottery to that associated with the 1277–80 deposits on Sites A, T and D, and that no masonry was present. No evidence for timberwork was found either, but this could be due to the denuded state of the inner bank. The amount of pottery (Table 18.7) found in the banks is remarkable, given that none was found in the soil or features beneath. Presumably topsoil with contemporary rubbish was being brought in from elsewhere, perhaps stripped from the lines of the roads which were being laid out. The flat basal layer, O14/P9 in the outer bank, O46/P12 in the inner, is neatly paralleled by the basal layer in the banks of the Town Ditch (Manley, 1987, Fig 5) and also by the inner bank at Flint (inset in Fig 8.4). The abundance of pottery at Gwindy Street contrasts with its absence from the Town Ditch banks. If the date suggested above of summer 1277 is accepted for the Town Ditch, work would have proceeded as Edward's forces were moving in. The Borough defences were constructed a little later, after the site had been occupied by an extensive army leaving large quantities of debris; it may be noted that pottery is found in features subsequent to the suggested partial levelling of the Town Ditch (Manley, 1987, 22, 26).

Edward, in correspondence about the transfer of the See of St Asaph to Rhuddlan (see below), refers in spring 1281 to the town of Rhuddlan 'Its site,....., is an outstanding one, spacious and very well protected' (Taylor, 1955, 44). Bishop Anian, writing on the same topic a few months later, says 'King Edward, who has built an important and well-frequented town in the neighbourhood and protected it with towers and earthworks' (*ibid*, 45). The significance of this reference to earthworks as the defence of Rhuddlan has not been commented upon before. Both King and Bishop, however, in the circumstances may well have presented the town as both more spacious and more complete than it was in 1281.

There is some evidence that the defences were still unfinished in March 1282 when Welsh rebels entered Rhuddlan, causing damage to the castle, to the church of St Mary (still on its Norman site) and the Friary. During 1282 timber was shipped to Rhuddlan to 'enclose the town and make dwellings therein'. By June 1283, however, materials designed for Rhuddlan were being forwarded to Caernarfon (Taylor, 1963, 323). The English reaction to the Welsh revolt of 1282 had been the conquest of all Gwynedd and the programme of castle and town building that included Conwy, Caernarfon, Beaumaris and Harlech. From 1282/3 Rhuddlan was no longer in a front-line position. Taylor considers that the reference to the enclosure of the town in 1282 indicated that the circuit was incomplete, and not a completed enclosure extensively damaged by rebels. This leads to the question of whether the circuit was subsequently finished, given Rhuddlan's comparative lack of importance after 1282.

The lack of any evidence for timbering in Site D might indicate that the circuit of the palisade at least was left unfinished, but only narrow strips were dug across the banks which had become heavily eroded. Excavation in DQ established that the ditch continues on the north east beyond the point to which it can be traced today on the surface. The line of this ditch, if projected, becomes Princes Road (Fig 1.2). Observation of a cable trench at H, at the junction of High Street and Princes Road showed neither bank nor ditch, suggesting an entrance through the defences, if these were completed, for the continuation of the High Street. The trench dug at Site S adjacent to the south west side of Princes Road indicated a cut or scarp of pre-17th century date (Fig 9.1) running down to the road which lies in a slight hollow – possibly the backfilled ditch. No trace of a bank was found on Site S, although the soft sandy soil would have rendered erosion quick and deliberate levelling easy; there was a line of postholes at the top of the scarp but these could not be dated. Excavations by the Clwyd-Powys Archaeological Trust at 'Fairmead', on the north side of Princes Road (Fig 1.2), in 1984 produced no clear evidence of bank, ditch or palisade (Brassil, 1984). A ditch of appropriate width and depth was found at Lôn Hylas, south of Castle Street in 1984 (Manley, 1985c) suggesting a junction with the castle just outside its main gate. This ditch was completely unsuspected, with no hint of its position on the

surface. It appears probable, on the evidence currently available, that the ditched circuit was complete. This at least is testable. Because the defences are so eroded it can never be established archaeologically whether the accompanying timber reinforcements were built all around the circuit.

The Edwardian Borough defences are similar to those at Flint, both built on almost flat sites which would be suitable for similar designs. The defences at Flint show clearly as a ditch between two banks, without a wall, on Speed's map of 1610. The south east side of the Flint defences were sectioned under salvage conditions in 1971 by T J Miles and H Quinnell (Cherry, 1971, 192). The ditch was 6.7m wide and 2.74m deep, with a bottom slightly more rounded than that at Rhuddlan. The inner bank, nearly 19m wide and 0.60m high, had a flat basal layer of material redeposited from the ditch (see inset on Fig 8.4); the available area did not extend to the presumed position of the outer bank. There were no datable objects from the bank or the primary ditch silt. The documentary record for Flint indicates, like Rhuddlan, a construction of earth and timber. None of the other Welsh Edwardian urban foundations are thought to have had defences without stone walls. The Borough defences at Flint and Rhuddlan built by Edward I owe their similarity to the same campaign of defence and to contemporary construction. From data presented by Beresford (1967) it seems unlikely that parallels would be found among the bastides of Gascony. It is assumed that earth and timber only were used because of the great need for masons on the Castles at Rhuddlan and Flint, and possibly because Edward was experimenting with ideas for urban defence which he may have developed during his travels abroad.

Comparison of expenditure on the urban defences at Rhuddlan and Flint helps little to determine whether the former was completed because of the different way the expenses were recorded for the two sites (Edwards, 1946). Flint had a ditch circuit of some 1550m yet only £171 is specifically recorded for the *Clausatura*. But the Flint records do not appear to divide expenditure between Castle and Borough until 1279. Before then a total of £2299 had been spent, at a time when most masonry seems to have been completed at Rhuddlan Castle; indeed Taylor (1963, 310) suggests that the £1000 spent in July and August 1277 may have been used to provide the main defensive circuit for the town. Rhuddlan's circuit was only 900m, with one side provided by the Clwyd. Recorded expenditure upon it was £1245.

Without knowledge of the disposition of the timber work it is not possible to understand how the defences were planned to work. Their most obvious feature is width, intended to keep attackers well out. The clay on the outer face of the outer bank may have formed both a revetment and a glacis. With timber fighting platforms and breastworks on the inner bank, and an outer bank forcing attackers into a prominent position, the defences could have been efficient. They were clearly original and experimental in design, in keeping with the other military works of Edward I in North Wales (Edwards, 1946).

After some royal-funded repair of the damage caused by the 1282 revolt, it is entirely credible that, in the later 1280s or during Rhuddlan's main period of prosperity in the 14th century, the defences were completed at the burgesses' expense. This was usual for maintenance of those town defences in which the King had little strategic interest. The ditch appeared to have been kept well cleaned for a while, with only a little primary silt, and a few Ewloe sherds within it. This would in itself argue for maintainence of the defensive circuit as a whole.

Site D revealed no evidence for an intra-mural road. The gully system R64 was dug following the curve of the inner bank and 4m within it. Its fill contained a lot of household refuse, some of which could be as early as late 13th century, and the gully may have served as the back boundary of a burgage plot. The 1428 extent (Jones, 1915) contains several references to burgages 'upon le Ditche' and a few curtilages 'against the Paleditch'. None of the sites excavated were in a position where structures built on burgage plots or boundaries between them might be expected. Gully O28, clipping the outer edge of the outer bank on Site D, intimates that agricultural holdings were soon laid out outside the defences. Sylvester (1955) has shown how extensive the strip field system was in the large parish of Rhuddlan (see 21.3).

It is probable that the Norman Church served the new Borough until the early 1300s. Taylor (1955) has discussed correspondence from Edward and Bishop Anian of St Asaph to the Papacy about moving the cathedral of St Asaph to Rhuddlan. This correspondence dates between the spring of 1281 and June 1282. There is reference to the King having offered 'an ample site' within the town and being prepared to 'appropriate to the chapter in perpetuity the church of the town to which the see was to be translated'. The church mentioned may either be the old church, which it was intended to maintain on its former site, or a new parish church to be established within the borough. The cathedral proposal was dropped after the war of 1282 moved the focus of administration away from Rhuddlan; the matter seems to have been decided before 1290 (Taylor, 1963, 323). The new church was under construction, with the old one presumably being demolished for its materials, soon after 1300, but the precise date of its consecration is not known. Its incumbent in 1306 had the Welsh name of Madoc (James, 1968).

21.3 The use of 'le Oldtown'

The term 'le Oldtown' is borrowed from the extent of 1428 (Jones, 1915). By that date all holdings situated there are described as land of certain extent, not as burgages. There are several references to land or 'places' in 'le Hemp(e)ditch' and one referring to '9½ separate acres of land curtilage upon le Hempendiche'. This might be a reference to the Town Ditch. Other land is described by its proximity to the 'door of the Friars Preachers'.

In the late 13th century structures were built on both Sites A and T. Both Houses on A appear to date to this period and perhaps continue in use until the early 14th century. They were built after all trace of rampart had disappeared, and therefore, following the argument presented in 21.1, after 1277. They have the same alignment, much the same size and method of construction, which may be unusual and archaic for its period (3.8.3). They may have been built to house craftsmen brought in to service the new works, possibly the smithing found on Site A which may, given the number of pits and features associated with it, have continued for some time. Drying kiln C3 is so similar to T61 and T50 (see below) that it may belong to this late 13th century period. Beyond the line of the former Ditch, and aligned on it, are a series of slots which interconnect with pits A56 and A57. They could be contemporary with the smithing activity and with the Houses. They form a sequence of boundaries maintaining the general line of the Norman Defences and some at least seem to have been structural. The most likely interpretation of the pit, at least in its A57 stage when stakes had held timbering, is as a latrine. We may see here the renewed boundary of a craft area designed to contain a latrine, with the craftsmen perhaps resident in Houses 1 and 2.

On Site T drying kilns T61 and 50 formed a gradually expanding sequence which was used mainly for the processing of oats. They postdate the sequence of slight slots in the Ditch top and so presumably should date towards the end of 13th century. Sand T14 was probably upcast from the kiln pits. The kilns, with their alterations, should have been in use for a few years. Despite the English rather that the Welsh style of their construction their use for oats reflects the predominant Welsh crop of the time (Davies, 1987, 154). After the kilns went out of use their area was surfaced with pebbles T22.

A little of soil T29 accumulated on surface T22 before the arrangement of slots T34/65/114 was cut. T114 (Fig 4.2) probably turned beneath the baulk to form an irregular enclosure about 10m across and of unknown length. It is described as a compound because it seems too large to have been roofed; there is even doubt as to whether timbers were set in the slots. The elaborate arrangement on the south east corner giving an angled entrance

2m wide might indicate a stock compound but there was none of the wear and mud usually associated with animals. The fill of T34 contained an Edward penny minted in 1281. Dolley and Boon (16.1) emphasise the large amount of currency circulating in Rhuddlan during the major building phase of the early 1280s. This makes residual finds very likely. The date of the compound relates to the next phase of activity in the area. This was a spread of clay, ash, charcoal and iron slag T80 with burning in places which sealed the infilled slot T114. It is probable that T80 represents the best preserved and most continuous evidence of an ironworking episode which affected much of the site – T21, 157, 243. A large amount of scrappy slag was found, but there were no smithing hearth bottoms as in the other smithing areas, of slightly earlier date, on Sites E and T. Probably activity was confined to the manufacture of objects from prepared blooms or scrap. Some rough shelters may be indicated by features such as slot T140. T80 and associated levels produced a large number of Type B horseshoe nails (Table 17.2), suggestive of the shoeing of horses. But Type B nails are unlikley to have been in use beyond around AD 1350 so the smithing area must have been well established by that date. This means that the compound beneath is unlikely to be later than a date early in the 14th century, or perhaps very late in the 13th.

The sequence on Site T covers about 70 years after Edward's arrival. After the initial Ditch infill suggested for 1277, it consisted of four separate episodes relating to different activities, the boundary slots, the drying kilns, the compound, and lastly smithing and shoeing. The Castle Friary Gate, on the south east of the Outer Ward, was blocked in 1301 (Jones, 1913, 16). This gate provided direct access from the castle to le Oldtowne. Its closure suggests a lack of official interest in the Oldtown area, and supports its use by burgesses. The smithing episode on Site T may therefore have been civilian as it is datable, most probably to the early 14th century. The population of Rhuddlan increased rapidly with 75 burgesses recorded for 1292 (Taylor, 1976, 157). Civilian use, with market interchanges, would account for gradual moves towards Welsh practices. The growing of oats and the use of a Welsh-style bakestone were contemporary with a Welshman becoming the parish priest. This accords with Soulsby's calculation (1983, 24) that Welshmen formed an average seventeen per cent of the inhabitants of all towns in Wales by 1300, the percentage being higher in the further parts of Wales, less near the borders. About three of the names in the 1292 Rhuddlan burgess list may be Welsh (Taylor, 1976), but people of non-Welsh origin must have adapted agricultural practices to local conditions and adopted local traditions in activities like cooking.

On Site V soil 2 was forming. There are no Type B horseshoe nails or anything to indicate date. On

Site soils G4 and then J16 built up over the AD 1280 lane G6. Rapid formation of even sandy mud on a lane surface is not suprising but accumulation was presumably accelerated by the amounts of soil disturbed by the digging out of the castle ditches, and the putative erosion of the inner bank of the Town Ditch. Soil G4 contained a large number of Type B horseshoe nails (Table 17.2). The area, despite its mud, was obviously still used as a track and, with the closure of the Friary Gate, must have provided a convenient way from the castle to the Oldtown and Friary, assuming there was an entrance at the junction of the Borough and the castle defences. This trackway eventually narrowed to the present day Lôn Hylas.

Site E probably ceased being used as a trackway when marker pit G135 was dug into soil G4; this seems to have formed the first marker for a long series of plot boundaries (Fig 6.2). North–south gully H27/G11 adjacent to G135 was infilled before the formation of any of the soil J16, as was G12 running east. Soil J16 contained many Type B horseshoe nails (Table 17.2) and was presumably accumulating during the first half of the 14th century around the marker post and boundary system. Boundaries appear to have been frequently renewed on Site E during the medieval period as soil, now less organic because the area was now agricultural and not a track frequented by draught and other animals, continued to build up.

Rhuddlan appears to have flourished during the earlier 14th century but to have been badly hit by the plagues of the 1340s. The reduction in population was probably never made up within the medieval period and must have left space within the Borough for activities which formerly had been carried out in le Oldtowne. This may be linked to changes on Sites A and T. By a date probably within the 14th century smithing ceased on Site T and soil T200 started its gradual build-up. The Houses on Site A had gone out of use early in the century, and there is no reason to prolong either the smithing there or the slot/latrine system far beyond the use of the Houses. The thick soil described on A as base of topsoil began to accumulate over the disused features. Soil formation on all the Sites, A,T, V and E was probably continuous from the 14th century until recently, agricultural use causing a gradual drift down the slope from the cliff edge along the Clwyd.

The *Conway Map of 1756* shows a system of strip fields along Abbey Road with their boundaries at right angles to it. The origin of Abbey Road is not known. It may not have been necessary for access to the Friary from the castle before the closing of the Friary Gate in 1301, although a route from the Borough to the Friary and then on to St Asaph would always have been needed. The general alignment of the main route to Spital (for documentation see J E Messham in Messham, Morgan & Manley, 1980) and on to Diserth (OS 1:25,000 Sheet SJ 07/17) is towards the centre of the Norman Borough; this was presumably the original route to Rhuddlan from the east. Its present line dog-legs between Diserth Road and Lôn Hylas (Fig 1.2) but the 1756 map shows the line broader and straighter with an open area at the junction with Abbey Road. That junction with Abbey Road is in a straight line with the outer east side of the Borough defences; it is likely that after their construction the practice started of turning south out of the main east gate, following along the outer side of the defences and then straight, the shortest route to the main Diserth road; the junction would then form a natural starting point for Abbey Road. The 1290 order (Taylor, 1963, 323) to 'make good the lack of a highway between St Asaph and Rhuddlan that it might be used for ever' would fit neatly with a late 13th century date for Abbey Road. By this argument the Road was in existence before 1300 and it would be natural for any boundaries in the Old Town and area enclosed by the Town Ditch to be laid out at rightangles to it.

It has been suggested that the area immediately outside the castle may have been laid out from marker G135 in the early 14th century. Plots for specific non-agricultural activities could have been laid out along Abbey Road from the 1290s. The strip field system there, overlying Site A and Site T east of gully T317 (see below), might be seen as appropriate for some period of recovery after the 1340 plagues. It has been suggested (3.11) that gullies A9 and A36, not directly datable in themselves, were especially deep-cut parts of a plot boundary system. The site of the Norman Church is glebe, shown as such both on the *Conway 1756 Map* and on the 1839 Tithe Apportionment Map. Its east boundary (that of the present school playing field) was the west boundary of the strip fields along Abbey Road; the land had presumably remained church property and its boundaries affected the laying out of new landholdings around it. (It is probable that with a careful study of these maps the original boundary of the churchyard could be established and tested for with a trial excavation.) The ditches found at Fairmead in 1984, not datable, may relate to another episode of strip field layout.

Once the Abbey Road strips were laid out, the land there continued in agricultural use until expansion of buildings in the present century. On Site E the boundaries up to the initial marker G135 continued to be renewed throughout the medieval period and beyond. Foundation trench H26 marks a stone-built structure, 8m by at least 10m, built in the corner of a plot (Fig 6.2). Material in its rob-trench suggested that it was out of use by the 17th century. Its date of construction could have been 15th or 16th century. The 1428 extent records Richard Motton holding '½ acre in le Oldetown where his barn is situated' (Jones, 1915, 71). It is the only such reference to a barn in le Oldtown in the extent (which may not not form a complete record because some properties were vacant). The date is perhaps early but the size of the holding is appropriate for that shown in this position in 1756.

At a date probably within the 17th century major boundaries in the Oldtown area were redug. The ditches are all substantial features with dark humic fills and may in some cases obscure earlier and slighter boundaries. These are H7 and G16 in E (after the demolition of the ?barn H26), V13 continuing the line of H7, T275 and T317. They were all cut after substantial amounts of soil had accumulated in their respective areas. The H7/V13 and the T317 line appear on the 1756 Conway Map, but only the T317 line on the 1839 Tithe Apportionment Map. The pattern presented seems to be the usual one of gradually increasing plot size.

21.4 The Borough after its foundation and the effect of Owain Glyndŵr

On Site D gully R64 inside the defences went out of use and some substantial timber structure was built involving R35,36, 26, 24 and 67 (Figs 8.2, 8.5). From its plan and size it might have been a granary or substantially built store. The defences are presumed to have been operational at this time, the 14th century, and so the inner bank may still have been in position on Site S.

In 1400 Rhuddlan suffered distastrous damage from two attacks during Owain Glyndŵr's rebellion in 1400 (Messham, 1968), from which it never recovered fully within the medieval period. There may have been some slighting of the defences during the rebellion. Layers such as 035 (Fig 8.4) were thought to be deliberate infill of the Ditch. Only above them did silt accumulate with a considerable quantity of domestic debris, perhaps because the Ditch, far from being cleaned out regularly, was regarded as a suitable rubbish repository. (Manley (1987, 22) recognized an episode of slighting in his excavation of the inner bank of the Town Ditch system, but this may probably be better explained by extension of agricultural activities in the early 14th century height of prosperity). On Site D both banks eroded rapidly in the late medieval period, filling the inner corner with clay soil R2 which contained a great deal of debris; erosion deposits from the outer bank contained less rubbish. The whole area appears neglected with the more accessible inner side being used for rubbish disposal. Subsequent, post-medieval features, indicate the area reverted to agricultural use.

Comprehensive slighting of the defences, and the lack thereafter of any attempt at repair or maintainence, would explain the disappearance of the inner bank from Site S and indeed the obliteration of the defences in the more populous south part of the town. The post line S11 etc (Fig 9.1) may best be explained as a late or post-medieval plot boundary. As the defences became obliterated in the south of the town it would become natural for the slightly sunken line of the former ditch to become used as a road. This route, the present Princes Road, was known as 'Street Newydd' in the eighteenth century (Clwyd Record Office Map of 1780 Ref NT/M/86).

Bibliography

Abercromby, J, 1912 *A Study of the Bronze Age Pottery of Great Britain and Ireland and its Associated Grave-Goods*, 2 vols. Oxford: Clarendon Press

Addyman, P V & Leigh, 1973 The Anglo-Saxon village at Chalton, Hampshire: second interim report, *Medieval Archaeol*, **17**, 1–25

Addyman, P V & Priestley, J 1977 (1978) Baile Hill, York: A report on the Institute's Excavations, *Archaeol J*, **134**, 115–56

Althin, C A, 1951 New Finds of Mesolithic Art in Scania (Sweden), *Acta Archaeologica*, **21**, 253–60

Andrews, P & Cook, J, 1985 Natural modifications to bones in a temperate setting, *Man*, **20**, 675–91

Arkell, W J, 1947 *Oxford Stone*. London: Faber & Faber

Ball, D F, 1960 *The Soils and Land Use of the District around Rhyl and Denbigh*. HMSO: Memoirs of the Soil Survey of Great Britain (England & Wales)

Barker, P A & Lawson, J, 1971 (1972) A pre-Norman field system at Hen Domen, Montgomery, *Medieval Archaeol*, **15**, 58–72

Barrett, J, 1973 Four Bronze Age cremation cemeteries from Middlesex, *Trans London Middlesex Archaeol Soc*, **24**, 111–34

Barton, R N E, 1986 Experiments with long blades from Sproughton, near Ipswich, Suffolk, in D A Roe (ed), *Studies in the Upper Palaeolithic of Britain and Northwest Europe*. Oxford: BAR Int Ser 296, 129–41

Barton, R N E, 1992 *Hengistbury Head Dorset Volume 2: The Late Upper Palaeolithic & Early Mesolithic Sites*. Oxford: Oxford University Committee for Archaeology Monograph No 34

Barton, R N E & Bergman, C A, 1982 Hunters at Hengistbury: some evidence from experimental archaeology, *World Archaeol*, **14(2)**, 237–48

Barton, N & Berridge, P J, in prep Waunfignen Felen, *Proc Hist Soc*

Bateman, J, 1976–77 (1978) A late Bronze Age cremation cemetery and Iron Age/Romano-British enclosure in the Parish of Ryton-on-Dunsmore, Warwickshire, *Trans Birmingham Warwickshire Archaeol Soc*, **88**, 9–48

Bay-Petersen, J L, 1978 Animal exploitation in Mesolithic Denmark, in P Mellars (ed), *The Early Postglacial Settlement of Northern Europe*, 115–45. London: Duckworth

Benson, D G, Evans J G & Williams, G H, 1990 Excavations at Stackpole Warren, Dyfed, *Proc Prehist Soc*, **56**, 179–246

Beresford, G, 1975 *The Medieval Clay-Land Village: Excavations at Goltho and Barton Blount*, Soc Medieval Archaeol Mono Ser, No 6

Beresford, G, 1987 *Goltho. The Development of an Early Medieval Manor c 850–1150*. English Heritage Archaeol Rep No 4

Beresford, M, 1967 *The New Towns of the Middle Ages*. London: Lutterworth Press

Berridge, P J, 1985 Mesolithic sites in the Yarty Valley, *Proc Devon Archaeol Soc*, **43**, 1–21

Bersu, G & Wilson, D M, 1966 *Three Viking Graves in the Isle of Man*, Soc Medieval Archaeol Mono Ser No 1

Biddle, M, 1976 Towns, in D M Wilson (ed) *The Archaeology of Anglo-Saxon England*, 99–150. London: Methuen

Blockley, K, 1985 *Marshfield: Ironmongers Piece Excavations 1982–3*. Oxford: BAR Brit Ser 141

Blockley, K, 1989 *Prestatyn 1984–5: An Iron Age Farmstead and Romano-British Industrial Settlement in North Wales*. Oxford: BAR Brit Ser 210

Blockley, K & M, forthcoming *Canterbury: Marlow Street Car Park 1978–82*

Bond, C J, 1987 Anglo-Saxon and Medieval Defences, in J Schoffield & R Leech (eds), *Urban Archaeology in Britain*, 92–116, CBA Res Rep 61

Bonsall, C, 1981 The coastal factor in the Mesolithic settlement of north west England, in B Gramsch (ed), *Mesolithikum in Europa. 2 Internationales Symposium, Veröffentlichungen des Museums für Ur and Frühgeschichte*, **14/15**, 451–70. Potsdam

Boon, G C, 1976 (1977) Segontium Fifty Years on: II the coins, *Archaeol Cambrensis*, **125**, 40–79

Boon, G C, 1988 *Welsh Hoards 1979–81*. National Museum of Wales, Cardiff

Brassil, K, 1984 Rhuddlan, *Archaeology in Wales*, **24**, 65–6. CBA Group 2 Annual Report

Brassil, K & Owen, W G, 1987 Abbey Farm and Ysgol Y Castell, Rhuddlan, *Archaeology in Wales*, **27**, 58. CBA Group 2 Annual Report

Brinkhuizen, D C, 1983 Some notes on recent and pre- and proto-historic fishing gear from Northwestern Europe, *Palaeohistoria*, **25**, 7–53

British Museum, 1905 *A Guide to the Antiquities of the Early Iron Age*

Britnell, J, 1989 *Caersws Vicus, Powys: Excavations at the Old Primary School, 1985–6*. Oxford: BAR Brit Ser 205

Britnell, W, 1976 Antler cheekpieces of the British Late Bronze Age, *Antiq J*, **56**, 24–34

Britnell, W, 1984 A 15th-century corn-drying kiln from Collfryn, Llansantffraid, Deuddwr, Powys, *Medieval Archaeol*, **28**, 190–4

Britnell, W, 1989 The Collfryn hillslope enclosure, Llansantffraid Deuddwr, Powys: excavations 1980–1982, *Proc Prehist Soc*, **55**, 89–134

Britnell, W, 1990 Capel Maelog; Llandrindod Wells, Powys: Excavations 1984–87, *Medieval Archaeol*, **34**, 27–96

Britnell, W J & Savory, H N, 1984 *Gwernvale and Penywyrlod: Two Neolithic Long Cairns in the Black Mountains of Brecknock*. Cardiff: Cambrian Archaeol Mono No 2

Bromage, T G & Boyde, A, 1984 Microscopic criteria for the determination of directionality of cutmarks on bone, *American Journal of Physical Anthropology*, **65**, 359–66

Bryant, G F, 1973 Experimental Romano-British kiln firings, in A Detsicas (ed), *Current Research in Romano-British Coarse Pottery*, 149–60. CBA Res Rep No 10

Bugge, A, 1935 Origin, development and decline of the Norwegian stave church, *Acta Archaeologica*, **6**, 152–65

Burgess, C, 1976 Burials with metalwork of the Later Bronze Age in Wales and beyond, in G C Boon & J M Lewis (eds), *Welsh Antiquity*, 81–104. Cardiff: National Museum of Wales

Burgess, C, 1980a The Bronze Age in Wales, in Taylor, J A (ed), *Culture and Environment in Prehistoric Wales*, 243–86. Oxford:BAR Brit Ser 76

Burgess, C, 1980b *The Age of Stonehenge*. London: Dent & Sons

Butler, L A S, 1974 (1975) Medieval finds from Castell-y-Bere, Merioneth, *Archaeol Cambrensis*, **123**, 78–112

Butler, L A S, 1987 Domestic Building in Wales and the Evidence of the Welsh Laws, *Medieval Archaeol*, **31**, 47–58

Butler, L A S & Dunning, G C, 1974 (1975) Wooden buckets, in L A S Butler, Medieval finds from Castell-y-Bere, Merioneth, *Archaeol Cambrensis*, **123**, 100–6

Calkin, J B, 1962 The Bournemouth area in the Middle and Late Bronze Age, with the Deverel-Rimbury problem reconsidered, *Archaeol J*, **119**, 1–65

Chapelot, J & Fossier, R, 1985 *The Village and House in the Middle Ages*. London: Batsford

Chaplin, R E, 1971 *The Study of Animal Bones from Archaeological Sites*. London: Academic Press

Chapman, S K, 1986 *Working with a Scanning Electron Microscope*. Kent: Lodgemark Press

Cherry, J, 1971 Medieval Britain in 1971: Post-Conquest, *Medieval Archaeol*, **16**, 171–212

Christie, H, Olsen, O & Taylor, H M, 1979 The wooden church of St Andrew at Greensted, Essex, *Antiq J*, **59**, 92–112

Clark, J, 1986 Medieval horseshoes, *Finds Res Group Datasheet*, **4**

Clark, J G D, 1938 Microlithic industries from tufa deposits at Prestatyn, Flintshire and Blashenwell, Dorset, *Proc Prehist Soc*, **4**, 330–4

Clark, J G D, 1939 A further note on the tufa deposit at Prestatyn, Flintshire, *Proc Prehist Soc*, **5**, 201–2

Clark, J G D, 1952 *Prehistoric Europe: The Economic Basis*. London: Methuen

Clark, J G D, 1954 *Excavations at Star Carr*. Cambridge: Cambridge University Press

Clark, J G D, 1972 Star Carr: A case study in bio-archaeology, *Module*, **10**, 1–42. USA Addison-Wesley Publishing Company

Clark, J G D, 1975 *The Earlier Stone Age Settlement of Scandinavia*. Cambridge: Cambridge University Press

Clarke, D L, 1976 Mesolithic Europe: The Economic Basis, in G de Sievking, I H Longworth & K E Wilson (eds), *Problems in Economic and Social Archaeology*, 449–81. London: Duckworth

Clarke, H & Carter, A 1977 *Excavations at King's Lynn 1963–1970*, Soc Medieval Archaeol Mono Ser 7

Claugher, D, 1988 Preparative methods, replicating, and viewing uncoated materials, in S L Olsen (ed), *Scanning Electron Microscopy in Archaeology*, 9–21. Oxford: BAR Int Ser 452

Clough, T H McM & Cummins, W A (eds), 1979 *Stone Axe Studies*, CBA Res Rep 23

Clough, T H McM & Cummins, W A (eds), 1988 *Stone Axe Studies*, **2**, CBA Res Rep 67

Coles, J M, 1971 The early settlement of Scotland: excavations at Morton, Fife, *Proc Prehist Soc*, **37**, 284–366

Cox, E W 1893-5 (1895) Diserth Castle, *J Chester Archaeol Soc*, **5**, 369–79

Cook, J, 1986 The application of scanning electron microscopy to taphonomic and archaeological problems, in D A Roe (ed), *Studies in the Upper Palaeolithic of Britain and Northwest Europe*, 143–63. Oxford: BAR Int Ser 296

Cook, M H R, 1982 The Hengistbury Head figurine reconsidered, *Proc Dorset Natur Hist Archaeol Soc*, **104**, 191–2

Cook, M H R, 1985 The Hengistbury whetstone, *Proc Dorset Natur Hist Archaeol Soc*, **107**, 178

Couchman, C R, 1975 The Bronze Age cemetery at Ardleigh, Essex: a further consideration, *Essex Archaeol Hist*, **7**, 14–32

Couraud, C, 1985 L'Art Azilien Origine – Survivance, *XXème Supplement à Gallia Préhistoire*

Courtney, P, 1987 Medieval pottery, in J Manley, Cledemutha: A Late Saxon Burh in North Wales, *Medieval Archaeol*, **31**, 27–31

Courtney, P & Jones, N W, 1988 The Clwyd-Powys Medieval Pottery Fabric Series, *Medieval and Later Pottery in Wales*, **10**, 9–32. Bulletin of Welsh Medieval Pottery Research Group

Cowgill, J, de Neergaard M & Griffiths, N, 1987 *Medieval Finds from Excavations in London: I. Knives and Scabbards*. London: HMSO

Crossley, D W (ed), 1981 *Medieval Industry*, CBA Res Rep 40

Crummy, N, 1983 *The Roman Small Finds from Excavations at Colchester*, Colchester Archaeological Reports, 2. Colchester Archaeological Trust

Curwen, E C, 1941 More about querns, *Antiquity*, **15**, 15–32

Darling, F F, 1969 *A Herd of Red Deer*, 3rd ed. London: Oxford University Press

Davey P J (ed), 1977 *Medieval Pottery from Excavations in the North West*. University of Liverpool

Davey, P J & Morgan, D E M, 1977 Hen Blas, in P J Davey (ed) *Medieval Pottery from Excavations in the North West*, 42–53. University of Liverpool

David, A, 1989 Some aspects of the Human presence in West Wales during the Mesolithic, in C Bonsall (ed), *The Mesolithic in Europe: Papers presented at the Third International Symposium, Edinburgh 1985*, 241–53. Edinburgh: John Donald

Davies, E, 1929 *The Prehistoric and Roman Remains of Denbighshire*. Cardiff: House of Lewis

Davies, E, 1949 *The Prehistoric and Roman Remains of Flintshire*. Cardiff: House of Lewis

Davies, J, 1963 A Mesolithic site on Blubberhouse Moor, Wharfedale, West Riding of Yorkshire, *Yorkshire Archaeol J*, **41**, 60–70

Davies, R R, 1987 *Conquest, Coexistence and Change: Wales 1063–1415*. Oxford: Clarendon Press

Davies, W, 1982 *Wales in the Early Middle Ages*. Leicester: Leicester University Press

Davison, B K, 1967 (1968) The late Saxon town of Thetford: an interim report on the 1964–6 excavations, *Medieval Archaeol*, **11**, 189–208

Dawkins, W B, 1874 *Cave Hunting, Researches on the Evidence of Caves Respecting the Early Inhabitants of Europe*. London: Macmillan

Dawkins, W B, 1901 The cairn and sepulchral cave at Gop, near Prestatyn, *Archaeol J*, **58**, 322–41

Dennell, R, 1983 *European Economic Prehistory: A New Approach*. London: Academic Press

Dolley, M, 1959 A note on the chronology of some published and unpublished 'short cross' coins from the British Isles, *Brit Numis J*, **29 Pt ii**, 297–321

Dolley, M 1963 The sequence of moneyers at Rhuddlan in the Short-Cross period, *Spink Numis Circ*, **17**, 226–7

Dolley, M, 1966 *The Norman Conquest and the English Coinage*. London: Spink

Dolley, M with Elmore Jones F & Lyon C S S, 1969 *Royal Coin Cabinet, Stockholm: Anglo-Norman Pennies*. Published with C E Blunt and M Dolley, University Collection, Reading (Sylloge of Coins of the British Isles, 11). London: The British Academy

Dreisch, A von den, 1976 A Guide to the Measurement of Animal Bones from Archaeological Sites, *Peabody Mus Bull*, **1**. Harvard: Harvard University

Dudley, D & Minter, E M, 1966 The Excavation of a Medieval Settlement at Treworld, Lesnewth, *Cornish Archaeol*, **5**, 34–58

Dumont, J V, 1983 An interim report of the Star Carr microwear study, *Oxford J Archaeol*, **2(2)**, 127–45

Dumont, J V, 1985 A preliminary report on the Mount Sandel microwear study, in P C Woodman, *Excavations at Mount Sandel 1973–77*, 61–70. HMSO, Belfast, Northern Ireland Archaeol Mono No 2

Dumont, J V, 1987 Mesolithic microwear research in northwest Europe, in P Rowley-Conwy, M Zvelebil & H P Blankholm (eds), *Mesolithic Northwest Europe: Recent Trends*, 82–9. Sheffield: Department of Archaeology & Prehistory, University of Sheffield

Dumont, J V, 1989 Star Carr: the results of a micro-wear study, in C Bonsall (ed), *The Mesolithic in Europe: Papers presented at the Third International Symposium, Edinburgh 1985*, 231–40. Edinburgh: John Donald

Dunning, G C, 1934 The swan's-neck and ring-headed pin of the Early Iron Age in Britain, *Archaeol J*, **91**, 269–95

Edwards, J G, 1946 Edward I's castle building in Wales, *Proc Brit Acad*, **32**, 15–81

Edwards, N & Lane, A (eds), 1988 *Early Medieval Settlement in Wales AD 400–1100*. (Early Medieval Wales Archaeology Research Group). Cardiff: Research Centre Wales, University College, Bangor & Department of Archaeology, University College, Cardiff

Edwards, T, 1912 Dyserth Castle, *Archaeol Cambrensis*, **12**, 263–94

Ellis, S E, 1969 The petrography and provenance of Anglo-Saxon and Medieval English honestones with notes on some other hones, *Bull Brit Mus Mineralogy (Natural History)*, **2**, 135–87

Fenton, A, 1978 *The Northern Isles: Orkney and Shetland*. Edinburgh: John Donald

Fieller, N R J & Turner, A, 1982 Number estimation in vertebrate samples, *J Archaeol Sci*, **9**, 49–62

Fingerlin, I, 1971 *Gürtel des hohen und späten Mittelalters*. Munich: Deutscher Kunstverlag (Kunstswissenschaftliche Studien Vol 46)

Fiorillo, A R, 1984 An introduction to the identification of trample marks, *Current Research in the Pleistocene*, **1**, 47–8. Centre for the Study of Early Man, Maine.

Fischer, A, 1974 An ornamented flint-core from Holmegård V, Zealand, Denmark, *Acta Archaeologica*, **45**, 155–68

Flints Ministers Accounts A Jones (ed), Flintshire Ministers Accounts 1301–1328, *Flintshire Hist Soc Pub*, **3**, 1913. Prestatyn

Fowler, P J & Thomas, A C, 1962 Arable fields of the pre-Norman period at Gwithian, *Cornish Archaeol*, **1**, 61–84

Fox, C, 1955 *Offa's Dyke*. London: Oxford University Press for the British Academy

Gardner, W & Savory, H N, 1964 *Dinorben a Hill-Fort Occupied in Early Iron Age and Roman Times. Excavations, 1912–69*. Cardiff:

National Museum of Wales

Geddes, J, 1982 The construction of medieval doors, in S McGrail (ed), *Woodworking techniques before AD 1500*, 313–25. National Maritime Museum, Greenwich, Archaeological Series No 7/Oxford: BAR Int Ser 129

Gelling, P S & Standford, S C, 1965 Dark Age pottery or Iron Age ovens?, *Trans Birmingham Warwickshire Archaeol Soc*, **82**, 77–91

Gent, H, 1983 Centralized storage in later prehistoric Britain, *Proc Prehist Soc*, **49**, 243–68

Gilbert, A S & Singer, B H, 1982 Reassessing zooarchaeological quantification, *World Archaeol*, **14(1)**, 21–40

Gillam, J P, 1970 *Types of Roman Coarse Pottery Vessels in Northern Britain*, 3rd edn. Newcastle: Oriel Press

Gillam, J P, 1976 Coarse fumed ware in North Britain and beyond, *Glasgow Archaeol J*, **5**, 57–80

Gillespie, R, Gowlett, J A J, Hall, E T, Hedges, R E M & Perry, C, 1985 Radiocarbon dates from the Oxford AMS system: Archaeometry datelist 2, *Archaeometry*, **27(2)**, 272–46

Giraldus Cambrensis *The Itinerary through Wales and the Description of Wales*. London: Everyman's Lbrary (1908)

Glenn, T A, 1914 Exploration of Neolithic station near Gwaenysgor, Flintshire, *Archaeol Cambrensis*, **14**, 247–70

Glenn, T A, 1915, Prehistoric and Roman remains at Dyserth Castle, *Archaeol Cambrensis*, **70**, 47–86

Glenn, T A, 1926 Recent finds near Rhyl, *Archaeol Cambrensis*, **81**, 199–203

Glenn, T A, 1935 The distribution of the Craig Lwyd Axe and its associated cultures, *Archaeol Cambrensis*, **90**, 189–218

Gob, A & Jacques, M-C. 1985 A Late Mesolithic Dwelling structure at Remouchamps, Belgium, *J Field Archaeol*, **12**, 163–75

Godwin, H, 1975 *The History of the British Flora*, (2nd ed). Cambridge: Cambridge University Press

Godwin, H & Willis, E H, 1959 Cambridge University natural radiocarbon measurements I, *Radiocarbon*, **1**, 63–75

Godwin, H & Willis, E H, 1964 Cambridge University natural radiocarbon measurements VI, *Radiocarbon*, **6**, 116–37

Good, G L & Tabraham, C, 1981 Excavations at Threave Castle, Galloway, 1974–78, *Medieval Archaeol*, **25**, 90–140

Goodall, A R, 1987 Medieval copper alloy, in G Beresford, *Goltho. The Development of an Early Medieval Manor c 850-1150*, 172–6. English Heritage Archaeol Rep No 4

Goodall, I H, 1973 Iron objects, in P J & R M Huggins, Excavation of Monartre Forge and Saxo-Norman Enclosure, Waltham Abbey, Essex, 1972–73, *Essex Archaeol Hist*, **5**, 168–75

Goodall, I H, 1975 Iron objects, in G Beresford, *The Medieval Clay-Land Village: Excavations at Goltho and Barton Blount*, 79–91, Soc Medieval Archaeol Mono Ser No 6

Goodall, I H, 1976 Iron, in T G Hassall, Excavations at Oxford Castle, 1965-73, *Oxoniensia*, **41**, 298–303

Goodall, I H, 1979 Iron objects, in P A Rahtz, *The Saxon and Medieval Palaces at Cheddar*, 263–74. Oxford: BAR Brit Ser 65

Goodall, I H, 1980a Iron objects, in A D Saunders, Lydford Castle, Devon, *Medieval Archaeol*, **24**, 165–7

Goodall, I H, 1980b *Ironwork in Medieval Britain: An Archaeological Study* (University College Cardiff, PhD thesis)

Goodall, I H, 1980c The iron objects, in P Wade-Martins, North Elmham Park, *E Anglian Archaeol*, **9**, 509–16

Goodall, I H, 1981 The medieval blacksmith and his products, in D W Crossley (ed), *Medieval Industry*, 51–60, CBA Res Rep 40

Goodall, I H, 1982 (1983) Iron objects, in J G Coad & A D F Streeten, Excavations at Castle Acre Castle, Norfolk, 1972-77, County House and Castle of the Norman Earls of Surrey, *Archaeol J*, **139**, 227–35

Goodall, I H, 1983a Iron objects, in J P Allan, *Medieval and Post-Medieval Finds from Exeter 1971–1980*, 337–8. Exeter Archaeol Rep 3

Goodall, I H, 1983b The small finds, in K Jarvis, *Excavations in Christchurch 1969 to 1980*, 76–7. Dorset Natur Hist Archaeol Soc Mono No 5

Goodall, I H, 1984 Iron objects, in A Rogerson & C Dallas, Eynsford Castle: the moat and bridge, *Archaeol Cantiana*, **88**, 76–105

Goodall, I H, 1985 Iron objects, in M Atkin, A Carter & D H Evans, Excavations in Norwich 1971–1978 Part II, *E Anglian Archaeol Rep*, **26**, 201–13

Goodall, I H, 1987 Objects of iron, in G Beresford, *Goltho. The Development of an Early Medieval Manor c 850-1150*, 177–87. English Heritage Archaeol Rep No 4

Goodall, I H, 1989 Iron objects, in T G Hassall, C E Halpin & M Mellor, Excavations in St Ebbe's, Oxford, 1967–1976: Part I Late Saxon and Medieval Domestic Occupation and Tenements, and the Medieval Greyfriars, *Oxoniensia*, **54**, 71–277

Goodall, I H, 1990 Iron objects, in M Biddle (ed), *Winchester Studies. Artefacts from Medieval Winchester. Part ii. Object and Economy in Medieval Winchester*, passim. Oxford University Press

Gordon-Williams, J P, 1926 The Nab Head chipping floor, *Archaeol Cambrensis*, **81**, 86–111

Grant, A, 1979 The animal bones, in B Cunliffe, *Excavations in Bath, 1950–1975*, 60–70. Bristol: CRAAGS Exc Rep No 1

Grant, A, 1982 The use of tooth wear as a guide to the age of domestic ungulates, in B Wilson, C Grigson & S Payne (eds), *Ageing and Sexing*

Animal Bones from Archaeological Sites, 91–108. Oxford: BAR Brit Ser 109

Green, H S, 1980 *The Flint Arrowheads of the British Isles*. Oxford: BAR Brit Ser 75

Greenhill, F A, 1976 *Incised Effigial Slabs*. London: Faber

Grigson, C, 1981 Fauna, in I G Simmons & M J Tooley (eds), *The Environment in British Prehistory*, 110–24. London: Duckworth

Grimes, W F, 1951 *The Prehistory of Wales*. Cardiff: National Museum of Wales

Gumbley, W, 1915 The Dominican priory of Rhuddlan, *Flintshire Hist Soc J*, **5**, 34–5

Haddan, A W & Stubbs W, 1869 *Councils and Ecclesiastical Documents Relating to Great Britain and Ireland*, **1**, 529–31. Oxford: Clarendon Press

Hall, R A, 1984a A late pre-Conquest urban building tradition, in P Addyman & V E Black (eds), *Archaeological Papers from York: Presented to M W Barley*, 71–7. York: York Archaeological Trust

Hall, R A, 1984b *The Excavations at York: the Viking Dig*. London: The Bodley Head

Harrison, H M & Davey, P J, 1977 Ewloe, in P J Davey (ed), *Medieval Pottery from Excavations in the North West*, 92–9. University of Liverpool

Hartley, D & Elliot, M M, 1928 *Life and Work of the People of England. The Fourteenth Century*. London: Batsford

Harvey, Y, 1975 The iron, in C Platt R Coleman-Smith, *Excavations in Medieval Southampton 1953–1969, 2: the Finds*, 276–93. Leicester: Leicester University Press

Haslam, J (ed), 1984a *Anglo-Saxon Towns in England*. Chichester: Phillimore

Haslam, J, 1984b The Towns of Wiltshire, in J Haslam (ed), *Anglo-Saxon Towns in England*, 87–148. Chichester: Phillimore

Haslam, J, 1984c The Towns of Devon, in J Haslam (ed), *Anglo-Saxon Towns in England*, 249–84. Chichester: Phillimore

Haslam, J, 1987 Market and fortress in England in the reign of Offa, *World Archaeol*, **19 No 1**, 76–93

Hawkes, C F C, 1935 The pottery from the sites on Plumpton Plain, *Proc Prehist Soc*, **1**, 39–59

Hedges, R E M, Housley, R A, Law, I A & Perry, C, 1988 Radiocarbon dates from the Oxford AMS system: archaeometry datelist 7, *Archaeometry*, **30(1)**, 155–64

Hewitt, N E & Morgan, D E M, 1977 Dyserth, in P J Davey (ed), *Medieval Pottery from Excavations in the North West*, 34–41. University of Liverpool

Higgs, E S, 1959 The excavation of a late Mesolithic site at Downton, near Salisbury, Wilts, *Proc Prehist Soc*, **25**, 209–32

Hill, D, 1974 The inter-relationship of Offa's and Watt's dykes, *Antiquity*, **48**, 309–12

Hill, D, 1981 *An Atlas of Anglo-Saxon England*. Oxford: Basil Blackwell

Hillman, G C, 1981 Crop husbandry practice in British prehistory: reconstructions from charred remains of crops, in R J Mercer (ed), *Farming Practice in British Prehistory*, 123–62. Edinburgh: Edinburgh University Press

Hillman, G C, 1982a Crop husbandry at the medieval farmstead, Cefn Greanog, *Bull Board Celtic Stud*, **29**, 901–7

Hillman, G C, 1982b Evidence for spelting malt, in R Leech, *Excavations at Catsgore 1970–1973*, 137–41. Bristol: Western Archaeological Trust Monograph No 2

Hillman, G C, 1984 Interpretation of archaeological plant remains: application of ethnographic models from Turkey, in W van Zeist & W A Casparie (eds), *Plants and Ancient Man*, 1–41. Rotterdam: A A Balkema

Hodson, F R, 1964 Cultural grouping within the British pre-Roman Iron Age, *Proc Prehist Soc*, **30**, 99–110

Holdsworth, P, 1976 Saxon Southampton; a new review, *Medieval Archaeol*, **20**, 26–61

Horsman, V, 1985 Rebuilding Saxon London, *Popular Archaeol* **(Oct 1985)**, 19–23

Houlder, C H, 1968 The henge monuments at Llandegai, *Antiquity*, **42**, 216–21

Housely, R A, 1991 AMS dates from the Late Glacial and Early Postglacial in north west Europe: a review, in N Barton, A J Roberts & D A Roe (eds), *The Late Glacial in North West Europe*, 25–39, CBA Res Rep 77

Hurst, J G, 1959 Middle-saxon Pottery, in G C Dunning, J G Hurst, J N L Myres & F Tischler, Anglo-Saxon Pottery: a Symposium, *Medieval Archaeol*, **3**, 13–31

Hurst, J G, 1969 (1971) in J G Hurst (ed), Red-painted and glazed pottery in Western Europe from the eighth to the twelfth century, *Medieval Archaeol*, **13**, 93–147

Hurst, J G, 1976 The Pottery, in D M Wilson (ed), *The Archaeology of Anglo-Saxon England*, 283–348. London: Methuen

Ingebristen, O, 1924 *Hjortens Utbredelse i Norge*. Bergen: Naturvidenska belige rekke No 6

Ireland, J & Lynch, F, 1973 More Mesolithic flints from Trwyn Du, Aberffraw, *Trans Anglesey Antiq Soc Fld Club for 1973*, 170–5

Jackson, D A, Harding, D W & Myres, J N L, 1969 The Iron Age and Anglo-Saxon site at Upton, Northants, *Antiq J*, **49**, 202–21

Jacobi, R M, 1973 Aspects of the 'Mesolithic Age' in Great Britain, in S K Kozlowski (ed), *The Mesolithic in Europe*, 237–65. Warsaw University Press

Jacobi, R M, 1976 Britain inside and outside Mesolithic Europe, *Proc Prehist Soc*, **42**, 67–84

Jacobi, R M, 1978 Northern England in the eighth millennium bc: an essay, in P Mellars (ed), *The Early Postglacial Settlement of Northern Europe*, 295–332. London: Duckworth

Jacobi, R M, 1980 The early holocene settlement of

232

Wales, in J A Taylor (ed), *Culture and Environment in Prehistoric Wales*, 131–206. Oxford: BAR Brit Ser 76

Jacobi, R M, 1981 The last hunters in Hampshire, in S J Shennan & R T Schadla-Hall (eds), *The Archaeology of Hampshire: from the Palaeolithic to the Industrial Revolution*, 10–25. Hampshire Field Club and Archaeol Soc, Monograph No 1

Jacobi, R M, 1987 Misanthropic miscellany: musings on British early Flandrian archaeology and other flights of fancy, in P Rowley-Conwy, M Zvelebil & H P Blankholm (eds), *Mesolithic Northwest Europe: Recent Trends*, 163–8. Sheffield: Department of Archaeology & Prehistory, University of Sheffield

James, J W, 1968 *Rhuddlan and its Church*. Rhuddlan Parochial Church Council

Jarrett, M G & Wrathmell, S, 1981 *Whitton: An Iron Age and Roman Farmstead in South Glamorgan*. Cardiff: University of Wales Press

Jensen, J, 1982 *The Prehistory of Denmark*. London: Methuen

Jochim, M A, 1976 *Hunting-Gathering Subsistence and Settlement: A Predictive Model*. New York: Academic Press

Jones, A, 1915 A fifteenth-century document of Rhuddlan, *Flintshire Hist Soc Publ*, **5**, 45–90

Jones, M, 1978 The plant remains, in M Parrington, *Excavation of an Iron Age Settlement, Bronze Age Ring Ditches and Roman Features at Ashville Trading Estate, Abingdon (Oxon)*, 1974–6, 93–119, CBA Res Rep 28

Jones, M V, 1977 Prehistoric salt equipment from a pit at Mucking, Essex, *Antiq J*, **57(2)**, 317–19

Jones, R, Wall, S, Locker, A, Coy, J & Maltby, M, 1981 *Computer Based Osteometry Data Capture Manual*, **1**. AM Lab Rep No.3342

Jope, E M, 1956 The tinning of iron spurs: a continuous practice from the tenth to the seventeenth century, *Oxoniensia*, **21**, 35–42

Keil, I, 1965 Farming on the Dorset estates of Glastonbury Abbey in the early fourteenth century, *Proc Dorset Natur Hist Archaeol Soc*, **87**, 234–49

Kelly, R S, 1982 The Excavation of a Medieval Farmstead at Cefn Graenog Clynnog, Gwynedd, *Bull Board Celtic Stud*, **29**, 859–908

Kinnes, I A & Longworth, I H, 1985 *Catalogue of the Excavated Prehistoric and Romano-British Material in the Greenwell Collection*. London: British Museum Publications Ltd

Lacaille, A D & Grimes, W F, 1955 The prehistory of Caldey, *Archaeol Cambrensis*, **104**, 85–165

Larsson, L, 1978 Mesolithic antler and bone artefacts from central Scania, *Meddelanden från Lunds universitets historiska museum 1977-1978*, **2**, 28–67

Lawson, A J, 1980 The evidence for later Bronze Age settlement and burial in Norfolk, in J C Barrett and R J Bradley (eds), *Settlement and Society in the British Later Bronze Age*,

271–94. Oxford: BAR Brit Ser 83

Leakey, L S B, 1951 *Preliminary excavations of a Mesolithic site at Abinger Common, Surrey*, Surrey Archaeol Soc, Res Vol 3, 1–44

Legge, A J & Rowley-Conwy, P A, 1988 *Star Carr Revisited: a re-analysis of the larger mammals*. London: Centre for Extra-Mural Studies Birbeck College

Le Patourel, H E J, 1973 *The Moated Sites of Yorkshire*, Soc Medieval Archaeol Mono Ser No 5

Levitan, B, 1984a The vertebrate remains, in S Rahtz & T Rowley *Middleton Stoney. Excavation and Survey in a North Oxfordshire Parish 1970–82*, 108–48. Oxford: Oxford University Dept of External Studies

Levitan, B, 1984b Faunal remains, in P Leach, *The Archaeology of Taunton*, 167–93. Bristol: Wessex Archaeol Trust Rep 8

Levitan, B, 1989 Bone analysis and urban economy: examples of selectivity and a case for comparison, in D Serjeanston & T Waldron (eds), *Diet and Crafts in Towns. The Evidence of Animal Remains from the Roman to the Post-Medieval Periods*, 161–181. Oxford: BAR Brit Ser 199

Levitan, B, 1989b (1990) A method for investigating bone fragmentation and anatomical representation, *Circaea*, **7**, 95–101

Lewis, J M, 1976 Field archaeology of Wales, AD 400–1100: some priorities and prospects, *Archaeology in Wales*, **16**, 25–8, CBA Group 2 Annual Report

Liversage, D, 1966 Ornamental Mesolithic artefacts from Denmark. Some new finds, *Acta Archaeologica*, **37**, 221–37

Lloyd, J E, 1939 *A History of Wales*. 2 vols. 3rd edn. London: Longmans

Lloyd Gruffydd, K, 1981–82 (1982) Coal-mining in Flintshire during the later Middle Ages, *Flintshire Hist Soc Publ*, **30**, 107–24

London Museum, 1967 *Medieval Catalogue* (reprint; original 1940). London: HMSO

Longworth, I H, 1976–7 (1978) The Bronze Age pottery, in J Bateman, A late Bronze Age cremation cemetery and Iron Age/Romano-British enclosure in the Parish of Ryton-on-Dunsmore, Warwickshire, *Trans Birmingham Warwickshire Archaeol Soc*, **88**, 16–19

Longworth, I H, 1981 Neolithic and Bronze Age pottery, in R J Mercer, *Grimes Graves, Norfolk Excavations 1971–72*, **1**, 39–59. Dept of Environment Archaeol Rep No 11

Lowery, P R, Savage, R D A, & Wilkins, R L, 1971 Scriber, graver, scorer, tracer: notes on experiments in bronzeworking technique, *Proc Prehist Soc*, **37**, 167–81

Lynch, F, 1969 The contents of excavated tombs in North Wales, in T G E Powell, J X W Corcoran, F Lynch, & J G Scott, *Megalithic Enquiries in the West of Britain*, 149–74. Liverpool University Press

Lynch, F (ed), 1975 Brenig Valley excavations 1974: interim report, *Trans Denbighshire Hist*

Soc, **24**, 1–25

Lynch, F, 1980 Bronze Age monuments in Wales, in J A Taylor (ed), *Culture and Environment in Prehistoric Wales*, 233–41. Oxford: BAR Brit Ser 76

Lynch, F, Waddell, J, Allen, D & Grealey, S, 1974 Brenig Valley excavations 1973: interim report, *Trans Denbighshire Hist Soc*, **23**, 1–56

MacDonald, A D S & Laing, L R, 1974-75 Excavations at Lochmaten Castle, Dumfriesshire, *Proc Soc Antiq Scot*, **106**, 124–57

McInnes, I J, 1968 The excavations of a Bronze Age cemetery at Catfoss, East Yorkshire, *E Riding Archaeol*, **1**, 1–10

Maltby, M, 1982 Mammal and bird bones, in R A Higham, J P Allan & S R Blaylock, Excavations at Okehampton Castle, Devon: Part 2, *Proc Devon Archaeol Soc*, **40**, 114–35

Manley, J, 1981 Rhuddlan, *Archaeology in Wales*, **21**, 58–60, CBA Group 2 Report

Manley, J, 1982a Rhuddlan, *Archaeology in Wales*, **22**, 34, CBA Group 2 Report

Manley, J, 1982b Rhuddlan and coastal evolution, *J Landscape Hist*, **3**, 1–15

Manley, J, 1983 Rhuddlan, *Archaeology in Wales*, **23**, 58, CBA Group 2 Report

Manley, J, 1984 The late Saxon settlement of *Cledemutha* (Rhuddlan), Clwyd, in H L Faull (ed), *Studies in Late Anglo-Saxon Settlement*, 54–64. Oxford: Oxford University Department of External Studies

Manley, J, 1985a The archer and the army in the late Saxon period, *Anglo-Saxon Stud Archaeol Hist*, **4**, 223–35

Manley, J, 1985b (1986) Early Medieval radiocarbon dates and plant remains for Rhuddlan, Clwyd, *Archaeol Cambrensis*, **134**, 106–19

Manley, J, 1985c (1986) Salvage excavations at Lôn Hylas, Rhuddlan, Clwyd: ditches of the Roman and Medieval periods, *Archaeol Cambrensis*, **134**, 230–5

Manley, J, 1987 Cledemutha: a late Saxon Burh in North Wales, *Medieval Archaeol*, **31**, 13–46

Manley, J & Healey, E 1982 (1983) Excavations at Hendre, Rhuddlan: the Mesolithic finds, *Archaeol Cambrensis*, **131**, 18–48

Manning, W H, 1985 *Catalogue of the Romano-British Iron Tools, Fittings and Weapons in the British Museum*. London: British Museum

Mason, D J P, 1985 *Excavations at Chester, 26–42 Lower Bridge Street 1974-6. The Dark Age and Saxon Periods*. Chester: Grosvenor Mus Archaeol Excav Survey Rep 3

Mayes, P, 1967 The Leeds kiln experiment, *Curr Archaeol*, **4**, 94–7

Mellars, P & Reinhardt, S C, 1978 Patterns of Mesolithic land-use in Southern England: a geological perspective, in P Mellars (ed) *The Early Postglacial Settlement of Northern Europe*, 243–93. London: Duckworth

Messham, J E, 1968 The County of Flint and the Rebellion of Owen Glyndŵr, *Flintshire Hist Soc Publ*, **23**, 1–33

Messham, J E, Manley, J F & Morgan, D, 1980 Excavations at Hendre, Rhuddlan 1978, *Flintshire Hist Soc Publ*, **29**, 113–41

Miket, R, 1974 Thirlings, *Medieval Village Res Group Rep*, **22**, 26–7

Mikkelsen, E, 1978 Seasonality and Mesolithic adaptation in Norway, in K Kristiansen & C Paludan-Müller (eds), *New Directions in Scandinavian Archaeology*, 79–119, Studies in Scandinavian Prehistory and early History 1. Copenhagen: National Museum of Denmark

Miles, H, 1971–72 (1972) Excavations at Rhuddlan, 1969–71: interim report, *Flintshire Hist Soc Publ*, **25**, 1–8

Miles, H, 1972 Rhuddlan, *Curr Archaeol*, **32**, 245–8

Miles, H, 1977a Rhuddlan, in P J Davey (ed), *Medieval Pottery from Excavations in the North West*, 60–1. University of Liverpool

Miles, H, 1977b Rhuddlan Kiln, in P J Davey (ed), *Medieval Pottery from Excavations in the North West*, 100–1. University of Liverpool

Mold, Q, 1979 The iron nails, in G H Smith, The excavation of the Hospital of St Mary of Ospringe, commonly called Maison Dieu, *Archaeol Cantiana*, **95**, 148–52

Monk, M A, 1981 Post-Roman drying kilns and the problem of function: a preliminary statement, in D O'Corrain (ed), *Irish Antiquity: Essays and Studies Presented to Professor M J O'Kelly*, 216–30. Cork: Tower Books

Moore, D T, 1978 The petrography and archaeology of English honestones, *J Archaeol Sci*, **5**, 61–73

Morris, E L, 1985 Prehistoric salt distributions: two case studies from Western Britain, *Bull Board Celtic Stud*, **32**, 336–79

Morris, J H, 1923 Finds of Neolithic and Bronze Age antiquity from under the submerged forest beds at Rhyl, *Archaeol Cambrensis*, **78**, 151–3

Morris, J (ed), 1980 *Nennius, British History and the Welsh Annals*. Phillimore: London & Chichester

Morrison, A, 1968 Cinerary urns and Pygmy vessels in South West Scotland, *Trans Dumfriesshire Galloway Natur Hist Antiq Soc*, **45**, 80–140

Murphy, K, 1987 Excavations at Llanychlwydog Church, Dyfed, *Archaeol Cambrensis*, **136**, 77–93

Murray, H, 1981 Houses and other structures from the Dublin excavations 1962-76; a summary, in H Bekker-Nielsen, P Foote & O Olsen (eds), *Proc Eighth Viking Congress*, 57–68. Odense

Murray, H, 1983 *Viking and Early Medieval Buildings in Dublin*. Oxford BAR Brit Ser 119

Musson, C R, 1991 *The Breiddin Hillfort: a Later Prehistoric Settlement in the Welsh Marches*, CBA Res Rep, 76

Musson, C R & Spurgeon, C J, 1988 Cwrt Llechrhyd, Llanelweddi: an unusual moated site in central Powys, *Medieval Archaeol*, **32**, 97–109

234

Musty, J, 1974 A classification of medieval kilns, in V I Evison, H Hodges, & J G Hurst (eds), *Medieval Pottery from Excavations: Studies Presented to Gerald Clough Dunning*, 41–65. London: John Baker

Musty, J, Algar, D & Ewence, P F, 1969 The medieval pottery kilns at Laverstock near Salisbury, Wilts, *Archaeologia*, **102**, 83–150

Nash-Williams, V E, 1950 *The Early Christian Monuments of Wales*. Cardiff: University of Wales Press

Neaverson, E , 1947 *Medieval Castles in North Wales, A Study of Sites, Water Supply and Building Stones*. Liverpool: University Press & London: Hodder & Stoughton

Newcomer, M H, 1975 Spontaneous retouch, in F H G Engelen (ed), *Second International Symposium on Flint, Staringia*, **3**, 62–4. Maastricht: Nederlandse Geologische Vereiniging

Newell, R R, 1981 Mesolithic dwelling structures: fact and fantasy, in *Mesolithikum in Europa, Veröffentlichungen des Museums für Ur und Frühgeschichte*, **14–15**, 235–85. Potsdam

Newstead, R, 1933 Medieval pottery and kiln at Ashton near Chester, *Liverpool Annals Archaeol Anthrop*, **21**, 5–26

Noddle, B A, 1985 The animal bones, in R Shoesmith (ed), *Hereford City Excavations: volume 3, the finds*, 84–96 and fiche m8.c8–m9.a13, CBA Res Rep 56

North, J J, 1963 *English Hammered Coinage*, **I**. London: Spink

O'Connor, R, 1985a On quantifying vertebrates – some sceptical observations, *Circaea*, **3(1)**, 27–30

O'Connor, R 1985b *Selected Groups of Bones from Skeldergate and Walmgate*. CBA, The Archaeology of York 15/1

O'Leary, T J, 1989 Pentre Farm, Flint, 1976–81. *An Official Building in the Roman Lead Mining District*. Oxford: BAR Brit Ser 207

Olsen, S L (ed), 1988 *Scanning Electron Microscopy in Archaeology*. Oxford: BAR Int Ser 452

O'Neil, B H St J, 1944–5 (1945) Criccieth Castle, Caernarvonshire, *Archaeol Cambrensis*, **98**, 1–51

O'Riordáin, B, 1971 Excavations at High Street and Winetavern Street, Dublin, *Medieval Archaeol*, **15**, 73–85

Oswald, A, 1962–63 (1964) Excavation of a thirteenth-century wooden building at Weolsy Castle, Birmingham, 1960–61, *Medieval Archaeol*, **6–7**, 109–34

Palmer, S, 1970 Second report on excavations at Portland Site I, 1967 to 1968, *Proc Dorset Natur Hist Archaeol Soc*, **92**, 168–80

Palmer, S, 1977 *Mesolithic Cultures of Britain*. Poole: Dolphin Press

Palmer, S, 1984 The Hengistbury Head figurine; further considerations, *Proc Dorset Natur Hist Archaeol Soc*, **106**, 127–8

Paludan-Müller, C, 1978 High Atlantic food gathering in north western Zealand, ecological conditions and spatial representation, in K Kristiansen & C Paludan-Müller (eds), *New Directions in Scandinavian Archaeology*, 120–57. Copenhagen: National Museum of Denmark

Peate, I C, 1946 (3rd ed) *The Welsh House*. Liverpool: Brython Press

Pennant, T, 1784 *Tours in Wales Vol 2*. London: Wilkie & Robinson

Pirie, E J E, 1964 *Grosvenor Museum, Chester, pt i; Coins with the Chester Mint Signature. (Sylloge of Coins of the British Isles, 5)*. London: the British Academy

Petersen, E B, 1971 Svaerdborg II: a Maglemose hut from Svaerdborg Bog, Zealand, Denmark, *Acta Archaeologica*, **42**, 43–77

Pitts, M W, 1978a On the shape of waste flakes as an index of technological change in lithic industries, *J Archaeol Sci*, **5**, 17–37

Pitts, M W, 1978b Towards an understanding of flint industries in post-glacial England, *Bull Inst Archaeol Univ London*, **15**, 179–97

Pitts, M W, 1979 Hides and antlers: a new look at the gatherer-hunter site at Star Carr, North Yorkshire, England, *World Archaeol*, **11(1)**, 32–42

Pitts, M W & Jacobi, R M, 1979 Some aspects of change in flaked stone industries of the Mesolithic and Neolithic in Southern Britain, *J Archaeol Sci*, **6**, 163–77

Platt, C & Coleman-Smith, R, 1975 *Excavations in Medieval Southampton 1953–1969: Volume 2 The Finds*. Leicester: Leicester University Press

Potts, R & Shipman, P, 1981 Cutmarks made by stone tools on bones from Olduvai Gorge, Tanzania, *Nature*, **291**, 577–80

Powell, T G E, 1973 Excavations of the Megalithic chambered cairn at Dyffryn Ardudwy, Merioneth, Wales, *Archaeologia*, **104**, 1–49

Powell, T G E, Corcoran, J X W P, Lynch, F & Scott, J G, 1969 *Megalithic Enquiries in the West of Britain*. Liverpool University Press

Pritchard, F, 1991 Small Finds in A Vince (ed), *Aspects of Saxo-Norman London: II Finds and Environmental Evidence*, 120–278. Museum of London/London & Middlesex Archaeological Society

Radcliffe, F & Knight, J, 1972–3 (1973) Excavations at Abergavenny 1962–9, ii Medieval and later, *Monmouthshire Antiq*, **3**, 65–103

Radford, C A R, 1963 The native ecclesiastical architecture of Wales: the study of a regional style, in I L C Foster & L Alcock (eds), *Culture and Environment*, 355–72. London: Routledge Kegan Paul

Radford, C A R, 1978 The later pre-Conquest boroughs and their defences, *Proc Brit Acad*, **64**, 131–53

Radley, J, 1971 Economic aspects of Anglo-Danish York, *Medieval Archaeol*, **15**, 37–57

Radley, J, Switsur, V R & Tallis, J H, 1974 The

excavation of three 'Narrow Blade' Mesolithic sites in the southern Pennines, England, *Proc Prehist Soc*, **40**, 1–19

Raftery, B, 1981 Iron Age burials in Ireland, in D O'Corráin (ed) *Irish Antiquity: Essays and Studies Presented to Professor M J O'Kelly*, 173–204. Cork: Tower Books

Rahtz, P A, 1969 *Excavations at King John's Hunting Lodge, Writtle, Essex, 1955–7*, Soc Medieval Archaeol Mono Ser No 3

Rahtz, P A, 1976 Buildings and rural settlement, in D M Wilson (ed), *The Archaeology of Anglo-Saxon England*, 49–98. London: Methuen

Rankine, W F, 1952 A Mesolithic chipping floor at the Warren, Oakhanger, Selborne, Hants, *Proc Prehist Soc*, **18**, 21–35

Reynolds, P, 1981 Deadstock and livestock, in R Mercer (ed), *Farming Practice in British Prehistory*, 97–122. Edinburgh University Press

Rigold, S E & Fleming, A J, 1973 Eynsford Castle: the moat and bridge, *Archaeol Cantiana*, **88**, 87–116

RCHME, 1972 *An Inventory of the Historical Monuments in the City of York*, **3**. London: Royal Commission on Historical Monuments England

RCHM(W) 1912 *County of Flint*. Cardiff: Royal Commission on the Ancient and Historical Monuments of Wales

Roberts, A, in prep *Aspects of the Mesolithic in South West Britain*: Oxford DPhil thesis in progress

Ruddy, H E, 1914 Summer excursions, *Proc Dyserth Dist Fld Club* for 1914, 14–20

Rutter, J A A, 1980 *An Important Collection of Pottery Wasters from the Arrowcroft Site 1979*. Unpublished note prepared for Chester City Council Amenities Commitee

Rutter, J A A, 1990 Pottery from the Dominican Friary, in S W Ward, *Excavations at Chester: the Lesser Medieval Religious Houses*, 138–63. Chester

Salzman, L F, 1967 *Building in England Down to 1540*, 2nd ed. Oxford: Clarendon Press

Sargent, H C, 1923 The massive chert formation of north Flintshire, *Geol Mag*, **60**, 168–83

Saville, A, 1977 Two Mesolithic implement types, *Northamptonshire Archaeol*, **12**, 3–8

Saville, A, 1979 *Towards a standardized classification for post-Mesolithic flints* (Unpubl paper presented at a meeting of the Lithic Studies Soc in Cheltenham, March 1979)

Saville, A, 1984 Palaeolithic and Mesolithic evidence from Gloucestershire, in A Saville (ed), *Archaeology in Gloucestershire: from the Earliest Hunters to the Industrial Age*, 59–79. Cheltenham: Cheltenham Art Gallery and Museums/Bristol and Gloucestershire Archaeological Society

Savory, H N, 1958 The late Bronze Age in Wales: some new discoveries and new interpretations, *Archaeol Cambrensis*, **107**, 3–63

Savory, H N, 1970 The later Prehistoric migrations across the Irish Sea, in D Moore (ed), *The Irish Sea Province in Archaeology and History*, 38–49. Cardiff: Cambrian Archaeological Association

Savory, H N, 1971a A Welsh late Bronze Age hillfort, *Antiquity*, **45**, 251–61

Savory, H N, 1971b *Excavations at Dinorben, 1965–9*. Cardiff: National Museum of Wales

Savory, H N, 1976 Welsh hillforts: a reappraisal of recent research, in D W Harding (ed), *Hillforts: Later Prehistoric Earthworks in Britain and Ireland*, 237–91. London: Academic Press

Savory, H N, 1980a The Neolithic in Wales, in J A Taylor (ed), *Culture and Environment in Prehistoric Wales*, 207–32. Oxford: BAR Brit Ser 76

Savory, H N, 1980b *Guide Catalogue of the Bronze Age Collections*. Cardiff: National Museum of Wales

Sheridan, R, Sheridan, P, & Hassen, P, 1967 Rescue excavations of a Mesolithic site at Greenham Dairy Farm, Newbury, 1963, *Trans Newbury Dist Fld Club*, **11(4)**, 66–73

Shipman, P & Rose, J J, 1983 Early hominid hunting, butchering and carcass-processing behaviours: approaches to the fossil record, *Journal of Anthropological Archaeology*, **2**, 57–98

Shoesmith, R, 1985 *Hereford City Excavations: volume 3, the finds*, CBA Res Rep, 56

Simmons, I G, Dimbleby, G W & Grigson, C, 1981 The Mesolithic, in I G Simmons & M J Tooley (eds), *The Environment in British Prehistory*, 82–124. London: Duckworth

Smith, B & George, T N, 1961 *British Regional Geology: North Wales*. London: HMSO

Smith, C, 1989 British antler mattocks, in C Bonsall (ed), *The Mesolithic in Europe: Papers presented at the Third International Symposium Edinburgh 1985*, 272–83. Edinburgh: John Donald

Smith, F G, 1924 Some evidence of early man within and near to the northern portion of the Vale of Clwyd, *Proc Liverpool Geol Soc*, **14**, 117–22

Smith, F G, 1926, Prehistoric remains at Bryn Newydd, Prestatyn, *Proc Llandudno Dist Fld Club*, **13**, 66–72

Smith, I F, 1965 *Windmill Hill and Avebury: Excavations by Alexander Keiller, 1925–1939*. Oxford: Clarendon Press

Smith, I F, 1969 Pottery and flints from sites A, B, C, D and M, in A Oswald (ed), Excavations for the Avon/Severn Research Committee at Barford, Warwickshire, *Trans Birmingham Archaeol Soc*, **83**, 33–7

Smith, I F, 1979 The chronology of British stone implements, in T H McM Clough W A Cummins (eds), *Stone Axe Studies*, 13–22, CBA Res Rep 23

Smith, R A, 1934 Examples of Mesolithic art, *Brit Mus Quart*, **121, Vol 8, No 4**, 144–5

Soulsby, I, 1983 *The Towns of Medieval Wales*. Chichester: Phillimore

Soulsby, I & Jones, D, 1976 *Historic Towns of the Rhuddlan District: Archaeological Implications of Redevelopment*. Cardiff: Urban Research Unit, Department of Archaeology, University College

Stanford, S C, 1982 Bromfield, Shropshire – Neolithic, Beaker and Bronze Age sites, *Proc Prehist Soc*, **48**, 279–320

Stenton, F M (ed), 1957 *The Bayeux Tapestry*. London: Phaidon

Stenton, F M, 1971 *Anglo-Saxon England*, 3rd edn. Oxford: Clarendon Press

Strahan, A, 1885 *The Geology of the Coasts adjoining Rhyl, Abergele and Colwyn*. HMSO: Memoirs of the Geological Survey of Great Britain

Stuiver, M, 1982 A high-precision calibration of the AD radiocarbon timescale, *Radiocarbon*, **24 No 1**, 1–26

Stuiver, M & Pearson, G W, 1986 High-precision calibration of the radiocarbon timescale, AD 1950–500 BC, *Radiocarbon*, **28 No 2b**, 805–39

Swan, V G, 1973 Aspects of the New Forest late-Roman, Pottery Industry, in A Detsicas (ed), *Current Research in Romano-British Coarse Pottery*, 117–34, CBA Res Rep 10

Swan, V G, 1984 *The Pottery Kilns of Roman Britain*. London: Royal Commission on Historical Monuments (England)

Switsur, V R & Jacobi, R M, 1975 Radiocarbon dates for the Pennine Mesolithic, *Nature*, **256**, 32–4

Sylvester, R, 1955 Settlement patterns in rural Flintshire, *Flintshire Hist Soc Publ*, **15**, 6–42

Tait, J, 1925 Flintshire in Domesday Book, *Flintshire Hist Soc Publ*, **11**, 1–37

Taylor, A J, 1955 Rhuddlan Cathedral: a 'might-have-been' of Flintshire history, *Flintshire Hist Soc Publ*, **15**, 43–51

Taylor, A J, 1956 *Rhuddlan Castle, Flintshire, Official Guide Book*, 2nd ed. HMSO

Taylor, A J, 1963 The King's Works in Wales 1277–1330, in H M Colvin (ed), *The History of the King's Works: The Middle Ages*, 318–27. HMSO

Taylor, A J, 1976 The earliest burgesses of Flint and Rhuddlan, *Flintshire Hist Soc Publ*, **27**, 152–9

Taylor, A J, 1984 A shipwreck near Rhuddlan in 1310, *Flintshire Hist Soc Publ*, **31**, 57–70

Taylor, P D, 1986 Scanning electron microscopy of uncoated fossils, *Palaeontology*, **29**, 685–90

Tester, P J & Caiger, J E L, 1958 Medieval buildings in the Joyden's Wood square earthwork, *Archaeol Cantiana*, **72**, 18–40

Thomas, C, 1968 Thirteenth century farm economics in North Wales, in *Agricultural Hist Rev*, **16**, 1–14

Thomas, C, 1981 *A Provisional List of Imported Pottery in Post-Roman western Britain and Ireland*. Camborne: Institute of Cornish Studies Special Report No 7

Thomas, H J & Dowdell, G, 1987 A shrunken medieval village at Barry, Glamorgan, *Archaeol Cambrensis*, **136**, 94–137

Tixier, J 1974 Glossary for description of stone tools, *Newsletter of Lithic Technology*, Special Publication No 1

Tringham, R, Cooper, G, Odell, G, Voytek, B, & Withman, A, 1974 Experimentation in the formation of edge damage: a new approach to lithic analysis, *J Field Archaeol*, **1**, 171–96

Turner, H L, 1971 *Town Defences in England and Wales*. London: John Baker

Tweddle, D, 1986 *Finds from Parliament Street and other Sites in the City Centre, The Archaeology of York*, **17**, fasicule 4, CBA for York Archaeological Trust

Tylecote, R F, 1975 Metallurgical report on padlock bolts, in G Beresford *The Medieval Clay-Land Village: Excavations at Goltho and Barton Blount*, 85, Soc Medieval Archaeol Mono Ser No 6

Uerpmann, H-P, 1973 Animal bone finds and economic archaeology: a critical study of 'osteo-archaeological' method, *World Archaeol*, **4**, 307–22

Unger-Hamilton, R, 1984 *Method in Microwear Analysis: sickles, blades and other tools from Arjoune, Syria*. University of London, Institute of Archaeology, unpublished PhD thesis

Vebaek, C L, 1938 New finds of Mesolithic ornamental bone and antler artefacts in Denmark, *Acta Archaeologica*, **9**, 205–23

Vince, A G, 1985 The Saxon and medieval pottery of London: a review, *Medieval Archaeol*, **28**, 25–93

Wainwright, F J, 1950 Cledemutha, *Engl Hist Rev*, **65**, 203–12

Wainwright, G J, 1963 A re-interpretation of the microlithic industries of Wales, *Proc Prehist Soc*, **29**, 99–132

Warren, P T, Nutt, M J C & Smith, E G, 1984 *Geology of the country around Rhyl and Denbigh. Memoir for 1:50000 geological sheets 95 & 107*. British Geological Survey. HMSO

Warrilow, W, Owen, G & Britnell, W, 1986 Eight ring-ditches at Four Crosses, Llandysilio, Powys, 1981–85, *Proc Prehist Soc*, **52**, 53–87

Waterman, D M, 1954 Excavations at Clough Castle, Co Down, *Ulster J Archaeol (ser 3)*, **17**, 103–63

Waters, W H, 1929 A first draft of the statute of Rhuddlan, *Bull Board Celtic Stud*, **4**, 345–8

Webster, G, 1960 A medieval pottery kiln at Audlem, Cheshire, *Medieval Archaeol*, **4**, 109–25

Webster, P V, 1976 Severn Valley Ware: a Preliminary Study, *Trans Bristol Gloucestershire Archaeol Soc*, **95**, 18–46

West, S, 1985 West Stow, The Anglo-Saxon Village. Volume 2: Figures and Plates, *E Anglian Archaeol Rep*, **24**

Wheeler, A, 1978 *Key to the Fishes of Northern Europe*. London: Warne

Whimster, R, 1989 *The Emerging Past: Air Photography and the Buried Landscape*. London: Royal Commission on the Historical Monuments of England

White, R B, 1978 Excavations at Trwyn Du, Anglesey 1974, *Archaeol Cambrensis*, **127**, 16–39

Whitelock, D, 1955 *English Historical Documents c 500–1042*. English Historical Documents 2. London: Eyre & Spottiswoode

Williams, J H, 1979 *St Peter's Street, Northampton. Excavations 1973–1976*. Northampton Development Corporation Archaeol Mono No 2

Williams, J L & Jenkins, D A, 1976 The use of petrographic, heavy mineral and arc spectographic techniques in assessing the provenance of sediments used in ceramics, in D A Davidson & M L Shackley (eds), *Geoarchaeometry; earth science and the past*, 115–35. London: Duckworth

Wilson, D M, 1976 Craft and Industry, in D M Wilson, *The Archaeology of Anglo-Saxon England*, 253–81. London: Methuen

Woodman, P C, 1985 *Excavations at Mount Sandel 1973–77*. Belfast: HMSO, Northern Ireland Archaeological Monographs No 2

Wymer, J J, 1962 Excavations at the Maglemosian sites at Thatcham, Berkshire, England, *Proc Prehist Soc*, **28**, 329–54

Wymer, J J (ed), 1977 *Gazetteer of Mesolithic Sites in England and Wales*, CBA Res Rep 20

Index

1 All page references are to Rhuddlan unless otherwise indicated.
2 Page numbers in *italics* indicate pages where an illustration can be found.

Abbey Farm 3, 82, 94
Abbey Nurseries *see* Site A
Abbey Road 5, 224, 225
　Site G 94
　see also Site A
Aberconwy, Treaty of 219, 220
Aberffraw, Anglesey 113
Abergavenny, Gwent 214, 215
Abergele, Clwyd 189
Abingdon, Oxfordshire 163
Abinger Common, Surrey 105
adzes *see under* axes
aerial photography *2*, 139, 145
Aethelflaeda 7, 212
agriculture viii, 3, 46, 50, 52, 56, 82, 139, 145, 146,
　218, 223, 224, 225
　crop husbandry 92, 161–3
　livestock rearing 43, 129, 153, 156, 159
　ploughmarks 33, 34, 87, 88, 90, 91, 144, 145, 209,
　　215, 216
　　Site T *27*, 31, 33, 34
　settlements 208, 209
　Site D 91
　Site E 70, 71
ale, brewing of 9
Aled reservoir 130
Alpine region 25
amber objects 125
Anarawad 7
Ancient Monuments 1, 72, 84
Ancient Monuments Laboratory (D of E) 72
Anglesey 7, 95, 113, 126, 127, 164
Anglo-Normans *see* Norman; Saxo-Norman period
Anglo-Saxon Chronicle: Mercian Register 7
Anian of St Asaph, Bishop 221–2, 223
animals
　bones *see under* bone
　for hunting 129–30
　livestock rearing 43, 129, 153, 156
　small mammals 130, 147, 157–8
　ungulates *see* cattle/sheep
　see also individual animals
Annales Cambriae 7, 34
antler 14, 110
　art form 125
　objects 130, 169–70, *171–2*
Archaeology in Wales (CBA) 1
archives 5–6
Ardleigh group, Essex 138

arrowheads 82, *106*, *113*
　flint 138
　iron 5, 188, *189*
arrows 110
artwork, Mesolithic 124–6
Ashton, Cheshire 56, 192
Aston hoard (coins) 217
Atiscross, hundred of 8
Audlem, Cheshire 56, 192, 217
auger bit, iron 178
aurochs 129
Aveline's Hole (cave) 130
awls *106*, *109*, 110, *111*–12
axes *106*, *112*
　adzes 113, *142*
　antler 125
　iron 178
　stone 139
Azilian pebbles 124

Baile Hill, York 178
bakestones *173*, 175, 224
baking, of bread 9, 173
Baldwin (Archbishop of Canterbury) 8, 216
Barford, Warks 138
barley 160, 161, 162
barrel padlock *see* padlocks
barrows *see under* burials
Barry, Glam 173
Basingwerk, Clwyd 7, 8, 165, 216
bass 158
Bath 154
Bayeux Tapestry 178
beads, shale 110
beans 10, 160, 161
Beaumaris, Gwynedd 222
Beeston, Cheshire 192
Benton Castle, Pembs 113
berms 210, 212–13
Bernard, Richard: appointed rector 8
binding strip, iron 180, *181*
birds 130, 147, *158*
　bones *152*
Black Death 9, 224, 225
blacksmiths *see* smiths/smithing
blades 5, 99, 100, 103, 104, *105*, *109*, 126, 128
Blaenau Ffestiniog, Gwynedd 67
Bleddyn ap Cynan (Welsh ruler) 8
Blubberhouse Moor, Wharfedale (Yorks) 98
boar, wild 129
bolts *181*, 182, 183–5
bone
　animal 6, 42, 92, 128, *148*, *156–7*, 211, 219
　　exploitation 153–9

quantification of species 151, *152–3*
taphonomic evidence 147, *149–50*
see also individual animals
as art 125
fragments 38
human 72, 77, 79–81, 82, 130, 134, 137
objects 124, *169*, *170*
tool cutmarks on 120
trial pieces 16, *169*, 209, 210, 213
working 110
Borough, Edwardian 43, 46, 56, 70, 82, 189
Defences 1, 5, 54, 84, *85–8*, 89–91, 144, 165, 212, 216
pottery 191
Princes Road 92
foundation viii, 1, 3, 4, 9, 10, 84, 219–23
later history 225–6
'le Oldtown' 223–5
Borough, Norman viii *2*, 139, 164, 214–18, 224–5
Defences 144, 209, 210, 212–13, 223
Site A 11–26
Site E 57–71
Site T 27–46
Site V 47–56
Borre style (bone trial pieces) 169
botanical remains *see* plants
bowls, ceramic 25, 138, 143, 144, 192, 193, *194*, 197–8, 207
bracken 113
bread
baking 9, 173
wheat 160, 161, 163
Breiddon, Mont 138
brewing 9, 10
bridge: Rhuddlan 9
Bristol 164, 175
British Museum 142
Bromfield, Shrops 136, 137
Bronze Age 145, 171
Earlier
lithics 110, 113
pottery 11, 59
animal bones 147
iron slag 189
lithic material *97*, *108*, 130, 138
pottery 84, 132, *133*, 134, *135*, 136–9, 140, 163
Sites 6, 11, 57, *59*
bronze objects *141*, 142, 165, 167
brooches 5, 146, 165
Broomhead 128
Moor 98
Bryn Llithnig, Cwn Diserth 169
Bryn Maelgwyn: Cnut hoard 164
Bryn Newydd, Prestatyn 130
Bryn Teg: Site S (Princes Road) 92, *93*, 94
buckets 183, 220
buckles
copper alloy 165, 188
iron 185–6, *187*
buildings/structures 34, 82
houses 11, 25, 144–5, 178
ironwork/fittings 180, *181–2*, 183

timber and viii, 14, 18, 20, *24*, 43, 45, 46, 139, 211, 213, 222
see also Grubenhäuser and under individual Sites
burhs viii, 2, 5, 7, 209–10, 212, 213, 214–15
burials 130, 145, 164, 212, 216
barrows 137, 138, 139
cemeteries viii, 9, 72, 136, 144
'grave pit' 79
horse 92
Site M *77–81*, 82–3, 189, 208, 215, 217
butchery 130, 151, *154*, *156–7*, 159
Buttington, battle of 7
buzzard bones 158

Cadw (Dept of the Environment) ii, 72, 84
Caernarfon, Gwynedd 9, 222
Caersws, Powys 142
candlesticks, iron *182*
Canterbury
Grubenhäuser 14
See of 8, 216
Capel Maelog Church: Llandrindod Wells, Powys 82
Caradog (King of Gwynedd) 7
Cardiff 214
Castell-y-Bere (castle) 183, 188
Castle, Edwardian (at Rhuddlan) viii, 1, 3, 45, 46, *47*, 54, 57, 145, 158, 164, 188, 191, 224
building 9, 66, 67, 176–7, 220–1, 222
defences 165
Castle Hill, Lôn Hylas: Site K 2, 93–4, *96*, 220
Castle Street (Rhuddlan) 5, 10, 221, 222
castles 158–9, 188, 190, 216, 217, 218, 222
at Rhuddlan 8, 9, 10
hillforts 138, 141, 144, 145
motte and bailey (Twt Hill) 1, 2, 8, 213, 214
see also Castle, Edwardian *and* individual castles
cats: bones *152*, 157, *158*
cattle: bones 147, 149, *150*, *151–2*, 153, *154–5*, 156, 159, 211
cauldrons 183
caves 130, 136, 139
Cefn Graenog (Gwynedd) 25, 161
Cefn-Y-Fedw 140
cemeteries *see under* burials
cereals 18, 139, 160–3, 210, 223, 224
grain store 139, 225
oats 10, 41, 43, 160, 161, 162, 163, 210, 223, 224
wheat 10, 160, 161, 163
see also kilns, corn drying
chains *182*, 183, 220
Chalton, Hants: house construction 25
charcoal 14, 16, 20, 24, 25, 26, 31, 33, 34, 37, 38, 41, 45–6, 49, 50, 52, 54, 66–7, 75, 76, 77, 160, 210, 220, 224
analysis: plants *162*, 163
for dating 127, 128
Site K 93–4
charter: Rhuddlan 9
Cheddar, Somerset 178
cheek pieces 171
chert 27, *96–8*, 99, *101–2*, *103*, *104*, *107*, 112, 126

Carboniferous chert 95, *97*, 98, 100, *101*, *105–6*, *108–9*, *111*, 113, 130, 138
   Gronant 95, 120
   industry viii
   struck 47, 57
   tools 5, *110*, 120, *121*, *122*, 123, 124, 126
   worked 11, 48, 72, 75
Cheshire 56, 140, 144, 193
   potters from 54, 217, 221
   pottery 192, 207
Chester, Earl of *see* Hugh of Avranches
Chester 7, 8, 56, 88, 207, 209, 210, 211, 212, 217, 219
   Grubenhäuser 14
   mint 164
   pottery 191, 192, 193, 217
   See of 215
chisels 142
Christchurch, Hants 183
Church Street (Rhuddlan) 221
churches 3, 8, 25, 82
   Norman Church 48, 72, *73–8*, *79–80*, 81–3, 164, 168, 189, 190, 212, 215, 217, 223, 225
   St Mary's Church 4–5, 9, 82, 222
claw hammers 178
clay 14, 16, 24, 26, 43, 50, 136
   burnt 25, 56, 189
   fired 34, 168–9
   pottery 132
Cledemutha ii, viii, 5, 7, 164, 209–13
cloth industry 178–9
   fulling 60
   spinning *172*
   weaving 60
   wool 155, 159, 178
Clough Castle, Co. Down 178
Clwyd Archaeological Record 2, 169
Clwyd Bridge 221
Clwyd County Council 5, 72
Clwyd Record Office 1, 82, 226
Clwyd, River viii, 2, 93, 94, 119, 145, 146, 164, 208, 209, 210, 217, 222, 224
   canalisation of 1, 9, 220–1
   ford 8, 214
   site of *Cledemutha* 7
   street alignment with 3
Clwyd-Powys Archaeological Trust ii, 2, 5, 92, 191, 222
Clynnog: Cefn Graenog, Gwynedd: farmstead 25
Cnut hoard (Bryn Maelgwyn) 164
coal 56, 66, 175, 189, 190, 220
Coal Measures 1, 45, 67, 119, 173, 192
cockle shells 65
cod 158
coffins 79, *81*
coins viii, 5, 79, *81*, 146, 164–5, 217, 218
   Edward I 38, 43, 46, 164, 219, 224
   Edward the Confessor 14, 164, 213
   William I 216
   William II 164, 215
   William Rufus 82, 215
Colchester 142, 171

Collfryn, Powys 43, 144, 145
combs 169, 178
Conway, Mad'm Elinor 1
Conway Map of 1756 1, 26, 46, 71, 84, 91, 92, 224, 225
Conway, battle of 7
Conwy 9, 161, 217, 222
Conwy: river and valley 7, 9, 208
cooking pots/vessels 165, 193, *194*, 197, 199, 201–2, 203, 205, 206
copper alloy 165, *166*, 181, 183, 184
   buckle 165, 188
   rin-headed pin 140
Coppergate, York 25, 211
cores *99–100*, *101*, 103, *104*, *105*, 126
corn *see* cereals
corn drying *see* kilns, corn drying
corvids: bones 158
Corwen, Clwyd 67, 82
Cotswolds 109
craftsmen 178, 179, 219
   masons 67, 176, 219
   potters 54, 217, 221
   woodworkers 178, 219
   see also smiths
cremations 59, 132, 134, 136, 137, 139
   see also burials
Criccieth Castle, Caernarvonshire 188
Criccin Farm: Maes y Groes 139
Cricklade, Wilts 210
crosses (St Mary's Church) 5, 82
crows: bones *158*
crusades 8
Culverhole, Glam 136, 137
Culverwell 124
cutlers 179
cwmydau (commotes) 208
Cwrt Llechrhyd, Powys 208
Cynddylan, line of 208

Dafydd of Gwynedd 8, 216, 217
dairying economy 153, 159
dating 126–8, 139
   animal bones 147
   pottery 138
   Site A 11, 13, 14, 16, 18, 20, 25, 26
   Site D 87, 90
   Site E 57, 59, 60, 64, 66, 67, 70
   Site M 75, 76
   Site N 82
   Site S 92
   Site T 33, 34, 36, 38, 43, 46
   Site V 48, 50, 54, 56
   see also radiocarbon dating
Davies, Melvyn 169
Daylight Rock, Pembs 113, 126, 127
Deceangli 146
decorated pebbles *see under* pebbles
Dee Estuary 67, 176
Dee, River 7, 8, 208, 218
deer 125, 129
   bones 128, 149, *152*, 157–8, 159, 169–70

see also antler
defences 5, 7, 84–91, 92, 165, 189, 209, 212
    Edwardian Borough *see under* Borough, Edwardian
    Norman Borough *see under* Borough, Norman
Deganwy 208
    castle 7, 8, 217, 218
Delamere Forest 9
Devon, east: lithic material 99
Dinorben, Clwyd 140, 208
    hillfort 138, 141, 144, 145
Diserth 9, 139, 146, 224
    castle 8, 54, 169, 188, 217, 218
dish: Buckley slipware 46
Dissolution of the Monasteries 3
ditches 2, 5, 54, 209, 210
    boundary 56
    Edwardian Defences 92
    Lôn Hylas 146
    medieval 31, 127
    Norman Borough 14, *15–16*, 25, 26, 139, 214–15, 217
    ring 137, 139
    Site A 134, 189, 214, 215
    Site D 84, 88, 90
    Site E 57, 60, *62–5*, 66–7, 189
    Site K 94
    Site M 72
    Site T *29*, *35*, 36, *37–8*, 41, 43, 45, 46, 189
    Site V 48
    see also Town Ditch
Dogfeiling 208
dogs: bones *152*, 157, *158*
Domesday Book viii, 1, 8, 77, 82, 164, 188, 214, 215, 216
Dominican Friary
    Chester 207
    Rhuddlan 3, 8–9, 94, 212, 218, 219, 222, 224
Dorset 143, 144
'drage' (mixed crop) 162
Dublin 7, 25, 165, 169, 170
Duffield Castle 183
Dyffryn Ardudwy, Merioneth 136, 137

Eadwine of Mercia, Earl 8
earthworks *see* Borough, Edwardian/Norman, Defences; Town Ditch
East Midlands 209
Eddisburg 7, 210
Edgar, King 8, 213
Edward I, King 1, 25, 190, 212
    coins 38, 43, 46, 164, 219, 224
    occupation 54, 189
    pottery 192
    reconquest 9, 218
    relocates church 8
    see also Borough, Edwardian; Castle, Edwardian
Edward the Confessor, King: coins 14, 164, 213
Edward the Elder 7
Edwardian Castle *see* Castle, Edwardian
Edwin ap Gronw (of Tegeingl) 8
Egerton, J 84

Eidsberg, Norway 175
Eldon's Seat 138
elk 129
elm *162*, 163
Elmham Park, Norfolk 184
Elwy: river and valley 7, 67, 139
Emma (wife of Dafydd of Gwynedd) 8
Englefield *see* Tegeingl
Essex 138, 141
Exeter 178
Eynsford Castle, Kent 186

fabricators *106*, *111*, 113
'Fairmead' 5, 92, 222, 225
fairs 9
farriers 178
ferrules, iron *182*, 183
field boundaries 31, 34, 145
Filpoke Beacon 128
fish 126, 130, 147, *152*, 158
Fishergate, Nottingham 43
fishing industry 158
flakes 95, 97, 100, *101–4*, *105*, *106*, 107, *112*, 113, 126
flax combs 178
Flint Castle 9, 222
Flint (town) 9, 173, 212, *219–20*
flint 27, 47, 57, 72, 75, 95, *96*, *98–9*, 100, *101*, *103*, *104–5*, *107*, *108–9*, *111–12*, *113*, 130
    arrowhead 138
    as artwork 126
    beach pebble 120
    cores 126
    flakes 107, 126
    scrapers *110*
    tools 120, *122*, 123, 124, 126
    worked 11, 48
Flints Ministers Accounts 9
Flints Plea Rolls 10
Flintshire 1, 192, 215
    coalfields 175
    County Council (now Clwyd) 72, 84
    County Record Office 72
    Historical Society ii
    Roman sites 146
food
    debris 159, 210, 219
    and diet 43, 158
    hunting/gathering 126, 129–30, 170
    marketing 10
    meat/meat consumption 113, 151, 154, 159
    preparation 9, 173, 179
    processing 109
    see also cooking pots
Four Crosses, Llandysilio, Mont 136, 137, 138
fowl, domestic: bones *152*, *158*
fuel: kilns 56, 163
fulling 60
furniture, household 180, 184

gaming counter, stone *172*
Gascony 222

geese: bones *152, 158*
geology viii, 1, 4, 11, 47, 67, 99, 119, 129, 134, 136, 139, 175–6
  Cambrian deposits 38
  Site D 84
geophysical survey 72, 82
Giraldus Cambrensis 8, 165, 216
glass *168*
Glebe 84
goats: bones 149, *150*, 151, *152*, *153*, *155*, 159
Goltho Manor, Lincolnshire 183, 184
Goode, Mr A J J (British Geological Survey) 119
Gop Cave 130
Gop, Prestatyn 130, 139
Gough's Cave 130
Graig Llwyd 139
grain *see* cereals
grain drying *see* kilns, corn drying
graves *see* burials
Great Orme 7
Greenham Dairy Farm, Berks 128
Greensted Church, Essex 25
Greyfriars, Oxford 183
Grubenhäuser 13, 14, 34, 36, 167, 169, 189, 211
Gruffudd ap Llywelyn of Gwynedd 8, 213
gullies 50, 127, 140, 144
  Site A 11, 13, 14, 24, 26, 145, 146
  Site D 87, 88, 90, 91
  Site E 65, 66, 70, 71
  Site M 75, *76*
  Site S 92
  Site T 27, *29*, 31, *32*, 33, 34, 209
  Site V 48, 49, 50, 56
Gwaenysgor, Clwyd 139
Gwernvale: Usk valley 130
Gwindy Street (Rhuddlan) 3, 221
  see also Site D
Gwithian, Cornwall 88
Gwynedd 8, 9, 25, 212, 215, 217, 219, 222
  expansion of 208–9, 213

Haddon-Reece, D 72
Halkyn Mountain 164
Halli (moneyer) 217
hammers 66, 178
Hammersmith 140
Hamwih 60
handles
  bone 169
  iron *182–3*
  wood 178, 179
hare: bones 153
Harlech, Gwynedd 222
Harold Godwinson 8, 213
hasps 184, 185
Hawarden: County Record Office 82
Hayes, P 72, 82
hazel 163
hazelnuts 57, 75, 127, 128, 130, *162*
hearths 20, 24, 49, 66, 76, 137, 188, 189, 210, 211, 212, 216, 223
hedge boundaries/lines 84, 91

Hen Blas 206
Hen Caerwys, Clwyd 183
Hen Domen, Montgomery 88
Hendre, Rhuddlan 5, 95, 98, 100, *104*, 105, 109, 129, 130
henge monuments 137
Hengistbury Head, Dorset 104, 124
Henricus (moneyer) 217
Henry I, King 8
Henry II, King 8, 164, 216, 217
Henry III, King viii, 54, 56, 193, 213, 217–18, 219
  pottery 192
  secures Rhuddlan 8, 216
Hereford 154, *155*, 191
hides 110, 112
High Street (Rhuddlan) 10, 221, 222
  Site H 92–3
hillforts 138, 141, 144, 145
hinges, iron 180, *181*
Holbaek district of Zealand (Scandinavia) 126
Holmegård V, Denmark 126
Holy Trinity Church, York 176
Holywell 164
hooks, iron 178–9
horse equipment 186, *187–8*
  horseshoes *67*, 186, *187*, 217, 221, 224
horsehair 43
horses: bones 92, 149, *152*, 157, *158*
horticulture 92
hospital: St John of Jerusalem 5
houses *see* buildings
Howells, Dr M F (British Geological Society) 99
Hugh of Avranches (Earl of Chester) 8, 164, 214
human bones *see under* bone
Humphries, P 72
hunter-gatherer communities 126, 129–30
Hylas lane 82
Hywel Dda 7–8, 213

Idwal, revolt of 7
industries 26, 66, 141
  chert viii
  Site T 45–6
  smithing viii
  waste 36, 37, 43
  see also individual industries
inhumations *see* burials
insects 161
Irish Sea 1, 7
Iron Age viii, 144–6, 208
  animal bones 147
  artefacts 140–2
  bronze objects *141*
  gullies 50
  ironworking 189
  pottery 11, 13, 137, 140–1
  Site A 11
  Site M 72, 76
  Site T 27, 31, 33, 34, *44*
  Site V 48, 49
iron objects viii, 14, 33, 36, 91, 189
  arrowheads 5, 188, *189*

buckles 185–6
building ironwork/fittings 180, *181–2*, 183
horse equipment 14, 186, *187–8*
knives/shears/scissors 60, 82, 169, 179, *180*
locks and keys 183, *184–5*
tools *142*, 178, *179*
iron panning 37, 76, 219
Ironmonger Lane, London 25
ironworking 77, 188–90, 212, 217, 220
smelting 66, 189, 215
smiths/smithing viii, 66, 178, 189, 221, 224
see also slag, iron
Ivinghoe Beacon 138
Iwerne Minster, Dorset 105

jars, ceramic 11, 138, 142, 144, 193, 201, 202, 205, 206
Jellinge style sculpture: York 169
jetons 165
John, King 8, 216, 217
Joydens Wood, Kent 185
jugs, ceramic 18, 20, 25, 26, 56, 193, *194*, 197, 198–205, 207, 221

Kent's Cavern (cave) 130
keys/locks 183–4, *185*
kilns viii, 5, 20, 26, *29*, 142, 172, 175
corn drying viii, 161, 163, 189, 223
Site A *16–17*, 18, 216–18
Site T *37*, 38, *39–42*, 43, 45, 223
pottery viii, *162*, 163, 191, 192, 200, 207
Site V *47*, 50, *52–3*, 54, 56, 193, *194–8*, *201–5*, 217, 221
knapping 100, 103, 106, 126, 130
knives
iron 36, 60, 82, 169, 179, *180*
Saxo-Norman 211

Lake District 1, 134
Lancashire 9
laws 7, 164, 216
le Botiler, Sir Johan 188
lead 34, 38, 50, 164, 165, 220
mining 10
objects *167–8*
leather 79, 164, 188
Lesser Garth, Glam 136–7
Lichfield 212, 215
Lille Knapstrup, Scandinavia 126
limestone 17, 20, 31, 38, 45, 46, 52, 56, 59, 65, 66, 70, 77, *80*, 124, 130, 188, 215
building 82
Carboniferous Limestone 18, 63, 67, 95, 134, 139
graves 79, 80, 81
Site S 92
linen smoother, glass *168*
lithics 5, 57, 75, 92
Bronze Age 138
Mesolithic 95–130 *passim*
Neolithic 84, 138
raw materials 95, *96–8*, 99
utilised/retouched pieces *105–13*, 114

waste material *99*, 100, *101–5*
see also chert; flint; pebbles; rhyolite; stone
Llanarth, Cards 137
Llanblethian, Glam 137
Llandegai, Caerns 136, 137
Llandegla, Denb 137
Llandrindod Wells: Capel Maelog, Powys 82
Llandysilio, Mont 136, 137, 138
Llanelwy *see* St Asaph
Llangollen-Corwen area, Clwyd 82
Llanychlwydog Church, Dyfed 82
Llywelyn ap Gruffudd of Gwynedd 8–9, 54, 218, 219, 220
Llywelyn ap Iorwerth 8, 217
Llywelyn ap Seisyll of Gwynedd 8, 213, 218
Lochmaben Castle, Dumfries and Galloway 183
locks/keys 183–4, *185*
Lôn Hylas 5, 146, 222, 224, 225
Sites E, T, V, K *see* Sites
London 165, 169, 180, 188
City: Pudding Lane 25
Ironmonger Lane 25
mint viii, 164, 215, 218
Museum 165
Longmoor, Hants 128
loomweights 36, 168, *169*, 209, 213
Lower Bridge Street, Chester 191, 211
Lydford, Devon 178, 210

Madoc (priest) 223
Maes y Groes (Criccin Farm): barrow 139
'magic' 38
Malvern 142
mammal bones *see* bone, animal
mammals *see* animals
Manchester 7, 210
markets 8, 9–10, 208–9, 215, 218
Marshfield, Glos 142
masons 67, 176, 219
mattock, antler 130
medieval period 6, 82, 95, 117, 145, 161, 162, 168, 169, 170, 176, 208–26
animal bones 147, 150, 151, 154, *155*
cemetery 144
corn drying kilns 43
ditch 127
Edwardian Castle 3
field boundaries 5
iron objects 178, *179–82*, 183, *184–5*, 186, *187*, 188, *189–90*
lithic material 172, 175
pottery 18, 26, 36, 66, 70, 82, 87, 88, 90–1, 94, 191–207 *passim*
Site A 25–6
Site D 87, 90–1
Site E 57, 59, 60, 65–6
Site S 92
Site T 31, 43, *44*, 45–6
Site V 47, 48, *49*, 50
sites and structures *3*, *4*, 25
stratigraphy 1
late, boundaries 70–1

Mediterranean imports 38
Meols, near Hoylake (Wirral) 164
Mercia viii, 7, 208–9, 210, 212, 213
Mercian Register (Anglo-Saxon Chronicle) 7
Mersey region 7, 193, 210
Mesolithic period 1, 5, 6, *162*, 163
   Early: lithic material 95, 100
   artwork 124–6
   chert blade 5
   decorated pebbles 115, *116–19*, 120, *121–2*, 123–6
   lithic material *97, 98, 99, 101, 104, 105–9, 110, 111–12*, 113, *125*, 126–30, 138
   occupation viii
   Site A 11, *22–3*
   Site E 57, *63, 65, 68–9*
   Site M 72, 75, *76*
   Site S 92
   Site T 27
   Site V 47–8
   Later: lithic material 5, 95, 100
metal
   objects 211
   Romano-British period 142
   tools/artefacts 120, 124
   see also bronze; copper alloy; iron
metalworking 66, 163, 188–90, 221
   see also ironworking
microburins 100, 104, *105, 106*, 110, 130
microdenticulates *106, 111*, 112–13
microliths 57, 95, *98–9*, 104–5, *106–8*, 109–10, 126, 127, 130
microwear analysis 99, 106–7, 110, 112–13
Middlesex 138
Middleton Stoney, Oxfordshire 150, 158, 159
mills 9, 10, 161
mining
   coal 175, 190
   iron 188
   lead 10
mints viii, 7, 8, 164, 209, 212, 215, 216, 217, 218, 219, 223
Moel Hiraddug 188
   hillfort 141, 144, 145
Mold, Clwyd: Shire Hall 2
moles: bone 158
Montgomery 136, 137
   Treaty of 218
Moore, Dr P (London University) 163
Morfa Rhuddlan (marsh) 1, 7, 146, 208
Morton, Fife 105
Mostyn, Clwyd 190
Motton, Richard 225
Mount Sandel, Co Derry 105, 106, 128
Mucking, Essex 141
mussel shells 14, 16, 25, 37, 38, 42, 63, 65, 67
Mynydd Hiraethog foothills 1

Nab Head, Pembs 110, 113, 124, 125, 126, 127
nails 50
   horseshoe 186, *187*, 217, 221, 224
   iron 178, *181–2*

Nant Hall Road, Prestatyn 130
Nantwich 140
National Library of Wales 1
National Museum of Wales ii, 6, 130, 147, 164, 169, 191, 194
Natural History Museum 120
needles 165
Neolithic period 130, 139
   art 125
   lithic material 84, 113, 130, 138
   pottery 137
   Later: lithic material 110, 113
Newmarket 7
Newry hoard (coins) 217
Nidlose, Scandinavia 126
Norfolk 138, 179, 183, 184, 186, 189
Norman
   Borough *see* Borough, Norman
   Church *see under* churches
   Conquest 13
Norman period 1, 8, 54
   see also Saxo-Norman period
Norse *see* Vikings
Northampton 165, 167, 168
Nottingham: Fishergate 43

oak *162*, 163
Oakley, G E 167, 168, 172
oats 10, 41, 43, 160, 161, 162, 163, 210, 223, 224
Offa (King of Mercia) 7, 164, 208, 209
Offa's Dyke 7, 208, 209
Ogof-yr-esgyrn, Brecks 136, 137
Okehampton Castle, Devon 158–9
Olby Lyng, Denmark 125
Ordnance Survey maps 2, *4*
Orkney and Shetland 161
Ospringe, Kent 181
Ostfriesland (Germany) 25
ovens 24, 43, 45
Owain Glyndŵr viii, 10, 91, 225–6
Owain of Gwynedd 8, 215, 216
Owen, M 67, 189
oxen 153
Oxford Castle 184

padlocks 38, 183, *184*, 185, 220
Palaeolithic period, Upper 124
palisades *27, 29, 31*, 36, 38, 88, 210, 212–13
Parliament Street (Rhuddlan) 5, 221
Parliament Street (York) 178
Paviland 130
peas 10, 160, 161
pebbles 95, 223
   Site A 11, 20, 115
   Site D 115
   Site E 57, 59, 115, *116–17*
   Site G 94
   Site M 72, 75, 76, 80, 115
   Site S 92
   Site T 27, 31, 33, 34, 38, 43, 46, 115, 117, *118, 119*
   Site V 47, 48, 49, 50, 115
   decorated viii, 27, 115, *116–19*, 120, *121–2*, 123–6

utilised *125–6*
Penberthy, I O 190
Pennant, T: tour (1784) 2, 3, 93, 220
Pentre, Flint 9, 142
petrological examination 134, 136–8
picks, iron 178, 179
pigs 129–30
  bones 149, *150*, 151, *152*, 153, *154*, 156–7, 159
pins, ring-headed, viii, 33, 140
Pipe Rolls 221
pipkins 193, *194*, 197, 198, 202, 205
pits 128–9, 146, 163, *175*, 189, 220
  C46 132, *133–4*, *135–9*
  lithic material *97*, *101*, *104*, *105*, *106–9*, *110*, *111–12*, 113
  plant remains 160, 161
  Site A 11, 20, 24, 25, 26, 95, 132, *133*, 134, *135*, 136, 142
  Site D 87, 90
  Site E 57, *59–60*, *63*, 65, 66, 70, 209
  Site M 72, 75, 76
  Site S 92
  Site T 31, 33, 34, *37*, 38, 41, 45, 46
  Site V 48, 52
plants 5, 6, 107, 113, 126, 130, 160–3, 210
Plas Newydd *see* Abbey Farm
ploughmarks *see under* agriculture
pollen 163
population 129, 224
port (Rhuddlan) 9, 10
Portland, Dorset 124
Post Office 84
postholes 128, 129, 132, 134, 144, 145, 209, 210, 211
  Site A 11, 14, 17–18, 24, 25, 139
  Site D 87
  Site E 57, *59*, 60, 66, 70
  Site M 72, 75, 76, 77, 140
  Site S 92
  Site T 31, 33, 34, 36, 38, 41, 45, 146
  Site V 49, 50, 54
pottery viii 219, 221
  Neolithic period 137
  Earlier Bronze Age 11, 132, 134
  Bronze Age 84, 132, *133*, 134, *135*, 136–9, 140, 163
  Iron Age 11, 13, 137, 140–1
  Roman/Romano-British 5, 33, 48, 50, 59, 77, 142, *143–4*, 145
  Saxo-Norman 14, 33, 34, 36, 145, 191–2, *193*, *198*, *201*, *202*, 211
  medieval 16, 26, 36, 46, 66, 70, 82, 87, 88, 90–1, 92, 94, 191, 192, 212
  post-medieval wares 192–3
  17th century 56, 70, 92
  17th/18th centuries 193
  18th century 70, 92
  18th to 20th centuries 90
  local 18th century wares 67
  alkaline-glazed bowl 25, 192, 207
  amphora (imported) 208
  black-burnished ware 76, 142

Buckley-type wares 46, 192–3, 205
calcite tempered ware 191–2
calcite-gritted 143
Cheshire fabric 140
Chester ware 191, 211
Coal Measures Fine wares 192
colour-coat beakers 144
Deverel-Rimbury wares 136, 138
Diserth 54
Ewloe type wares 46, 64, 70, 192, *201*, 202, *203*, *205*, 206, *207*, 223
Fine wares 192
food vessel 134
grey wares 11, 143, 144
imports 25, 26, 67, 191, 192, *198*, 199, *201*, *202*, *203*, *207*, 208, 217
'Irish Sea ceramic zone' 138
kiln V type 26, 38, 46, 64, 67, 70, 90, 94
maiolica 192, 201, 207
Mancetter-Hartshill mortaria 142, 143, 144
Mediterranean wares 192, 199, 201, 207
mottled ware 193
New Forest beaker 143
Peterborough (Mortlake style) 139
St Neots ware 191, 209
Saintonge ware 26, 67, 192, *198*, *201*, *202*, *203*, *207*, 217
salt containers 33, 34, 48, 76, 140–2, 144, 145
samian 5, 33, 76, 82, 84, 142–3, 144, 146
sandy wares 54, 191, 192, 193, 207
Severn Valley Ware 142
shelly ware 191, 193, 209
slipware 193
urns 57, 59, 132, 134, 136, 137, 139
Wroxeter 144
  see also kilns, pottery *and under* Sites
pouches 79
Powys 43, 82, 144, 145
  Kingdom of 7, 208
prehistoric period viii, 46, 59, 75, 115
  lithic material 95
  pebbles 124, 126
  Sites 6, *48*, 76, 84, 87, 88
  late 72, 76
Prestatyn, Clwyd 7, 34, 95, 105, 130, 139, 140, 142, 144, 145, 146, 189, 216
Princes Road (Rhuddlan) 226
  see also Site S
'Priory Mount' (Abbey Road) 5
props, kiln 193, *194*, 197
proton magnetometer (Elsec) 72, *73*
Pudding Lane (City of London) 25
pulses 160, 161
purses 79

quarrying 95
querns 76, *125*, 140, *141*, 142, 145

rabbits: bones 158
radiocarbon dating viii, 6, *125*, 127–8, 130, 136, 138
  Site M 75

Site E 57
Town Ditch 5, 210–11, 212
railways 10
reeds 56
Remouchamp, Belgium 124
rents, for mills 9, 10
Rhodri Mawr (king of Gwynedd) 7
Rhos Ddigr 139
Rhos (kingdom) 208
Rhuddlan Bridge 9
Rhufoniog 7
Rhyd-y-Boncas, ford of 94
Rhyl, Clwyd 1, 130, 209
rhyolite 95, *96*, 99, *111–12*, 113, 136
Rhys ap Gruffudd 8
Rievaulx Abbey, Yorkshire 182
ring ditches 137, 139
ring-headed pins viii, 33, 140
Ringerike style (bone trial pieces) 169
'ripard' 144
roads 87, 90, 94
Robert of Rhuddlan 8, 164, 214, 215
roker (thornback ray) 158
Romano-British period viii, 1, 144–6, 171, 208, 210
    animal bones 147
    artefacts 6, 142–4
    bronze objects *141*
    ditch: Lôn Hylas 5
    gullies (Site A) 24
    kilns 56
    metal 142
    pebbles 117, *118*, 124
    pottery 5, 33, 48, 50, 59, 77, 142, *143–4*
    querns 140
    Site A 11, 13, 24
    Site M 76–7
    Site T 33, 34
    Site V *48*, 49
    stone 142
Romsey 124–5
roves, iron 182
rowel spur, iron 188
Royal Commission (RCHM) 2
rubbish/waste 16, 25, 37, 42, 45, 54, 128, 139, 159, 169, 210, 219
Runcorn 7, 210
Runneymede Bridge 138
rye 160, 161
Ryton-on-Dunsmore, Warks 136, 137, 138

St Asaph 2, 94, 165, 215, 224, 225
    Cathedral 8, 9
    Chapter House Museum 169
    market granted 9
    See of 8, 9, 216, 221
St Bride's Major Church, Glam 188
St Govan's Head, Bosherton, Pembs 137
St John of Jerusalem: hospital 5
St Katherine's Priory, Exeter 150
St Mary's Church 4–5, 9, 82, 222
St Peter's Street, Northampton 165
salmon 158

salt containers, ceramic 33, 34, 48, 76, 140–2, 144, 145
sandstone 20, 124, 126, 134, 136, 140, 172, 173, 191
    Carboniferous Sandstone 18, 45, 46, 67, 176
    coarse-grained 64
Saxo-Norman period
    iron objects 179
    knife 36
    pottery 14, 33, 34, 36, 145, 191, 211
    Site A 18
Saxon period 1, 7, 60, 168, 169, 170, 189, 209, 220
    building 25, 34
    burh 2, 5
    coins 164
    corn drying kilns 43
    iron objects 178
    late: pottery 193
    see also Cledemutha; *Grubenhäuser*
scale-tang knives 179
Scandinavia: building construction 25
Scandinavians see Vikings
Scanning Electron Microscope (SEM): pebble analysis 119–24
scissors, iron 180
Scotland 134
    west of 1, 138, 183
scrapers *98*, *106*, 107, *109*, *110*, *111*, *113*, 138
sculpture 169
sea shells 219
seeds 126, 160, 161, 163, 210
Segontium 165
Severn Basin/Valley 139, 144, 145
shale 110, 124
shears, iron *180*
sheep: bones 147, 149, *150*, 151, *152*, *153*, *155–6*, 159, 211
shells
    cockle 65
    hazelnut 57, 75, 127, *162*
    mussel 14, 16, 25, 37, 38, 42, 63, 65, 67
    sea 219
Shetland 161
Shire Hall (Mold) 2
Shotton, Professor F W 139
silver 164, 165
Site A 1, 5, 11, *12–13*, *22–3*, 25–6, 38, 43, 54, 57, 145, 146, 208, 210, 213, 220, 221, 225
    corn drying kiln *16–17*, 18, 216–18
    Houses *18–20*, *21*, *24*, 25, 219, 223, 224
    industry 66, 169
    lithic material 95, *96*, 99, 113, 115, 129, 138
    Norman Borough defence ditches 14–*15*, 214–15, 217
    pits 128
    pottery 132, *133*, 134, *135*, 138–9, 142, *143*, *198–200*, 211
Site C 6
Site D 3, 5–6, 54, 84, *85–9*, 90–1, *92–3*, 145, 146, 208, 209, 216, 219, 221, 222, 223
    boundaries 215
    lithic material *96*, *98*, 100, 113, 115, 129, 138
    pottery 132, *135*, 139, 144, 191, *202–4*, *205–6*

Site E 5, 38, 54, 56, 57, *58–69*, 72, 146, 163, 164, 175, 208, 219, 220-1, 224
  buildings 70-1, 139
  lithic material 95, *96*, *99*, 100, *104*, 107, 109, 110, 112, 113, *125*, 126, 127, 129
  Norman Borough Defences 60-1, *62–5*, 66-7, 210, 214-15, 216, 220
  pebbles 115, *116–17*
  pits 128, 209
  pottery 132, 134, *135*, 138, 139, *143*, 202, *203–4*
Site G (Abbey Road) 94
Site H (High Street) 92-3
Site K 2, 93-4, *96*, 220
Site M 6, 57, 140, 145, 146
  burials *77–81*, 82-3, 189, 208, 215
  gullies 34, 225
  lithic material 95, *96*, *99*, 109, 112, 115, 129
  Norman Church *see under* churches
  pits 128
  pottery 132, 138, 139, *143*, 144, 202, *204*
Site N 82
Site S 6, 92, *93*, *96*, *206–7*, 222, 225
Site T 6, 18, *27–32*, 47, 54, 57, 72, 164, 210, 212, 214, 218, 219, 220, 221, 225
  drying kilns 38, *39–42*, 43, 223, 224
  gullies 48, 49
  industry 66, 189
  later medieval activity 43, *44*, 45-6
  lithic material *96*, *99*, 109, 129
  Norman Borough Defences 26, *35*, 36, *37–8*, 215
  pebbles 115, 117, *118*, *119*
  pottery 140, 142, *143*, *200–1*, 202, 211
  Structures 33-4, 36, 43, 45, 46, 144-6, 208, 209, 211, 213, 223
Site V 6, 27, *47–9*, *51*, *55–6*, 57, 71, 145, 146, 224
  gullies 34
  lithic material *96*, 110, 115, 138
  pottery 140, 143, 211
  pottery kilns *47*, 50, *52–3*, 54, 56, 193, *194–8*, *201–5*, 217, 221
  Structures 49-50, 54, 145, 209, 211, 215-16
'skate' 158
slag 37, 79, *80*, 81, 82, 83
  iron 25, 26, 45, 54, 66, 67, 72, 76, 77, 188-9, *190*, 215, 216, 219, 220, 224
slate(s) 38, 67, 82
smelting 66, 189, 215
Smithfield 165
smiths/smithing viii, 66, 178, 189, 221, 224
Snowdonia 99
South Witham, Lincolnshire (monastic grange) 182
Southampton, Hants 165, 170, 175, 185
Speed's map (1610) 222
spindle whorls, stone *172*
spinning 172
Spital 5, 224
spurdog 158
spurs 14, 167, *187–8*, 211
staples, iron 180, *181*
Stapleton, James 1
Star Carr 105, 110, 129, 130
stone 65, 70, 93, 142

analysis *see* Scanning Electron Microscope (SEM)
decorated 27
and Edwardian Castle 66, 67, 176-7, 221
kilns 43
objects *172–6*
querns 140, *141*, 142, 145
tools 120-4, 139
utilised *125–6*
weight *172*
see also lithics; pebbles
stratigraphy 1, 5, 6
  Site A 11, 13-14, 16-18, 20, 25-6
  Site D 84-5, 88, 90
  Site E 57, 59-60, 65-7, 70
  Site K 94
  Site M 72, 75-6, 77, 79
  Site S 92
  Site T 27, 33-4, 36, 38, 43-6
  Site V 47, 48, 49-50, 56
straw 43, 160
structures *see* buildings
studs, iron 91, *181*
Stump Cross 128
Suffolk 169

taphonomic evidence: animal bones 147, *149–50*
Taunton 154
  Castle 183
taxes 9, 215, 218
Taylor, Dr R (British Geological Survey) 119
Tegeingl (Englefield) 7, 8, 208, 213, 214, 216, 217, 218
tenterhooks 178-9
Thames: river and valley 124-5, 138, 140
Thatcham, Berkshire 103
Thelwall (*burh*): Merseyside 7, 210
Thetford, Norfolk 179, 183, 186, 189
Thirlings, Northumberland: house construction 25
tiles, roof 179
timber 113, 161, 168
  castle 8
  as fuel 56
  houses 18, 20, *24*, 25, 211
  mortuary house 139
  nails 181, *182*
  pit settings: Site E 59-*60*, 209
  ramparts 210
  Site A 26, 214
  Site T 36, 37, 38, *41*, 42, 43
  structures/buildings viii, 14, 43, 45, 46, 213, 222
  for town defences 9
  see also trees; wood
Tithe Apportionment Map (1839) 71, 84, 225
Tomas (moneyer) 217
tools *see* arrowheads; awls; axes; cores; fabricators; microdenticulates; microliths; scrapers
Toot/Bonc Hill *see* Twt Hill
topography 1, *3*, 14
town defences *see* defences
Town Ditch 2, 5, 11, 93, 94, 129, 209, 210-11, 212, 213, 218, *219–20*, 221, 224, 225
trade 9-10, 38, 146, 207

trees/woodland 128, 129, *162*, 163, 178, 219
Treworld, Cornwall 173
trial pieces, bone 16, 169, 209, 210, 213
trout 158
Trwyn Du, Aberffraw (Anglesey) 113, 126, 127
tub gurnard 158
Twt Hill 1, 72, 82, 146, 216, 219
   motte and bailey castle 1, 2, 8, 213, 214
   palatium 8, 213
Tybrind Vig, Denmark 125

Upton, Northants: *Grubenhäuser* 14
urns, *see under* pottery
Usk valley 130

Vale of Clwyd 1, 7, 95, 129–30, 139, 145, 146, 215,
   217
Vale of Pickering 129
vegetables 25, 210
vertebrate remains *see* animals; bone, animal
Verulamium area 143
Vicarage (Rhuddlan) 5, 139
Vikings 7, 8, 168, 169, 170, 182, 209, 213

Waltham Abbey, Essex 181
Warcock Hill 128
waste flakes 95
Waterford 165
Wat's Dyke 7
weaver's pit 60
weedhooks 179
weeds/weed seeds 160, 161, 162, 163, 210
weight, stone *172*
Welsh
   Owain Glyndŵr's rebellion viii, 10, 91, 225–6
   wars 7, 8–9, 54, 213
Welsh Church Records 10
Welsh Marches: William the Conqueror 8
Welshpool, Powys 2
Weoley Castle, Warwicks 183

Wessex 7, 210, 212, 213
West Midlands 137, 138, 191, 192
West Stow, Suffolk 169, 170
whale bones 158
wheat 10, 160, 161, 163
whetstones 38, 124, *162*, *174–6*
whittle-tang knives, iron 179
whorls, spindle *172*
wicker framework 43
William I, King 8, 216
William II, King *81*, 164, 215
William of Louth (clerk) 221
William Rufus, King viii, 79, 82, 215
Williams, Dr D F 191, 192
Winchester 179, 183, 186
Wirral 7, 164
wood
   handles 178, 179
   objects 38, 79
   paddle 125
   woodworking 110, 112, 178, 219
   works: Rhuddlan castle 8
   see also timber
woodcock: bones *158*
Woodeaton, Oxfordshire 140
woodland *see* trees
wool combs 178
wool production 155, 159

York
   Baile Hill 178
   Coppergate 25, 211
   Holy Trinity Church 176
   Jellinge style sculpture 169
   Parliament Street 178
   Viking 7, 169, 170
Yorkshire: Mesolithic assemblages 98
Ysgol-Y-Castell
   playing fields *see* Site M
   Sites E; V; T *see* individual Sites